Black Boys

Black Boys

The Social Aesthetics of British Urban Film

Clive Chijioke Nwonka

BLOOMSBURY ACADEMIC
NEW YORK • LONDON • OXFORD • NEW DELHI • SYDNEY

BLOOMSBURY ACADEMIC
Bloomsbury Publishing Inc
1385 Broadway, New York, NY 10018, USA
50 Bedford Square, London, WC1B 3DP, UK
29 Earlsfort Terrace, Dublin 2, Ireland

BLOOMSBURY, BLOOMSBURY ACADEMIC and the Diana logo are trademarks of
Bloomsbury Publishing Plc

First published in the United States of America 2023

For legal purposes the Acknowledgements on p. x constitute an extension of this
copyright page.

Cover design by Clive Chijioke Nwonka and Eleanor Rose
Cover image: Ashley Walters in *Bullet Boy* (2004), dir. Saul Dibb [BFI ID 696133].
Courtesy of the British Film Institute

Bloomsbury Publishing Inc does not have any control over, or responsibility for, any third-
party websites referred to or in this book. All internet addresses given in this book were
correct at the time of going to press. The author and publisher regret any inconvenience
caused if addresses have changed or sites have ceased to exist, but can accept no
responsibility for any such changes.

A catalog record of this book is available from the Library of Congress.

ISBN: HB: 978-1-5013-5282-9
PB: 979-8-7651-0584-9
ePDF: 978-1-5013-5284-3
eBook: 978-1-5013-5283-6

Typeset by Deanta Global Publishing Services, Chennai, India
Printed and bound in Great Britain

To find out more about our authors and books, visit www.bloomsbury.com and sign up for
our newsletters.

For the Nwonkas of Port Harcourt, River State, Nigeria, and of North West London.

Contents

Illustrations

Acknowledgements

This book is the outcome of what I want to describe as a community of ideas – the product, or produce, of a mobile, interchangeable and continuously accumulative affinity space. The general orthodoxy of academia, it seems, is to describe our intellectual works in terms of their contribution, an intervention into a particular paradigm or discipline. This may be so; however, I would like to also think of this book as something born of an inheritance, or a composite of offerings. By this, I understand this book as a gift that I have been given, that has been bestowed on me rather than one that has been produced solely through my own endeavours. The thinking and writing of this book spans a number of years, institutions and intellectual and disciplinary phases that, it is hoped, have come together into a coherent but equally heterogeneous and multi/interdisciplinary analysis of Black British urban identity and representation across film, TV and its social, cultural, political and institutional geneses, but one that is drawn not just from academic departments at the London School of Economics and Political Science, Columbia University, University of York and University College London, but the countless organic cultural experiences, encounters, geographies and existences. These continue to inform my own academic practice and efforts to achieve a horizontality between the elite, extractive and exclusive spaces of academia and the very identities, geographies and existences that academia draws its knowledges, research, social importance and economic value from. It was an absolute pleasure to not only share my work but also to have it critically questioned from a range of positions, perspectives and voices who all, knowingly or unknowingly, have influenced this book though their teaching, research, collaborations, discussions and informal conversations, gestures, the extending of their networks and at times, simply their presence. It is sadly beyond the scope of this brief acknowledgements section to be able to thank them all.

I would firstly like to thank my brother Kevin, who many years ago encouraged me to watch a DVD copy of *Bullet Boy*, which was being shared among his friends and catalysed my intellectual interest in not just the urban as a form of authentic representation but also the why, and the where and the from. This gesture proved to be so important. My thanks are also due to Katie Gallof at Bloomsbury for her patience and editorial support with this book that was written through a period of interludes and unprecedented global change; to Anamik Saha, an immensely supportive brother and colleague; to Sam Mejias who, be it in Holborn, London or Queens, New York, has and remains a tremendous source of support and perspective; to David Forrest, who throughout nearly a decade of intellectual sparring over the shifting meanings of cinematic realism, has been a great friend, colleague and someone whose immense body of work has been a source of continued engagement; to Paul Gilroy for our talks within the neutral spaces of Lincoln Inn Fields Café that were significant beyond measure, and whose writings and thinking continue to greatly inspire and, importantly, challenge; to Suzi Hall, whose constant reminders that redemption, restoration and justice are to be found within the intellectual work we produce, and whose integrity, critical loyalty, mutuality, delicacy in the art of listening, and interrogative spirit, which refuses to invest in the unproductive common-sense logics that seem to possess and orchestrate so many, is everything that is extremely rare and extremely valuable in academia – as you said so many times, the writing prevails; to Les Back, whose generosity with his time, anti-hierarchal sensibility and collegial presence are important features within my own academic life and began with his missing a speaking event at Goldsmiths to continue a late and impromptu discussion in his office with me on Stuart Hall, Black film and the very idea of a politics of representation; and to David Scott, whose sharing of his deep thinking on the multitudinous voices of Stuart Hall remains a valuable resource. I also want to thank those colleagues and friends who provided a platform for discussing the themes of this book in its various nascent stages: Shelley Cobb, Neil Ewin, Joy White, Laura Mee, Jack Newsinger, Maria Korolkova, Richard Martin, So Mayer, Lanre Bakare, Caspar Melville, Jana Melkumova-Reynolds and Amber Lascelles. My thanks are also due to LSE's Black security and cleaning staff in and around both St Clements and the Centre Building, whose moments of recognition and appreciation for the early Saturday morning to late Sunday evening writing sessions in the otherwise deserted spaces of LSE were a great source of personal and cultural recognition. This acknowledgement was sometimes as subtle as a silent gesture or as overt as an embrace or a spud, but always tremendously meaningful. I hope that my own recognition and appreciation of their presence and labour was felt. There were so many others during the writing of this book who created a generative intellectual space and a harmonious institutional structure where my work and ideas could flourish: Coretta Phillips, Abenna Owusu-Bempah, Tess Thorsen, Nima Paidpady, Erica Carter, Charlotte Brunsdon, Laura Mulvey, Nick Anstead, Verity Treadwell, Nicola Lacey, Liza Ryan, Suki Ali, Pat McGovern, Alexandra Antonopulou, Charis Thompson, Helene Neveu Kringelbach, Phil Drummond, Lee Grieveson, Mel Hoyes, Orson Nava, Julian Henriques, Phil Wickham, Emma Sandon, Steve Presence and Tariq Jazeel. My thanks also go to David Graeber (1961–2020), an amazing thinker, colleague and friend. Our extended conversation in the middle of Oxford Circus became a pivotal moment in both my navigation of academia and my own reminder of the anti-racist principles that were in need of defending; to John Hills (1954–2020), whose sense of equality, justice, integrity and decency within an institutional context where the politics of self, visibility and subjective interest renders such principles as antithetical to the logics of academia, remains an example to all those who were around him; to Farah Jasmin Griffin and the Department of African American and African Diasporic Studies at Columbia University, where as a Visiting Academic, I wrote some of this book and drew from the university's rich scholarship on Black film, culture and identity; and to all the students whom I have taught, tutored and supervised whose engagement with and inquisitiveness towards the material to be explored in this book has contributed greatly.

I'd like to reserve the final, highest thanks for Shakuntala Banaji, without whose time, counsel, support, critical loyalty and institutional interventions in the service of anti-racism within academia, this book would not have been possible. There are very few days when that period does not occupy my thoughts, and that, to borrow (or maybe reappropriate) from James Baldwin, I do not wish that *Houghton Street Could Talk*. Of course, given the myriad ways in which our voices can become compromised by the incorporating power of institutionality, there is no real certainty that Houghton Street would say what it really saw, and these thoughts are occasionally fissured by other, more generative thinking. I remain convinced that the racial justice that was collectively fought for will one day come to pass. And I hope that I am able to repay some of the effort and time she, and many others, gave me in some way. I accept that given the magnitude of these efforts, such a gesture may be an unreachable horizon, and one that will ultimately find its presence through written words, with all their limitations and finite capacitates. But perhaps the publication of this book, dealing critically with some of the very issues that were identified as problematic and worthy of continued challenge, this being the racialized characterizations of Black men, can go some way towards this endeavour.

Introduction

The Black British urban identity as a visual identity is a particularly labile social, historical, cultural and political formation, one that has been assumed, consumed, examined, but insufficiently analysed in the context of either fictive or non-fictive work. In broad historical terms, what I term as the 'Black urban text' in specific British contexts can be understood as a generic approach to the representations of Black identities within the inner city, with its primary themes and characterization constructed upon an association with a specific form of social deviance, representations that often register an overt engagement with the dominant images, understandings and narratives around Black, mostly masculine and ostensibly working-class identity. This book is the first focused analysis of the construction of Black urban identity within British screen culture. The urban can be understood as a generic approach, a sensibility or an implied visual identity. Given its fundamental role in the normalizing of particular images of multiracial Britain, it is a formation that requires far more critical attention than it has so far enjoyed. Its scholarly disregard can be attributed to what, as Stuart Hall argued, is deemed to be the vulgarity of the popular that cannot be accommodated into the esoteric and often circuitous readings of British cinema, of which the more experimentalist forms of filmmaking in the Black workshop movement of the 1980s and early 1990s has been granted entry. What I am arguing is that this has been the framework (rather than the optic) through which all other forms of Black film, in all its definitions, have been assessed in terms of critical value, and which subsequently disallows the urban film from being afforded a similar degree of analytical attention. As a result of this textual and interpretative purity, I contend that the Black urban text has often been engaged with in terms of classification and association rather than individual analysis and judgement, a consequence of its reliance on a televisual mode of realism, its youth-focused orientation, the apparent simplified forms of narration and plot, the uninventiveness of its production techniques and its general assessment as the reductive product of the instrumentalist clamour of cultural/racial diversity. But the aim of this book is not simply to articulate a space of analytical and interpretative value within the canons of film and television analysis. It is, instead, an attempt to understand the complex genealogies of Black urbanity as a corpus of representation. Resultingly, the book is necessarily extensive in its analysis and interdisciplinary in its framework. In drawing on film studies, cultural studies, political science, Black Studies and social theory, it seeks to establish a normative centre from which one can develop an understanding of the Black urban text as a social aesthetic; this is to refer to the contingent elements involved and implicated in the production of its themes, characterisations, formal strategies, representative logics, and crucially, its function once circulated within a range of publics from which the text, and the triangulation of ownership it is embedded within, attempts to assert a cultural value from its claim to authenticity, truth-telling, self-authorship, counter-hegemony and representational difference.

There lies in this formulation of Black urban cinematic and televisual identity a highly complex synchronism, and we naturally arrive at a number of pertinent but very complex issues for us to work through that also bring into the discussion the purposefulness of our analytical tools. The dominant modes of analyses of Black film, particularly its Black British variant, have even in its more esoteric manifestations relied upon a set of interpretive frames that esteem the sociological facets and elements of Black textuality which, in reference to the disciplinary agility of cultural studies, stress the contextual issues that may inform and produce certain kinds of Black filmic representations that for many exhibit a neglecting of the actual textual study of the films – what the Black texts themselves mean and the close reading of the text's formal and aesthetic properties that allow us to arrive at this meaning. These perspectives, subtle enough to be concealed and undetected within the accepted orthodoxies of film analysis but so rooted in the violent and obstinate instinctive of racism are, at least to me, unable to constitute a substantive or systematic point of argument at this particular conceptual nodal. By this, I'm gesturing towards the historic and often imperceptible stability of the Eurocentric analysis of Black film as the definition of a cultural practice that equally performs as the definition of a culture. My criticism of the paradigmatic pre-eminence of Eurocentrism that has framed the dominant readings of Black filmic representation is located in what such evaluative languages are able to conceal, a concern with the ethics of film analysis that is often simply a demonstration of ahistorical Eurocentric aesthetic theory masquerading as an uncomplicated universalism, although it should also be acknowledged that the paramount textual concern at this point is not to organize my analyses within a prioritizing binary between the question of formal aggrandizement and contextual deconstruction, but to open up the analysis of the popular Black urban film to a set of substrates and provisional formulations. What are these formulations? Perhaps as an outcome of its corporeality, the Black British film text, with some variations, possesses a limited materiality, beyond its obvious physical elements associated with its mode of exhibition, *prior* to its necessary processing by an already socially conditioned spectatorship. Paradoxically, it is in this same ecology of meaning and perception that reveals the contradictory nature of Black cultural politics is both internal and external to the text and its deep attachment to the question of cultural identification and cultural value that the Black text is rarely *immaterial* and posits some kind of significance and purchase on the social world within which this conditioning occurs. However, we should note that this conditioning is neither homogeneous nor uniform in its effect and uptake, and the ability of Black imagery to produce a topology of relative meanings provides some means of understanding the ways in which Black filmic representation can be organized to engage its divergent audiences in particular ways placing the social context at the very axis of this contradiction. Thus, my situating of the Black urban text and its various components within a larger political economy of Black film does not necessarily pose an analytical threat to any notion of the primacy of aesthetics or film form as the means through which an understanding of the multi-referentiality of the popular urban film can be constructed. Instead, it is precisely through a political economy of Black urban texts that allows us to explore how the presence of the various and interacting social forces, discourses and tendencies that construct Black British cinematic representation as a social aesthetic and its defining textual features are implicated in a *preformation* of the popular Black British urban film. I should be clear on the specificity of the popular Black British urban text and its aesthetic and narrational conventions that are determined by its preformation. The Black British film text is constitutive. Of course, the degree to which the text is constitutive of the social and cultural context within which it exists remains dependent on its generic form and thematic interests, the heightened nature of Blackness as a source of social and cultural debate and the contingencies that emerge within the industrial constructing of Black identities. Attendantly, such an analytical trajectory necessarily ventures beyond the instinctive, standardizing and racially fused generic lores that have historically collapsed Black British films into an uninventive and comparatively retrograde surveying of its cinematic realism, but a preformation that is derived from the idea that the Black urban text and representations of Black urbanity are organized and formed by the existence and circulation of previous images, characterizations and narratives, re-emerging and similar Black social materials, the propelling of recurring social motifs and cross-mediatized representations of Blackness that are able to latch onto new and emerging cultural and social patterns and trajectories and shifting contexts. In this sense, the concept of the Black urban text as a social aesthetic gestures to not merely the formal and stylistic sensibilities that speak to the modality of cinematic realism and the issue of Black mimesis and indexicality, but equally fashion the Black urban text as constituted by and imbricated in a contradictory and multi-intentional tapestry of discourses – where at one moment we have the disavowal of films with Black lead casts as mono-racial, particular discourses now open up the possibility for an urgent desirability to be ascribed to the production of racially densified films and narrational themes.

It is in cognizance of the analytical dangers to be found in the inconsideration of the fugitivity of Black screen representation and how the unexamined classification of the didactic Black film can produce a certain political over-indexing and textual overdeterminism, that it is necessary to acknowledge that the intention on the part of the directors and their films analysed in this book may not have been for the films to be read through the optic of political science or sociology. In addition, in demanding such inclusions, we risk placing the precise 'burden of representation' afflicting notions of black cinema Mercer (1988) identified, in which black films are compelled to represent a particular sociopolitical perspective. Such perspectives are often declared as the homogeneous, authoritative voice of Britain's Black population, a Black Britain that for Hall (1988) was no longer unified under the political category of Black but fissured by, *inter alia*, class, sexuality and political alignment. Further, and in recalling the very structure/culture nexus Wilson presented in his analysis of the (in)ability of the general public to understand the complexities of race and poverty in the urban locale, therefore rendering behavioural explanations more palatable (2009), it may be that analytical space should be created to accommodate the idea that directors may consider the impact of any oppressive social structure on the agency of their urban protagonists as unworthy of commentary, or one that can't be accommodated to within the narrational scope and generic bounds of an urban film cycle that operates predominantly at the more visible, recognizable and accepted representational contexts of Black British youthhood. Finally, there is also the recognition that the urban film must exist within the specific *industrial* volition governing its production, a set of restrictive conditions that find linearity with Hall's notion of Black film's 'regimes of representation' (1988), which are, as we will encounter in the chapters concerned with the popular Black urban text's development and production context, informed by a combination of cultural, industrial, generic and economic rationalities that are not necessarily indexed to any ambition the film's creative team may have to position social inequality as the urban film's primary antagonist. In other words, the degree to which the urban film's politicized Blackness emerges as a determining factor in its character's often tragic fate is an outcome informed by its generic demands.

Before commencing an analysis of the Black urban text, one that will attempt to evidence how such film and televisual representations are organized by an ongoing exchange between hegemonic obedience and ontological suture, I wish to clarify that while my effort to re-theorize the concept of black-on-black representation as a highly contradictory and multifaceted visual encounter, and as a result one that is distinctively Hall(ian) in orientation, in arguing that the aesthetic reification of Black Otherness within the framework of Public Service Broadcasting (PSB) resituates the popular urban text as a site for Black creative participation, the text's invaluating claim to *authenticity* is also informed by the organization of the film as a counter-hegemonic filmic experience. Attendantly, the potential for the popular Black urban text to serve as a site for an ontological and epistemological nuancing of the dominant narratives of Black violence relies on an aesthetic and thematic continuity, here made viable by the provision of relatively permissible production conditions. The Black urban film text's thematizing of habitual violence as organic Black subject matter to some degree accentuates the need for actors cast for the production to bring certain aspects of their own experiences into its forms of characterization. I find that such contingencies render the Black urban text as a distinctive and permissive performative sphere, and create the conditions for a practice of performative improvisation, which can generally be understood here as the absence of scripted dialogue or any pre-prepared or predetermined dramatic instruction or delegation. There is, of course, a plethora of approaches to the practice of improvisation, and we find historic examples in the films of the French New Wave which pursued a practice of improvisation in the use of sparse scripts that was to permit productions to be alive to the natural capturing of the fortuitous organic flows of unanticipated street activity. In other examples, it is the methodological predilections of the practitioners that are in themselves informed by the specific social and political context that the improvisatory methods of Italian Neorealism and the French New Wave influenced filmmaking traditions such as Cinema Novo, which applied the idea of improvisation to develop a political praxis that, while drawing on its basic principles of non-scripted, extempore dialogue and dramatic spontaneity that displayed an alignment with documentary film modalities, achieved a degree of horizontality in which its performers are embedded in a broader political project which, in permitting actors to improvise their dialogue and reactions to other performers, establishes a mode of film practice that reflects the very radical ideals they have for the society the films are depicting. Thus, there is a political impetus behind the idea of improvisation as a participatory practice. Different variations of such methods have been taken up by British directors and can, of course, be identified in the films of Ken Loach and Mike Leigh and, in more recent years, Andrea Arnold, Clio Barnard, Shane Meadows and Sarah Gavron have described a process of improvisation that has produced moments of natural, emotional expressivity and organic relationships with and between young actors on screen, developed through a process of workshopping where director, screenwriter and actor(s) participate in the negotiation of ideas for the creation of dramatic performance conducive to their various iterations of cinematic realism. That the above directors are generally associated with low-budget and culturally valuable filmmaking and at the textual level invested in the portrayal of socially marginalized and peripheral identities is of relevance to the popular Black British urban text, as while its performers are compelled to perform within a compressed thematic structure in that the taut indexicality of the Black urban gun crime thematic curtails any potential for the popular Black urban film's iteration of improvisation to be completely at the mercy of dramatic circumstance, the generic demand for a sense of spontaneity and realness via an organic dramatic intercourse allows for a theoretical reconsideration of the function of filmic improvisation. The casting of the non-professional actor is by no means exclusive to the Black urban film, nor in the broader British social realist tradition, however, and as will be expounded upon further in the following chapters, there is a particular industrial, cultural and social significance in the idea of dramatic improvisation. Here, I am concerned with how the structuring of thematic concerns of the popular Black urban drama is able to bring the actors in a state of performative disinhibition where they are actively required to bring their real-life experiences and identities to the screen, and in doing so reveal the relations between the idea of the popular Black British urban film as constructed from a constellation of social aesthetics and the practice of improvisation. The aforementioned aspects of social aesthetics make it particularly germane to any analysis of Black British urban representation in its most participatory utterances, since improvisation, at least in the context of film, TV, theatre and other forms of dialogical dramatic performance, can be understood as a form of social inclusivity. And while the creating of a deeper sense of authenticity can be conceived as the primary contribution to the popular Black urban drama, dramatic improvisation can also be seen as demonstrative of a participatory process on the part of white directors who possess limited knowledge of the specific idiosyncrasies of the subject of filmic depiction, an imperative to be brought into being in the casting of non-professional actors and the providing of minimal direction so as not to impinge on the natural and innate understandings and experiences of the particular social milieu or thematic issue they are endeavouring to bring to the screen, rendering improvisation, and its aesthetic outcomes, in themselves a practice of social participation. The spectacle of authenticity as the popular Black urban drama's most cherished and commodifiable criterion of value becomes the entry point through which the practice of improvisation allows Black performers to possess an authorial or contributory stake in the film's production, a practice of dramatic improvisation that can be interpreted as a *social address*. The genre's reliance on untried and new ethnic minority talent, combined with the culturally specific nature of Black gun crime as Black subject matter provides the kind of sociocultural engagement that the subsequent performance of Black hegemonic symmetry demands, while at the same time excessing the image of the Black urban Other and its synonymous violent acts as the recognizable unknown, an aesthetic of Blackness that displays a specific intentionality – the instrumentalization of Black representation within film culture as a social corrective and mode of representational authenticity.

My dichotomizing of the Black urban text and the textual representation of Black urbanity is therefore not without a specific purpose. For a related issue is found in the means by which textual approaches to the narrating of Black British identity accrues meaning and authenticity from a mimetic association with narratives and images circulating within the popular imagination – the ways that Black urban film texts attempt to augment the reality and perceptibility of their narrative, plot or aesthetics through their attachment to media themes that may immerse the spectator in a perceptible, rather than a purely perceivable social environment. Further, how and by what means did the historic cultural and biological associations between Black British urban identity, crime, violence and premature intra-racial death come to disturb the contemporary social imaginary and in doing so, establish what I describe as a performative corporeality through the Black body at a particular conjuncture? By exploring this, I'm attempting to think beyond the critique of the stereotypical nature of Black urbanity, and the discourses that constitute it as such, to how Black urban identity textually functions as a demonstration of an otherwise denigrative set of recognizable thematics and social knowledge that spill into a series of racial antitheticalities and become positioned at the very basis of Black filmic characterization. It is this analytic engagement with the above-mentioned preformations that prepares for a understanding of how cinematic representations of Black life and corporeality become camouflaged within the abject phenomenology of Black death as an inferential media spectacle, and in doing so, condition the social and cultural grounding for the popular Black urban text to emerge as accommodative of or /and existing within new or pre-existing hegemonies, social mores, prevailing sense-making logics and racial lexicons.

The Black urban text's cinematic portrayal of criminalized Black youths within the urban environment, while distinctive in its geographical setting, is, of course, no novel characterization, and as congruent with capitalist machinery of the film industry, such texts found industrial and cultural habitation through an attachment to an identifiable generic model. I'm recalling the period of the early 1990s, which saw a body of film projects from African American writer-directors commissioned by major Hollywood studios, who identified the commercial potential of the amalgamating that characterized the genre of 'hood dramas', characterized by stories of gun crime and violence among Black working-class identities and depicted in *New Jack City*

(Mario Van Peebles, 1991), *Boyz In the Hood* (dir. John Singleton, 1991), *Menace II Society* (1994), *Fresh* (1994) and *Above the Rim* (1994). Such productions were termed as 'crossover' films as a result of their hybridizing of cinematic devices and aesthetic techniques that were demonstrative of a distinctive independent film production practice married with mainstream generic qualities and a popular ambition. American hood films were also described as 'crossover' as a result of their ability to appeal to the desires of the white imaginary through the mainstream consumption of Black cultural forms, cultural products and subcultural practices, a commodificatory impulse as similarly asserted by Kara Keeling (2007), who conceives the genre in more pejorative tones in her definition of 'ghetto-centric' films as 'a historically specific reaction to and articulation of a cinematic social reality (the post-industrial city's ghetto) produced at the juncture between globalizing capitalism and contemporary US racism' (120). Keeling's contention that the ghetto-centric hood films are created at the intersections of capitalism and racism exhibits a number of aesthetic, thematic and contextual linkages with the popular Black urban drama, at least at the level of their dominant characterizations of Black masculinity, inferential thematics and their distressed images of Blackness and the Black existence. In addition, the idea of crossover is also a reference to the use of notable Black performers from other cultural mediums, and as seen for example in *Bullet Boy*, the plausibility of its depiction of Black British urban masculinities is secured through the iconography of its central star, Ashley Walters, as an embodiment of all that the 'urban' had at this point come to represent within the popular imagination.

Although this form of crossover, among other thematic factors, allows us to acknowledge their thematic and narrational continuities, it is important to note that the popular Black British urban film is also dissimilar in important respects, not least in terms of the surrounding industrial logics and production values, but by a departure located in the very concept of PSB. Whereas the underlying rationale for the Hollywood investment in the ghetto-centric hood dramas of this period was engaged in a model of racial representation that for the African American intellectual Cornel West was reflective of an adjective 'nihilism' within America's Black community (1993), there was also a powerful generic momentum that was motivated by profit, a factor that, as argued by Massood, accompanied its arrival into the mainstream of the American film industry. This, for Massood, is exemplified in films such as *Do the Right Thing* and *Boyz in the Hood*, and while the former offers for Guerrero (1993) a more nuanced account of the contradictions of race within the American social fabric, individualism and personal responsibility, and accompanying this, a less fetishist image of Black death in depicting the murder of Radio Raheem as the direct outcome of systemic police racism, it finds continuity with the latter in that both secured significant crossover potential through the intertextual absorbing of the increasing mainstream popularity of rap music and black popular culture. For the British offshoot, its dependency on public subsidy via National Lottery resources necessitated an approach that, while undoubtedly influenced by the commercial success and public visibility found in the American ghetto-centric hood dramas, constructed a differentiated form of cultural crossover upon the proliferation of Black youth subcultural practices and the instrumentalist impulses of the cultural and creative industries that situate the popular Black urban text at the nexus of black urban violence, and at the level of context, the accompanying diversity and inclusivity ideals of the black British film, or the idea of the Black urban film performing as a faux intervention into the whiteness of both its figuration of national cinema and its volitional acceptance of Black and ethnic minority creative authorship. While this renders the popular Black British urban text, of which *Bullet Boy* is at this sociocultural nodal our primary exemplar, as constitutively distinct from the US ghetto-centric films, they remain bound by the thematic investment in the narrative of Black male deviance.

Black Boys is not an exhaustive analysis of the British urban film genre, nor does it offer a holistic reading of the representations of Black urbanity across film and television, and this is a decision not of neglect but by design. The rationale for this is somewhat implied in my classification of the urban texts as the *popular*. By this, I refer to films in receipt of institutional support through public funding bodies that carry with it a number of agendas, imperatives and aims, all of which underpin the Black urban text's status as a *social* aesthetic, for it is where we can observe most clearly how these institutional entanglements and the ideologies, logics and desires that its aesthetics are constituted by, register a powerful and often deterministic presence at the level of *text*. Of course, given that since the tangible emergence of the British urban text as a concerted generic model from the early 2000s, and the new modes of production, distribution, exhibition and spectatorship afforded by digital technology, the categorization of the urban film is now vast and heterogeneous and renders the mainstream as no longer the centrifugal force to which Black urban films are drawn and are consumed. However, this book's historicization of the Black urban text necessitates an analysis that adjoins its production with the cultural shifts and conjunctures that are informed by and inform political and institutional investments in racial difference as a cultural product. To embrace the popular Black British urban film as a *social* aesthetic, as this book will argue throughout, is to accept these preformations as a constellation of formal, industrial, cultural and political imperatives that determine the Black urban text's form, style, and both corresponding and incommensurable forms of meaning.

Resultingly, the following chapters are thematic in structure. Rather than adopting an approach that frames its analysis through a singular, universal framework to be applied to a range of texts, my reading of the Black British urban film, while remaining chronological to trace its genealogies and shifts, is an attempt to situate the texts in a number of analytical and theoretical contexts. Chapter 1 opens this book with an analysis of the racial politics of the late 1970s and 1980s that brought into being a number of racial myths of Black identity, which became schematized into the representations of Black urbanity. I want to argue that the Black urban text as a spectacle of Blackness finds its basis in historic attempts to situate Black urban identity within the physical geographies of the Black community as a natural, unredeemable savagery within its Black characterizations. Here, I locate the thematics of Black urban rebellion and racial crisis that become the central dramatic feature for the televisual reconstruction of the Black 'event'. In Chapter 2, I examine the invisibility of Black British films and performers towards the late 1990s and the idea of hegemonic symmetry, applied here to describe a representational schema where race is consequential to performance. This became a tension-laden sphere within which Black performers attempted to reject the hegemonic logics of the screen industry, but which equally became the modality through which the urban film was able to consolidate its place within British film and television. Chapter 3 examines the conjunctural shift in the nature of Black cultural politics that was to mark the New Labour government's interest in the cultural and creative industries. With a particular interest in the screen sector and its absorbing of the macro-political agendas of cultural inclusivity, I identify forms of racial capitalism in how the screen industries' social and economic interest in racial difference, at a moment of industrial change, set the social, cultural and institutional contexts for the emergence of the popular Black urban text. Chapter 4 applies the Derridian concept of hauntology to describe how the Black urban Other as a historical figure of social anxiety becomes resignified through new discourses and representations of Blackness and fatal criminality that perform as useful fictions of race. Here, in challenging the cohesiveness of Blackness and gang and gun criminality, I consider how the Metropolitan Police's Operation Trident anti-black-on-black gun crime unit in the early 2000s as the dominant spectre of Black violent otherness fed into popular narratives and visual aesthetics to service the hegemonic reading of Black urban criminality in terms of national identity and unbelonging. This allows for a phenomenological reading of Black urban identity and its central position in the construction of social anxiety and allure, that being Black violent death, as the natural, mediatized outcome of the Black urban existence. Chapter 5 offers an analysis of an early manifestation of the popular Black urban film drama. Examining the emotional life of Black youth identity and questions of parenthood, the BBC feature-length drama *Storm Damage* is a significant text in that, in exhibiting a number of binary characterizations and themes relating to the experiences of young Black men, it serves as a progenitor of the popular Black urban film in its theatrical guise, while demonstrating narrational, formal and aesthetic departures from its more popular iterations. Chapter 6 analyses the development of the urban as both a racial categorization and a commercial pseudonym, and how the popularity of urban music subculture in the early 2000s was opportune for the racialized associations between Black urban music and crime to emerge as contemporary examples of moral panic. However, in nuancing the concept as advanced by Cohen (1972), Hall et al. (1978), and others, in the identification of both deviance and evil as two individual characteristics within the practice of 'folk devilling', mainstream media's ascription of the latter term to Black urban masculinity in the period is essential to the understanding of the racial distinctions and connotations embedded in descriptions of Black urban existence. Chapter 7 explores PSB's attentiveness to the questions of inclusion, diversity and innovation as a legislative concern that allowed for an expansion of the institutional framework for the representation of urban subculture. Here I examine the BBC Three documentary series *Tower Block Dreams* (2004), which is set in council estates in and around London and captures the grime and rap music subcultures emerging from them, and the artist's involvement in, and attempts to, escape from various forms of criminality. I want to consider how the production's descriptive language of 'raw' and 'honest' is ballast in a reliance on the excessive depictions of urban malevolence within a segregated PSB space mandated to appeal to the sixteen to thirty-four target audience. Chapter 8 conducts an analysis of the 2005 film *Bullet Boy* as an amalgamating product of much of the preliminaries that constitute the popular Black urban text, demonstrating how the film's production context, marketing language and forms of narration attempt to dissect the hegemonic narratives of gun violence through the concept of 'ontological suture', a narrational and aesthetic practice that attempts to intervene in public knowledge of black-on-black gun crime through the sub-narratives of family, friendship and hyper-locality. In doing so, it exhibits both a textual and contextual engagement with the primary form of Black urban signification in its depictions of Black internecine violence and Black death. Chapter 9 offers a reading of the urban text as a transmedia genre marked by its interactions with different audiovisual mediums. What we see here is the interchangeability of the urban as a description for a range of cultural practices under the auspices of urban multiculture. Here, I interrogate the idea of the urban as an uncontested sphere of multi/interraciality through an engagement with Paul Gilroy's concept of conviviality and how the theory of agnotology, the study of deliberate ignorance, becomes salient in a consideration of One Nation Conservatism as a political culture in the latter part of the 2000s that provided a thematic basis for the representations of urban youths within the genre as a challenge to the discourse of Broken Britain. Arguing that the popular Black urban film develops an overt political critique through a generic departure, Chapter 10 investigates the British Sci-Fi film *Attack the Block* (2011) as a radical exploration of racial and social tension, anxiety, nationhood and resistance. The chapter focuses on its realist/representational lexicon and argues that a metaphorical critique of race and class antagonism is developed through an allegorical examination of the crisis that emerges by the intrusion on the tower block by extra-terrestrial power. An attempt is made to forgo the inordinate analytical focus on the formalistic features of cinematic realism (a focus which Forrest (2020) asks us to disavow in favour of a conceptualization of 'New Realism' that permits the elevating of the more poetic and haptic qualities of British realist cinema) that evacuate larger narrative questions of organization, style and intention, for a reading of the film that considers the various approaches that reside outside of cinematic realism but could be understood as a *critical* realism, inasmuch as taking the spectator into a racial and sociological understanding of the world of its making, all the while giving the film a new-found *generic* significance. By interpreting the characters' use of Wyndham Tower's architectural features as a defence against an extra-terrestrial force, the film's allegorical critique of social stigma also performs as a reclamation of Black Britishness. In Chapter 11, through the use of Hall's analysis of Black popular culture, I consider the unprecedented cultural permeation of the urban drama series *Top Boy*. In attempting to account for the various positions and meanings ascribed to the series in its transition from Channel 4 to Netflix, I argue that the representations of criminality and Black violent death cannot be understood simply as the negative depiction of Black urban experience, but also as part of an important sphere of Black cultural visibility that accompanies its entry into the popular and, with it, the hyper-performance of a criminalized Black urbanity as an essentializing strategy to consolidate the position of Black vernacular representations. Our engagement with the series equally allows for a number of acceptable contradictions that become present in its endeavours to address aspects of the Black experience, and in drawing its cultural relevance through its interactions with other mediums, it renders the Black urban as an aggregating sphere of authenticity and realness as it moves from a position of cultural invisibility to visibility. This being the case, *Top Boy* characterizations demonstrate what I see as the disruption of the urban male norm, and I consider the ways in which the series attempts to attend to issues of race(ism), gender and sexual difference.

A note on the book's use of the term Black. Throughout the book, I use capital B for Black in acknowledgement of my racial and cultural identity. However, and relatedly, Black is lower- cased when using the term 'black-on-black' in a disavowal of its racialized, ideological function as the linguistic means through which Black death is made distinct purely by our melanin differential. The lower-casing of black-on-black in this book is to reject its use as a descriptor for the spectacle of Black death and attendantly, as the nomenclature for anti-Blackness.

1

Black British Filmic Identity, the Symbolic Location and the Extractive Choreographies of the Black Mytheme

Why Broadwater Farm?. . . .You've got many other reasons but if the riot never took place, you would not be here, talking to me right now. You wouldn't know I existed, would ya?
—'Scenes from the Farm', Channel 4/Allegra Productions, 1988

the glances of the other fixed me there, in the sense in which a chemical solution is fixed by a dye. I was indignant; I demanded an explanation. Nothing happened. I burst apart. Now the fragments have been put together again by another self.
—Franz Fanon, *White Skins Black Masks*, 1952

The filmic and televisual representations of Blackness, particularly depictions of Black identity created through the white imaginary, find its genealogies in a number of beliefs, understandings, and associative interpretations of racial difference. By beliefs, I am speaking of the historical narratives and fictions of Black savagery and non-being that find some registration in myth. For Barthes (1972), as for Lévi-Strauss, myths are a powerful form of structuring the beliefs of a society through both speech and discourse and, importantly, visual language. In Barthes's semiotic reading, myth is seen as the combinational outcome of a hierarchical order of signification: first, denotation (the literal meaning of a text) and its second order, connotations (its implied, associative meanings). Lévi-Strauss's thesis insists that myths are made active in the transformation of one myth to within another, and with this, myths are to be understood as possessing limited independent meaning; myths are brought into being through their relations with other myths. In both understandings, myth is seen as a discursive language that subsumes and obfuscates reality, and visual culture has been a primary space for the interaction of various myths, and in this visual sphere as *public* sphere, the distortion of the realities of Black identity for the representation of Black people, geographies and acts. The 1970s and 1980s were a period of a particular race politics in the UK most visible in the instances of mass Black British youth rebellion within the inner cities against a system of racial violence and harassment, and given that we are concerned here with the nature of myth as a process of diachronic transition, film and television are transitionary practices where racial myths become woven into a system of denigrative characterizations and associative readings to be placed onto the image of the Black body. There, of course, lies a body of readings within a sociological/cultural studies paradigm that examines the media representations of Black British youths, and is to be located in the work of scholars such as Stuart Hall (1981) and, later, Paul Gilroy (1987) and John Solomos (1988). For them, the media representations of Black youths could be seen as being structured by two processes: first an othering process through its depictions of criminalized, violent and improvident Black existence, and in a second phase of this representational technology, such portrayals significantly impacted Black youth's discriminatory experiences within Britain. These representations are not singular, and despite their medium specificities, a corresponding portraiture of race can be drawn from multiple texts and their interactions; the narrational and textual modalities where the production of cultural and racial stereotypes are also structured by the binaries between 'civilization' (white) and 'savagery' (black) (Hall, 1997: 243). This suggests that the perceived physiological and biological particularities of race that we encounter in televisual texts help to establish mythical polar differences between the human and non-human. Further, in Hall's analysis, discorded, mythical Black representations can be crafted into the narratives of certain racially associative acts to make natural Black (and often but by no means exclusively masculine) savagery; it becomes both instinctive and irredeemable. 'Naturalization', in this sense, 'is therefore a representational strategy designed to *fix* "difference", and thus *secure it forever*. It is an attempt to halt the inevitable "slide" of meaning, to secure discursive or ideological "closure"' (245). This chapter is concerned with how the historical construction of Black criminality as myth can be identified in film and television representations of Black urban identity that produce a restorative alignment between the public understandings of moments of civil disobedience within the racial politics of the 1980s, which, I argue, are a critical point of the interaction between PSB and the representation of racial difference. In our understanding of the popular urban text of the 2000s, one must first consider the racial tensions of the period, the social incidents that became opportune for the projecting of Black identity as a savage non-being through a range of thematics within the sphere of British television as the naturalizing vector for the public's engagement with, understandings of and responses to the myths of Black identity and corporeality. In this endeavour, Lévi-Strauss's concept of 'mythemes' becomes a valuable framework for considering how a body of Black myths becomes unified within filmic and televisual representation as a thematic that, crucially, centres the housing estate as the natural site for both the Black urban 'event' and the demonized Black urban figure.

It is not necessary to rehearse what I feel is the well accounted for analyses of Black British film and representation during the 1970s and 1980s; however, the position of the popular urban text as one that, in the broadest interpretation of the term, finds its genesis in the historical constructions of Black masculine identity; the representations that would come to constitute the urban film genre from the 2000s exhibit a number of textures that can be observed within the history of what can be understood without contention as

Black British cinema. *Pressure* (dir. Horace Ové, 1976), *Blacks Britannica* (dir. David Koff, 1978), *Dread, Beat an' Blood* (dir. Franco Rosso, 1979), *Babylon* (dir. Franco Rosso, 1980) and Burning an *Illusion* (dir. Menelik Shabazz, 1981) can all be seen as depicting some aspect of the urban; however, these are representations of the urban that are thematic in the sense that they are situated within the geographical sphere of Black social and economic marginalization, unemployment and perpetual police harassment with an overt commitment to the inclusion of institutional and habitual white racism as an antagonistic feature within its narrative universe and aesthetic practices. The symbiotic relationship expressed in these texts (and many others) between Black British identity, our social and economic conditions and geographical location is of particular importance in the context of the 1980s, as a result of both the existing racial tensions within British society and the portrayal of Britain's Black population as a natural landscape of violence, social decay and non-belonging, which was to become a dominant feature within British television's constructions of racial difference (Pines, 1992; Mercer, 1988; Nwonka, 2022).

The idea of British television's investment in Black Britain throughout this period as revealing a denigrative interest in race and the physical environment is to suggest that such representations, be they through mainstream news reportage, factual documentary practices and dramas, once inscribed within the text's mise en scène are able to produce a set of racial meanings once situated within what had now come to be understood as their natural habitat, that of the 'symbolic location'. This was a descriptive and inherently racialized term that was applied by the then Metropolitan Police Commissioner Kenneth Newman in a report to the Conservative Home Secretary William Whitelaw in 1983 that identified areas marked by crime and violence, high unemployment and drug dealing and abuse. There was an instinctive racial connotation present in the categorization of such locations as 'no-go areas', where the presence of outsiders in the form of police and law and order was met with hostility and violence, and resultingly as an un-policeable physical and social terrain, and the symbolic location became an all-encompassing shorthand for the public denigration and violent stigmatizing of Black communities, given the geographies the terms was ascribed to: All Saints Road in Notting Hill, which had been the location of the Mangrove Restaurant where in 1970 the Mangrove Nine would be arrested after years of resistance against racist police harassment; Railton Road in Brixton, the site where the Brixton Riots had begun (Figure 1.1); the Stonebridge Estate in Harlesden, and the Broadwater Farm Estate in Tottenham, two densely Afro-Caribbean locales that had been firmly established within racist media discourse as landscapes of lawlessness and Black youth malevolence, but for the estate's Black residents, were experienced as sites of habitual police harassment and violence. Eventually, and performing the necessary ideological practice in the implanting of the hegemonically unified language of race, crime and environment into the social lexicon, the symbolic location would become a descriptor for any housing estate within the inner city with a large proportion of Black people and, therefore, be subjected to disproportionate hyper-policing. But the assertion that the state-endorsed categorizing of the symbolic location represented a varied modality of racism and anti-Blackness can be further affirmed in that the description was not limited to the physical environment of the estates but also to the mobile cultural spaces

Figure 1.1 Brixton Riots. Courtesy of Getty Images, Keystone/Stringer, 1981.

where Black people congregated in the form of the Notting Hill Carnival which, as was most evident in 1976, had historically been seen by the police as the battleground for the violent curtailing of Black cultural expressions.

For Solomos and Back (1996), in building on Gilroy's reading of the ascription of criminality to Black youths to accentuate the indelible association between Blackness and non-Britishness, such language simply served as an aggregating element to be placed within an existent racial discourse in which 'Black youth are thus defined as constituting a social problem' (182). It is this threat of the potential explosion of the Black social problem, and the benign and culturally suppressive practice of race relations through the late 1970s that failed to ameliorate the Black youth's existence within a geography of concentrated poverty, unemployment, social marginalization and police brutality that would lead to the uprising of 1980–1 in St Paul's in Bristol; London's Brixton; Moss Side in Manchester; Chapeltown in Leeds; Toxteth in Liverpool, and many other towns across the UK that conditioned the racial and sociopolitical climate of the early 1980s. At the same time, major institutional changes within the cultural arena would prove conducive to the implementation of particular Government initiatives that would chime with the remedial language of The Scarman Report into the Brixton Riots, published on 25 November 1981 (Scarman, 1982). While the report would acknowledge that Black youths within the inner cities had been subjected to forms of social disadvantage, it would generally avoid any kind of condemnation of the Metropolitan Police or the identification of institutional racism, instead opting for a rationale rooted comfortably in accentuating the self-destructive pathologies of the Afro-Caribbean family and as its index, the criminalized pathologies of the Black youth that would provide further consenting momentum to the Thatcherite discourse of law and order, albeit one to be rhetorically accompanied by a practice of community policing and the continuation of the late 1970s technology of race relations. It is this latter imperative, that certain forms of cultural participation may remedy a sense of alienation among Britain's Black youth population by providing a more productive expressive outlet, and in this endeavour fulfilling the Scarman dictate for a 'comprehensive, grounded political programme of accommodating cultural minority needs' (Vinen, 2010: 90), that would find a somewhat serendipitous manifestation through the establishment of Channel 4 in 1982 with a distinctive remit to represent those on the periphery of British society. A direct outcome of the Annan Report (1977), established by the newly elected Labour Government in 1974 that would recommend a fourth independent terrestrial channel to respond to the representational needs of Britain's minority audiences, was implemented by the Conservative Party as an Act of Parliament through the 1980 Broadcasting Act that had given the Independent Broadcasting Authority (IBA) responsibility for the establishing of Channel 4 and with this, the decree that the channel was to fulfil a number of obligations in its programming to fulfil its specific PSB obligations. This positioned Channel 4 not just at the centre of a struggle over representations of Black and ethnic majority/minority identities, but the channel was also positioned to become the platform through which Britain would be provided with a PSB framework for the dramatic departure in the form and nature of the textual depictions of Britain's marginal societies, demographics, regions and cultures through new formal and narrational approaches in the representation of Blackness and racial difference. This new visual language was to be most dramatically experienced in the independent Black film and video workshop collectives that were to emerge in the early- to mid-1980s. The outcome of an agreement between the newly established Channel 4 and the Association of Cinematograph, Television and Allied Technicians (ACTT) would result in the 1982 Workshop Declaration that would aid the development of Black film collectives, such as the Ceddo Film and Video Retake, Black Audio Film Collective and Sankofa Film and Video; with the sustained financial support from Channel 4 and the Greater London Council, such film and video collectives were able to work within an industrial context that proved favourable for filmmakers who saw screen media as a counter-hegemonic tool against the dominant narratives of race (Mercer 1988). There is a tremendous heterogeneity to be observed in the films that were produced by these collectives throughout the period in texts such as *Territories* (dir. Isaac Julien, 1984), *The Passion of Remembrance* (dir. Maureen Blackwood/Isaac Julien, 1986) and *Handsworth Songs* (dir, John Akomfrah, 1986), which through the mosaic use of archival footage, stills, interviews and soundscapes, offered a subversive account of the Handsworth riots that occurred in the Afro-Caribbean/Asian area of Birmingham the previous year (Figure 1.2). The Black workshop movement can be understood as an inherently diasporic project aligned with a shared exploration of the broad dimensions of Black identity and the Black experience through the intersections of race, gender, class and sexuality that, for Kobena Mercer, allowed for the filmmakers to be described as 'cinematic activists' (1994: 53). Operating within a praxis of 'political Blackness' as an ethnically cohesive term that, in the specific context of the 1970s and 1980s, allowed

Figure 1.2 *Handsworth Songs* (dir. John Akomfrah, 1996).

Black and Southern Asian identities to coalesce through a shared experience of and a unified fight against white British racism, the Black workshop movement created a body of films that were visually, culturally and politically agitative to the lacerating racial politics of Thatcherism, but in such a way that, rather than simply countering the normalization of racist social beliefs towards Black identities through the presenting of a positive Black imagery, but also exposing the myths at the centre of Britain's treatment of Black people through an interrogation of the neocolonial conditions of Britain's Black communities, which was approached in ways both narrationally and *aesthetically* antithetical to British television and film's ideological project of the creation and dispersal of denigrative racial characterizations.

The question of myth is central to exploring the meaning of Black representations within the castigatory function of the symbolic location, and as Lévi-Strauss argues, the nature of myths cannot be understood in their singularity but through an ecology of relational meanings. One of the symbolic locations that had been included in the Newman taxonomy was the Broadwater Farm Estate in Tottenham, North London, which would be the scene of the most severe moments of civil disobedience and in UK history, and a critical point of state/civilian racial conflict (Figure 1.3). The estate had been built in the late 1960s upon marshes that required the buildings to be built above ground level to avoid flooding, creating an estate comprised of elevated buildings marked by a series of overhead walkways, underground car parks and secluded spaces that made it particularly opportune for criminality. These were just some of a number of design flaws that rendered Broadwater Farm one of the most undesirable housing estates in London, a claim to be made by Alice Coleman in her book *Utopia on Trial* where Broadwater Farm would occupy a central position within the social lexicon as a 'sink estate' through its associations with Coleman's taxonomic analysis of similar housing estates, inspired by the architect Le Corbusier, and its various social problems

Figure 1.3 Broadwater Farm, 1985. Courtesy of Getty Images/Julian Herbert.

(1985), and one which eschewed any analysis of social inequality and poverty for a thesis that assessed crime and social decay within such estates as an outcome of a failed architectural imagination. Despite the subtle legislative changes to particular aspects of policing after Scarman, notably the promise of more contextual, community-based policing, and the residents own modes of self-organization in the creation of the Broadwater Farm's Youth Association, the disproportionate application of 'Sus' law, SPG raids without prior community or council liaising, simply exposed Broadwater Farm's Black youth to an unaltered system of militaristic policing (Rose, 1992). This set the climate for an inevitable moment of Black rebellion that was to be catalysed by the death of Cynthia Jarratt, a 48-year-old Black woman who died of a heart attack on 5 October when four officers from Tottenham Police Station unlawfully gained entry to her home and conducted a speculative search for stolen goods connected with her son Floyd Jarratt, whom they had wrongly arrested earlier that day for theft and assault (no stolen goods were found and Floyd Jarratt was later released without charge). However, Cynthia Jarratt collapsed and died after allegedly being pushed by officers as they searched her home. The incident, which exacerbated a deep-seated system of racial antagonism towards the local Black community from the Metropolitan Police, had followed a number of anti-racist uprisings that autumn in the Handsworth Riots in Birmingham on 9 September and the Brixton Riots on 28 September after a Black woman, Cherry Groce, was shot and left permanently paralysed after police had raided her home looking for her 21-year-old son Michael in connection with a gun incident. This would be followed by riots in Peckham, South London, on 30 September and Toxteth, Liverpool, the following day. On the evening of 6 October, Broadwater Farm Estate erupted in violence, when 600 policemen were deployed in the area where they clashed with the estate's youths (Glifford, 1989; Rose, 1992) (Figure 1.4). During the rioting, a small police unit, which had been deployed to escort the London Fire Brigade into Broadwater Farm's Tangmere House to put out a fire in one of the shops on the upper deck, came under attack by a group of rioters. One of the officers, PC Keith Blakelock, fell as his unit retreated from the Tangmere block out of the estate where he was set upon by what was reported to be up to 30 rioters armed with knives, machetes and iron bars (Gifford, 1989) and sustained forty-three separate wounds, including a knife lodged in his neck and a horrific wound to his jawbone that the investigating pathologist believed to be the result of an attempt at decapitation (Rose, 1992).

Figure 1.4 Riot police at Broadwater Farm Estate, 6 October 1985. Courtesy of Getty Images/ Julian Herbert.

The unprecedented degree of public emotion, outrage and horror caused by the murder of a police officer was accelerated by the media's dissemination of the circumstances, nature and physical facts of the killing, and the existent anti-Black sentiment was to be portrayed through a number of racial thematics in the displays of overt racism within the media's reportage of the riot. This was manifest through a range of race fictions: the construction of Broadwater Farm as a site of racialized polarization through the propagation of the idea of the existence of an unrelenting culture of fear inflicted by Black youths upon Broadwater Farm's white residents, and the sustained racist characterization of the Black Labour Councillor for Harringey, Bernie Grant, who was to be likened to an ape in the tabloid press (Glifford, 1986; Rose, 1992). However, and central to my identification of mytheme in the development of the social idea of Black savagery as indexical to the symbolic location, our urtext is to be identified in the circulation of the image of Winston Silcott, a 26-year-old Black resident of the Broadwater Farm Estate who had been arrested for the murder of Blakelock alongside two teenagers, Engin Raghip (aged nineteen) and Mark Braithwaite (aged eighteen), who would come to be understood colloquially as the Tottenham Three. All would have their murder convictions overturned in 1991 after forensic analysis revealed gross miscarriages of justice by the police, including the fabricating of written evidence and the drawing of confessions under extreme duress and oppressive interrogative practices. What is encoded in the figure of Silcott as the symbolic location's symbolic target? My argument here is that the mythic creation of Black savagery is not necessarily assured through the fact that he had been identified by the police *a priori* as the primary suspect in the murder of Blakelock, but in the symbolic product of Black myth made tangible both by the image and the methods through which the image was captured. According to Silcott (BBC, 2004), having been arrested days after the murder, he had been asleep in his cell when he was dragged out by several officers and taken into a custody room where a camera and a tripod had been set up. After momentarily struggling, he was then suddenly let free by the officers, where a photograph was then taken of the startled Silcott with his hands raised slightly by his side (Figure 1.5). What also interests me here, if we are able to momentarily put to one side the disturbing, racial choreography of the image that was to be circulated by the police to the mainstream tabloid media in the lead-up to the 1987 trial (Gilford, 1986) is how the mythic construction of the urban as a geography for the spectacle of an unassimilable Black urbanity can be approached through the framework provided by the structuralism of Lévi-Strauss in his idea of mythemes, the constituent units of a myth at the basis of a narrative structure from which myths are both constructed and actioned (1978). Lévi-Strauss's theory asks that the mytheme should be understood as the unification of theme, characterization and event, and such a formulation is conducive for a reading of the mythical portrayal of Silcott in which 'atavistic racial imagery lay close to the surface' (Rose, 2004). My contention here is that the racial identification to be extracted from Broadwater Farm as the embodiment of pathological beastliness is manifest in the interaction between location, race and masculinity, which is encapsulated in the photographic image that works to define and secure Silcott in the public imaginary as the 'beast of Broadwater'. Further, and producing associative feelings dispersed by the unsettling power of the

Figure 1.5 Winston Silcott, 'The Beast of Broadwater'. Courtesy of Press Association, 1985.

monochrome image of Silcott in its forced choreography of racial menace, as advanced by Hall, the ahistorical acceptance and association of the figure as the Black savagery antagonist in the mythical narrative of a haunting Black non-being becomes animalistic in nature, and in considering how myths are anchored in meaning by the use of captioning as argued by Barthes, the photo finds its correspondence with the racial logics within tabloid media representation in the accompanying text where Silcott is described as a 'monster' and 'beast' (Gilford, 1986). The photo of Silcott, and all it claims to represent in what Hall describes as 'the conjunction of image *and* text' (229), is equally where its racialized meanings arrive at a point of ideological closure. In doing so, the image secures into its publics the 'beast of Broadwater' as a natural creation of the symbolic location.

In drawing attention to the processes through which the iconographies of Black savagery created from the interaction between the Black symbolic location, the position of the Broadwater Farm riots as the primary critical vector through which white Britain would construct and secure the normalization of beliefs and ideas of a natural Black savagery into the social episteme, I wish to term the literal and referential thematic of Broadwater Farm, in the specific context of the 1980s, as the 'extractive choreography of the Black mytheme'. Of course, the 1970s and 1980s and their technology of anti-Black violence and harassment provided many examples of how collective Black struggle and anti-racist rebellion were purposefully reframed as a collective and unredeemable Black urban menace in Brixton, Handsworth, and beyond, through which they produced the mythical properties for the naturalizing of Black people as a negated identity, but it was the singular act associated with Broadwater Farm – the killing of PC Blakelock, and in such horrific circumstances – that became the pathologizing 'event' that unifies Black identity within the white imaginaries of Broadwater Farm. Associatively, it is in the particular image of Winston Silcott that we can observe the aggregation of mythemes that 'created a monster to stalk the nightmares of Middle England' (BBC, 2004). Thus, the extractive choreography of the Black mytheme refers to how a relational body of racial myths became implicated in the dramatizing allure of a moment of Black social crisis that becomes the basis for mainstream televisual and filmic representation, which carries with it specific forms of social meanings when presented to us within PSB/terrestrial contexts – the instances of Black urban violence that are used as the source material for a range of Black textual characterizations. In the context of the media's racist narrating of the racial crisis of the 1980s, Broadwater Farm became a particularly labile Black thematic for the televisual representation of the symbolic location as a natural lair of Black urban savagery. However, the provisions created by Channel 4 throughout this period meant that both countering and neutral perspectives were able to produce their own discursive space for the alternative portrayal of Broadwater Farm, its events and its inhabitants as racialized subjects. Thus, the Broadwater Farm riots, and the public's understandings of it, were to be contested in a number of texts. From one perspective, the Broadwater Farm riots become a site of representational counter-hegemony in Ceddo's *The People's Account* (dir. Milton Bryan, 1985), a documentary that would investigate the events at Broadwater Farm and the immediate aftermath but, crucially, narrated from the perspective of the estate's residents to counter the hegemonic framing of the estate and its indigenes that would challenge the dominant racist framing of Broadwater Farm in public discourse and media narratives in presenting 'the antagonistic relationship between the police and the residents and how the media colluded with the police in distorting the real causes of the uprising' (Friedman 1993: 131). However, the IBA, who would take particular umbrage towards the documentary's description of the Metropolitan Police's actions, both on the day and historically, were rooted in a technology of racism and the interpretation of the riots 'as a classic example of self-defence by a community' would demand significant editorial changes before the documentary could be aired. Refusing to accede to the editorial demands made by the IBA, *The People's Account* was subsequently pulled from Channel 4's scheduling and would never be shown on terrestrial television. A less politically contentious depiction of Broadwater Farm was to be found in *Scenes from the Farm* (1988), a Channel 4 documentary that featured as part the channel's True Stories series, a fly on the wall current affairs programme. This was directed by the anthropologist filmmaker Melisa Llewelyn-Davies, who had spent much of her career making documentary films on the Maasai people, a Nilotic ethnic group indigenous to Kenya and Tanzania, for Granada TV and the BBC. Resultingly, *Scenes from the Farm* exhibits a similarly detached and holistically observational documentary approach that captures the estate in its diurnal moments; artwork on the estate has been defiled by National Front insignia, a heated discussion between residents, their representatives and the Harringay Council is filmed where plans to outsource employment contracts for the estate's building work in the aftermath of the riots are challenged by the estate's unemployed, mostly Black indigenes; Black fathers discuss the domestic teaching of Black culture to their children; and local residents are filmed reflecting on the conditions of their existence on the estate. Rather than being a vessel for the organic articulation of the counter-factualities of the Broadwater Farm riots, the documentary's representational schema is an ethnographic account of the community's attempts to rebuild physically and emotionally from the events of 1985. Thus, it is through the broader organization of the film as a political project that a claim to a radical participatory documentary can be observed, and one that can't necessarily be achieved through the mere framing of Broadwater Farm's *politicized* residents through anthropological documentary practices. This important factor renders the documentary as markedly distinct from the form of polemical truth-telling that can be observed in *The People's Account*, and such a comparison is of particular salience, as in the tension between framing Broadwater Farm from the outside, and the production of organic forms of narration from within, the estate and its meaning are fixed at the centre of an *endogenous* and an *exogenous* representational dialectic. Both Ellis (1982) and Fiske (1994) have questioned the efficacy of anthropological television, specifically the subsuming of a distinctive visual practice under the paradigm of scientific knowledge that is uninvested in the specificities of the medium, and indexically, is devoid of any attunement to both the dynamics of the audience/text relationship and the context of its spectatorship. This has been noted by Grimshaw (1997), who, in an analysis of Llewelyn-Davies's anthropological oeuvre, concedes that such a modality possesses what she describes as 'a tremendous conservatism in the forms or media used for the transmission of anthropological knowledge; and it sets up a fundamental contradiction at the heart of any project concerned with anthropological television' (51). In some senses, *Scenes from the Farm*'s aesthetic form can also be contrasted with *Handsworth Songs*, which serves as a counterpoint to the orthodoxy of representing Black British identity through the mirror-optics of documentary realism as argued by Pines (1991). The ethical dynamics in the representation of Black urbanity within the symbolic location can be observed in the opening moments of the documentary where a Black resident, while being filmed in his flat, challenges Llewelyn-Davies when she claims the film crew have decided to film the residents because 'it seems like an interesting place where a lot is going on' when asked directly 'what is your purpose for being here?' However, she would then concede when pressed that the motivation for her documentary is 'partly because of the riot', a confession that is attempted to be made less disingenuous and strategically extractive by an accompanying claim that this interest is shared in equal measure with the community organization work being done on the estate. His response is a subtle but precise and persistent evisceration of the absurdity that the work of the community associations and the spectacularizing allure of Black urbanity within the symbolic location so heavily inscribed within the public imagination of the Broadwater Farm riot can be held within a balancing equivalency of thematic and then public interest and allure. Briefly looking away from the camera, he replies with 'partly the riot? . . . that the *only* reason you're here init?' (my emphasis). Llewelyn-Davies responds with 'it's not the only reason', and it is here that the camera zooms in on him, in an effort to highlight this very tension in the relationship between Black urban identity and televisual anthropology as a representational visual strategy. As he replies, 'well, you've got many other reasons but if the riot never took place you would not be here, talking to me right now. You would not know I existed, would ya?' The documentary does not allow for her response to his assertion, and in many respects, this is unrequired, for there is a mutual acceptance that the public castigation of Broadwater Farm is the axis upon which the engagement between the filmmakers and the residents, in all its verticality, is constructed. The specific point I wish to make here, and one crucial to the broader relationship between the historical development of the spectacle of urban disorder, Black 'social' issues and the primary thematic interest of the popular Black urban text is that the televisual and filmic interest in Black urban identity within the frames of PSB is determined solely by the presence and degree of stigmatization within the public imaginary of the symbolic location as a site for Black social, and therefore *national*, crisis.

I want to consider the possibility that the period's audiovisual construction of Black urban savagery can be understood as a kind of mytheme in the fictitious iteration of Broadwater Farm as a televisual culture that, as argued, secures the verisimilitude of its dramatic material from a heightened point of Black urban crisis and mythical Black savagery, and is to be observed in the feature-length television drama *London's Burning* (dir. Les Blair, 1986). The singe drama, aired on London Weekend Television (LWT) on 7 December would attract 12.5 million viewers and, on the basis of the film's success, would be commissioned as a television series running between 1988 and 2002 that at its peak would draw an 18 million audience share. Written by the British playwright Jack Rosenthal, who had written episodes of the long-running British soap Coronation Street, Rosenthal had been motivated to write a drama about the fire brigade through daily conversations with the husband of the family's au pair, a North London firefighter who lived with them. Rosenthal, who had lived in Muswell Hill, where, indeed, Keith Blakelock had patrolled, would then be inspired by the nearby Broadwater Farm riots, which became what Rosenthal termed as 'the dramatic framework: a fictional centre that could make the fact all the more true' (2005: 331). My analysis here is concerned with the indexical use of the Black event within the symbolic location that, as recognized by Vice, becomes its 'factual structure' (76). This thematic imperative positions the drama as firmly embedded within the period's attendant race politics in that it is its sensationalist Black subject matter that becomes primed for the spectacle of the Black Other to be included within the white imaginaries of televisual and filmic representation. While the film is marked by a tragicomic tonality most evident in its framing of the often juvenile antics of the Blue Watch fire crew based in Blackwell, East London, the factual elements of the Broadwater Farm riots that provided the film with 'particular dramatic and political opportunities' (72) are exploited through the character of Andreas 'Ethnic' Lewis (Garry MacDonald), the sole Black firefighter who lives on a crime-ridden South London estate and would serve as the text's constitutive link to the Black urban. Ethnic is immediately situated within the positive exemplars of the local Black community; the opening sequence begins with an image of a young Black boy sitting on the pavement within what appears to be a distressed urban location. The mobile camera then follows a Black man from the street into a populated Black community hall where Ethnic is shown playing the saxophone among other mostly Black young musicians in a reggae band to joyous members of London's Windrush Generation. This opening of the drama to a Black density permits me to find particular narrational significance in the broader placing of the symbolic location at the centre of a thematic contestation over Ethnic's own sense of his racial and national identity and, crucially, the identities conferred on him by others. For example, Ethnic is subjected to frequent racial abuse by his 'bantering' white colleagues who have given Ethnic his nickname, and prior to this, Ethnic is seen going through the routine of applying hair cream, then placing a durag over his afro hair, a demonstration of a Black cultural practice within the whiteness of the station that for Ethnic, coexists *with* rather than being contradictory *to* his own claim to Englishness. Earlier, Ethnic is antagonized by the estate's unemployed Rastafarians who interrogate him after a forceful inspection of his work uniform (he tells them he's a cleaner) lead them to suspect that Ethnic is as an agent of Babylon. This prompts them to pressurize the reluctant Ethnic to verbally declare his devotion to Rastafarianism as both a racial affirmation and, in the context of their existence under police racism and brutality, a political posture, with the evasive Ethnic eventually saying 'true to Jah'. Given that Ethnic's default dialect is an assimilatory South London accent when among the all-white fire brigade, it is acceptable to interpret this as a moment of double consciousness, and one equally reflective of Du Bois (1903), Fanon (1952) and Gilroy (1993) in inflection in that his opting to speak in patois during this particular exchange can be seen as an instinctive code-switching strategy to navigate the Black vernacular decrees of the estate and the whiteness of the station. The film exhibits an interest in the personal, socio-spatial and institutional dimensions of Ethnic's Black identity that, at least in its opening scenes, appears to be the drama's paramount concern in specific relation to race. However, given the film's close fidelity to the events of Broadwater Farm, the drama can rightly be understood as an actual *reconstruction*. Indeed, Rosenthal had spent time speaking with residents on Broadwater Farm about the riots while writing the script, and there is an engagement in the period's race politics in its depictions of Black representational authenticity; the narrative is fissured with instances of police harassment and racism towards the estate's Black youths, although this is subsequently negated by its simultaneous depictions of Black men involved in drug dealing on the estate. Within its factual universe, Broadwater Farm and the aesthetic of Black urban 'race' rioting becomes the film's dramatic climax (Figure 1.6). Narrationally altering what is understood to be the

Figure 1.6 Reconstructing the riots in *London's Burning: The Movie* (dir. Les Blair, 1986).

planned nature of the riot and the police's response, who from 28 September were 'expecting riots in areas with large Black populations in the week following Brixton' (Glifford, 1986: 97), two beat police officers are lured into the estate at night where they are attacked by a waiting group of Black youths – indeed, the scene immediately preceding the attack shows Black youths preparing for the conflict by breaking concrete slabs to use as weaponry and setting fire to a car to goad the police. Like the popular images of Black urban disorder that were symbolic of the events of Broadwater Farm, the images of burning vehicles within the symbolic location serve as a signifier for a moment of civil disturbance that allows for the involvement of Blue Watch, who are deployed to put out a number of fires on the estate only to come under violent attack by the rioters, who, just as reported in the media about the circumstances surrounding Blakelock's killing on Broadwater Farm's Tangmere block, at a moment of urban conflict with state institutions within the symbolic location, one makes no distinction between the firefighters and the police. Relatedly, the film finds its social and moral address in the dramatic utility of the dead Black body. Having taken the day off before his last shift the following day (he had recently got a promotion to Archway Fire Station) as Ethnic watches the rioting from his balcony, he witnesses the police savagely beating a young Black youth to an inch of his life with batons. Ethnic, now reduced to tears, runs down to the ground level to assist. However, at this point he then sees a large group of Black youths attacking the simpleton Charisma (Gerald Horan), whom one of the chasing rioters refers to as a 'dirty white git'. The camera hones in on Ethnic as he is faced with a particular dilemma – come to the aid of the Black youth, germane to the estate, before he is beaten to death by the police, or to the aid of his (white) work colleague. He chooses the latter, intervening and pushing the youths away. What we see next is the decisive moment when the most associative aspect of Broadwater Farm is inscribed into the film's tragic mise en scéne. After the beaten Charisma is led to safety, we now see that the incident has been observed by some of the rioters from the walkway above, who draw Ethnic's attention by shouting out 'Oi, traitor!' As Ethnic looks up, the camera oscillates from the POV of Ethnic to that of the perpetrator as a concrete pavement slab is dropped from above onto the head of Ethnic, who falls to the ground. If this sequence's formal denotations are in the framing of the scene, where the slab seems to be on the verge of penetrating through the screen and signifies, as Vice observes, the moment of death, the connotative meanings to be extracted in the following shot-reverse-shot sequence between the prone Ethnic and the returned Charisma register a key moment of diegetic and non-diegetic suture as he is confronted with a colleague's death. Unable to attend to Ethnic, who at this point is now dead and therefore cannot return Charisma's look, the scene becomes a site of several, interweaving planes of meaning: the futility of Ethnic's intervention; the white guilt carried by Charisma that would spill into the film's concluding and emotional high point where he breaks down in front of his colleagues, unable to eat the celebratory Ackee and Saltfish dinner that they had prepared for Ethnic's leaving; the usually boisterous canteen (and the food they eat) now a source of silent tribute/mourning; and finally, the symbolic location as an inescapable environment of Black conflict, savagery and inevitable violent death.

Congruent with the footage and imagery encountered within television reportage and print media on the morning of 7 October, the now quiet estate is populated by burned out cars, debris and, crucially, the police, who preside over what is now a murder scene while the estate's Black community dwell, discuss and mourn against the audial backdrop of incidental music. Such a scene underpins my rejection of Vice's claim that 'the film has no pretensions to documentary status' (77) made in response to some of the film's critical reviews that Rosenthal's drama strives for a documentary realism that, in the absence of what was termed as 'psychological accuracy or moral analysis' (Walsh, 1986), it subsequently fails to attain. *London's Burning* occupies a nebulous space between documentary and drama, and given the film's screening just over a year after the events at Broadwater Farm, the drama engages with the essences of docudrama in the facticity of the (very recent) historical event that cannot be negated by Vice's observation that the selective and strategic use of *cinema vérité* aesthetic devices in the film can support the insistence that the drama can be detached from the question of realism and the dramatized re-enactment of factual events, despite the racial topicality of Broadwater Farm as its extractive value (indeed, it is the film's most dramatic moments that are presented to us under these formal auspices). Rather, the film presents an aggregational documentary realism that

Figure 1.7 Ethnic watches on as the estate explodes into violence in *London's Burning: The Movie* (dir. Les Blair, 1986).

is not determined solely by the presence of any documentary realist formal techniques but also by the authenticating augmentation that is accentuated by the indexicality of depictions of race and Blackness through which the film accrues an immediate cultural, social, political and, therefore, *representational* associativity. By this, Vice's analysis reveals a critical lacuna in her aim to stress formal and aesthetic determinism, for this disregards the crucial questions of the exceptionality of race and Blackness, given its centrality to the film's dramatic and 'factual structure' and the relationship to the audience's understandings of the Broadwater Farm events as both the sphere of discorded Black identity and the source of its production of verisimilitude, both generic and cultural (Neale, 1990), and, subsequently, how its interpretations and meanings are secured by racially organized gazes. The question of *London's Burning*'s textual and representational facticity is not dependent on an analytical triumph over its generic categorization as a docudrama, but in such a formal approach's communicative purpose and, crucially, its *intentions*. This means we must be cognizant of the analytical lenses that are surrendered or eviscerated in any effort for the question of race, its representational alterity, the conjunctural and contextual dimensions and cultural dynamics through which its representations exist and the thematics and characterizations that secure its degree of identification and plausibility, to be analytically segregated, as Vice attempts, from an understanding of the drama as possessing a claim on actuality, irrespective of its realist stylistic techniques being preserved for solely 'fictional purposes' (77).

I am in agreement with Rosenthal's insistence, as concurred by Vice, that Ethnic 'experiences a conflict between incompatible moral actions' (76). However, such an incommensurability is one not limited to the moral conflict between what Rosenthal asserts is a loyalty to 'his ghetto community and to his fellow-firefighters' (2005: 12), and in the emotive knowledge of Broadwater Farm and the killing of PC Blakelock within the public imaginary in the lead-up to the Tottenham Three trial (Gilford, 1986; Rose, 1992), the text becomes implicated in the hegemonic construction of the symbolic location and the savagery of Black youth within it, while the film extracts an array of meanings to deposit within the diegesis by its dramatizing of an extra-diegetic facticity. Whereas Vice identifies a plot and character alteration where 'the real-life murder of PC Blakelock during a riot has been transformed into the death of a Black firefighter living on the estate in question' (2009: 77) that is to be used as a defending exemplar of a dramatic moment 'where fiction has priority' (2009: 77), this cannot serve as a mitigating defence against the reading of the film as a documentation of the most paramount moment of the riots as, crucially, Vice neglects a consideration of how the film's thematic use of Broadwater Farm serves as a powerful, dramatic point of public identification and emotional investment, for it can be argued that its very *raison d'etre* as a television drama is structured on its potential impact upon its socially conditioned audience, be them imagined or empirical (Brunsdson, 1981). Nor can it articulate a formal space that is divorced from its entanglements with the events and characterizations of the riot as its source of facticity, as the fundamental positional transformation that takes place is of Charisma and PC Blakelock, who are both unified in their status as members of the emergency services and public servants, and in the context of the riots as a response to the oppressive racist actions of the state, they are the embodiment of authority, institutionality and its synonymy with whiteness, a set of factors that are antithetical to the Blackness that populates the quasi-fictitious frames of the film. Thus, it is Ethnic, and the environmental and epidermal mythologies that his representations within the facsimiled realism of Black urban rioting and savagery that his character embodies, that is placed in a position of fixity and non-transformation. While it is indeed Ethnic who is killed at the hands of the rioters rather than Charisma, whose innocence and, in returning to the Hallian extrapolation of Saussure in that we arrive at an understanding of the meaning of Black not through the presence of a Black *essence* but through its contrast to its immediate opposite (whiteness) and its denotative readings and connotative associations, his sense of antithetical non-place is accentuated by both his uniform and the Blackness of the symbolic location, it is PC Blacklock's death and the Broadwater Farm's symbolic meaning that provides the film's factitious textuality. Ethnic is compelled to occupy the void of a public outrage and mourning towards the tragedy of Broadwater Farm, and with this, attend to the denigration of a symbolic location voided of morality – *surely is not one of them capable of intervening?* It is the social, and racial spectacle of the Broadwater Farm riots, and the specific killing of PC Blakelock that accentuated the universal application of the myth of the Black savage in terms of theme, plot and character that *London's Burning* is stencilled from as its immediate and holistically encouraged narrational and aesthetic point of factual reference. Here, and in returning to how the narrational and aesthetic investment in the racial crisis of the 1980s allows for the Black mytheme to become centrally positioned in the textual construction of a malevolent Black urban identity, it is through the public encounter with Broadwater Farm as Black thematic, character (s) and event that the film performs an associative and perceptive Black urban realism, whether telegraphed formally through docudrama or otherwise. And with this, Ethnic is placed at the centre of the film's, and consequently the public's, imagined intervention in a historical event of racial, social and national tragedy.

2

Hegemonic (A)Symmetries of Black British Filmic Identity in the 1990s

> We keep coming back to the question of representation because identity is always about representation
>
> —bell hooks, *Reel to Real: Race, Sex and Class at the Movies*, 1996

A central proposition that Stuart Hall poses to us in *Representation: Cultural Representation and Signifying Practices*, one that becomes particularly salient in regard to understanding the popular Black urban film's intra-diegetic narrational intentions and its extra-diegetic critical and cultural framing, is 'does visual language reflect the truth about the world which is already there or does it produce meanings about the world through representing it?' (1997: 7). The question of visual language that concerns us here at this point specifically is the ability of film texts to present a reliable account of the conditions of Black life in Britain, to reveal truths or untruths about the nature of our existence and to refer to some of the examples touched upon in the previous chapter, to represent our experiences as devoid of equality or, indeed, presence. As a form of meaning-making, film, and in particular drama, is a highly contested visual and narrational system that is not only able to construct our social identities through a range of ideological representations but also define our relationship to the social, the political, our histories and the present. These powerful forms of mediation that films generate bring us to the question of British national cinema as a mode of filmic narration that is attuned to the dynamics that organize our social relations. In relying upon this figuration, to accept this perspective is to acknowledge that at every moment, juncture and sphere of the Black existence within the nation is an experience not of a cohesive multiracial society or of a cultural multiplicity, but of a continuous and violent evisceration. It is in keeping with Hall's proposition that we think deeply about the forms of meaning construction that are embedded within visual language and its ability to contain within its diegesis a reflection, a refraction and an idealization of the nation that, if we are to examine the social identities that comprised the more dominant and circulated forms of cinematic representation throughout the 1990s, we will find ample and evidential cause to conclude that there were no Black people living in the UK. In regard to questions over the representation, or underrepresentation, of Black identities within the mainstream of the UK film and television sector, I again use film and television as an adjoined visual medium, in this instance not to provoke the analytical legitimacy of the study of what are two distinct visual and narrational languages. Instead, I use them as a unified and integrated representational form that not only points towards the critical body of ethnic minority representation captured within public service broadcasting's historic investment in British film production, but equally acknowledges the presence of the migratory and organic textual features that point to the specificity of race and racial difference in rendering television as a medium of cross-pollinatory textuality, meaning- making and spectatorship. These have always centred on the heavily contested issue of causality: that the entire system of Black industrial and textual erasure is an outcome of benign underrepresentation, a deficit of the prerequisite skills and capabilities among Black people, cultural apathy or, alternatively, an outcome of a concerted, wilful and performed *practice* of racism. It may be useful at this stage to think of British cinema, if we can retain the idea that the function of national film is, *inter alia*, the assisting in the external construction of social identities through the authoring and authoritative power of textual representation and a continuous site of contestation, as afflicted by the coexistence of these two regimes. In this endeavour, we find that we are in some ways drawn to an engagement with Hall's identification of the challenge to both the denial of access to the means of cultural production and the objectifying of the Black imagery that comprise the relations of representation. But even if we are to reduce this specific aspect of the Hallian critique to its very essence – that the purposeful denial of Black people's rights to access the means of mainstream film production bears a material consequence in the presence and nature of Black images – we find that when isolating the concern with the fetishizing Black imagery and its 'positive' countering, the issue of on-screen (non) representation is equally conditioned by a certain comorbidity. It feels absolutely true to me that, in engaging with Back who, via both Hall and Fanon's reading of the overlapping elements of racial ideology, points to the existence of 'no one monolithic racism but numerous historically situated racisms' (1996: 9), when engaging with the question of race and its implicit/explicit manifestations which are highly organized by the social and institutional arenas within they are practised, any referral to the theoretical dichotomizing of racism is prefaced by the recognition that our use of the manifold conceptual prefixes and hyphens that allow for the necessary nuancing and complicating of the nature, expressions and circulation of racism(s) possesses little or no experiential or diminutive bearing, that the anatomy of racism reveals no differentiation in its origins, pathogens or genetic make-up and that the various descriptive categories of racism are emptied of all difference at the level of *affect*. This encourages me to place a momentary analytical emphasis on the textual implications of race thinking, and to conceive of film production as a site of a comorbid racial contestation becomes a more figurative way of arguing that the film and TV industry produces a variant of the racism that, while present in its more recognizable forms within the organizational cultures and structures of Britain's screen institutions, at the textual level is performed, energized and, crucially, disguised through the feints and deceptive rationalities within the film form and its racialized authorship. This idea that the racism that underpins the representational absence of Black Britain within British cinema enjoys an almost decoyed and therefore acceptable structuring invisibility allows for the erasure of Black identity to become encoded within the generic, stylistic and formal fissures of filmic grammar that Lola Young terms as a variant of an 'aversive racism' (1996). For Young, in relocating to the question of Black British cinematic representation the psychological hypothesis on the subtle but no less consequential forms of racial discrimination expressed towards African Americans by educated white individuals within workplace environments and settings in the United States as advanced by Gaertner and Dovidio (1986), aversive racism is a system of racial avoidance and distancing enactioned by the dominant racial group within liberal societies to secure a kind of non-malignant segregation in specific arenas. A crucial aspect of the idea of aversive racism that in many ways reaffirms its adequacy as a theory for working through the invisibility of Black people in British film is that it is characterized by ambivalence; rather than an overt racial hatred, aversive racism is demonstrated by white groups within social and cultural spaces, social practices and workplace cultures that would otherwise project a progressive or racially tolerant self-image. By this, we can come to understand aversive racism as an uneasily detectable and therefore easily refutable and disguisable practice, particularly when performed though the fragile normative structures and subjective social mores of the UK film sector. It is in the varied specificity of aversive racism that Young argues, in the context of the film industry in the decades leading up to the late 1990s, is essentially designatory and preservative in its marking out from British society the territories and customs of a reluctant multiculturalism. In erecting the film industry as an alternative and resistant social sphere that can protect the idea that cinematic language is an inherently white idiolect, British film's contribution to the repertoires of aversive racism is one that does not privilege any of the formal, generic and stylistic categories that organize our primary experience of film culture. Rather, it operates as a permeating and pernicious rationality for racial exclusion and erasure and is therefore an expressive practice to be identified firmly within the disinclining cultures of the overwhelmingly white custodianship over British film production, for as Young observes, 'the practice of aversive racism may be seen as a significant feature of white British mainstream, independent and "art" cinema' (1996: 27). From a comparative perspective, while acknowledging the differentiating production cultures and the corporeal and historically determined textualities that are found in the filmic representations of Black America, a similar manifestation of the practices of aversive racism as a decoying logic supporting the denial of Black cinematic identities is explored by James Snead (1994). In his reading of Black representation within the dominant frames of Hollywood cinema, Snead finds a concerted practice of racial denial in the manoeuvres of filmic 'exigency' as the system by which Black identities are erased and/or reduced in significance, range and visibility under the protected logic of an alleged incompatibility with the intricate aesthetic, narrational and generic conventionalities of cinema that works to veil over the racist ideologies at the centre of the production of filmic images. It is perhaps this description of cinematic image-making and narration as a variant of the existent racialized power dynamics that hold Black representation as vulnerable to the subjective intricacies of film aesthetics, which leads Snead to conclude that 'since editing, framing and cutting out are the exigencies of filmic and aesthetic practice, it is possible to hide the ideological motivated distortions under the auspices of artistic economy or exigency' (7). In both Snead and Young's identification of the highly clandestine techniques of racism within the film industry, the primacy of white textual authorship and its accompanying orthodoxy of Black invisibility as an aesthetic normality help us to come to an understanding of how film texts are able to circumvent the reality of the multiracial society within which they are situated through the exigencies of on-screen depictions and the aversive organizational practices that govern such depictions.

My reading of the condition of Black British representation within film and television in the early 1990s may appear ambiguous given the status of Channel 4 as the locus of the representations of multiracial Britain. However, the period saw the erosion of the channel's original remit for a neoliberal model of PSB as a result of the 1990 Broadcasting Act, which, during the following decade, would produce an array of structural and economic changes imbued by the decree to sell its own advertising that would include a shift from the radical television culture of the 1980s to a more populist, mainstream orientation (Brown, 2007; Hobson, 2007). This would also see a reduction and redefinition of multicultural representation that would result in the withdrawal of specific, mandated support for Black content providers and, subsequently, autonomous Black cultural representation within an economically competitive marketplace. This change was to be glacial in its manifestations, however, and the continuation of the channel's commitment to racial difference throughout the early 1990s as the moment of multiculture had given the impression that Black Britain was entering into a period of optimism, when, having previously existed on the edges of a nation that saw racial difference and British only in terms of mutual exclusivity (Gilroy, 1987), Black Britishness could be accepted as a cohesive identity. However, while we observed a new politics of recognition in the visibility of Black music subculture and the representations of Afro-Caribbean identities within popular culture, the period's optimism was to be curtailed by an unprecedented moment of public outcry over racism that would rupture the fragile technology of race relations. On 22 April 1993, Stephen Lawrence, an eighteen-year-old Black student from Plumstead, would be stabbed by five to six white youths while he stood waiting for a bus home at the junction of Well Hall Road and Dickson Road in Eltham, South East London. This was just one of a number of fatal racist attacks in the Greenwich area of South East London, a region described by Hewitt (2005) as the 'white hinterland' during this period – the murder of fifteen-year-olds Rolan Adams in Thamesmead in 1991, and Rohit Duggal in Eltham (1992), on the very same road upon which Stephen Lawrence would be murdered. For many (Cathcart, 2000; Hewitt, 2005), the tremendous increase in racial attacks in the area was attributed to the presence of the British National Party headquarters in Welling in 1989, that would later see a councillor elected in the nearby Millwall by-election in September 1993. Indeed, such a climate did not free us from the kinds of treatment recruited from the myth of a natural Black criminality where even in a moment of racist attack, Black youths remained subjected to most recognizable forms of racist characterization. For in the immediate aftermath of the incident, as Stephen Lawrence lay bleeding to death on the ground on Well Hall Road, the Metropolitan Police officers who arrived at the scene pursued a line of questioning to Duane Brooks that suggested that both he and the prone Stephen had naturally been involved in gang conflict (Macpherson, 1999). Indeed, and as argued by Hall (1999), the treatment of the nation's Black population exhibited an adherence to the necessary logic of race and crime, necessary in that the investigation remained comfortable in the implausibility of Black victimage and the inconceivability of innocence; the Lawrence family's very own liaison officers assigned to them after the murder exhibited a set of behaviours that implied that Stephen had been involved in gang-crime, and would ask the Lawrences if Stephen owned a pair of leather gloves that were recovered near the scene (Macpherson, 1999; Cathcart, 2000). This pointed to an institutional defect that finds its genealogy beyond not only the immediate racisms of the Metropolitan Police's handling of the murder (indeed, the liaison officers would come under a scathing condemnation at the subsequent enquiry in 1999, where they would insist that the murder was not racially motivated), but also the very racist textures of the British Criminal Justice System. Notably, as the far-right would gain political legitimacy in the early 1990s, the racial climate was further exacerbated by the comments made by Sir Paul Condon, the Metropolitan Police Commissioner in 1995, that the vast majority of muggings in the capital were carried out by young Black males (Mills and Ward, 1995).

It is not erroneous to describe British society within a New Labour political project as a political culture not holistically defined solely by the project of nation building, but of nation branding, where visual language, culture and narration would be an essential part of the new cultural zeitgeist that New Labour would maximize as a primary exemplar of a postmodern break from the past in the feel-good euphoria of Cool Britannica. This seemed to bask in a highly polarized national imagery where the realities of a multicultural Britain were to be located in an alternative sphere unrequired for the more palatable portraiture of whiteness as the sole racial identity of the official forms of popular culture. Indeed, in some of the films that have been argued to capture the various essences of the New Labour's political project either economically or thematically such as *Trainspotting* (dir. Danny Boyle, 1996) and *Billy Elliot* (dir. Stephen Daltry, 1999), films that for Wayne (2002) 'add to working class life the all-important ingredients of aspiration, individual ingenuity and transcendence of class boundaries' (44), what we encounter is a cultural landscape where Black filmmakers, narrative themes and characters were subjected to an ossified system of 'visible invisibility', and support for Black and Asian filmmakers during the 1990s was a neglected issue in the UK film industry throughout the decade (Korte and Sternberg, 2003, Arnold and Wambu, 1999) despite the presence of Black filmmakers attempting to make incremental interventions into the whiteness of UK screen culture. Of course, one can cite *Young Soul Rebels* (dir. Isaac Julien, 1991), and *Welcome to the Terrordome* (dir. Ngozi Onwurah, 1995), the first UK feature film to be directed by a Black woman, as demonstrative of films that centred questions of race and Blackness within an otherwise white industrial landscape, although the latter film would be subjected to widespread critical denigration. However, such criticism was also underpinned by issues of race and gender; notably, in an Empire Magazine review that was laden with racial undertones, its author would describe Onwurah as male throughout. Our understanding of Channel 4, particularly in its first ten years, can be conditioned by its position as both the vanguard of narrational Blackness and a site of cultural contestation – an arena of struggle against forms of cultural hegemony. This being so, the reference to Channel 4's changing relationship with Black Britain in the 1990s allows for a discussion of the Independent Film and Video Unit, run by its Commissioning Editor, Alan Fountain, and, later, Stuart Cosgrove, which was a unique department within Channel 4 and had a long and admirable track record commissioning a wide range of documentaries and low-budget dramas. *Independent* became a key term here, as the department encouraged programme makers and filmmakers who worked within an independent cultural tradition, through political conviction and cultural difference. However, the changing economic and mandated face of Channel 4 in the 1990s can be located most strikingly within the department. By 1992, in its third season of ten new British films, the average budget per film was £270,000. The department's annual budget was to be reduced to £1.5 million in 1996, and by 1997 it was in the region of £800,000. In 1998 this allocation was less than £500,000 (Johnson, 1992). As acknowledged by Fountain at the time, this was not a fertile economic condition for fiction film of any kind, particularly one invested in contemporary Black Britishness. However, it was from within the Independent Film and Video unit that *We Are The Ragamuffin* (1992), director Julian Henriques' first film, acted as a vignette for the director's embryonic ideas for *Babymother*. *We the Ragamuffin* was shot on a budget of £180,000, using improvised regional dialogue and local musicians essentially playing themselves in a story of two armed gangsters who are driven out from a peaceful and vibrant West Indian community in Peckham, led by a group of local reggae musicians. The thirty-minute film was broadcast on 7 September 1992 on Channel 4 in its third season of ten British independent fiction films on its 10.00 pm Monday night slot. However, its claim to *Britishness* became a point of contestation within the production and, crucially, its exhibition; Channel 4 would broadcast the film with English subtitles, against the wishes of its creative team. That the film was screened with subtitles is of particular significance. Channel 4 felt that the organic accents, vernacular and idioms might restrict a broader section of the television audience from comprehending the film, a stance challenged by the film's screenwriter Russell Newell, who would state: 'These people are speaking English. The subtitles have been applied with total indiscretion. Basically, we're being treated as foreigners' (Johnson, 1992).

The question of racial density is also found in the 1998 film *Babymother* (dir. Julian Henriques), described as the first Black British musical exploring the world of reggae dancehall music among the working-class Black community on the Stonebridge Estate in Harlesden, North West London. Given the condition of Black representation during the period, *Babymother* is a significant text in its construction of identity and Black Britishness, representations that were themselves underpinned by broader social and political contestation over multiculturalism and the purposes of British film culture within Channel 4 in the mid-to-late 1990s. Questions of the film's crafting of identities cannot be separated from those of gender relations, as one of the central characteristics of the film is that of gendered subjugation and the confinement of women to domesticity. The plot of *Babymother* is interwoven and laden with questions of identity, and revolves around the story of Anita (Anjela Lauren Smith), a young Black 'babymother', a term that at its most cursory definition describes a single mother with a fractured and temporal relationship with her spouse. Here, Anita struggles to balance raising her two young children while pursuing her ambitions of a career as a reggae artist. But her ambitions are not motivated by escapism, but by existence and resistance. Here, race and class are made tangible through fortitude – the initial Manichean binary between Anita and her middle-class older sister Rose, the opposition to her career pursuit by her babyfather and more successful reggae artist Byron, the mourning of the death of Anita's mother and the impact of this on Anita's mental well-being. The characters are bound to Harlesden's localized economy, which in turn produces limited scope for and means of economic sustenance. *Babymother* offers a particular construction of the everyday, the mundane and the unspectacular to those outside the area's indigene. It presents a set of conditions that are germane to Black life within Harlesden. In a particular critique, the BFI's online journal *Screenonline* would assert that 'whilst *Babymother* captures the vibrant Black dancehall culture of Harlesden, it does so in a strange vacuum, where no white faces intrude, and no attempt is made to engage with the wider world. Some critics identified this as the film's greatest weakness, removing an important level of conflict' (Wambu, 2003). What is presented to us in this critique is both the fragile value and politics of Black cinematic representation when set within a space of geographic Black density. Indeed, to stress the absence of the wider world, of conflict, as performing politics, is to prescribe a synthetic politics, to claim that a cinematic Blackness can exist only when defined by cultural trespass, when in proximity to whiteness, and to advance a position that is unable to conceive cinematic Blackness on its own terms, and through its own epistemologies.

If the 1990s were marked by what Alexander (2000) describes as a period where, in an analysis that shares the identification of the UK film sector's erasure of Black identities as the systemic outcome of practices of aversive racism and exigency as diagnosed by both Young and Snead, and cites an equally sophisticated but no less lacerating system of visible invisibility in the textual subsumption of cultural difference with 'the presence of ethnic characters in otherwise periphery roles' (97), for Malik (2002), who retained the use of 'Black' as the politically cohesive and encompassing term for those racialized identities unified in their oppositional challenge to the racially subjugating politics of Thatcherism, assesses the invisibility of Black and Asian directors, writers and performers within British film and television as structured 'patterns of exclusion' (171). Both Malik and Alexander's diagnosis of the conditions of Black cinematic representation formed part of a critical literature on the increasingly politicized nature of Black film funding that places analytical significance on the institutional context of Black film culture throughout the 1990s, with Alexander's reading of the period being one that marked a glacial departure from the supportive frameworks of the 1980s that was born of the multicultural remit of Channel 4 and its particular role in the development of both the Black independent film sector and the more general visibility of Black and Asian identities within key presenting and editorial positions and programming (171). With a specific interest in Black performers, it is indicative of the combinational logic of aversive racism and racial exigency that the peripherality of presence that Alexander points to is observed in the nature of on-screen representation. The period witnessed an intensified response by Black acting talent against a film and TV production culture that strived to make tangible the seemingly inconceivable possibility of Black performers as lead actors in the kinds of large-budget films that had characterized British film throughout the decade, with Black actors maintaining a tokenistic presence devoid of depth or dimensionality, or playing atypical criminal roles. Such is the kind of industry lore through which Black actors were subjected to the patterns of exclusion that motivated the exodus towards the end of the decade of Black British screen talent such as Marianne Jean-Baptiste, Sophie Okonedo and Adrien Lester to what appeared to be the promise of a much more permissive and heterogeneous acting landscape for Black performers in the United States. Notably, Lester, who starred in the American comedy film *Primary Colours* (dir. Mike Nichols, 1998), would state that the situation in the UK film and TV sector for Black actors would compel him to leave Britain to find roles with 'IQ-value attached' (Quoted in *The Guardian*, Tuesday, March 26, 2002). Whether Lester's statement, in his desire for intellectually laden film roles, was in response to the second challenge within relations of representation, here, an intervention that imagines a different obligation by the film industry towards Black actors that allows for the full circulation of the uncontested breadth of performance enjoyed by white actors, or the expression of his own individual sensitivities towards the accommodating aversiveness of the industry in the form of typecasting as criminal characters, the general point of Lester's disaffection can be examined through the very public umbrage he took towards the declaration on the purpose of on-screen Black Britishness made by the white British director Guy Ritchie. In a May 2000 interview in the *Evening Standard* magazine, Ritchie would further contribute to the already infertile industry conditions for Black British screen performers as evaluated by Lester by stating that 'there are no black actors around. The ones I've seen all speak Shakespeare beautifully but that's not the point'. We should pay particular attention to the protracted politics of race implied in Ritchie's statement, evocative of what was argued by Hall as the challenge against the fetishized nature of Black cinematic imagery through a counter-hegemonic imagery that populates the relations of representation. Without wishing to reconvene what are now historical and undoubtedly regurgitated critical readings and subjective positions on the genesis of the debate specifically, and the infinite question of what could ever constitute Black more generally, the comments display a version of aversive racism that functions here as an equilibrating logic that asks for Black identity to be bound within the generic orthodoxies of Black cinematic representation, and holds a particular relevance to the study of Black urban film at the beginning of the decade. Somewhat paradoxically, this draws from a cross-pollinating set of meanings inscribed within both Ritchie's dissatisfaction with the sparsity of Black British actors and the affronting expansion of Black cinematic identity and Lester's response, which included tearing up a copy of the *Evening Standard* interview on stage at the 2000 Emma Awards before an applauding audience. Blackness, for Ritchie, and its gradual entry into the white domains of the UK film industry, is seen here as a defilement of the traditional cinematic image systems that organize and/or correspond with our perceptions of racial and cultural difference, with the abundance of Black actors who now adopt a Shakespearian vernacular performing simply as a metaphor for the encroaching of Blackness into the preserved bastions of Englishness. Be it through performance, class position or the degree of mobility, transcendence and social acceptance secured through received pronunciation, film casting and characterization are collapsed into a reductive set of racial equivalences, in which the presence of Black actors in roles where race is either inconsequential or not defined by assumptive ideas of class position, results in the immediate shedding of any Black identity. For Lester and others, Richie's singular vision for Black cinematic images devoid of subjectivity is one that cannot be easily accommodated within the demands for a multiplicity of Black cinematic representations, representations that arose at the point of renewed critical debates on the question of Black subjectivity and difference (Hall, 1988). However, we should also be alive to a particular structure of value that is central to this challenge, as Lester's specific criticism of the fixity and reductivity of Black filmic performance implied in his polemic is that the orthodoxy of on-screen characterizations and narratives of Blackness – we can suggest with a degree of authority that his pursuit of intellectually rich acting roles is in reference to the dominant portrayals of Black males within the UK screen industry as one-dimensional, peripheral and/or criminal – possesses no intellectual or creative availability and subsequently is stripped of desirability or the potential for displaying acting *craft*. The articulation of these two positions – Black filmic characterization as indexical or as devoid of value – therefore formulates a construction of filmic Blackness that remains in an irresolvable reflection/refraction binary. This is a crucial contextual and, in many ways, preparatory argument as it allows into the theoretical and analytical frame a study of the Black British urban film – and the Black identities that would come to constitute the texts – that would be structured through what I describe as a hegemonic asymmetry. I want to expound further on my attempt to problematize the racial correspondence implied in Richie's comment through the use of the Gramscian prefix to describe what may be read as a trivial concern with the way film texts may respond to the common understandings of different cultural identities, for this asymmetry is *hegemonic* in the sense that the nature of Black cultural politics implied in the demand for Black representational subjectivity is a challenge that is constructed against an industrial orthodoxy that privileges the accepted and prescribed singularity of the Black British experience and identity. This idea of Black filmic representation as an outcome of a hegemonic asymmetry provides the conceptual grounding for an analysis that possesses less interest in Lester's response as a demonstration of a decamping politics of respectability that endeavours to assert its independence from what are the negative characterizations that assist in the white denigration of Black life, the disavowal of the generic and thematic exigencies that strive to pull Black representation towards a Black filmic indexicality and away from cinematic performances that are unbounded by race and ethnicity, and speak to the material conditions that accompany our experience of Black modernity. To invest analytically in this possibility would also be to perform a denial of the individual subjectivity and difference, both indicative of the central critique located within Stuart Hall's analytical shift from race to ethnicity as the critical dimension at the heart of what he saw as the 'immense diversity and differentiation of the historical and cultural experiences of black subjects' (1988). The idea of Black cinematic representation being subject to the logics of a hegemonic symmetry that in many ways assists the description of the popular Black British urban text as a necessary and useful fiction of race as its governing adjective, authenticity, means the Black urban film is precisely esteemed as such as a consequence of such texts' spectacularizing accounts of Blackness that are easily subsumed into a homogenizing logic of representational symmetry. However, this is accompanied by an alternative set of cultural and industrial justifications and arrangements that would result in the general denial of the Black urban text as possessing any kind of critical value beyond the mirroring of Black social issues, the indulgence in the propagation of racial stereotypes, or the way that the urban film as framed as a Black text is able to attend to the agendas of cultural policy that attempt to regulate the volume and nature of Black cinematic representation. From this perspective, I choose a framework that contextualizes the question of where and how Blackness should be represented cinematically within the fragility of Black cultural politics that Mercer and Julien (1988), in an analysis that builds on Gilroy's surveying of incorporation to within the corresponding and mimetic aspirations of the state (1988), interpret as a 'tension between representation as a practice of depiction and representation as a practice of delegation' (4). I use such a tension here to further illustrate how the structuring of Black filmic identity, termed here by Mercer and Julien as 'representational democracy' (4), within a hegemonic asymmetry as a normative frame for the positioning of Black cinematic characterization is anchored in a larger cultural politics. For Ritchie's perturbation, which should be considered as an amplification of the UK film industry's unrelenting valorization of Black visual labour, not only brings into question the very legitimacy of Black actors as viable members within the profession of acting itself, but also proscribes an industrial situation in which the burden of representation lies with the already marginalized Black actors themselves to resist the temptation to perform the ultimate transgression: attempting to dismantle the determining scaffolds of Black cinematic representations that discourage the Black British cinematic identity to transcend its hegemonic indexicality (this being in simple terms a desire to exist outside the designated and comfortable area of race and class mimesis, be it motivated by puritanism, plurality or the wholesale rejection of preordained generic configurations). This is premised on an instinctive and reductive mimetic practice of cultural representation that, within industry lore, Black actors are expected to exhibit an indexical correspondence with the real – in this example, the hegemonic continuum of the Black male (and Black Britishness more broadly) as socially peripheral and resultantly, their representations should accord with a general understanding of Black life forms. To borrow from an alternative intellectual project, the dialectic over Black filmic performance as a hegemonic symmetry seems to me to be indicative of what Pulwar (2001) sees as the racialized 'somatic norm' through Black typecasting as an acquiescence to a symmetric codifying of Black identity to represent a dominant and desirable extratextual reality. This orthodoxy of popular Black filmic characterizations fulfilling a hegemonic expectancy was, of course, in existence both before and beyond

Richie's ubiquitous predilections towards the dramatic range of Black British actors who, at the time of Richie's comment, had in both of his feature films *Lock, Stock and Two Smoking Barrels* (1998) and *Snatch* (2000) exhibited an affirmation of Black male identity's use-value as sub-characterized members of violent criminal gangs. Indeed, in a recognition of the highly contingent nature of Black filmic representation that compels us to acknowledge a plausible but no less mitigating and equally problematic rationale, Richie's lamentation over the misconfiguration of the designatory representational function of Black actors may also be the outcome of their embedding within a particular fictional setting and generic convention, to which the aforementioned films are a reference. To again recall the critique of how the dominant representations within film and visual culture are constructed to ensure the hyper-visible invisibility of white ethnicity by Richard Dyer (1997), within our domain of British film, IQ-stripped filmic representations are cordoned as the natural preserve of Black British male actors. What comes into view here is how the issues of both Black British film production and the struggle over the aesthetic fixity of Blackness seem to coalesce over a conjunctural moment of Black representational politics that remains heavily implicated in a post-multicultural demand for a heterogeneity in which Black cinematic portraits can open up to questions of class, or at least the *perception* of class difference, as the sociocultural dividend of a postmodernist and liberally pluralistic Black Britain. Within both these refrains – Richie's denigration of the hegemonic asymmetry of Black British filmic performance and his accompanying and unqualified positioning as the Black British acting hegemon, and Lester's public condemnation of the denial of subjectivity and the trammelling of an expansive form of Black representation by the indissociable cinematic orthodoxy of Blackness and crime – is a shared embeddedness in a racialized somatic dialectic. We are confronted with a version of Black cultural politics that places demands for representation which pushes against the primitiveness that is ascribed to Black urbanity as a narrational theme, its associative acting roles and, with it, the disallowing of the subjectivities of race and class.

Somewhat ironically, the Black British actor Lennie James, who had appeared in Ritchie's film *Snatch* as the leader of an armed gang of Black criminals (Figure 2.1), would in the same period comment on the limited scope for Black actors in Britain. The solution proposed was one that finds some relationship with both the acceptance of a hegemonic symmetry as a structuring logic in the historical race thematic that delegates Black Britishness's presence within film and TV and Mercer's description of the unresolved dilemma faced by Black filmmakers and producers in the evading of the ghettoizing impulses of the film and TV industry and embracing the broader distribution potentialities that are afforded to Black practitioners in existing 'within conventional patterns' of production vis-à-vis the independent and locally orientated experimentalist approaches that define the Black film workshops and set the integrated and culturally horizontal conditions to address Black British audiences through what he terms as 'a specific community of interests' (1994: 80). For James, writing and directing his own films, as a semi-autonomous mode of film production, in many ways a reflection of Sue Horrick's emphasis on the importance of Black authorship as Channel 4's Multicultural Programming head at

Figure 2.1 *Snatch* (dir. Guy Ritchie, 2000).

its establishment in 1982 (Hobson, 2007), Black writing and directing could be a means of ensuring a practice of thematic and casting homophily that would, in the devising of film projects by Black British actors through the maximizing of fragile industrial links, ensure some kind of continuity of presence to essentialize the portrayal and representation of Black people. I use the term 'essentialize' with some degree of elasticity in its re-appropriating of a practice that, of course, finds a central position in Hall's critique of the issues that accompany the uncritical positive framing of the Black subject (1988).

This practice, even within this nascent encounter within the Black representational politics of the early 2000s, can easily be understood as a substantive problem *a la* Hall if we are to move forward with a singular interpretive use of essentialism. Of course, a more industrially administered practice of racial essentialism would emerge as a primary repertoire in the version of Black cultural politics that would enter the 2000s under the description of diversity and inclusion. Lester's essentialism can be redeemed if applied, as in this example, as a pragmatism that attempts to replicate the uninterrupted practice of racially fissured homophily that had remained the preserve of whiteness and reconfigure the white institutional structuring of the film industry through the creation of affinity space where the representational marginalization of Black actors and Black narrational concerns and interests can be realized within the development of a critical mass of Black penned and directed films. While James would register a less castigating explanatory perspective on the causality question in electing to define Black exclusion in less deliberate and explicitly malignant terms than that pursued here, his own forecasting of the impending erasure of Black identities from the frames of British film would draw on the same modality of Black representational evisceration via aesthetic decoy as identified by Young and Snead. As he would state:

> The industry's attitude is not malicious, it stems from ignorance. I only began to get properly cast as an actor in my own right 10 years after I left drama school. The US has huge race problems, but at least in US culture everyone gets a chance. Here, we are side-lined and insulted. Denzel Washington said at the Oscars that there was a time when black actors were filmed so they could be cut from the final product in certain US states. The way we feel in Britain is not far off that. (quoted in *The Guardian*, Tuesday, 26 March 2002)

We should at this point return to my general reading of the popular Black British urban film as one birthed from a coalition between the competing dilemmas of positive/negative Black characterization and the question of mimesis and indexicality, a coalition that is equally positioned at a paradoxical interplay between the mainstream conventions and antennas of race-making and the circulatory language of inclusion and cultural participation that would emerge in response to the demands for ethnic minority representation, which would continue into the 2000s. However, it is the sparsity of opportunity within the industrial landscape that would compel a number of Black British actors to leave the United Kingdom for the United States and the promise of more expansive and substantive acting roles, a venture that would be premised on the notion that the arriving British actors would benefit from an extensivity of the now more favourable industry conditions for African American actors, directors and producers who had been able to find fissures of opportunity within an economically incomparable film production culture and film production velocity. What remained for Black British actors in Britain was to accede to the centripetal race logics of the UK film industry, and in this acquiescence, be content, and almost grateful for their peripheral presence through existing within its marginalizing valorization of Black identity and cultural representation. Despite the presence of these representational *cul-de-sacs* in the film sector, the opening gestures as an industrial methodology at this conjuncture are to be observed in the launching of the short-lived film initiative Spirit Dance, a film development/production company devised by Film Four in collaboration with the Black American actor Forrest Whitaker in 2000 with the specific aim of supporting Black and ethnic minority filmmakers in Britain. This was an ambition that would be encouraged to produce a rare material outcome through a 'first look' agreement on projects with the broadcaster. However, that no feature films were made under the auspices of this production scheme during its lifespan, with the forensic traces of the Spirit Dance initiative themselves remaining obscure within even the various retrospective analyses of Channel 4 (Nwonka, 2015) suggests that the idea of racial inclusion, even at this nascent stage, was highly subjective in its definition and application and, resultingly, was marked by an unwillingness to disturb a resistant industry culture. Again, only once we have engaged with the politics of anti-racism as subsumed and redefined within the language of diversity can we begin to develop and understanding of how industry policymakers were able to successfully convince ethnic minority filmmakers and cultural workers that there is a dividend, be it cultural or political, to be gained from the relinquishing of what was the foundational principles of what Hall saw as 'the struggle to come into representation' (1988) for the persuasive but only partially generative practice of cultural plurality through inclusion initiatives.

This chapter has advanced the idea of hegemonic (a)symmetry as a way of engaging with the tension-laden bidirectionality of Black screen representation as an industrial logic in the early 2000s. Indeed, we see that the two elements related to the issue of race, racism and the popular Black urban film that concern us here, the different kinds of value placed upon the idea of Black cinematic particularity and the film sector's valorizing of Black representation, become crystallized in the industrial experiences of the Black British actor Trevor Thomas, who had featured in both an early Black British directed film, *Black Joy* (1977) and Horace Ové's *Playing Away* (1987) and would state, 'I just submitted a script to a major British film and television funder and it came back with a note saying it was too "mono-racial".... It had black, Indian and white characters in it but the leading roles were black' (quoted in *The Guardian*, Tuesday, 26 March 2002). Insofar as the UK film industry has practised a historical evasiveness, be it through textual exigency or industrial aversivity towards Black led, Black authored or Black populated film, the analysis of the popular Black urban film finds a theoretical attraction towards the idea of 'mono-racial' film productions and texts as the platforms for the inclusion within film and TV culture of Black stories and Black actors. The question of what kind of thematic interests constitute mono-raciality in the occasions when such stories become desirable and compatible with the commercial/cultural hybridizing agendas of the UK film industry is appealing to the genealogical study of the formation and constitutiveness of the popular Black British urban film as a filmic and narrational approach constituted by the nexus of the irresolvable contestation over Black representation and an aestheticizing of fetishizing Black subject matter that, when drawn from the ever-available reservoir of Black social issues circulating within the popular consciousness, offers an instant and plausible visual and thematic Black *density*. By this, as will be explored further in the following chapters, I am referring to the accumulative logics that combine at a critical social, political and industrial conjuncture to make viable through film and TV drama the dramatizing of the institutionally beneficial pathogens of an imagined, or very real Black social phenomena.

3

Black Cultural Politics and the Management of Racial Difference

Within culture, marginality, though it remains peripheral to the broader main-stream, has never been such a productive space as it is now. And that is not simply the opening within the dominant of spaces that those outside it can occupy. It is also the result of the cultural politics of difference, of the struggles around differ-ence, of the production of new identities, of the appearance of new subjects on the political and cultural stage

Stuart Hall, 'What Is This "Black" in Black Popular Culture?', 1993

When considering some of the issues that have concerned the previous chapter, such as the forms of affect produced by Black textual representation, the intersubjective relationships claimed between the creation of filmic images and Black identities in the context of history, politics and the systemic manifestations of racism, the meanings contained in the struggle of hegemonic symmetry/asymmetry, or the organizing of Black cinematic narratives within the frame of cultural governance, we are engaging with the constituent elements that become the unified social practice that we've come to understand as the management of marginality, and I want to return to the questions that are presented to us within what Hall argues is the residual and overlapping character of Black cultural politics. Hall, in drawing our attention to the 'historical specificity' of the cultural strategies and policy logics that act as an intervention within the heavily negotiated terrain of Black popular culture (1993: 104), observes a certain transcendence and a mobility of presence and form once finessed through a field of institutional procedures, in that they are not simply constructed anew but are built upon the remnants of previous attempts at bringing the fragmenting representations, experiences and definitions of Black cultural practices into some kind of productive homology. I'm interested in the way that Hall describes the unrepetitive and specific nature of the procedures that inform Black cultural struggles over representation and its ability to make reference to different social processes and features while remaining within the uninterrupted corpus of Black cultural politics, and its relevance to my own thinking on the propelling of particular forms of Black urban masculine identity into the popular cultural aesthetic – a conceptual reliance that may be seen as a demonstration of analytical atavism is how Hall invites us to think of the bureaucratic and institutional structuring of Black cultural politics as a shifting and contingent politics that opens up new and nodal spaces of Black cultural contestation while maintaining a specificity structured by the conjunctural *moment*. This, the reliant, contradictory and temporal nature of Black cultural strategies and the receptiveness to the existent social dynamics that enables the moment to produce a new politics of difference characterized by a convergence between the familiar and unknown is certainly a tendency that would define the Black cultural politics that emerged with its own specificities from the early 2000s, and the period saw a politics of race where the murder of Stephen Lawrence would be the basis of a new modality of racial politics that would be characterized by a discursive shift from anti-racism to a politics of inclusion. In what can be described as the processes through which the political context was able to pull the consternation over the visibility of Black film and TV representation to within its influential spheres (Nwonka 2015), I identify a pervasive discourse of 'post-Macphersonism' as a broad descriptor for the new social and cultural phase of Black and ethnic minority representational politics arising at the point of the public inquiry into the police investigation into the killing of Stephen. The Macpherson Report, published on 24 February 1999, would conclude that the investigation conducted by the Metropolitan Police into Stephen's murder had been 'marred by a combination of professional incompetence, institutional racism and a failure of leadership by senior officers' (quoted in Thomas, 2011: 65). While the Macpherson Report would secure its position as a landmark ruling in its identification and condemnation of institutional racism as a practice specifically located within the Metropolitan Police, we find that the wider effect of the inquiry was a policy focus towards racial inequality as a political imperative directed not just towards the reform of discriminatory policing practices but also to a range of rhetorical and symbolic approaches to purge its manifestations within the broader spheres of British society. Two critical facets of the Macpherson Report become valuable for our understanding of how its dissemination set the social, cultural and institutional conditions for the pursuit of racial inclusion within the film and television industry, both of which were to be inscribed in Government legislation. First, the report informed the 2000 Race Relation Amendment Act, which in effect required public bodies to adopt a much more systematic and proactive stance against discrimination and racial inequality in the workplace. Second, in what can be interpreted as the opening gestures of diversity and inclusion was the system of race monitoring in the advent of Equality Impact Assessments, requiring all public bodies to 'demonstrate that they are actively combating racism and promoting equality of opportunity and good race relations in all areas of their employment practices and service provision' (Thomas 2011: 66). These critical developments in many ways embodied the 'new anti-racism' which Hewitt (2005), in identifying what he has described as the rehabilitation of previous attempts to sustain a state-focused and ethnically coalitional praxis against British racial hostility and violence, displayed modalities that were developed to some degree upon the legacies of the 1980s Thatcherite anti-racist politics. The first modality was observed as the class-determined disavowal of racial discrimination found in the 'popular, press-led condemnation of racist violence' through the media (52). The other modality, which displays an interaction with the first, was for Hewitt an equally 'class inflected' practice that was seen in the 'incorporation of anti-racism within the less contentious "social inclusion" framework' (2005: 52). Indeed, Hewitt's criticism of the nature of this new 'non'-anti-racism as pursued by New Labour is not specifically directed towards the distribution of a templated and easily implementable version of racial inclusion within areas such as the civil service. Rather, it is the modalities of race relations observed in the rapid racial and ethnic diversification of workforce personnel within public sector environments and institutional spaces that are able to succeed in the creation of a racially plural portraiture in the engineering of a seductive but painfully acetate image and experience of inclusion but unable to agitate, let alone dismantle the fundamental forms of racism that were to repel the post-Macphersonist impetus of the early 2000s and New Labour's eager cultivation of a racially cohesive national vista. In my thinking on the arrival of the issue of cultural representation within this new racial politics (2015), we encounter an analysis that chimes with both of the modalities cited by Hewitt, and despite film and TV culture being the subject of my analysis, I take a critical position on the impact of Macpherson as a panacea for the various manifestations of racial discrimination the new anti-racisms were constituted to attack. As I argue, in an analysis that finds a variant of Hewett's new anti-racism as a social inclusion framework in the creative and cultural sector, the public reaction to Labour's official declaration of British racism as institutionally practised works to support the description of post-Macphersonism as a political intervention characterized by an abundance of highly visible institutional responses towards representational cultural diversity within media, culture and cultural production and a corresponding erasure of any acknowledgement of or intervention towards actual racism. Such an analysis equally remains in conversation with Hall's idea of the overlapping nature of the management of Black culture in that the description of the phase of post-Macphersonism as a political culture that spirited a desire for a racially cohesive inclusivity within the film and TV industry contained within its logics a number of elements, actions and modalities that were cyclically drawn from the very same reservoir of Black cultural politics. The argument here is that New Labour's approach to institutional racism proved conducive to the elemental political practice of the gutting of the more confrontational aspects of the anti-racism challenge from the 1980s and 1990s, with the accusation of an ossified racist ideology as dyed throughout British society's infrastructures as its most distinctive feature, and the thrust of a new anti-racism as a heightened appreciation of cultural plurality within the cultural and creative industry would implore Ambavalander Sivanandan, in a typically eviscerating analysis to summarize the post-Macphersonist thrust as a 'shibboleth of cultural compensations and euphemisms as the antidote to racism and established institutional racism instead as the problem that needed to be tackled' (2008: 170). The cynicism expressed by Sivanandan, which essentially sees the New Labour race politics as a benign modality of anti-discrimination that is collapsed into a comfortable range of cultural compensatory sentiments, points to how the idea of racial equality was devoid of any adequate theory of how an anti-racist Britain could be realized in practice beyond the aforementioned legislative decrees and the developing rhetoric of a post-racial utopia. Thus, the recourse to culture and cultural production as a post-racial vista where one is able to invite into the popular Black and Asian cultural practices from its space of marginality can be understood as a key part of New Labour's realpolitik that, unwilling to further disturb the fragile race-determined social relations that had welcomed the new Government's legislative recognition of institutional racism, was most observed in the thrust of 'white backlash' that had shaped the crisis of multiculturalism of the 1990s, and in a strategic effort to circumvent right-wing accusations of ethnic minority preferential treatment and racial inclusion by way of protocol that could prove an electoral threat by energizing the existential Conservative fear of a liberal descent into identity politics, ethnic minority cultural provision and celebration becomes the basis for the systematic distortion of the depths of racism in Britain. Such an argument has since been given additional credence as a result of the release of previously unpublished Cabinet papers in 2022 that would reveal that a White Paper detailing a ten-year strategy for the eradication of racial inequality by Home Secretary Jack Straw just prior to the publication of the Macpherson Report would be vetoed by Tony Blair as 'OTT'. A political investment in cultural (in)equality is instituted as the decanting vector of the racial inclusivity prescriptive, and the ways in which cultural policy was brought into the frame of representational difference is identified not just by the Macpherson Report's indirect interest in the cultural and creative industries as a politically vacant modality of new anti-racism at the point of the emergence of the sector as an economically lucrative form of cultural production, but also by its possessing a utilitist dimension in its potential to capture the unrealized and unrecognized creative ambitions of a racially marginalized section of the nation. This discourages an unsophisticated reading of post-Macphersonism as politically conspiratorial, but certainly politically opportunistic in that it is able to accrue considerable social currency in a moment of multicultural crisis and rethinking, assessed here by Lentin and Titley (2011) as the arrival of 'culture and the celebration of difference to mask the structures of power associated with the production of class and ethnic inequality' (16). These critical developments in the political field inaugurated a new social enthusiasm for racial and ethnic difference, and in doing so, cultivated a novel and responsive climate of institutional investment, however rhetorical and piecemeal it proved, in culturally diverse cultural production that provides some account for how publicly funded cultural institutions would become so absorbent of the post-Macphersonist race discourse. We cannot begin to construct a reliable paradigm by which an interrogation of how the questions of film, film culture and Black representation were to be brought within the capacious purview of the race politics of New Labour without this more definite understanding of the institutional conditions and practices that were to prove essential in shaping post-Macphersonism's most pastoral offering to a deeply fractured British society: the bestowment of new anti-racism as the comfortable rehabilitation of Britain's racialized identities through the policy activities of a cultural and creative industry now readied for the production, presentation and celebration of racial and cultural alterity. Hall is keen to qualify his critique of the contradictory and at moments counterintuitive visibility strategies of Black popular culture in reminding us that it is the expropriating and incorporating power of capital, rather than simply an exhausting of the Black struggle to come into representation, that compels Black cultural politics to deposit a faith in the fragilities of the management of difference that, as pessimistically asserted by Slavoj Žižek, become a series of multiculturalist protocols introducing a modality of integration premised on a conditional tolerance where the dominant identity positions marginal existences to move only to the customs of racial aversiveness and the maintaining of neo-segregated cultural arenas and racially enclosed social relations. This is an argument which Saha and Van Lente (2022) and Pritcher (2012) reject as highly reductive in that Žižek observes in multicultural policy a version of anti-racism as serviceable only to capitalism, a myopic argument that neglects a conceptual engagement with the realities of the incorporating nature of capitalism to both enable and curtail anti-racist action, provided such practices exist only within capitalism's volition. There is a role, with some necessary qualifications, for both the cynicism towards postmodernity's interest in racial difference as a capitalist enterprise as expressed by Žižek and Saha and Van Lente and Pitcher's examination of capitalism as the axis upon which racism/anti-racism is permitted in an analysis of the construction and integration of new modes of Black British cinematic representation via the post-Macphersonist zeitgeist to within the UK's screen industries. As we'll engage with later in this chapter, their utility refers to the questions of what anti-racism is when filtered through the restructuring and finessing logics of cultural policy/production, the racial specificity of the social architecture it seeks to integrate anti-racism in and the other social forces that the conjunctural climate negotiates. The important point here, however, is that racial equality emerges as a flexible cultural plurality that establishes culturalism as the prevailing genre of post-Macphersonist anti-racism, a sublimating race politics that revels in a definition of racial inequality as a malfunction of representation rather than representation as a decision of racial inequality, a discourse of post-racialism further normativized by the evacuation of the politics of racism as the structuring dimension to the realities of Britain as a landscape of habitual social antagonisms and racially ossified divisions of power. It is these, as paradigmatically argued by Hall, that are the specificities of a moment where Black cultural politics was resituated within an inchoate set of desires and imperatives that attempted to reconcile emergent cultural institutions with the terms of a new anti-racism.

We may wish to bring into question the highly generative and seemingly straightforward discursive thrust of post-Macphersonism as outlined here – specifically that the moment of heightened racial debate in British politics is able to consciously produce a new climate of race and race thinking in which macro ideas of racial inclusivity are able to seamlessly cascade from a form of governmentality to within the logics of a developing cultural policy that could respond to the issue of racism. There is a quite deliberate use of the term 'conjunctural' throughout this reading, one that, in its reference to what Hall described as the social effects produced by the unexpected convergence between different and at times opposing circumstances and tendencies that come to inform and shape existing structures of powers within a specific period of time, also prevent us from developing an overdetermined understanding of the post-Macphersonist thrust. The identification of an ideological practice within the social inclusion framework of the new anti-racism asks for a reliance on an Althussarian understanding of how we are to link particular developments in the specific post-Macphersonist social constituting of institutional racism as an ideological outcome in which political discourses are absorbed and filtered through state apparatuses, in this context, the UK film industry as a site of various kinds of social participation where dominant beliefs and ideas eventually find a certain manifestation within film texts. Certainly, an ideological mirror language can be observed in the rhetorical permeation of concepts of diversity and the overtly public demonstrations of a positive and progressive 'race making' that would chaperone both the arrival of the New Labour government and the ways in which the decree that the agendas of the cultural and creative industries would also come to find a secure, and at its advent, a relatively uncontested habitation within the cultural logics and agendas of the UK film and television sector. By the late 1990s, at a moment where the CCIs were devoid of any sustained or concerted practice of cultural inclusivity, these significant changes within the wider figuration of British politics impacted on the British film industry in the advent of a new commercial structure for UK film. Following the 1997 General Election success, New Labour's first Culture Secretary, Chris Smith, would announce the project of the wholesale transforming of the UK's cultural sector that would trade upon the continuing zeitgeist of Cool Britannia that had proved so valuable as a socially palatable companion to New Labour's election campaign, a transformation that was characterized by a decisive shift towards the monetization of the UK's cultural and creative industries. New Labour's paramount interest, as noted by others (Hesmondhalgh et al., 2015), was to be observed in the emphasis on the economic dimension of cultural production and participation, and as was proclaimed in his authored manifesto *Creative Britain*, Smith would state that 'as a new Government, we have recognised the importance of this whole industrial sector that no one hitherto conceived of as "industry"' (Smith, 1998: 26). For the film sector, the decisive interventions that New Labour made upon entering government emphasized the particular importance of the economic viability of film production, an imperative that was seen in the appointment of the first ever Minister for Film. For example, July 1998 saw the rebranding of the Department for Culture, Media and Sport (DCMS), which had formerly been the Department for National Heritage, and in the same period would declare its embryonic plans to create a new lead body for film funding in Britain. The United Kingdom Film Council (henceforth UKFC) represented an amalgamation of the key functions of British Screen Finance, which had received £4 million in public funding annually for its UK-focused and European co-productions, and the film funding/production unit of the more culturally and educationally orientated BFI. The intention here was to establish a UK-wide body with the primary objective of overseeing the strategic investment of public resources into British film production. It is worth returning momentarily to the question of how the issue of cultural representation and plurality within the film industry become implicated in the post-Macphersonist politics of race. The Macpherson Report made no specific reference to the significance of the cultural and creative industries as a utility for racial equality and inclusion. Yet, as a body in receipt of public resources, the UKFC (like the vast majority of UK cultural and creative institutions that are dependent on financial subsidy from public funding bodies such as Arts Council England and others) were, in the context of New Labour's broader social agendas that very much sit within the Athussarian Ideological State Apparatus (ISA) model, were to be in dialogue with a public commitment, however rhetorical, to the prevailing social inclusion agenda, of which racial inclusion was very much part of its performative repertoire. It may be worthwhile, given the nature of issues of race and cultural identity when they emerge within the UK film industry, that we think of ideology in a less linear fashion to evade the construction of crude linkages between the judicial identification of institutional racism and the attendant rhetorical commitment to the eradication of racial discrimination as a political imperative and the emergence of the cultural inclusivity agenda within the arena of creative production. This being the case, the vernacular of cultural participation expressed by the UK film industry under the guise of racial inclusion does provide us with a concrete Althusserian example of the ideological process of the institutional uptake and practice of political ideas – here, the political and cultural interaction through institutions that allow for the social participation in material institutions of the state. In attempting to evidence the relationship that is established between the strategic aims of the UKFC and the broader focus of the UK cultural sector in its alignment with the macro-beliefs of the state, I am suggesting that the political sphere registers a powerful influence at the level of economic policymaking, and such a focus prepares the analytical terrain for a consideration of how New Labour's broader economic programme advocated a mixed economy approach that, while it is tempting to conceive this as an inherently Third Way conception that strived to reconcile the economic structure of society with the varied social realities of postmodernism, was actually located in the ideas of Anthony Crossland and the Labour revisionism movement that found some purchase within the Labour governments of the 1970s and which, in simple terms and with some notable points of resistance, conceived the relationship between the State and capitalism in non-antagonistic ways. For this analysis, and in recognition of the social dimensions of the economy – the socio-economic structure of the economic structure – it is the socio-economic dynamics of capitalism and the social forces that drive the idea of economic plurality that defines the relationship between New Labour and the creative sector, and Chris Smith would later expound his vision for a new economic model for the film industry by stating:

> The new labour government is committed to giving our creative industries the support they need to realise their full potential as we enter the new millennium. Developing our film and audio-visual industry is a key component of that strategy. I look forward to working closely with filmmakers from Hollywood and around the world to deliver our fundamental aim of a strong, profitable and sustainable British film industry. (Smith, 1998: 90)

Here, Smith naturally makes no comment at this point on the role of a national cinema that could provide an equally valuable function in being representative of a film culture more attuned to the social relations and dynamics of a fractured nation, a somewhat critical culture that brings into the frame a mode of social intercourse pursued through narrative conventions and production values antithetical to the kind of productive functions the DCMS had envisioned for the film industry as a flourishing 'sunrise economy' that would develop in its economic importance. There exists no universal or affirmative paradigm within which I can conceive this ideological relationship. However, and reflective of New Labour's supply-side economics doctrinal, we find that the Government's trickle-down effect exhibits a filmic specificity through the provision of the £27 million of annual public investment in the UKFC via government grant-in-aid, attractive tax breaks that cultivate the fertile industrial conditions for international co-production and the demands for commercial returns on investment (ROI), through which film productions would be required to generate a degree of profitability, and in turn registering an influence, to some level, on the formal and narrational sensibilities such an economic logic esteems. Cascading from somewhere within this economic strategy would be the agenda for film as a mode of social inclusivity and betterment. Because we are exploring a quite varied and complex political and cultural terrain from which the economic and social elements of New Labour's programme become unified in film, we can arrive at a more stable formulation of film as an arena where the economic and the societal are brought to an ideological fusion if we are to identify the social dividends from the emphasis on business, trade and enterprise that would comprise New Labour's fiscal policy: growth, productivity, employment, and through this, the elevation of poverty and social inequality. This, in drawing a correlation between New Labour's economic principles and cultural/creative practices, encourages us to consider the functions of the film industry through the Marxist model of society and socio-economic relations where Wayne (2020) suggests that film can be positioned as both base and superstructure in that its conditions of production are constituted by the bidirectional relations of both economic and social determinations. With this in mind, what emerges as one of the rationales for New Labour's interest in the creative sector, and the film industry specifically as a sunrise industry, was that the box-office success and mainstream acclaim achieved by film productions would perform a similar social function for the pluralist aims of British cinema. In more specific terms, and in allowing for an analysis of the political impetus behind cultural governance through the Marxist dialectical model, what is revealed to us, and perhaps encoded in the persuasive promise of industrial sustainability, is that the economic prosperity of UKFC would come to subsidize independent and domestically ambitioned British film productions and the related societal benefits of the creative sector. Thus, the establishment of the UKFC signalled the intentions of the New Labour government to assist in the application of market principles to UK film production. This economic model attempted to unify the business imperatives of film production and the potential of film as a socially cohesive practice within the new modality for British cinema that could be responsive to new social realities; the most obvious pillar of this new model was the idea that film, like all forms of cultural and creative engagement, could also possess distinctive sociocultural effects. Just how one would assess the social contribution the cultural and creative sector is able to make is, as one could expect within the still developing postmodernist vernacular of cultural participation, instrumentalism and impact, quite difficult to convey in tangible terms, and a particularly imprecise idea to be expressed through a prevailing language of economic profitability. However, Smith would attempt to expound on the social benefits of the industry, stating that film could 'contribute to social cohesion by developing networks and understanding, and building local capacity for organisation and self-determination' (Smith, 1998: 135). Here, we find that the enacting of the New Labour film-as-social-cohesion discourse through the use of figurative language cloaked in the broader Third Way idioms of self-actualization and societal betterment positions the industry as a transformative vector, which in practical terms was to be produced through education and upskilling, the availability of new forms of cultural access and the opportunities for marginalized identities to become immersed in diverse cultural expression. Thus, Smith's vision of social cohesion was to be realized through cultural participation and a heightened appreciation of diverse creative production (Brook et al., 2020; Nwonka, 2015). The industry's amalgamation of commercial desires and social concerns can be observed in the two strategic aims that were foregrounded within the publication *Towards a Sustainable UK Film Industry*, the manifesto that was released at the launch of the UKFC. First, the UKFC's most public agenda was the investment in the idea of a sustainable UK film industry, a primary UKFC sound bite that, while never applied with any kind of precision, seemed to imply *a la* Smith a need to achieve a degree of economic sustainability through a new commercial imperative for British cinema that, in the identification of the global film industry as a simple but specific variant of any other competitive economy, esteems film production as a trade interest that needed to be adequately resourced to compete with other international territories for Hollywood studio inward investment. The second strategic aim was centred on encouraging a parallel but less prominent and certainly economically de-emphasized recognition of the *cultural* value of film, primarily pursued through the expansion of access to film culture in the digitalizing of cinemas and a wider circulation of films through an investment in film exhibition, film literacy and education. Of course, the coexistence of these agendas does not automatically ensure that they retain an equivalency in emphasis, and it is through the UKFC's restructuring of UK film production as an overtly economic practice, albeit one that is organized by a range of social and cultural relations, that the instrumentalist cohesivity of cultural production and participation could be actioned, although as we see, it was the socially cohesive benefits bestowed by the commercial imperatives that were to commandeer this dialectic interaction. There is a general consensus among even those scholars who take a more ambivalent analytical stance on the UKFC's commercial/cultural dyad that the UKFC can incontrovertibly be described as an 'arms-length' body (Moody, 2017; Kelly, 2016) and its status as a government quango is crucial for an understanding of the ideological permeation of the idea of racial equality and inclusion across some of its functions as a policy agenda. The relative devolution of power that quangos enjoy is seldom accompanied by the bestowment of complete conceptual autonomy, and the idea that quangos maintain an adherence, be it explicit or implicit, to the overlapping flows of government mandates is particularly useful as it allows us to understand the UKFC's *modus operandi* as being aligned with the particular ideological imperatives of both the monetization of the creative industry and the cohabiting possibility of socially cohesive outcomes, and works to support the interpretation of the UKFC as 'an iconic New Labour creation' (Doyle, 2014: 133). While such a description invites an Althusserian framing for both the economic and social/cultural impetus behind the UKFC's mandate, I am also mindful that an unvaried application of Althusser's ISA to the UKFC's policy mandate brings with it an invitation to interrogate its suitability as a theoretical model that is able to capture the orientations of a film industry that is highly fragmentary and compartmental in its organizational structures and plural in its primary functions, its forms of labour and the modes by which different facets of society are able to participate. This encourages us to perhaps see the influence of New Labour's racial politics as displaying less of a cascading ideological pattern and, instead, one characterized by different points and forms of social and cultural interaction, influence and pressure. To be precise, and in developing this reading through the status of the UKFC as the lead body for film in Britain, while quangos are reflective of a classic power structure and organizational framework, the specificity of cultural institutions, the cultural products they create and the multiple stages of cultural interaction they allow, open up a number of entry points in which the pragmatic momentum of Black cultural inclusion attempts to stake its claim on the fragile post-Macphersonist industrial landscape through a demand for racially diverse cultural production, if not so much at the point of government policy and political discussion, then certainly at the point of institutional management and the cultural and social consumption of film. By pursuing this alternative paradigm, I place the UKFC at the centre of a circulatory ideological apparatus, or an ideological ecology, in which the UKFC is influential to and influenced by both the official Macphersonist directive against institutional racism and, crucially, the struggle for racial representation through the renewed impetus of a Black cultural politics that has equally been pulled into the post-Macphersonist frame as a kind of strategic essentialism. The result of this interaction finds the UK film industry's social inclusivity rhetoric travel in a vertical trajectory that develops initially from this point as a mandated cultural policy and becomes concretized within film funding streams now attentive to the needs of Black cultural workers, creatives, practitioners and audiences, and grassroots organizations, but in retaining my contention that demands for a more racially inclusive film industry exists within the very same ideological sphere, Black cultural politics is collapsed within the defining logics of post-Macphersonism, this being the incorporating of the more palatable aspects of the demand for cultural representation that had been witnessed in the 1980s and 1990s. We should not discount the use of the term 'rhetoric' in describing the nature of the film industry's racial inclusivity language as it holds particular analytical value in forming a critical understanding of both the cultural industry's interwovenness with the broader politics of race in the UK and, more specifically, the UKFC's instrumentalizing of film culture as a socially cohesive experience; the propagation of the ideology of Britain as a landscape of post-racial inclusivity and access functions as a lacunar discourse in that it relies on the circulation and subscribing of fallacies and contradictions that are revealed as such only when brought into practice. Thus, the ideological nature of the UKFC's racial inclusion agenda within the film industry is derived not so much from post-Macphersonism as a political discourse as from the official command from which it was born: *the eradication of institutional racism.* Undoubtedly, while New Labour's intentions were to create the impression that such a command could function as a universal principle across all areas of social, cultural and economic life, such an ambition is unable to serve as an affirmative philosophy for the highly contingent relationship between film and cultural identity, the prosaic reality being that the instinct of the film industry as a particularly variable apparatus is to place the decree of ethnic minority inclusion in its full lacunar guise, within a plethora of subjectivities, manoeuvres and temporalities. In other words, and to again recall Young and Snead, the competing ideology of racial inclusion becomes subsumed into the already present infrastructural ideology of racism that, thriving on the ambiguity and fluidity that the discourse of racial inclusion affords, places Black identities through a system of racial aversiveness at the level of institutional governance and commissioning, and racial exigency at the level of film authorship and textual representation. This is an important formulation of the ideological relationship between New Labour's race politics, Black cultural production and, more specifically, film, that presents an interesting schematic abstraction of the base/superstructure model: post-Macphersonist new anti-racism as an ideological endeavour influencing everyday material and social relations possesses persuasive elements that evade the collapsing of the transformative processes of the State to within a structuring binary of either force or consensus. For example, if the new thrust of racial inclusion as an outcome of government legislature through the 2000 Race Relations Amendment Act that proceeded from the Macpherson Report, and in tandem with the Commission for Racial Equality as a non-department public body that sought to inscribe racial equality as a concerted professional practice offers a more imaginative understanding of forceful persuasion through (loose) legislation, the general thrust of New Labour's post-racism and its dependency on the production and circulation of a certain figurative language required for the social uptake of the political idea of a harmonious, racially inclusive Britain; visual imagery, narration, experience and expressivity for the essentializing of racial difference work to support description of film, film culture and its outward-facing institutional practices as a consensual mode of social influence. By adopting such an analysis of post-Macphersonism, the politico-institutionalizing of racial inclusivity as a shared social value through cultural policy implementation allows us to arrive at an understanding of the racial inclusivity aims of UKFC as informed by these two regimes of societal persuasion. In the political recognition of the cultural and creative industries and their products as a site of social interaction, it is this potential for the defining of social identities and meaning construction contained within film and screen culture that positions the film industry as prime for the instrumentalism of the post-racial utopia.

The renewed identification of the cultural and creative industries, even in its now politically valuable and celebratory stage, as producing a continued system of cultural deprivation within marginalized communities also chimed with a developing challenge to the exclusion of racial and ethnic minorities within the sector developing in the broader political sphere, primarily the 2000 publication of the Parekh Report by the

Commission on the Future of Multi-Ethnic Britain in collaboration with the race think tank The Runnymede Trust. The outcome of a two-year study emerging just a year after the Macpherson Report, the iconoclasm of the report's demand for a paradigmatic shift in the dominant understanding of Britishness and British identity would also capture in its analysis an uncovering of a system of racial discrimination in the exclusionary structures of cultural participation, and would reveal tremendous racial and ethnic inequalities across a number of sectors with a particular emphasis on the cultural and creative industries and the disparities within public funding towards Black and ethnic minority cultural projects (Runnymede, 2000). Notably, it is within two of the thirteen objectives that were mandated for the UKFC by the DCMS at its inception that hold particular value for an analysis of how the institutional context of cultural governance was immediately responsive to both the legislative essences of the Macpherson Report and the more germane issue of racial exclusion within the film sector. For the UKFC, perhaps relying on an indexical definition of Black film practices (or any other mode of ethnic minority representation) in its responsiveness to the relations of representation as producing an affective relationship between Black access to film production and the nature of Black filmic imagery, its post-Macphersonist objectives were to be found in two specific policy aims that would speak directly to the interests of Black filmmakers in the UKFC pledge to 'support innovative film-making to develop film culture and encourage creative excellence and nurture new talent', and 'support and encourage cultural diversity and social inclusiveness' (Film Council, 2000a: 10). We can ascribe both of these pledges to the ideological resonance of a post-Macphersonist Black cultural politics that overlap and cross-pollinate at the point of their mediation within the specificities of a given product, practice or industry, and if Hall argues that the strategies of cultural politics that have attempted to organize Black creative practices and cultural expressions within their own space of marginality are subjected to a continuous set of discursive phases, we find within the strategic aims of the UKFC a similarly regurgitative modality of cultural policy in the public promise of infrastructural support for Black film/filmmaking in the UK. I accept that this promise, in the context of Hall's reading of the static, non-static, extemporaneous and bidirectional tendencies towards the management of the politics of difference, at least prior to the moment of the discursive shift to post-multiculturalism in the early 2000s, is neither new in its origins nor departing in its general techniques. What does represent change and departure, in an argument that remains within the same Hallian paradigm, is in the conjunctural specificity of the moment that produces, rather than emerging alongside, what Hall sees as the 'specificity of the question' (1993: 104). The question that was being posed to British society, in a new moment of a race politics, was how the official aggrandizement of cultural plurality could perform as an intervention into the racial divisions and underrepresentation that structure its public institutions, a question that allows one to conceive the film sector as a cultural space that is constructed by a range of motivations, justifications, predicaments and interests – the hegemony of the new anti-racism that would be the official political instructive of the Macpherson Report and would inaugurate a culture of hastened visibility within the UK's public institutions, the hyper-capitalization of the cultural and creative industries that provides a politically flaccid but socially advantageous strategy for the institutional governance of cultural difference and the degree of consent it is able to accrue from the fatigued and still-dependent remnants of the previous moment's Black cultural politics. Given this, and anchored by the progressive political utopianism that is implied in the general description of the racial inclusivity agenda in the film sector as an industrial, and therefore a social intervention, we observe an important conjunctural dynamic where divergent social and material forces seem to coalesce over the official agenda against racial exclusivity in the film industry as a cultural predicament, and therefore one that I am unable to understand as anything other than the outcome of a relational discourse. Again, in my identification of cultural participation and access as the migratory tenet of post-Macphersonism, the lexicalizing of terms such as 'cultural diversity' and 'racial inclusivity' to within film industry policy requires further theoretical supplementation to account for its encoding in film language, and in drawing on what Frederick Jameson has interpreted from the concept of mediation as the transitory process that permits an analyses of how forms and practices born from one context can exist within the context of another (1981), the dynamics of capitalism's socio-economic dimensions and the new political discourse on race enter into a mediating relationship within an ideologically receptive state-funded film institution that is able to preserve what renders film institutional practices and the films they produce as unique, and creates the permissive but equally regulated conditions through which film culture is able to encourage the development of its own distinctive textual response to a social circumstance, trend or a commonly identifiable and anxiety-inducing situation. Of course, there exists an array of variations and contradictions to this mediating dynamic, primarily determined by the unfixed and multilayered nature of Black cultural politics when centred towards the question of filmic representation. Allow me to venture into a more abstract interpretation of the socio-economic dynamics organizing the film industry that draw from two intellectual positions on capitalism and their usefulness in the analysis of the cultural management of race. For what is not unique in my observation of the institutional conditioning for the renewed politics of racial representation and the necessary function of economic logics to this development is the presence of the natural reflex of capitalism to excess cultural difference as part of its extractive processes of racial codification, a reading that of course reflects the particular anti-Eurocentric thinking of Cedric Robinson (2000 1983)) where in a rejection of the narrow internationalism of Marx and Engels's forecasting of the determining nature of capitalist development, Robinson would argue that the unconsidered material force of the ideology of racism would suffuse throughout the social relations, consciousness and structures that capitalism would construct. This is a challenge that for Saha and Van Lente (2022), in an application of Robinson's theorization of racial capitalism onto the question of the UK cultural institutions' production of racial diversity as a commodifying spectacle of inclusion, the ambiguity that is created by the primacy of post-racialism as the organizing principle for the diversification of racially discriminatory cultural institutions necessitates a more complex and racially nuanced analysis of capitalism in that 'rather than a mere by-product of capitalism, racism helps capitalism expand while capitalism in turn keeps racial hierarchies in place' (2). This understanding of racial capitalism becomes a particularly valuable framework for the analysis of the popular Black urban film as indexed to the range of political and cultural imperatives that populate the institutional context, for the new economic impetus behind the UK film industry places capitalist extraction at the centre of a conjunctural encounter with a number of macro-political and social tendencies that are able to reshape the modalities of multiculturalism through film culture, and liberalism takes refuge in the social functionalism of film as an ideological chaperone, in which culture provides a less politically convoluted but equally scenic pathway into the New Labour chimera of a racially cohesive social imaginary, here adorned with the images and artefacts of a new enthusiasm for racially diverse cultural production. But equally, and as demonstrative of the forms of power that are harnessed within capitalist modes of film production, Black creative labour can be subjected to a process of mediation, and this gestures towards the kind of socio-economic logic that Wayne terms as capital's 'abstract quantum' (2020: 84). In a Marxist reading of the tensions that arise as capitalism attempts to convert both creative labour's use value and exchange value into a cultural commodity, Wayne's conceptual project centres capitalist profit at the nexus of the relationship between the natural economic instincts of film industrial activity and the kind of craft-like labour that he terms as 'aesthetic-cultural production' (2020: 84) and invites another way of thinking through the socio-economic acclimating of the industrial conditions that become crucial in the negotiation of Black cinematic representation, Black filmic density and, resultingly, the popular Black urban film. Remember that I am developing an analysis of Black urban identity as an excessed filmic experience through a conceptual apparatus that frames the popular Black British urban text as comprised of interacting and conjunctural-dependent situations and agendas, and as a result of how this interaction becomes reconciled, realized and made material once lexicalized within the filmic text, I am describing a set of social aesthetics that paradoxically, are both intra- and extra-industrial. Building on this, the primary position of Blackness and Black spectacularizing to the filmic experience that I argue are constructed from this social aesthetic is an analysis that does not, and cannot, stress economic determinism as the sole foundational logic commandeering this cohabitation. Rather, it is because the various imperatives invoked in this cohabitation are interdependent and somewhat horizontal that its analysis can be located in Robinson's theory of racial capitalism, through which Saha and Van Lente insist that, in a reading of the contradictory and tension-laden impetuses behind the practice of racial diversity in the media, capitalism under the guise of racial inclusion practices can purport to be assisting anti-racism while simultaneously creating and sustaining racism itself. This is an insistence that, in the context of any comprehensive interrogation of the liberal embrace between race and the cultural industries, calls for an analysis in which 'racism and capitalism need to be understood as two distinct historical forces that are inextricably intertwined' (2022: 2). It is by this bidirectionality of racism and anti-racism within the post-Macphersonist film industry sphere and the presence of capitalism at its axis that places the ideological permeation of racial inclusivity as a political mandate that the economic and social predilections of the UK film industry and Black cultural politics is able to enter into a kind of convergence. Such an approach should not be seen as a particularly novel synthesis, and we should note that, at least in the specific context of Black filmic representation, other analyses have exhibited an alternative understanding of variable capitalism that conceives the qualitative value of Black British film as embedded within a triangulation of ownership that draws the practitioner, the institutional funder and its spectatorship/ cultural value into some kind of dialectic mutuality and alignment (Nwonka and Saha, 2021). This triangulation is by no means fixed or hierarchal in structure, and while race and racism are not necessarily cited as part of Wayne's framework for the analysis of capitalism and the film industry as a simple variant of capitalist production, there is a contribution to be made in considering the racial specificity of the three components that make up this triangular relationship embedding Black British film within Wayne's paradigm, and can be located in the textual features of film that Wayne argues are the qualitative elements of variable creative labour. In Wayne's formation, acting and on-screen performance is seen as the primary variable creative labour to be turned into a cultural commodity that appears to esteem film production as the quantitative variable with a lesser regard for the kinds of value to be extracted in film distribution, exhibition and its circulation within societies as a means through which capitalism is able find an extractive economic, cultural and social profit. This is a particularly convoluted conceptual juncture that we are working through, and one that offers no linear pathway for arriving at an understanding of cultural commodification that can fully account for the paradoxical cosmopolitanism of capital and its quite unpredictable mannerisms and modes of operation when centred on racial difference. However, there is the potential within such an analysis of the abstract quantum of capitalism to extract from its commodification of a variable creative labour through film a qualitative variable that is attuned to the filmic *text*: in this context, the most recent version of Black cultural politics, the demand for inclusion in the newly massified UK film industry, and the identification of Black as a *thematic* value. This is reflected in Wayne's partial acknowledgement of a characteristic tendency in which capitalism's attempts at quantifying variable creative labour into a cultural commodity becomes negated if devoid of the crucial qualitative dimension that would make the commodity appealing to the filmmakers as a site for creative expression and the demonstrating of their aesthetic sensibilities and a 'consuming' use value, which Wayne suggests holds particular appeal for different audiences. It is this latter imperative of capitalism, its interest in the creative variables of film production, that brings the idea of film culture as an abstract quantum into dialogue with Hall's critique of the fragile and contingent nature of Black cultural politics and the endless and therefore ever-evolving and contradictory set of modalities, meanings and purposes that are embedded within the very idea of Black film. This being said, while Wayne wants to conceive the process of cultural commodification as a relatively straightforward contestation between capitalism and labour that takes place within the process of creative production, the introduction of the issue of race and the post-Macphersonist iteration of Black cultural politics to within the analytical frame re-renders cultural commodification as a contestation located *both* within the process of creative production that Wayne essentializes as the sole variant that imbues the cultural commodity with a qualitative value and at the point of *cultural* production – its circulation under the auspices of a Black dialogism within a range of publics at specific and opportune social and political conjunctures. What is presented to us here is an intriguing synchronism between the cultural policy interest in Blackness and racial difference, and the increasing accumulativeness of the UK film industry as a site of both economic power and cultural significance, and presents a much more complex matter than the forms of Black cultural exploitation that can be easily attacked through an all-encompassing and, at points, cursory critique of racial capitalism. Instead, and demonstrative of how capitalism's socio-economic dynamics are able to make insertions within Black cultural practices, capital's insatiable need to assert control over such creative variable inputs and with this, institute film as the industrial mechanism for the production of both cultural products, identities and forms of social meaning, positions film institutions as the constitutive machinery through which the desire for Black British filmic narration is to be realized. However, and as Hall observes as the instinctive process of commodification in which Black film, like any form of Black cultural expression, is inevitably drawn into 'the circuits of power and capital' (1993: 108), the result of this capitalist machinery, in proceeding through Hall with a conceptually valid positioning of the film industry as a 'dominant technology' is that the need for institutional support for Black film, be it motivated by the protracted struggle for recognition via Black cultural politics or the post-Macphersonist racial inclusivity agenda, can be brought into being only through the standardization of the forms of Black narration and representation. Put differently, the aggregated desire for Black filmic visibility that becomes the locus of racial capitalism's abstract quantum and the logic of excessive racial differentiation that motivates its attraction to Black film production as a viable commodity must rely on a Black thematic contemporaneousness, or its hegemonic symmetry if you will, as an underwriting guarantor for the economic and/or sociocultural investment in its production. It is only through an understanding of this more complicated iteration of race politics that a number of salient questions pertaining to textual representation can now be posed: What is particular and distinctive about Black British identity and sociality that would both justify its presence within mainstream film narration and representation and supplant its value as a socio-economic and cultural commodity under the rubric of the post-Macphersonist racial inclusion directive, while equally alive to the social textures of the specific conjunctural moment? What can be extracted from the facticity of Black British existence, useful Black fictions or, as Hall terms it, the defining and common discourses and dominant representations that can also form part of the 'Black repertoire' (1993: 109) into the standardizing logics of film production? Relatedly, in the aestheticization of Blackness as a novel and essentialized filmic spectacle, what is first understood hegemonically about Black life, and the Black body in particular, that holds within it the kinds of narratable material necessary for the sketching out of new forms of Black cinematic identity that can be refined as commodifiable, valuable in the conjunctural sociopolitical situation and subsequently, secure a spectarorial obedience, desire and expectation? Here, I am arguing that it is undeniable that the interaction between the hegemony of post-Macphersonism and the social inclusivity aims of the cultural and creative industries embodied a new phase of Black cultural politics. This being the case, I remain in concert with Hall (1988) in that despite the phasemic and temporal nature of Black cultural politics, the official cultural strategies that accompany it and are birthed from the specific moment do not necessarily inaugurate a reversal or disposing of the previous moment's modality or logic, but are composed of antecedents, and retain the constituent fragments of historical and more recent modes and iterations of Black cultural intervention and provision. In a similar vein, we should also be cognizant of the easy assumptions and crude associations that can be arrived at through the underdeveloped reading of the ability of the industrial environment to produce particular textual expressions and representations of Black identity. This is particularly salient in an examination of the multi-dimensional factors that assist in the filmic aestheticization of Black urbanity, and as Wayne advises, as with all forms of capitalist production, one being film making as a social or cultural practice, the conditions of production do not *necessarily* occupy a pre-determining function in the (textual) outcomes of such conditions. Of course, and as the central argument within Saha's framework for dissecting the overt and more clandestine modes of cultural domination within the multifaceted relationship between Black and Asian film and TV representation and Britain's publicly funded screen sector (2018), the institutional context does, indeed, possess a powerful and historic command over the visibility, volume and nature of Black British filmic encounters through its production cultures, industry policies, commissioning decisions and funding provisions, but it is only through its interaction with the political ideologies, social relations and the discourses on race that permeate the social/cultural climate that the institutional context becomes inscribed within Black textual representations. For us, and returning to Hall's theoretical refinement of the quite nebulous field of cultural strategies that shape and occasion the textual visibility of Black identities, Black cultural politics becomes difficult to conceive as process of displacement (2018) but a process that is characterized by an accumulativeness, a discursive layering, and in this specific conjuncture, the hybridizing of radically opposing positions on racial equality and cultural visibility. The outcome of this is that the institutional context, comprised of all that is demanded and promised within the postmodern vista of a pluralized British cultural identity, is able to create apertures in a Black cultural field that is by its very nature contradictory, paradoxical and inconsistent in its behaviour. What does this mean for the exploration of the genesis of the popular Black urban film and its narrative account of the contemporary Black social realities that were to become hegemonically codified in its recrafting of both organic and socially conferred Black identities? In the Black urban film, we encounter a text that must be understood as a highly contingent aesthetic in which forms of political appropriacy, liberal altruism, Black cultural struggle as a strategic contestation and racial capitalist self-interest are able to coexist within the dynamics of a conjunctural moment of race politics that derives a political and social value from both diverse cultural production and, crucially, its consumption. The Black cultural intervention promised by the UKFC at its advent may appear as a disintegration of the binary racial oppositions that had incited the historic demands for Black filmic recognition and industrial inclusion, but the imposing post-racial architecture it is constructed upon and the historically fixed and racially determined structures of identification that authorize Black cinematic representation open up, invite in and reconfigure the terms and aims of Black cultural struggle and with this, the two points of contestation that occupy Hall's relations of representations.

What comes into view as a result of this chapter's exploration of the relationship between the various agendas that furnish the logics of cultural institutional governance as a point of both change and continuity and the industrial conditions from which we can trace the development of the popular Black British urban text as a distinctive Black filmic experience of the early 2000s are conditions that are themselves the outcome of a complex and contingent set of political and social agendas. The unification of these agendas, and their integration within the developing cultural attentiveness of the UK screen industries, produced a new phase in the management of difference that retains the ability to both challenge and sustain racism through the racial compartmentalization of its workforce, commissioning practices and, importantly, on-screen representations. The question of the filmic representation of racial difference holds particular significance in that a fuller understanding of the social and political factors underpinning the industrial context now asks us to consider the textual and narrational implications of the reconfigured and ideologically ossified conditions of film production and the kind of production cultures, logics and fictions that become positioned as conducive to the inclusion of Black identities. However, in the context of the post-Macphersonist strategies of the UKFC, it is insufficient to assume that a more accommodating industrial landscape under both the forceful and consensual persuasiveness that would accompany a more permissive vista of racial inclusivity is the primary factor in the commissioning and popularizing of Black British film and the generic and thematic offshoots that would come to occupy the popular and critical imagination as Black British film's defining exemplar from this period. As I've argued throughout, the cultural participatory mandate for the UK's creative industries is just one way to account for how the film sector became responsive to the renewed momentum of Black cultural politics from the early 2000s that is itself constructed of both historical and more recent approaches to Black and ethnic minority cultural inclusion, which are brought into dialogue with a constellation of social aesthetics that structure the production context, the thematic content and the intended social meanings of the popular Black urban film. Of course, the image systems and modes of narrative communication by which film becomes a source of meaning construction is never a complete, independent or intra-textual process, and is a relational practice that is secured by the level of social participation integral to film and visual culture that insists on the spectators to complete the circuit of meaning through their own system of cognitive organizing, which is not simply the populating of vacant social imaginaries with nomadic and disconnected fictions, but is anchored through an attachment to the public narratives and images that define our social and cultural identities. Rather than remaining on the outer parameter of this process, this is a sequential architecture that places both spectator and text at the centre of a concentric arrangement involving a multitude of imperatives in the diversification of racially majoritarian cultural institutions. It is the social and political context in all of its totality that comes to organize the popular Black urban text and the representational practices through which Black Britain has been negotiated. This points to the significance of the institutional context that draws us towards the conceiving of film policy, institutional practices and their textual products as a site of mediation between Black cultural politics, the cultural compensatory altruism of post-Macphersonism and the interests of the subjective and insatiable desires of capitalist commodification as inherently synchronous; in the instrumentalizing of carefully cordoned areas of the UK film industry as adaptive to the new modalities of racial equality, cultural plurality and social cohesion, the mediacentric choreographies of Black existence that would come to populate the primary forms of Black British cinematic representation give accent to the status of the film industry as a social and political site of racial facilitation. In chiming with Hall's observation of the bureaucratic logics by which 'Black' is brought into the *popular*, Black film as a useful race fiction, a cultural rationality, and a narrative structure must be populated with the easily identifiable and consumable images and metanarratives and Black identity, Black representational currencies or the excessive Black conventions that are staked out and claimed as the dominant frame for our understanding of racial difference. The institutional sphere, its essentializing of Blackness and racial difference, emerges as the outcome of a politics of resistance that coexists within the hybridizing political, social, cultural and textual embrace that allows film to become opportune for the post-Macphersonist cultural politics of race and inclusion.

4

The Hauntological Black Urban Other

a ghost never dies, it remains always to come and to come-back
Jacques Derrida, *Specters of Marx*, 1993

I want to remain momentarily with the exploration of what I feel is particularly generative in the idea of Black facticity as a cultural commodity that can be useful for the bringing into my analysis of the primary image that shapes our filmic encounters of Blackness and Black existence, that of the Black body. In this endeavour, a reading of the Black contemporalities and hegemonic symmetries that are to both inspire and justify the popular representations of what has become accepted as Black British identity can be approached through a phenomenological interpretation of the Marxist model of commodity fetishism, and the performance of the Black body within mainstream visual narration that attempts to consolidate the validity of this symmetry is particularly relevant given the previous chapter's exploration of the industrial, political and cultural contexts which I term as the *preliminaries* of the Black British urban text that moves towards the capitalist nature of film production and its usefulness in imagining a different purpose for Black identity and existence. For to engage with Marx's idea of commodity fetishism is to understand how our experience of the Black body as an entry point into the filmic and televisual experience of Black identity (as an object) can also be grounded in what Wayne has invited us to think of as the quantum abstract profit of creative labour and, in particular, film production. As Wayne interprets through Marx, artisanal labour and matter, the two elements that Marx insists the commodity is comprised of are both active in a process in which the commodity is made present through the labour required for the converting of such matter into a material and tangible form. For us, and in the recognition that the labour involved in film and television production can also be made valuable by its interaction with the politics of race and cultural difference, the conversion of what I describe as Black matter, or material, into some kind of standardizing form furnishes the commodified object with a degree of use value to be derived from its intrinsic value – its seductive and emblematic worth to be found in the depiction of the themes of Blackness as a commodity that draws in its consumer and from which its value is secured by the symbolic and cultural impact rather than just its human labour – alongside its exchange value. There is an important formation to be observed here, for the commodification of Black identity and the way the Black body in its most predicable representative forms has come into aestheticization, visuality and screen narration has been the primary lens through which we have been able to observe what Wayne terms as the 'magic' of variable creative labour (2020). As I've argued, both Wayne's and Hall's thinking as applied here – the identification of the ways in which the qualitative and quantitative elements of film production are drawn to within the variable logics of capitalism and its attendant interest in the real and inauthentic repertoires, vernaculars and practices emanating from Black popular culture – offers a teleology that helps formulate the critical transition of not just the qualitative aspects of Black cultural production from creative labour to form, but also the qualitative aspects of Black British urbanity as a televisual and filmic theme and the ways in which the alterity of the Black urban existence as a form of dramatic narration are able to be extracted and commodified from the aestheticization of the Black body. This transition occurs within the ensemble of agendas created by the new phase of race and cultural difference that are to be found in the social, political and cultural imperatives of the post-Macphersonist sphere. Resultingly, the liminality of the commodifying transition to a useful race fiction means that the Black body cannot be fully materialized until it has been articulated through the crucial constitutive element of capitalist profit's most racially satisfying and justificatory interest in Blackness as an extractive value from the quantitative nature of film and visual culture, and its qualitative elements in its gaze of Blackness – the *spectacular*, and the standardizing normalization of this spectacular – remembering that we are placing the nascent development and popularizing of the popular Black urban film within an ambivalent relationship between capitalism, the politics of race and its ideological uptake within the cultural and creative industries and the renewing thrust of Black cultural politics that all remain subject to the specificities of the conjunctural moment, these being the new forms of race politics and Black cultural representation. This conjuncture, occurring during the early 2000s as a liminal space reveals all kinds of convergences, and the new forms of Black filmic representation in the popular Black urban film as one index of creative labour demands not just the commodification of Blackness and the Black body as an independent and autonomous visual experience for its conversion, but the development of the popular Black urban text in a useful fiction of race also demands an interactive commodification of both instances of and the imaginary ideas within the social Black crisis and catastrophe. In mobilizing such a phenomenological reading of the Black body's meaning and function in the popular Black urban text as useful fictions of race, I want to argue in this chapter that an unprecedented political and social interest in the heightened instances of Black social violence and Black death becomes part of the substrate of social aesthetics that underpin the popular Black urban text. In this effort, before we are able to fully understand the social and cultural dynamics involved in the development of the popular Black urban text, we must also examine the development of Black conflict and social trauma as a narrative thematic that prepares and propels the spectator through the Black body and onto the Black world as a mediation between the seemingly dialectical poles of Black filmic presence and absence. Here, I am concerned with how the filmic and televisual construction of

Black urban identity as a useful fiction of race is secured from its extrapolation of Black social tragedy that structures the popular Black urban text's fabula: its characters, their stories, movements, vernaculars and relations; its incidents, events, plots and dramatic action; and the thematic conventions that organize their character's interactions with others, their functions, narrative trajectories and fates.

That films are able to draw their stories and characterizations from the immediate social world into which they are embedded is, of course, no novel occurrence, and in the very nature of film language we find that indexicality, the idea that film narratives and images are to register a correspondence with the world of their making, is part of the cultural process of story craft assisted by the involvement of creativity and an adherence to the conventions of narrative structure that provide the audience a sense of relevance and identification. As I have described in my opening chapter, much of what we have come to accept historically as Black film registers a close and at times an indissociable indexicality – certainly at the level of text and certainly at the equally related and consequential level of context, and by this I am referring to the social and cultural dynamics, relations, logics, circumstances and human conditions that penetrate our everyday existences and find narrative form within the language of film. This being the case, what I'm attempting to argue is that what is exceptional about the indexical relationship between the emergence of the popular Black urban film and its claim to function as a repository of the Black British experience is found in the ritualistic nature of its image-making and its construction of visual representations that are animated by the most dramatic elements of the Black existence and offered back to us through the structuring optic of white imaginaries, which are themselves framed by the amplification of narratives and images of Black hyper-criminality that are presented as a habitual feature of the natural world. How can the conjuncture's most excessive and fetishistic modality of Black representation provide the useful fiction of race with new serviceable untruths that function as both denigrative and reparative when they draw so heavily from the official circulation of anti-Black anxiety and expressed through both the spectacular and the sensational cultural representation of Black bodies, and Black death? This question is one that asks us to situate our reading of Black filmic representation and the narrational investment in Black abjectness that occasion and justify its production through the analysis of how the social proliferation of ideas and accounts of Black social catastrophe and the denigrative meanings associated with Black urbanity governed our primary understandings of Black identity, how this came to serve the practice of filmic and televisual realism, how it is ascribed a value, presence and meaning within a phenomenological understanding of the Black body and how the Black body is placed at the centre of how we understand politically, socially, culturally and aesthetically, the Black urban life world.

In the opening chapter I drew attention to the figure of the Black urban Other as a construction of eighteenth-century racist mythology and the proliferation of images of urban unrest and protest, and the permeating race fiction of a genetic Black malevolence that requires the consenting practice of authoritarian policing. In this figuration, I want to argue that the social, political and cultural preoccupation with Black urban identity in the early 2000s that established violent Black masculinity as a specific filmic and televisual theme was determined by historic conditions and ideas that exhibit an interaction with a version of race politics that seems to intensify the interest and strategic investment in the depiction of Black urban masculinity and its illustration of the Black urban Other as a perennial symbol of social anxiety, unease and spectarorial desire, and in doing so are able to propel the reincarnated Black urban malefic as a primary candidate for the central figure of condemnation within a number of social crises, race fictions and various forms of visual narration. What really concerns me here is how the construction of the Black male Other within popular Black urban texts is a construction of a recurring racial unease, a construction of hauntology, and this critical framing invites us to turn to the work of Jacques Derrida (1994). In an abstraction of Marx's imaginative description of Communism as a social ideology permeating throughout Europe as a kind of *spectre*, Derrida presents the idea of hauntology to describe the affectivity and nature of past social thought as a spectral permeation in the production and circulation of forms of social knowledge throughout a social and political episteme. For Derrida, in its establishing of gradual and at times infinitesimal connections upon our social imaginations, memories and understandings, this interpellation of historic ideas within the current social sphere is understood as the ghostly disturbance of the present. David Marriot, in the use of the Derridian formulation for examining how the recycled ideas and images of African slavery continue to disturb Black modernity, applies the concept of hauntology to explore how Black people are experienced as 'spooks', scary figures that become a haunting feature within visual cultures and practices. We find a less explicit reference to Derrida in Avery Gordon (2008) who, in exploring how the spectre registers a temporal disjuncture in rupturing our experience of the past and the present and frightens everyday life and social relations by a similar sense of ghostliness, describes haunting as the social condition where 'a repressed or unresolved social violence' announces itself within an episteme through dominant systems of power that are able to place relic ideologies and abusive practices back onto the contemporary social imaginary – it moves from the abstract to the material. The conceptual task of renovation through a Derridian deconstructivism that has been undertaken by scholars from a plethora of different intellectual fields, theoretical paradigms and disciplines that find interpretive favour in the deliberately loose application of hauntology as a critical framework encourages me to advance a description of hauntology as the recurring presence of ghosts – images, ideas, spheres and figures born of the past that maintain a haunting effect on the present. We can think of this affect as a harming presence and consuming ghostliness, and through the version of haunting as described by Gordon, illustrates that the violence suffered by Black people in the period of slavery, colonialism and beyond is re-experienced in the repetitive racial injustice and death confronting Black Britain, not just through their habitual experiences but also through the beliefs, ideas and images resurrected from history that find manifestation in the powerful narratives of the media and popular culture.

The analytical pathways that are opened up in the attempt to work through the edifice of Black denigration in the use of the Derridian spectre have a particular significance for our interest in the Black urban Other as a continuing social concern that has a hauntological persistence in the racialized imaginaries of whiteness, performing here as the physical embodiment of ceaselessly recrudesce social ideas and reimaginations. In as much as I am suggesting that the idea of hauntology allows for a framework for understanding the continuous public denigration of Black urban identities, my analysis is equally cognizant of the areas of departure and separation in the theoretical application of Derrida's concept of hauntology to the racially bound processes of Black othering. An obvious point of disjuncture from Derrida's theoretical construction of the ghost as a haunting spectre is in the rigid atemporality of the hauntological Black urban Other. While Derrida's project in its most original form (and despite my own recognition of its temporal disjunction) is drawn from a metaphorical reading of the Marxist evaluation of the spread of communist thought and is politically and, therefore, socially situated, the Black hauntological figure is transcendental, and finds its presence throughout a number of political cultures and postmodern experiences and, in contrast to the Derridian formulation, whose ghost is homogenous and is bound by the opacity of history and contemporaneity, this hauntological presence of the Black urban Other, in its ability to both defy and define temporality, has a permanence and is metaphysical in texture. Further, I want to contend that an additional area of disunity is found in the acceptance of the temporality of ghostliness as suggested through Derrida, for where the spectre of the recurring ghost emerging from beyond the grave would accrue a degree of affective knowledge production, social affect, and then eventually wither and pass, the volume of social malevolence that embodies the Black male as a hauntological spectre is rendered distinct and particular not simply through its Blackness itself, but also through the absence of mortality. The hauntological Black Other can never be truly dead or diminished; this would take us into a somewhat counterintuitive and hegemonically malfunctioning understanding of Black Othering and accompanying this, the partial acknowledgement of the humanness of Black people, an acceptance that would represent an affront to the very ideological foundations of racism when we consider that infra-humanization has been and remains so fundamental to the structuring logics of white negations of the Black existence. Anti-humanness, part of the white intercessions of the Black life form, can be critiqued within a regenerative analysis of hauntology, and in my arguing that an understanding of the Black urban Other as a figure of a haunting social spectre as finite and mortal triggers an autoimmune crisis within the episteme, social knowledge becomes open to the possibility of dismantling the organizing structures of Black antitheticality, of dispelling its figmental but material construction as an existential and unredeemable threat to the otherwise placid and harmonious white normality. To accept wholesale that the original and unadapted Derridian formulation of hauntology can also capture in its conceptual sphere the manifold questions of Black corporeality that for Gilroy, in drawing from the practice of colonial rupture indexed in Fanon's idea of epidermalization as the principle through which social relations and existences become classified within what Gilroy terms as a 'color-coded humanity' (2004: 46), is to allow the hauntological Black Urban Other to enter into a process of human identification, recognition and, ultimately, dispellment and demystification. Rather, Black urban Otherness as a hauntological figure permeating throughout our social world retains an eternal life and sustained presence across a number of social formations, situations and crises and, as critical to my argument that the Black urban Other exists as a haunting spectre that is orchestrated by the heterogeneity of the prevailing racial discourse, with varying levels of intensification. Let me imply that this idea of hauntological Blackness as a spectre that is both immortal and restless is indicative of what Hall has conceived in his enduring analysis of race as the 'floating signifier'. In this theoretical project offered by Hall, 'signifiers refer to the systems and concepts of the classification of a culture, to its practices for making meaning' (2021 [1997]: 362). It is in his understanding that the symbols and systems recruited in these processes of race meaning-making are unable to be 'transhistorically fixed' and are able to accrue different and multiple interpretive codes and classifying language that Hall then asks that we think of the floating signifier and its configuring of race not as an independent and autonomous process but as one that is made impactful only through its interactivity. For as Hall continues, 'And those things gain their meaning, not because of what they contain in their essence, but in the shifting relations of difference, which they establish with other concepts and ideas in a signifying field' (2021 [1997]: 362). What is crucial to my theoretical interest in Hall's idea of race as a floating signifier is that he isolates the contingent character of signification in the use of *floating* as the critical adjective that creates the opportunity for the theoretical consideration of the instinctive and necessary relationality of signification; the practice of racial signifying possesses a transience and a mobility, for the signifier

> is subject to the constant process of redefinition and appropriation: to the losing of old meanings, and appropriation and collection of new ones, to the endless process of being constantly resignified, made to mean something different in different cultures, in different historical formations at different moments of time. (2021 [1997]: 362)

This description of race as a montaged and versatile system of meaning-making and comprehension asks for an understanding of the hauntological Black urban other as unfinished and continuously subject to the shifting and epidermalizing classifications of a given culture, as for Hall, race is a dependent signifier; the means of racial signification and its meaning are enacted and brought into being through its vulnerability to the insatiable demands of the continuously shifting and repossessing racial discourses and racial frames. However, allow me to occupy a position of slender disunity towards the hauntological/signifying inscriptive, as located in my analysis of the Black urban Other are several points of departure that emerge in the conceiving of the Black hauntological figure through the theoretical synthesis of Derrida and Hall that should be engaged with. First, the hauntological Black urban Other, as aligned with Hall's own understanding of the nature of signification, is never fully autonomous in movement or independent in presence, nor can it enjoy a detachment with the structuring signifying field, be liberated in its existence or be haphazard or unpredictable in its functions and mannerisms; the hauntological Black urban malevolent cannot roam freely within the social situations it is placed in, although this does not imply that the

Black urban identity can never exist as extra-hegemonic, or *attempt* to re-represent itself within a positive/negative binary. To fatigue this understanding, and referring to the ways through which meaning-making processes seek to codify Black identity within a system of both categorization and characterization, the hauntological Black other is unable to exist outside of the strict orchestration of the dominant discourses. Rather, the hauntological Black figure is accumulative, and both accrues and has ascribed upon itself its social purposes, functions and connotative meanings and contemporary anxieties by the resignifying and regenerative codes of the 'discursive structure' (Hall, 2021: 362). Second, while Derrida's hauntology is a concept that posits the spectre of ghost as a figure of non-origin, the overriding logic servicing the process of racial signifying presents to us an understanding of the Black malevolent figure as inscribed and secured in nature, and this fixing bestows the hauntological Black Other with a certain stability. By this, and remembering that we are confronted here with an alternative understanding of stability and fixity, not as a kind of immutability of identification – as I've argued, paradoxically, the hauntological Black urban Other is neither monolithic in meaning nor transhistorical in its cultural purpose and function and is bound to the volition of the material and symbolic processes of reification that come into figuration and meaning through its inscription in the centre of various social situations, anxieties and ills. In this sense, the Black urban Other retains a versatile atemporality, or to term this in more direct accents, the hauntological Black urban Other is never of *status* (which would again imply a permanence of time and history) but of a transcending *condition*. Instead, the Hauntological Black Urban Other is a construction of a fixity and stability that is a decision and outcome of the preordained characteristics, habitats and pathways that have been marked out for the Black existence, which are consciously templated against the racially normalizing framework of whiteness; the Hauntological Black Urban Other is fixed and stable in nature only in its anchoring within the impatient and ideological signifiers of a continuous and epidermalizing Black antitheticality. In other words, the hauntological Black urban figment accrues its solidity in its aestheticization, its lexicalization within a range of publics and useful fictions, narratives and discourses, and in the context of Hall's identification of the reifying processes of signification, as a constant source of social perturbation; it becomes material and is made meaningful both by the signifying field and through it.

There is a particular intentionality and purpose in pursuing the analysis of the period's crafting of Black identity once placed onto the signifiers of Black urbanity through a Derridian hauntology. I previously described the Black urban Other as a mythical figure that casts a constant haunting presence across generations, social and cultural periods and political situations. Here, and indicative of the shifting nature of race as a signifier that resists time and temporality, the prevalence and proliferation of Black male malevolence as a hauntological energy finds both favour and, crucially, habitation, within the cyclical racial discourses. It is in the emphasis placed on the question of racial identity in securing Black urban masculinity as a social anxiety that I find a similar sense of hauntological othering in some of the ideas on racial aversion presented by Sivamohan Valluvan (2020), who, in an eclectic but sociologically ballast theorization of the ubiquitous racial politics that characterize contemporary Britain, pursues an ontology of nationalism as the identificatory and associatively accusatory ideology 'by which primary culpability for significant socio-political problems, whether real or imagined (depending on one's political leanings), is attributed to various "alien" ethno-racial communities' (5). Like the atemporal nature of hauntological racial othering, this kind of ascription is born of a certain melancholia, and as argued by Valluvan, it is a modality of racial signification that is dependent on an official polarization between the whiteness of the nation, and those of non-belonging, of *non-being*. It is through the idea of an accentuating of the demonizing of racial difference by its attachment to a highly palatable and consensusing social crisis or ill that I find a nationalistic character to the processes of racial signification that are able to recreate and assign the Black urban Other to host a hauntological set of ideas, mystifications and descriptions; the hauntological Black figure, in this sense, is reified with a congenital reproductivity. We should remind ourselves that we are approaching an analysis of signification as one that, as Hall argues, is in a continuous 'sliding of meaning' (2021: 362). Its emptiness is by the necessity of its relationality and the re-laying of its meaning; there always remains something yet unsaid to be said about, or ascribed to, race. Signification, by this description, is the systemic and systematic process that produces, reproduces and reorients identities to official and approved social relations, conditions and positions, and is thus an inherently semiological endeavour and, in the context of race, one of a pernicious outcome. It finds its genetic origins and relations in the symbolic, which for the purpose of accounting for the social othering of Black urban masculine identity, its racial meaning gains a material presence by the attribution of the Black body to a tangible social idea, concern, narrative or image system. This is where we are indeed confronted by what Les Back terms the 'cultural contradictions of racism' (1996: 8) that, in drawing on Hall, place racial Others within a corresponding simultaneity of desire and denigration, at one moment functioning within the white imaginary as an object of intrigue and another categorized as a 'violent savage' (1996: 8). The idea that a complex dualism structures the white gaze when fixated on the malevolent Black body introduces an important point of consideration about the kind of narratives that are generated in the service of the useful fiction of race. As informed by Fanon (1952), these have been found within particular forms of narration, where Black masculinity is fictionalized in fatal sexual mythologies that craft the Black male as born of an instinctive and insatiable Black sexual lust and savagery that is impelled to carry out the cardinal transgression in daring to cross the forbidden thresholds of white intercourse and, as we observe in the enduring narrative of white supremacy and deliverance in *Birth of a Nation*, provokes an intervention marked by the possessive bulwark of white patriarchy that establishes the phenomena of interraciality as the ultimate defilement of white female purity, or the resistant and official characterization of Blackness as an unassailable threat to the safety, functioning and prosperity of normal society and civility. I'm touching upon some quite visceral examples of Black Othering and denigration, but they reveal the central argument within my analysis, for what the Hauntological Black urban Other possesses is a certain epistemic bilingualism that in its spectral embodiment of

Black identity as an excessive spectral force within these race fictions, secures in the popular imaginary the image of the Black urban male as a regenerative construction of representation, of memory, of fear, of expectation and of discourse.

This conceptual grounding of the exploration of the genealogical basis and processes of Black urban othering and signification within a Derridian theorizing of hauntology is important in a critical analysis of the thematic structures and characterizations that become the vernacular principle of the popular Black urban film, as it lends itself to an understanding of the extra- and intra-textual versions of Black male identity they hold, just as with the idea of the popular urban film as social aesthetic, as the outcome of a novel cultural, political and textual syncretism. For what we encounter in the very public crisis of Black masculine identity and existence in Britain that was to emerge towards the end of the twentieth century was not an inherently new iteration of the Black urban male problematic, but a return to an all too familiar image, and given that the hauntological Black urban Other once ushered through the signifying field possesses an accumulative adaptability, it is infused with an additional set of characteristics, capabilities, apparels and, crucially, *à la mode* repertoires. What I am arguing here is that the processes of resignification imbue within the hauntological Black figure a certain hegemonic vitality of presence and function that becomes necessary for the hauntological Black urban figure to be centred within a set of dominant race discourses that, as Hall argues, is a primary conductor to the dependent mobility of race as a floating signifier. In other words, the regenerative omnipresence of the malefic Black hauntological figure is one formed of the coexistence of older and more recent processes of Black othering that both invent and reinvent a host of social crises in the purpose of the positioning of the Black urban figure as the antagonist/protagonist required for the devising, narrating and propagation of useful race fictions, and the mid-to-late 1990s would witness the glacial but no less significant entry of a regenerated and hegemonically potent version of the hauntological Black urban Other into the inscriptive signifying field of ethicized criminality and fatal violence. Like the race uprisings of the early 1980s that were both created from and were met with the force of violent racist policing, we find the political discourse of race-natural criminality at the centre of a triangulation of anxiety, fear and the remedial impulses of law and order provide the nationalistic dimension to the official categorizing of the Black urban male as of non-being, but in an argument that invites us to momentarily reflect on Hall's revision of hegemony as a consensus-securing strategic practice (1978) provide justification for the renewed centrality of the Black masculinity problematic within the strategic narratives, images and both the liberal and illiberal, but continuously racially sutured commentaries of the British media. As a policy response to a number of violent gun killings in London that were attributed to the presence of Yardies, a descriptive, all-encompassing and highly racialized euphemism for Black, male criminal gangs originating predominantly from Jamaica and residing within the UK's Black inner cities, the Metropolitan Police would launch Operation Trident in 1998, a dedicated, Central Metropolitan Police Unit that would sit within the Serious Crime Directorate and whose remit was the investigating, solving and preventing of what would become hegemonically understood as 'black-on-black' gun-related murders and incidents in which both the victim(s) and suspect(s) are Black. It is in the continued fidelity to my own demand that the analysis of the Black urban text and its attendant and undergirding dimensions pursues a form of intellectual dexterity that evades the understandable and easily drawn charge of essentialism that I should make clear, even at this nascent point in my analysis, that my critical reading of Operation Trident as an ideological product of the racial logics of British policing is not an attempt to deny the very real and devastating impact of the increasing gun-related violence within London's Black communities during the late 1990s and the Metropolitan Police's rhetorical dissatisfaction towards the low detection and conviction rates that encouraged the highly imbalanced strategic cohabitation of an overtly racially programmed, armed and subsequently fatal form of law enforcement with, at least within the residual late-twentieth-century imaginaries and fragile logics of the Metropolitan Police, elements of consultative 'community-level' policing. However, and while I will generally resist the obvious, well-rehearsed and in many respects justified review of the broad and voluminous critical perspectives on the logics of Black policing, in a continued adherence to what Martin Glynn argues is the necessity of a 'Black criminology' (2021: 3) that, drawing on the work of Phillips and Bowling (2003) who contend that the introduction of questions of race and racism to the critical orthodoxy allows significant methodological and analytical frames to emerge that may disturb a paradigmatic slumber most comfortable in the containment of violent criminality in a range of Black pathologies, the idea of a Black criminological imagination as an essential part of any substantial analysis of race and crime allows us to form a critical understanding of the sociology of criminal activity and its placing onto the contested terrain of Black urbanity. For Gilroy (1987) the very concept of a Black criminality as an enduring stereotype is derived from the historic and ideological archive of Black marginalization and unwelcoming. Turning some years later to what he describes as 'Yardie-phobia' (*The Guardian*, Wednesday, 8 January 2003), Gilroy would contend that the crisis of Black urban gang and gun crime that emerged in the early 2000s is simply the most recent in a long history of decontextualized commentaries that reveals the 'consistency in the way that it is always crime which tells the British people what racial differences add up to' (*The Guardian*, Wednesday, 8 January 2003). Operation Trident, just as the hauntological Black identities that occupy its centre, is equally the product of a historical and melancholic clamour over Black identities that provides the ideological basis for a practice of policing race, and it is through Gilroy's reading of the protracted struggle over the idea of a Black criminality that we can find this haunting in the programmatic structures of law and order, such as the Metropolitan Police's aptly titled Yardie Squad in 1990; Operation Dalehouse, an informant-reliant unit for the investigating of Yardie activity in South London that was disbanded in 1993 after, in a response that is indicative of the kinds of community-centric policing that Gilroy terms as a 'commentary strategy' (1982), it reported poor conviction rates that its lead detectives would attribute to a lack of cooperation from London's Black communities; the Drugs and Related Violence Intelligence Unit (DRVIU), a title which, given its specific remit that was identical to its previous incarnations, served as a synonym for Black gang and gun violence (The *Independent*, Thursday, 30 June 1994); and Operation

Dibri, an ancillary investigation unit launched in 2008 within the broader Operation Trident directive that would specifically target armed Black gang activity within and around Tottenham's Broadwater Farm Estate. From its launching, Operation Trident set in motion a programme that beyond simply incentivizing, specifically *required* the heightened police presence in the Lambeth and Brent areas of London, with the latter centred on the housing estates of St Raphael's and Stonebridge, two disproportionately Afro-Caribbean locales, and placing it on the continuum of racially programmed policing practices. Thus, this official process of increasing the consensusing social anxieties over an instinctive Black non-beingness through the racial categorizing of crime targeted towards London's Black communities exhibited a significant tendency to inflame already existent notions of Black violent criminality. In a moment where New Labour policymakers would begin to publicly declare an unprecedented policy investment in programmes of urban renewal and regeneration, child poverty alleviation initiatives and social welfare reforms (Hills, 1998), we observed a simultaneous embracing of the continuation of historically racially specific crime control policies as a means to overpolice working-class Black people, who were to find themselves, just as the generations before them, cast as a veritable and violent social disease. This identification of the police as the state infrastructure where Black identity is placed under hauntological pursuit is congruent with my initial chapter's exploration of the official, unofficial, overt and covert modes of racial subjugation, harassment, violence, prejudice, corruption and injustice performed by the police under the protective but transparent structuring discourse of law and order and abetted by a media ideology committed to the denigration of Black masculine identity, which combine to construct, develop and contain within the racial spheres of the nation the mythology of the Black urban Other as an instinctively problematic and alien culture necessitating the racially specific approaches to law and order (Hall, 2021 [1981]; Solomos, 1988). In other words, race, racism and racialization has always been an essential facet of British policing. This invites us to think beyond the more concrete examples of Black policing found in the Scotland Yard's anti-Yardie directives mentioned earlier and towards its more heterogeneous manifestations. In this expansive understanding, we can refer to the continuum of violent colonial authority that would become systematized within the brutal police practices that were to be inflicted upon the West Indian communities as the fulcrum of the nation's management of post-war immigration, the 'official' apathy displayed towards the 1981 New Cross Fire where thirteen Black British children would perish in a house blaze during a birthday party that was widely believed to have been the result of a racist arson attack, to the habitual state-endorsed and state-administered violence towards Black youth identities within urban locations in the 1970s, 1980s and 1990s that *inter alia* institutionalized the violent curtailment of Black childhood. This latter point is particularly salient to the analysis of the formations of early twenty-first-century Black urban youthhood as a criminalized subject and an attendant film and television thematic. Extensive analysis of the wilful acceleration of Black childhood to youthhood for the primary benefit of British policing is found in the critical analysis of racism in 1970s Britain by Errol Lawrence (1982), by which the police's racist assumptions of an inherent Black criminality through the physiological assessment of Black adolescence work to dispatch Black children prematurely into the very adult and therefore potentially fatal realms of suspicion, threat and congenital violence that conceive Black boys as the natural progenies of the genetic and cultural characteristics of a malevolent Blackness, propagated by the extended and durable white supremacist logics of the police and stabilized through the equally hauntological optic of the infrahuman Black problematic. This, of course, is not solely an affliction situated within the racially barbed parameters of Black Britain, and we encounter a similar critical analysis of the planetary existence of the baleful instincts of the police within the North American Black Studies paradigm by Walcott (2021), who, in a lucid but mournful theorizing of the dispersal of police violence throughout the Black diaspora, reconfigures the organic and placid environments and geographies of Black childhood as places of innocence as 'sites of antagonism'. In this compelling thesis, the healthy and productive functioning of the technology of anti-Black policing demands the criminalization of Black childhood vernacular practices and normoactivities found in parks, streets, playgrounds and schools, which become what Walcott terms as 'the terrain of black death' (21). Thus, whether found in the subjecting of Black children to the violence of adultification, or the historic and habitual practice of Black profiling in urban areas of London, policing, one of the primary institutional processes that define racism in the twenty-first century, the socio-historic practice of law and order as a dividing practice that can be understood through the W. E. B. Du Bois's notion of the 'colour line' (1989: 13) [1901] finds its contemporary manifestation as social violence in the form of racially concerted law enforcement that, gaining its cohesive modes of social consent through its reliance on the preservation of a verticality between racial identities, assists the justification for the differential treatment towards white and Black Britain. It is necessary here to further contextualize my argument. If the specific value of a Black criminology is that it is able to situate an interrogation of the relatedness of Black people and crime within the analysis of racism, rather than just race, and through a number of disciplines and paradigmatic optics, its efficacy in this example as an agile and generative modality stems from the fact that both urban sociologists and criminologists coalescing within a Black criminological approach have been able to bring into serious question both the validity of the Metropolitan Police's explanatory account of the city's Black gun crime and its accompanying policing practices within the neo-segregated Black communities in areas such as Brent and Lambeth (Operation Trident would later be expanded to cover all of London). Indeed, a sustained analysis of the police's constructed account of the presence and potency of gangs is found in the work of Claire Alexander (2008), who offers a sociological interrogation of the lack of precision and reliability in the Metropolitan Police's advancing of gun crime as a distinctive *cultural* practice and its natural and incontestable synonymy with gang (Black) culture. Here, the official commentary of gang activity in the UK that strives to implant Blackness itself as the organizing principle for gun violence is in itself made problematic not solely by the logics through which the idea of gangs is racialized, but in the very validity of the term 'gang' itself. In Alexander's reading of the hysteria surrounding Black criminal gangs within officialdom, she finds an ontological crisis in the dominant framing of Black male criminal activity and its fixity through UK policing and its cursory application of the term 'gang culture', one seen as problematic as 'we know very little about the gang in the UK: about how a "gang" might be defined or understood, about what being in "a gang" means, even whether there are "gangs" in any accepted sociological and criminological sense at all' (3). My use of the term 'culture' as a reference to the codes used within the official race lexicon that work to stress an automatic fixity in the popular imaginary of the Black urban Other and a set of behavioural patterns that are able to unify Blackness and fatal criminality have a specific and important value in the attempt made here to describe the processes of parallelism that equates, without rigorous analysis, informal Black criminal activity with the formal structures of organized gang violence.

To return to the reading of the nationalistic dimension to the criminal signifying of the hauntological Black urban Other, it is the transnational policing variant found within Operation Trident's construction of gun violence as a Jamaican diasporic criminal activity that sets the justificatory context for the armed policing of Black communities. The natural assumption here is that the Metropolitan Police's finite evaluation of armed gang violence as racially distinct is buttressed by an official and incontestable identification of a localized drug trade at the basis of London's violent gun crime phenomena that necessitates a strategy that enlists the collaboration of local Caribbean police forces who may possess an organic and authentic analytical position towards the issue of violent gun crime with distinctive cultural and ethnic specificities. For Bowling (2009), Operation Trident's primary transnational measures involve 'intelligence sharing, dispatching detectives to the Caribbean to interview witnesses and attend the funerals of homicide victims, as well as hosting Jamaican officers in London' (156). It should be of particular note that this examination of the useful fiction of race that is revealed in the identification of Jamaica as the birthplace of gun-related murder and, through this, a stable description of London's gun and gang activity within urban environments as a natural crime of an uniquely Black origin, remains in concert with the Hall(ian) reading of the obfuscatory potentialities of hegemony that work to sever the visible and unrepentant chords that bind racism with the political and social injustice. Echoing the critique by Gilroy on how the relationship between Blackness and criminality is extracted from any historical analysis of Black life by its detachment from the colonial conditions of the nation, nationality adds another dynamic and anxiety-inducing layer of othering to the already ballast set of apparent cultural and biological impulses that sustain and justify the so-called black-on-black criminality phenomena. As much as some segments of Operation Trident's justificatory narrative retain a degree of credence, this being that the period indeed witnessed an increase in gun- and drug-related murders, an empirical study conducted within the London Borough of Brent, which by the early 2000s would record one of the highest number of violent gun-crime offences within London, revealed that the reality of gun and gang culture posited a much more nuanced and, crucially, multiracial relationship than the racially singular master narratives of black-on-black gun crime permits. In the area of Brent, which by 2001 would register the second most ethnically and racially diverse Local Authority in England, where 18.3 per cent of Brent's Black and ethnic minority population (54.7%)

were Black Caribbean or Black African, and where 86.1 per cent of those accused of murder/attempted murder between 1998 and 2003 were IC3 (Black) men, 24.4 per cent of murder/attempted murder victims in Brent where a Firearms Feature Code was noted were actually of non-IC3 categorization (Hales, 2005). Such realities call upon the Black criminological work of Bowling, Parpar and Phillips (2003), which has called into question not just the legitimacy of the instinctive black-on-black criminality officialdom but also the consequences of the creation and distribution of inaccurate, counterfactual and sensationalist accounts of violent Black crime to be faced by Black identities through militaristic policing practices and the increasing of racially predicated surveillance strategies. Of course, this cannot serve as a basis for the wholesale rejection of some of the realities of gun activity among the city's Black environs, nor can this claim to an ontological crisis of black-on-black gun crime be sufficient for the development of an affirmative counter-narrative. This is not the intention, and in drawing attention to this empirical but of course highly situated data on gun crime in Brent does not contend that our official encounters with the fallacious Black gun-crime narrative can be fully comprehended and remedied through a more racially fissured portraiture of gang and gun-crime in London, but that the failure of official narratives to attend to the more multiracial nature of urban crime within the symbolic locations of London reveal a particular morbidity in the propulsive flows of the Black urban gun violence discourse. The evisceration from official narratives of gun violence as a crime that cuts across racial lines even within the symbolic geographies works exclusively to the service of a useful fiction of race, as such portrayals are drawn from the hauntological Black archive and, crucially, position the Black body at its ontological foundation, revealing how the discourse of black-on black violence became so secured within our publics just as the historical facticity of Black catastrophe as an outcome of white structuring was to become even more obscured in our social memory. In what ways does the mono-raciality of gun violence as advanced by the socially conditioned discourse of black-on-black crime assist in an examination of the meanings to be extracted from and placed onto the Black body for the purpose of inscribing an epidermal mnemonic within popular accounts of Black urbanity as a useful fiction of race? This understanding of the black-on-black gun-crime social illness as a specific social and cultural configuration may be the point where I, like Hall, see the idea of the conjuncture in much more departing and substantial ways than Gramsci had accounted for. I want to insist that the propagation of a savage Black urbanity as a useful fiction of race and the necessity of the Black body as the immediate representative of gun crime cannot be understood without first entering into an ontology of the very term applied to Black crime. This, I propose, is a critical engagement that must be based in the rejection of the term 'black-on-black' gun violence, for in the specific context of the proliferation of the black-on-black colloquialism as the synonym via the Black body for intra-racial death, 'black-on-black' is the nomenclature of *anti-Blackness*. This claim is premised on a singular role for the Black being where, unlike the uncontested innocence of white mortality, Black life is forcefully placed within an expected and desirable outcome, that of a violent and criminal death. The symbolic zone of Black urbanity is a zone of the natural and inevitable production of Black death. My rejection of the hegemonic language of black-on-black criminality and the insistence that the aestheticizing of Black death and urban existence functions as a useful fiction of race is not to enter into a relativist analytical position that calls for the denial of intra-racial violent death as a feature of our Black environs, but that the *practice* of Black death within the symbolic zone of Black urban existence is a practice of anti-Blackness that lexicalizes black-on-black as the incontrovertible, indissociable and uninterruptable index of Black life. I, of course, acknowledge the experiences of Black men and women, young and old, who reside within the geographies of murderous conflict as a real and veritable issue and the cycle of devastation gun violence inflicts upon UK's Black working-class and underclassed communities. Equally, my disavowal of black-on-black as anti-Black takes a much different pathway than the violent psychosocial incubus within Black America as diagnosed by Wilson (1991). Rather, and in drawing on the dissection of the logic of anti-Blackness by Costa Vargas and Jung (2020) in which 'Black people's embattled bodies, spaces, knowledge culture, citizenship and humanity have served as the counterpoints to safety, rationality belonging and life' (8), the commodity value of black-on-black fatality and Black precarity as a serviceable useful fiction of race works to affirm the universality of whiteness, for the secured invaluation of white life is illuminated only by the aesthetic of Black death, and allows us to understand how anti-Blackness is so implicated in the everyday Black existence as an evacuated and excavated corporeality. Within the practice of anti-Blackness as Black death's structuring logic, and found deeply in the preoccupation with black-on-black fatal conflict as the natural sequela of the inner city, the Black body is emptied and made hollow, is consigned to the *a priori* position of abjectivity within prevalent race discourses, made the subject of vituperative public denigration, becomes bound in spectrality and fixed through the narrative image of the Black body as the effigy of fatal Black violence in nature, culture and geography. Anti-Blackness is fixed to the Black body, but principally because its habitat is the violent and normatively antagonistic and distressed social landscape. Black-on-black as anti-Blackness is the way in which captive Black bodies are prepared and mandated to accentuate our own social disappearance caused by the spectre of Black non-being, which, as Walcott (2014) has informed us in his observation of a historically resistant anti-Black condition curtailing our claim to humanness, black-on-black is the discourse that makes legible the dead Black body upon which whiteness performs its own anatomy, but does so only by denying, rejecting and concealing our own. Thus, just as Costa Vargas and Jung argue that anti-Blackness is a distinctive framework from racism in that it can account for how Black people are subjected not only to the logic of racial domination but also of 'social and ontological abjection' (2020: 8); black-on-black as the essential preliminary of Black death is not just the disappearance of the Black body, but also the disappearance of Black life and life capacity from the everyday public lifeworld that invigorates both the socio-historic system of racial othering and the assisting socio-aesthetic project of legitimizing anti-Black non-humanness , to be realized by the codes of meaning that are held within the narrative of interracial Black death and the aestheticization of the dead Black body.

The popular image streams of Black ganghood and violence that are meted out within official commentary, which I argue perform as the canonical perception of Black British working-class identity and the key indexical conductor in the construction of useful race fictions, exhibit all the hallmarks of the kind of media practices that necessitate a 'narrative criminology' for which Glynn, in developing a taxonomy of the critical perspectives that have yet to enter the mainstream of the criminological study of race and Blackness, interrogates the ways through which stories of crime via media narratives influence and shape both crime itself and the attendant 'harm doing policies' (7). For Alexander, mainstream media's unabated construction of Blackness as indelibility and essentially affiliated with gun- and gang culture represented a denial of the complexity of Black identity, sociality and experience within a fixed and dominant racial frame. In many ways Alexander's analysis of the Black gangs narrative unveils an identical ideological practice to the Hallian idea of mugging as a crime that gains its credence through its reliance upon the pre-existence of substantive 'institutional links' between 'those who define and control crime and those who report it as news' (166). For Hall, the media are seldom independent in the processes of crime reportage, and their construction of the narratives that create crime as a fearful but alluring spectacle are dependent on these definers: the police, the courts and the policymakers that officiate the accepted notions of crime and punishment. There is a continuity with this interdependency Hall identifies to be observed in the placing of Black urban gang culture within a similar ecology of meaning production that, and as aligning with Alexander's observation, the repetitious, sensationalist and pre-constructed narrative schema of Black gun- and gang-crime can be equally understood as a consequence of what Hall refers to as the 'inferential structure' of the media's position in this nexus: its active role in the constructing of the very crime that then becomes the subject of its own sensationalism. Despite Hall's study being primarily interested in the media narratives found in news reportage, we must, of course, include film narratives in this unificating interdependency, as it is this inferentiality of Black gun crime media narratives and its intercourse with the hauntological form of the Black urban Other that creates the silhouette of the Black violent male that is stencilled into the prevailing discourse of gang culture and gun violence, that in turn becomes primed as the most dramatic and mimetic element of the useful fiction of race. Again, we see how the hauntological Black urban Other is a regenerative figure of social castigation that finds a material presence through new modalities of racial signification to be readied for the attachment to new forms of social crises. As Alexander goes on to argue, 'it seems that simply being a young, male and minority ethnic victim is sufficient itself to warrant the label gang-related' (2008: 5). The specific ways through which we can observe media's complicity in the development and permeation of gun- and gang-crime as racial phenomena that would be essential to the popularizing of Black urban identity is discussed in greater detail later in this book, but at this analytical juncture the racist alterity that underscores the condemnatory signifying of the hauntological Black urban other finds some relation with Gilroy (2004), who traces the development of a new racism that seeks to bring a restorative equilibrium to the crisis of national identity resulting from postcolonial Britain's race politics. For Gilroy, the effectiveness of the restructuring agenda of this new racism is premised on the identification and castigation of 'alien' Others to be returned to live 'in the environments that matched their distinctive cultural and therefore national modes of being in the world' (24). We hear the echoes of this critique of new racism in Valluvan's account of nationalism's desire to identify the racial Other's non-belonging and non-being as the primary source of an indiscriminate range of social problems and anxieties, and in the new racism of nationalism as observed by Back, who offers a similarly Gilroy-informed description of the nation where 'Blackness and Englishness are reproduced as mutually exclusive' (2020: 9). This racial distinction of both nationality and crime through alleged cultural factors chimes with Gilroy's reading of how the hegemony of a Black criminality has been fundamental to the process of 'washing the discourse of the nation as white as snow and preparing the way for repatriation' (1982). Operation Trident and the description of gun- and gang-criminality as a Black instinct finds its supportive energy in *The Guardian* in the identification of Jamaican males as the avatar of gun violence that, in referring back to the significance of national identity to the securing of the idea of Blackness as a spectral inheritance through criminality as asserted by Gilroy, attributes their expanding criminal presence within the Black enclaves of London as the outcome of 'illegal immigration' (*The Guardian*, 26 August 2001). This is no counter to the truth of any analysis of illegal immigration as a correlative to certain instances of violent criminal acts, although the very value of Gilroy's assertion in my reading of the criminal characterization of Jamaican males and its synthetic but ideologically productive link with illegal immigration is that gun grime and its associative abhorrent acts are not to be understood as a natural outcome of race and Blackness *per se* but as a procedural and legislative failure. The argument that the sensationalist instinctiveness of the useful fiction of race seeks to privilege the issue of immigration and racial identity over the very real contextual factors for its narrating of Black crime is one that finds absolute validity in the example of Delroy Denton, who was convicted of the horrific 1995 sexual assault and murder of a 24-year-old mother of two, Marcia Lawes, in Camberwell. Denton, a Jamaican national who had been imprisoned there for a number of armed crimes, had entered London from Kingston in the early 1990s using false details. It is as a direct result of the Metropolitan Police's apocalyptic assessment of the uncontrollable scale of Yardie criminal activity in London that, facing deportation upon his arrest for drug offences in Brixton, and despite the UK Home Office declaring Denton *persona non grata* and rejecting his asylum claim on the basis of the nature of his crimes, Scotland Yard detectives would collude with senior immigration officers to ensure Denton was able to remain in the UK as a *quid pro quo* exchange for agreeing to work as a police informant for their ongoing anti-Yardie initiative, effectively granting Denton impunity to carry out further violent crimes, including the killing of Marcia Lawes, under the protective cloak of his informer status. It is possible that it is the highly publicized nature of these failings that may have later motivated Operation Trident's insistence on transnational collaboration as Jamaican policing officials, who were in pursuit of Denton and held an extensive inventory of his violent misdemeanours, were not informed by the Metropolitan Police that Denton was in London being employed as their informant.

The mediatizing of this incident is crucial to the way we can understand both the method and functions of useful race fictions, as while the failures of the Metropolitan Police are the primary concern of *The Yard's Yardies*, a *World in Action* documentary on the case and the broader phenomena of Yardie criminality (ITV, 1 February 1997), the deliberate and systematic use of the term 'Jamaicans' as a descriptor for the Black antagonists throughout the documentary serves an inferential purpose. Here, this violent murder is presented less as a consequence of a system of illegal immigration *per se*, in which in this instance the Metropolitan Police are solely culpable, but as the simple presence in the UK of Black men emerging from Jamaica. In this useful fiction of race, Black non-being and non-belonging are central to the construction of Black gun crime as representative of inherited or/and imitated Black cultural characteristics, and while there are undoubtedly many other forms of signification through which we are to observe how the Black body functions as a mechanism of denigrative racial meaning, the ubiquity of Operation Trident's signifying construction of Blackness, and its subsequent pathologizing of black-on-black murder as a gendered anti-Blackness, reveal an extensivity that we can again align with the conceptual vocabulary advanced by Ambikaiparker (2021) that insists that anti-Blackness is not just the dehumanization of Black people but also the abjection of all that is ascribed to, associated with and allegedly produced just by us – in this spectral instance, the dead Black body as an image of Black non-being. With the moment's unprecedented political, social and cultural lexicalization of Black gun crime, Operation Trident's black-on-black project expands the connotative scope of the term 'Yardie' to incorporate the hauntological amalgam of visual representations of Black bodies and becomes thrust into the useful race fiction that affirms and assists the validity of armed police forces operating in London's dense Black communities that remain vulnerable to the homogenizing visions of the Black urban existence conceived and sustained by racism. In essence, Operation Trident's *raison d'etre*, be it through the transnational activity that enlists Jamaican collaboration in their efforts against Yardie gang violence in London or the policing of its British-born descendants, was constructed upon an already racialized State infrastructure and punitive policing apparatus, and in the context of Operation Trident's strategic presence in sections of the city with a critical mass of Black residents, Black urban identity is recalled, resignified and reassigned to a central position within a useful fiction of race, where they become spectacular enough to generate national media attention. We must pay particular attention to the inclusion of the term *useful* as the adjective that acts as a modifying attribute to the fiction of race, as it is a variable race fiction that in a similar vein to Hall's dissection of race as a floating signifier, is a term that points to the subjectivities of perception and context that equally gesture to the polysemicity of film and media texts, which can serve different functions and structures of meaning. One of the clear modalities of the fiction of race in its useful form is when it is created to accentuate the level of social unease expressed towards Black urban masculinity. In this instance, the useful fiction of race is conducive for the portrayal of the genetic nature of Black criminality, where 'alien' Jamaican Yardie criminals can be placed symbiotically alongside Black British subversives within a corresponding and non-conflicting sameness, with any cultural and behavioural differentials becoming irresolvable only when placed against a white framing of the nation. We encounter such a version of this fiction of race in the 2007 Virgin1 series *Crime Invasion: Britain's New Underworld* in an episode titled 'Yardies' (25 October 2007). Its presenter/narrator, Rageh Omaar (who is Black and of Somali origin) immediately sets about the task of presenting Black criminality as a pervading threat within British normality by listing off empirical data on the increasing number of Yardie-attributed drug/gun crimes that have taken place in Cambridgeshire, Hampshire, Gloucestershire and Hertfordshire while on a National Rail journey (we presume at this stage to one of these locations). We should not disregard the powerful modes of racial meaning construction embedded in Omaar's citing of the county, rather than the city of these crimes, as such a linguistic device works to secure into the audience's imaginary a juxtaposing image of chaotic and armed Black men rampaging within what are accepted as the idyllic and mono-racial spheres of Middle England. It is against this contrasting narrative framing that the documentary takes its audience to the market town of Hereford, where the arrival of a small group of Black men simply termed as 'Jamaicans' distributing crack cocaine has caused unprecedented terror in an otherwise placid and exclusively white corner of rural England. However, its attempts to augment the narrative of Black gangs descends into fallacy when an interview is conducted with a white former drug addict who, while suitably filmed working on a large farmhouse located among vast green fields, offers an account of the moment when, having been unable to source any crack cocaine through his traditional networks, he was told that its only availability was through the seemingly novel discovery of five 'blacks' living in the town. As he then states, 'It was the Yardies and the blacks that first brought it to Hereford, because that's their drug to sell them. They'll use machetes, knives, sometimes even guns' before concluding with details of the numerous violent acts inflicted upon would-be customers by the town's Yardies. That the man had, by his own admission, been obtaining crack cocaine well before the unprecedented arrival of Black men in Hereford does nothing to dislodge the documentary's editorial investment in the truth-apt of his metanarrative, and as exemplified through the testimonies of both him and local police, the documentary exhibits a mode of investigative journalism that is concerned less with the actual presence of a localized drug economy in Hereford than the idea that the economy is being orchestrated by undesirable Black immigrants of non-belonging, in both rural Hereford and Britain. The documentary's conjectural narrative now shifts from an account of Black gun crime rooted in racial juxtaposition to cultural verisimilitude, and in a following segment the camera frames Omaar stood against the backdrop of Tangmere House on the Broadwater Farm Estate. The episode now draws on the powerful suggestiveness of the narrative of Yardie gun- and gang-violence when situated within the corresponding plausibility of a symbolic location by returning to the more cognitively palatable settings of Black urban London, via a graphic account of the high-profile violent crimes carried out by Black gangs in Tottenham offered by an Operation Trident detective, crimes that would be described in the media as the work of 'malign and corrosive gangsters' (BBC News, Friday, 17 May 2002). The documentary, in a communicative device that undoubtedly fulfils the criteria that would necessitate a narrative criminology, attempts to fortify the

Figure 4.1 The use of subtitles in *Crime Invasion* Episode 4 – 'Yardies' (Vashca, 2007).

authenticity of its argument with an ethnographic predicate in interviewing two Black men whom Omaar introduces as reformed former Yardies, with the narrator prefacing the interview by stating that the interview will present parallel perspectives on the violent nature of Yardie gangs framed by an interest in the question of its national and cultural origin in Chris, a Jamaican national and the other, his British-born friend Watchman. However, despite the documentary's overriding framing of Yardies, violent gangs and drug crime as a non-domestic invasion that finds its immediate genesis in Jamaica, the camera's primary interest here is in the British-born Watchman (Figure 4.1). Speaking in a thin Jamaican patois, the documentary compounds its useful fiction of racial alterity by the use of subtitles to translate what is a generally comprehensible personal account of the motivations behind the British-born Black youth's attempt to match, if not exceed, the levels of violence exhibited by his Jamaican counterparts, an intra-racial competitive tension that for the documentary becomes one of the motivating factors at the root of black-on-black violent conflict. The use of subtitles in itself may appear to be indicative of little beyond the racialized editorial logics we encountered in *We Are the Ragamuffin*, where the (un)acceptance of the organic forms of Black vernacular cultural expression into the normative visions of the British experience (through filmic means or otherwise) becomes a decision of dialect rather than actual language. However, this becomes a much more substantive and racially signifying mode of visual communication when considered within the context of Gilroy's analysis of the marginalization of Britain's Black population as a people apart through the concept of a Black criminality, Valluvan's account of nationalism as an ideological technology of racial and ethnic othering, and my own reading of Operation Trident as an all-encompassing Black signifier that prepares the hauntological Black urban other for its dispersal across a range of race fictions. These conceptual interactions reveal a complex racial signifying practice at play. While the segment initially bounds itself within an over-polarizing narrative structure, in which the documentary attempts to hold Jamaican Yardies and their British-born 'copycats' within a competing binary through the identification of some subtle geographic differences, this is only a temporary disjuncture, and the documentary's description of British-born gangs through what Omaar insists is their versing in 'Yardie tactics', their exhibiting of 'Yardie characteristics' and the relative speed and ease with which British-born Black criminal gangs have become accomplished in 'Yardie techniques' re-adjoins them as simply two facets of the same evil brand. At its very essence, its uncomplicated, inferential distribution of the term 'Yardie gangs' posits no substantial distinction between the Jamaican Yardies, their British-born criminal offshoots and an even younger generation of Black youths of school age residing within London's symbolic locations ready to occupy the vacant spaces that are opened up by Operation Trident's purging of the city's intra-racial gun and drugs crime epidemic. In a certain sense, the documentary's serviceable race fiction of an inevitable and generational uptake of Black gun crime is reflective of a pheromonic analytical framework that asserts that the simple presence of Jamaican men is sufficient to produce a secreting affect within Black symbolic locations as the aggregating environment of Black violent criminality through which the murderous activities of Jamaican Yardies leave a biological trail to be followed by and identified in the criminal behaviour of an identical but younger cultural species, Black men become equally unified within the same narrative corpus. And in its use of the Black body as the biological source of violent criminal acts, the mediagenic instituting of Yardie as the dominant signifier for Black maleness performs as a collective identity adjoined by the already developed social permeation of the haunting spectre of Blackness, a method of reification observed in Omaar's repetitive use of the specific term a 'unique brand of criminality'. What specifically qualifies either for this description is left to the audience to discern through the documentary's image system and its narrating of gun murder as a Black spectre, but the perpetual description of British-born Black gang violence as one of 'new horrific levels' suggests that the audience, just like the police and the media, should regard 'black-on-black' violence as a separate and distinctive mode of criminality. Thus, the documentary's emphasis on nationality, birthplace and race, and the invasion of Yardie activity as an outcome of Black culture, legitimizes the nationalistic structuring of Black urban Otherness and the idea that gun violence is somehow a specifically Black contagion. Here, Black men, Jamaican or otherwise, and their relation to symbolic locations combine to produce a common Black affliction in their alien predisposition to a unique form of violent crime, which is simply reproduced in the eager desires of younger Black boys. In other words, we are presented with a unified construction of Black men and criminality as a useful fiction of race that locates their gun and gang violence, and its *sui generis* nature, specifically in their epidermal relations. It is the specificity of Black gang murder as a racialized crime of no reasonable or identifiable cause or underpinning factor that is the sense of unknowability through which race fictions are able to retain a degree of speculativeness and uncertainty which, having therefore established Black*ness* as the only plausible and satisfactory *fons et origo* of Black gun crime, cultivate the social and cultural conditions through which anti-Black anxiety can most thrive. So as expressed externally through Operation Trident's generative function as an exorcizing signifier that, in its sensationalizing of gun, gang and drugs-related murder, interplants the hauntological Black malevolent spectre into postmodernity, here the crisis of Black intra-racial gang warfare and Black ultra-violence as the spectral condition of white Britain to be addressed in the conjuncture of the early 2000s as a state of emergency.

Throughout this chapter, I have been pursuing an analysis of the various social preliminaries servicing the reification of Black criminal identity as a structuring thematic for popular Black urban textual representation, and it is an analysis that attempts to make legible a genealogy of the early 2000s official abjection of Blackness through a set of cursory exemplars of the relationship between Black gun crime and gang violence. These preliminaries were to emerge as alluring to the orthodoxies of Black British film analysis, and the situating of the popular Black urban text's aesthetic preliminaries within a socio-historical examination of Black Othering and reification in the interrogation of Operation Trident as a practice of racial signification allows for what I feel is the necessary nuancing of the processes through which the depictions of Black identities in audiovisual narration come to exhibit a simple correspondence with the specific conjuncture's modes of Black characterization. I am again making reference to the gestures of Eurocentric film analyses that display a superficial engagement within the paradigm of sociological and cultural studies. These more cosmetic interests in the social context of Black filmic and televisual identity, as touched upon in my first chapter, hastily arrive at a textual evaluation in which Black film represents an uncomplicated practice of mimesis in the absorbing of the popular representations of Black existence and with it, the texts become implicated in the continuation of the historic reductionism of Black identity in the reproduction of the stereotypes and oversimplifications that constitute the prejudicial existences of Black people. This, of course, has been and remains the foundational practice of the white racial framing of Black identity that we have been subjected to as the dominant optic in our approach to the study of Black cinematic and televisual representation. My analytical departure from this practice stresses the need for a more comprehensive interrogation of the historical and social dynamics that precondition the popular Black urban text and such an approach, while very congruent with the idea that racial mimesis is a central tenet of the visual representations of Black urbanity, is a contextualization of the conditions, motivations, sources and ethical principles of Black 'representation' itself, a term that, as Hall argues through a critique of mimetic theory, refers to the imagining of 'a reality that exists "outside" the means by which things are represented' (1988: 27). It is highly significant, in the context of my later analysis of the narrative style of the popular Black British urban film, that by the end of the twentieth century, the hegemonic representations of black-on-black gun crime exhibit an adherence to the master narratives of Black gun violence as provided by Operation Trident in its definition as a *singular* social phenomenon. By this, I'm referring to how the official and therefore popular examination of Black urbanity and crime, be they through the promulgation of black-on-black gun violence in the public campaigns and operational strategies of the Metropolitan Police or via inferential media narratives, is denied any kind of etymology; social relations are de-emphasized or disregarded, influencing political and economic structures are not dissected but airbrushed from the preferred and spectacularizing portraiture of the Black urban existence. I should draw focus towards what is to be discerned from the hegemony of this singularity, which displays some degree of consonance between the spectrality of the Derridian hauntological Black urban othering and what is specifically adaptive for us in Hall's idea of race as a floating signifier – that the hegemony of Black fatal crime that cannot find any kind of generative materiality without the inferential narratives of black-on-black violence, which synonymizes the Black urban male and the Black body with the inevitability of violent death. As the discourse of violent Black criminality interpellates the Black urban subject into the reliable common-sense symmetry, the spectacularizing narratives of black-on-black gun violence are able to secure ideological consent not just through the signifying field of official race policing operations and its allied narratives in the media, but also through the equally persuasive reifying of Black criminal identity and culture within the normalizing fictions of Black filmic and televisual representation. But our encounter with Black urban Otherness through the narratives of a self-inflicted Black social decay is to also experience a certain kind of reification. The Black body, so historically fixed as violent within the public imaginary, is rarefied as an object of inferential public representations that seek to attain a level of spectatorial and perceptive equilibrium, and the polysemicity of race meaning construction renders Operation Trident as a cognitive field of racial signification in language as the criminalized understanding of Black urban masculinity is subjected to the whiteness of official and dominant image-making through which popular filmic and televisual representations of Blackness are resourced. Indeed, we may find this to be indicative of the very racial desire/denigration simultaneity Back identified as a central facet of European racism that acts as an exemplar of the multiculturalist celebration of the Other, which Back reminds us may retain 'liberal intentions' (1996: 8). Of course, the permeation of such liberal intentions finds a primary vehicle within film and television culture as a space of consolidation, where popular images are intimately related to political power bases and existing social relations and therefore serve as a repository for the hauntological spectre of Black urban othering, the consequential outcome being that such liberal intentions find easy habitation within the Black urban text as both a useful and necessary fiction of race and become instituted as the dominant perspective within which the social anxieties that the hauntological Black urban Other as a criminalized encounter evokes, with all its racial meanings, can be articulated and find a degree of cultural resonance. This places a significance in film and television narrative as an important variant of popular visual culture that is primed for the reincarnation of the hauntological Black Other and is a contingent outcome that can be attributed to a post-Macphersonist inflection of racial and cultural difference, as capitalism's abstract quantum, as a textual encounter of social significance, value and urgency. Indeed, and in returning to my reading of thematic value to be derived by capitalism from what is perceived as recognizable Black subject matter, the unprecedented social and cultural permeation of Operation Trident as a signifier for violent Black male identity and the facticity of Black death performs as another contribution to the pre-existing and expanding archive of the fiction of race, an archive that once reified through the signifying field and reduced to a topology of standardizing

Black haunting essences – violent, criminal, savage, murderous, depraved, *non-human* – is to be readied for the decontextualizing, condensing and distilling of what are the narratives and projections of Black men as a discorded menace into what now becomes convertible Black material. But as I am pursuing a pragmatic application of the idea of useful fictions to explore the circulation of black-on-black as a form of narration, it is worthwhile at this point to again expound on the meanings of the adjectives of 'useful' and 'necessary' that prefix my analysis of Black criminality as a version of race fiction. I describe the narratives of criminalized Black urbanity once rarefied into a form of visual storytelling as the *useful* fiction of race, in that the fictions of Black urban violence can be described as useful when they are primed to assist and supplement the dominant understandings of Black as an imagined, destructive community, and as *necessary* when most opportune for both the contingent interests of the liberalism of the film and television sector and the sensationalizing hegemony of Black urban violence as a spectral and spectacular matter of urgency and the establishing of black-on-black as a public narrative. It becomes a necessary form of social and cultural knowledge, sociology and, at some level, pedagogy. Beyond the general function of the narrative of urban gun crime as a method of Black signification and social identification as capitalism attempts with evident success to individualize and decontextualize social, political and economic relations, the specific ways by which Operation Trident as an official signifier for the unifying of Black masculinity and Black death within the symbolic locations of London that position Blackness itself as its own pathogenesis are in some ways also determined by a claim to pedagogy, and Black-specific policing would come to inscribe itself within the fabrics of the popular Black British urban text via the evocative and subject-forming ecology of social preliminaries involved in the creation of Black urban identity as a social aesthetic where the signifiers of dangerous Black urban identity, the inferentiality of the media and the enduring political and social practice of racism are able to congregate in the most tremendously generative and unpredictably accumulative ways in that they all become unified to make powerful deposits into the Black hauntological *archive*. The dramatic function of the Black hauntological archive is the negotiation of the affects of anxiety and desire that have been prepared by the capitalist accumulation of Black identity. The Black hauntological archive in this sense departs from a more traditional understanding, as the archive is not a depository of documentation or of memorialization, but as a resourcing and productive public archive of racial identification and signification for the creation of spectacular and sensational Black narrational material that works to consolidate the position of whiteness as the universal identity upon which Black people's protracted claim to humanness is denied but also the primary beneficiaries, one could say, of the propelling of Black urban criminality as a site of spectral knowledge production and circulation, where whiteness also becomes implicated in the process of Black hauntological archivization as the signifying field through which Black identities become rarefied as images of distain. This is thus a colonial archive that possesses an adaptive value in that it provides access to both the past and the controlling and consequential ideas of the present. Black urban identity becomes subjected to a range of decontextualizations, associations and identifications for the purpose of useful race fictions, rendering the hauntological Black archive as an expansive, revising and politically constituted space to be exhausted and gutted of all that it holds. Therefore, it is the multi-dimensionality of the hauntological Black archive that allows for the homogenization of Black social identities through the conventions of filmic and televisual practices that have recourse to crude mimetic representations, and in the context of a paradigmatic reading of Black British film, an inherently indexical practice possessing racially connective properties that are implied in the mono-racial composition of the popular Black urban text's Black (self) representations.

Let me reaffirm my central proposition at this point. The popular Black urban film as a site of cinematic Blackness was brought into being within the ecologies of black-on-black as an anti-Black non-existence, resignified the Black body as a spectral image of desirable and undesirable alterity and was subsequently reappropriated as a method of Black popular representation that draws its validity through the spectre of the hauntological Black urban figure. Of course, spectrality is by no means specific to the Black urban text, and it could be argued that most of our ontological and aesthetic encounters with film are populated with narratives and images that possess and facilitate a ghostly and haunting engagement for the audience. But, and reminding ourselves that the intensification of useful race fictions serves as a powerful mode of subject formation, it is the sedimentation of black-on-black gun crime accelerated by replication and repetition that emerges as the rationalities through which such hauntological notions of Blackness are facsimiled onto the new discourse of violent Black criminality. These, I argue, are the social practices by which Black urban identity as a useful and necessary fiction of race became schematized into a new aesthetic project. This may not be precisely what Hall, in favouring a syntagmatic reading of the modes through which the production of a story is able to circulate as a product (2021 [1973]), had in mind when he identified film, alongside other communicative processes, as a 'material substratum' (248) that is the signifying apparatus needed for the necessary refining of the symbolic into the material, or in other words, the story in narrative form prior to its arrival as a 'communicative event'. However, the negotiating between the stories of Black urban fatality and its visibility within British film and television production are processes that are by no means sequential, although the tonalities produced in the aesthetic use of filmic realism accentuate the spectacle and spectre of Black urban death and the Black body as a communicative event or, to be specific, as a useful fiction of race. Black death is an embodied event in the creation of images and forms of narration, but this process is relational and interpenetrating only within a relational set of social, political and cultural discourses that account for how Operation Trident as a signifier for Black urban male gun crime would become present and material as both an intra- and extra-diegetic narrative thematic, an intertextual image system, a stencilled form of characterization and an aesthetic principle. Black urban identities become subject to the excessive representations of screen culture and serve as an example of the commodification of race and Blackness that Saha (2021) suggests is the conditional basis of racial difference's inclusion into the cultural and creative industries via the politics of diversity. I intend to return to the modes in which the development of Black urban criminality as a moral panic and its forceful association with the popularizing of Black urban subcultural practices display an interaction with the inferential schemas of the media and, finally, filmic and televisual narration, at a later point in this book. Here, I want to remain with the public dispersal and uptake of racialized social ideas that seemed to justify popular screen culture's interaction with the hegemony of the black-on-black conflict and capture the impulses of the hauntological Black urban Other as a multi-constituted spectre prior to its lexicalization within the pluralities of both filmic and televisual storytelling. What does this imply in the appraisal of the socio-historical, racial and cultural factors that are present in the emergence of the popular Black urban film? Is it not possible for Black British filmmakers and screenwriters to display a resistance to the narratives, characterizations, thematics and fictions to be drawn from the hauntological Black archive? We again find the answer to this question in the assemblages that constitute Black urbanity as a narrative experience, as while it is the social aesthetics that inform, populate and constitute the popular Black urban text, it is in the tri-directional imperatives and needs that popular Black urban filmic and televisual representation becomes constituted as a useful, and at times necessary fiction of race. In momentarily isolating the term *needs*, I want to suggest that such engagements are determined not just by the interests of the spectral discourses of Black criminality and inferential logics of the media, but also by the idea that the dramatizing of excessive Black urbanity within film and television can be responsive to particular cultural desires. From one perspective, a very compelling philosophical framework for exploring how the aestheticization of the Hauntological Black urban Other is able to be fashioned as a progressive cultural praxis can be found in the development of Magnus Ezensberger's theories on cultural consumption as a spectacle servicing a social climate of utopianism by Richard Dyer (1977), who offers a schematic for understanding how the social immersivity of film texts renders the film industry as a resource for the dissipation of a topology of positive and remedial feelings. I accept that Dyer's paramount analytical interest in musicals as a particular genre where one is able to access pleasurable feelings may not appear to naturally correspond with the analysis of the denigrative filmic and televisual depictions of Black urbanity. Nevertheless, Dyer's conceptualization of how films can be responsive to feelings of social scarcity does provide a relatively stable paradigm from which we are able to develop an understanding of how the film and TV industry's extractive interest in the irresistible Black hauntological archive at the specific conjuncture of race and cultural representation could implore Black filmmakers, writers, acting talent and audiences to persevere with a certain inverse utopia. But these feelings, emanating from real social tensions and conditions of alterity, lack and fragmentation and that for Wayne (2020) infuse such feelings of entertainment and experience with a crucial sociopolitical dimension, posit a different set of meanings and outcomes when considered in the context of Black filmic representation and the narratives of violent Black urban crime and trauma as responsive to a body of textual and industrial utopias. Identification, arrival, a semblance of cultural recognition and the satisfaction of familiarity are all feelings of a Black creative and spectatorial utopianism that can be situated within my reading of the contradictory modalities of the ever-renewing Black cultural politics and Hall's exploration of capitalism's homogenizing command of what at this conjuncture is the commodification of useful fictions of black-on-black violence that the inferential desires of the media strive to conceive as a simple variant of Black culture. I realize I am skirting quite close to the unresolvable analytical zone of homogenizing both the Black British experience and our spectatorial interests, but my emphasizing of the idea of Black filmic utopianism as a conjunctural possibility is at least one way to rescue my analysis at this point from an impasse, and utopian feelings both from within and through film are able to service and attend to a social deficit or lack that has developed, in accordance with Hall's understanding of cultural politics as instinctively contradictory, through its own practices of racial exclusion. This contradiction suggests that mainstream screen culture is able to configure Black urban criminality as an emancipatory thematic that can appeal to the utopian desires of Black British film and television representation, meaning that the popular and most mimetic representations of Black urban identity can also perform as an intervention into the predictable monotony of peripheral Black characterizations and the aversive and exigencial absence of Black British identities within our mainstream filmic experiences. By reconstructing Black filmic and televisual representation as a post-racial provision at the nexus of the new politics of race and the evolved Black cultural politics of the early 2000s, and as a multicultural representational right throughout the previous decades, Black visual practitioners are compelled to acquiesce to the same archival reservoir that has been cultivated to develop a hauntological image that can be moulded and illuminated to service a range of interconnected agendas, imperatives and fictions. But this also brings into question both how the representational norms of Blackness, as conjured by the spectres of the past, make insertions into the mediatized landscape of Black urban crime and bring with it a generative and mutually beneficial dimension and, relatedly, how the socio-aesthetic signifiers of a contemporary and deadly Black British identity have become inextricable from the Black body, which is engaged to consolidate the images of violent criminality to be observed in popular representations as being 'Black'. This, I argue, implies that the Black hauntological archive, and the hauntological Black urban Other as the central and textually aestheticized embodiment of its raw Black material is a socio-historical formation of Blackness that should be understood as meta-representational; in other words, the popular Black urban textual representations and their characterizations of the Black urban Other are representations *of* representations.

With this in mind, what is revealed in considering Black British practitioners' involvement in the authorship of the popular Black urban textual experience is a constant need to be cognizant of its own citational politics. What kinds of Black image streams and descriptive language forms are engaged with when aestheticizing the discourse of black-on-black criminality that affirms popular Black urban representations as a citational practice? What does it mean for us to aestheticize the Black urban experience through the mediums of film and television when our primary sources are the very Black archival entries that signify the Black body to supply the hauntological Black urban repertoire? How can filmic and televisual counter-investments in the Black body be enacted within the historical fixity of the Black body that disrupts and reconfigures the phenomenal existence of Blackness? Such questions are again located within Hall's idea of race as a mobile and evolving signifier, and leads me to contend that the popular Black urban text, despite all of the social, cultural and industrial and ideological agendas that populate its social aesthetics, can never be fully constituted by the archive. There is always something that remains outside the archive's collection, beyond the hauntological purview, that has evaded the ornamentation of Black criminality as a useful and necessary fiction of race – the continuously shifting meanings located within the productive and regenerative hauntological Black urban Other once entered into the signifying field means that there will always be something new and/or previously unexplored to be aestheticized about the Black urban condition and experience to summon the anxiety and fetishist desire held within the episteme as a source of knowledge production. The popular construction of Black masculine urbanity as a spectre of unknowability also adds an additional *participatory* dynamic to the useful fiction of race. In this regard, Black urban identity becomes a utopianist and aesthetic hauntology in that it affirms the master discourse of black-on-black gun violence as a reliable witness for the realist homogenizing of the Black urban Other, and the capacity for film and television narratives to conceive the representation of Black urbanity as an intervention into the peripherality of Black identities within British screen culture and the ability of excessive violent Black interracial conflict to provide film and television narratives with the required forms of dramatic action suggest that Blackness's own participation in the aestheticization of Black urban textuality is a decision of both representational lack, and representational excess. Marginality, to use a more decisive term, imposes an important institutional state for consideration at this point of my analysis, as it is the re-signification of the hauntological Black urban Other into the present-day sphere of Black criminality and the aestheticization of Black death and the utopianist needs to be satisfied through the norms of Black filmic and televisual representation that allows for the spectre of black-on-black violence and death to move from the *spectacular* to the *quotidian*: the habitual, everyday and fixed Black subject as an expected and natural occurrence and where the Black body is epistemologically flattened within the very regime of powerlessness Hall identified as the unilateral *quid pro quo* accompanying Black filmic and televisual representation's incorporation into the popularizing frames of capitalism.

This asks us to bring into question the ability of the popular Black urban text to operate as an instinctive and affirmative point of counter-factuality, counter-narration and supplanted social knowledge, although this is what is generally purported to be the Black urban film's justifying criterion of value, its horizon of expectation or, as we are reminded by Back (1996), racism's cohabiting liberal intention. PSB becomes the arena where a number of agendas are unified in a negotiation over what is presented to us within the popular Black urban text's complex fabula and where the Black perspective, while by no means occupying a fully autonomous authorial position, is able to offer some organic insights into the experiences of Black masculinity within the geographies of gun violence, and establishes the popular Black urban text as a site for the reclaiming of arrested Black urban realities, narratives and Black representations. With this in mind, the thrust of Black filmic utopias will inevitably come into conflict with the expectancies, demands and conventions that secure the stories of Black urban conflict as a spectacle of desire and anxiety for televisual and filmic consumption. This means that we are able to understand the very public hauntological Black archive itself as a space of representational struggle over Black identity. But the idea of PSB representation, which has always sourced its ideas, narratives and images from the hauntological Black archive, as a theatre of contestation also encourages us to think beyond the sociopolitical, industrial and cultural factors that organize the popular Black urban text as a social aesthetic, and towards the impact of racial othering at the level of Black characterization, in that being both seen and unseen, and known and unknown is part of the alluring nature of the Black figure as a hauntological threat that draws our attention towards its aestheticization in filmic and televisual form. However, the verbatim adaptation of the public narratives of black-on-black violence and death as a useful fiction of race on its own serves as an unreliable witness to the official narratives of Black criminal existence when presented within frames of PSB and its rhetorical claim to be a repository for the broad experiences and perspectives of the nation, and at this conjunctural moment, of cultural diversity. Perhaps this is the outcome of the social, political and industrial conjuncture of the new phase of identity as so incisively formulated by Hall (1988), as I discern a set of contingencies where Blackness's *own* aesthetic investment in the popular urban text would come to exhibit an altered tonality. And while there is, indeed, a differing motivation to be registered in this involvement of the organic Black perspective, given that black-on-black crime is being theorized here as a hauntological spectre permeating within society and concretized in discourse, such authorial investments will inevitably draw from, while mining *through*, the climate of paternalism, sympathy and social attentiveness to the issue of Black urban casualty and death that maintains some presence within both the spectre of anti-Blackness through Operation Trident's lexicalization of black-on-black gun crime and, accordingly, in film and television narratives. Such narratives, as I have argued, emerge as a form of race fiction within the fissures of the disintegrated boundaries between the spectatorial desire for images of racial alterity found in the depiction of fetishized pathologies of Blackness and the ventilation of contemporary moral issues, an alignment most prevalently identified in public service broadcasting single dramas and its occasional interest in race. *Authenticity*, and the cultural and textual credibility that is accrued from the popular circulation of Black representation when termed as a 'realistic' experience becomes the language through which the hauntological Black urban Other is able to satisfy the interests of both the capitalist rarefication of Black criminality as a spectacle and the utopian needs of the imagined Black audience. Black filmic and televisual identity is crafted as a return to the innocent notion of the Black subject, a return that, rather than simply recrafting the figure of Black criminal urbanity in the counter-depiction of Blackness through an unstable cultural politics in which filmic Black identity is constructed as instinctively good, positive or uncritically worthwhile, is one that is couched in a concern with the young, the very demographic of Black youths that have been identified as vulnerable to the undisruptable genetic passing on of causeless interracial Black malevolence. Here, and with specific regard to PSB drama and its key function in exploring, framing and affirming our individual and collective social identities, it is the fictitious and non-fictitious investment in the stories and experiences that are not captured in the inferential media accounts of Black urbanity, the micro-narratives *within* the macro-narrative of Black urbanity, that allow the primary representations of black-on-black violence, the Black body and Black death to be adapted to the temporalities of film and television as a site for the creation of public narratives. It is this negotiation, or cohabitation, with the liberal sentimentality to be observed in the overexposure of fatal Black trauma as a form of PSB representation and the spectacularizing logics of race and racial alterity that the visual narrative evidences and places Black urbanity into a series of silhouettes and caricatures that set the terms for the popular Black urban text as a necessary and useful fiction of race, and demonstrates how the Black urban Other is aestheticized through a body of thematics, images and characterizations that exist both outside *and* within the colonial storyboard.

5

A Storm in Angell Town

Black Youth Delinquency in *Storm Damage*

Black People Die Differently
> Rinaldo Walcott, 'Death and Freedom', in *The Long Emancipation: Moving Toward Black Freedom*, 2021

I want to be clear that the primary assertion in my analysis of the preformations of the Black urban text and the centrality within this formulation of the hauntological Black urban Other, one that further affirms the conceptual value in the extended reading of the ideological practices of Operation Trident's lexicalizing of Black gun and gang crime, is that the immediate political and social context was alive to cognizant of and responsive to its own development of the crisis of Black urbanity and criminality as an inferential discourse just as the orientation of the UK film and television industries exhibited a shift towards the representation of a new portraiture of Black working-class urbanity as a new iteration of Black cultural politics and, resultingly, new creative rationalities. As a social institution, PSB film and televisual practices become the primary repository to further concretize, intensify and vary the conditions for the repetition of the signification of the Black urban Other as a recurring, familiar and haunting national spectre into a system of aestheticization, although sometimes with altruistic motivations. The Black urban Other is caught within the entanglements of the assumptive innocence of the Black subject and becomes schematized as a liberal project. Despite what may have appeared to be an analysis of the historic permanence of the criminal synonymy of Black sociality and identity, the Black urban figure as a hauntological Black Other is never an antiquated image or one that is exhausted of its meanings, connotations or purposes, and its presence works to inaugurate a new, necessary and useful fiction of race when, rather than rejecting the urban text as a Black textual mono-raciality, through the commodifying use values of Blackness and the liberal desire for inclusion, mono-raciality is able to secure institutional legitimacy for the bringing into being and into aestheticization Black urban identities and vernacular practices. To return to Dyer's reading of the film industry's logics in the context of the production of utopian sentiments at moments of social and cultural deficit, representations of Black urban identity at its most hauntological, most othering and most abhorrent are able to replenish the affliction of Black representational lack.

In considering the key functions of PSB drama, specifically its unique ability to represent and interrogate the fabrics of contemporary social life and draw its spectatorship to within questions of national belonging and identity, we can point to the indexical relationship between Black British film and PSB, most notably in Channel 4, which performed a critical function in the expanded production of Black British film and television representation and producers throughout its first decade in the 1980s, aided by its unique independent commissioning. By the turn of the century, British television became an ideological structure for a plethora of post-Macphersonist imperatives for racial diversity and cultural plurality, where the UK's public service broadcaster's responsiveness to the broader politics of Black representation found manifestation in its increasingly public rhetoric on diversifying its on-screen talent, with less emphasis placed on attending to the poor racial composition of its off-screen workforces, which would continue to be an unaddressed condition within the film and TV sector throughout the decade (Nwonka, 2015). However, by the early 2000s, PSBs became attuned to the narratives emerging from Britain's Black urban youth identities. One of the first films to explore this experience was the BBC feature-length drama *Storm Damage* (dir. Cellan Jones, 2000), screened on BBC Two on 23 January 2000. Written by Black British actor Lennie James, whose own personal experiences of the foster care system after the death of his mother are inscribed within the story, and produced by Ian Madden of BBC Films, *Storm Damage* would go on to win a Royal Television Society Award and a BAFTA Television Awards nomination for Best Single Drama. The film's production context is an important area where we can observe the discourses of authenticity and realness that would permeate the popular Black British urban film, and press coverage of *Storm Damage* prior to its screening would pay specific attention to the drama's claim to realism and truthfulness through a journalistic emphasis on the social, emotional and industrial circumstances that would entice James to turn what was described as 'his shocking experiences' into a film (*The Guardian*, Thursday, 20 January 2000). James, who was thirty-three at the time of writing *Storm Damage* and had established himself as both an actor and a screenwriter having been the first Black writer to write an episode for the long-running ITV police procedural drama *The Bill* (1983–2010), had written *Storm Damage* after attending the funeral of a teenager from the home. Indeed, the film, while not an obvious challenge to the hegemonic symmetry of the Black British text, exhibits a set of epistemologies that register a connective between screenwriter/director and text through the semi-biographical nature of the film which, as we will encounter in many other urban texts, becomes the popular urban film's criterion of value. As he went on to explain, 'If I'd written 20 scripts this would be the important one, because almost everything the film's about actually happened' (quoted in *The Guardian*, Thursday, 20 January 2000). Here, in James citing of the truthfulness of the events that populate the film, we can observe how Black urban actuality becomes an appropriate filmic theme structuring the realism and authenticity of its account of the troubled experiences of predominantly Black teenagers within a care home, rendering

Storm Damage as a particularly visceral account of the lives of Black youths within the urban locale.

One can locate in *Storm Damage* some of the central tenets and narrational repertoires that would come to constitute the urban film, repertoires that are informed by both textual and contextual imperatives. Indeed, the film's opening sequence reconciles the audience with the more novel formal elements of the cinematic/televisual hybridity that can be seen as a rejection of the social realist aesthetic strategies of Black British drama, and through a roving kinetic camera work that ventures at pace through a seemingly pleasant London street before turning into a large driveway and bursting through the doors of Number 66. It is here that we are introduced to the film's central characters via a fourth wall address as their various personas are captured in a narrational roll call: Paul (Roland Manookian), a troubled white working-class youth whose emotional sensitivity, timidness and fear of the dark is concealed within a seemingly unaffected and confident exterior as he cheerfully opens his bedroom door and ushers the camera towards the next character; the sexually promiscuous (and pregnant) fifteen-year-old Massive (Jackie Williams) who playfully displays her cleavage to the camera; Stefan (Ashley Walters), the home's dominant personality, who tussles with Paul over a large portable stereo he is carrying before finally dragging it off him (we later learn that Stefan has Paul and other young members of the home shoplifting for him); Analise (Ashley Madekwe) spraying hairspray at the camera as it intrudes on her as she is getting ready in her bedroom; and finally, Leon (Ashley Chin), one of the youngest members of the household, lying in bed as Agnes lifts the duvet from over him, where he is seen in a still in his school uniform. He attempts to get up, lifting his hazed face up to the camera in a close-up before collapsing back into his bed (the film later reveals that he is addicted to sniffing aerosol cans). To conceive the opening sequence in Brechtian terms, its dismantling of the fourth wall that performs as the imaginary barrier between story and spectator and, with it, the transgressing of the aesthetic binds of the 'classic realist text' (MacCabe, 1974), render the characters in *Storm Damage*'s Number 66 as instinctively *gestural*. The direct camera address performs as a narrational device capturing the chaos of an atypically dysfunctional morning in Number 66 where the idea of privacy and personal space within the confines of the home is simply unimaginable, as the youths (and their adult carers) sit around a frantic, crammed breakfast table, with the camera still hovering intrudingly around its activity (Leon throws some of his cereal at the camera) at the completion of an opening sequence that possesses all the hallmarks of what will be an ensemble drama. However, despite the apparent equivalency of plot attention suggested by this opening, the film's paramount narrational concern is the contestation over the future of *Storm Damage*'s main protagonist, the aggressive and troubled Black youth Stefan, fought between two appropriately antithetical Black male identities: the local gangster Bonaface (played by James himself) and the well-spoken English teacher Danny (Adrian Lester), who we soon learn had spent a significant part of his youth at Number 66. Set in Brixton's Angell Town, *Storm Damage* opens to a Steadicam aesthetic as the fluid movement of a roaming camera captures the disinterested activity of a number of pupils in the class, providing the spectator a full scenic immersion in the room, one akin to documentary surveillance of the class, as Danny, sitting on the edge of his desk, holds a poetry crit in a predominantly Black South London comprehensive classroom. Indeed, cultural juxtaposition and contrast are employed as an expositional device as the camera circles the room via a pupil, Patrick (Alexis Rodney), as he recites his poetry, telegraphed in a raw and distinctive inner-city Black youth dialect as the mobile camera momentarily hones in on the back of his head, revealing the distinctive pattern shaved into his afro hair before eventually returning to the impressed Danny. Suddenly, three youths (Stefan, Paul and a friend, MacDaddy) burst into his class and threaten Patrick, or Shinehead as he is known informally, over a girl they are both involved with (Stefan is in a relationship with Shinehead's ex-girlfriend and the mother of his baby daughter). In attempting to defend Shinehead, Danny is himself then threatened at knifepoint by the group's ringleader, Stefan, before they leave vowing to deal with the seemingly unintimidated Shinehead. However, Danny, shaken and seething at the incident, physically confronts Shinehead, forcing him to reveal who the youth is. After learning from Stefan's disinterested mother Cynthia that he lives at Number 66, he returns to the home where he is embraced by his neglected former foster mother, Agnes. However, it is Danny's interest in Stefan's transgressive behaviour that emerges as the central focus of the narrative. The paternalistic, mentoring attitude Danny immediately adopts towards Stefan, despite Stefan's continued hostile rejection of it, is an attempt to present Danny as a paragon of respectability through his status as an outwardly successful Black male, a teacher and a former resident of Number 66, whose interventions may transcend the limitations of race and class and offer an authentic and organic analytical (and indexically, a remedial) position in relation to Stefan, an intervention made just as Stefan begins performing criminal acts for the influential 'Yardie', Bonaface. Such a level of admiration for the villainous Bonaface is solidified when Stefan and the Number 66 youths witness Bonaface humiliate an associate who pulls a gun towards him in a packed nightclub, forcing the gunman to slowly retreat and rendering him a pathetic figure incapable of carrying out the shooting among the watching crowd, as Bonaface laughs while throwing pound notes at his armed rival. This demonstration of power, control and confidence reaffirms the dangerous allure of a criminalized but no less influential and respected notoriety within the hyper-locality of South London's Black community. For Danny, who made an unappreciated attempt to shield Stefan from the incident, his own reconciling with Number 66 and through this, the development of his disproportionate concern with Stefan's welfare as entwined with his recognition of his own troubled youthhood in Stefan's behaviour results in his resigning from his teaching post and taking a job as a care worker at Number 66. Here, the home represents a chance of both a personal redemption through guiding Stefan away from a life of violence and confronting the unresolved psychological tensions born form a childhood maternal loss that continues to dictate his relationship with his past and, as we see, the care home youths and their parents.

Stefan's aloofness towards Danny, and the former's rapid descent into the amoral and criminal embrace of Bonaface is both contextually and narrationally plausible. The classic binary required to set up a dramatic conflict between characterizations through antitheticality are informed both by Danny's perceived class status – despite his own identical domestic background to Stefan's, and his entering the respectable profession as a secondary school teacher offers a perceived pathway to righteousness to be followed or rejected. Indeed, Bonaface himself makes reference to the moral dilemma Stefan is confronted with in the youth's desire for the geographically situated respect and fearfulness Bonaface has accrued as they drive through late night South London, the journey in Bonaface's expensive open-roof car also serving as a metaphorical passage as they head towards the point of a crossroad for the youth: an acceptance of the economically rewarding but potentially fatal existence under the tutelage of Bonaface, or a relative placidity but ultimately nondescript reformation through the guidance of Danny and his status as the vanguard of morality, decency, conscientiousness and self-actualization. *Storm Damage* is notable for its elaborate use of a specific form of Black working-class vernacular that further underscores the film's claim to authenticity, achieved through what would become a standard within urban films in the casting of the mainly non-professional and unestablished young acting talent. This authenticating of the film's representation of its specific Black, working-class cultural milieu is brought into being in combination with Nicholas Knowland's cinematography, which oscillates between a cinema verité documentary realism and, as we can observe in *Shoot the Messenger* (2006) as a novel feature in Black PSB drama, the introduction of distinctively non-realist aesthetics. Indeed, both a number of tracking shots and dolly zooms are employed to accentuate a character's sudden moment of realization, leading to an emotional transition in the immediate aftermath of dramatic action, often involving violent confrontations with Stefan. It is through these aesthetic strategies, which circumvent the production of a naïve realism (Masood, 2003), that the film presents a mosaic cinematic realist schema that captures a number of tragic but everyday vicissitudes and incidents that characterize young lives within both the care system and the broader distressed social fabrics of South London. This said, *Storm Damage* relies on an array of filmic devices to add a subtlety to the difficulties and negative experiences of teenage urban existence; for example, when Annalise dies in hospital after overdosing on solvents at a New Year's Eve party (her friend is encouraged to leave her as she lies unconscious by her boyfriend Shinehead). Here, the function of death as provoking a dramatic shift in tonality relies on a less elaborate, de-dramatized mise-en-scene that may appear contradictory to my own positioning of *Storm Damage* as the proto-type for the popular British urban film, if not yet in overt generic conventions, thematic concerns or a combination of both, but in the more subtle use of its soundtrack, and the status of *Storm Damage* as a PSB terrestrial drama allows for the addressing of the film's use of non-associative music. By this, I'm drawing attention to the non-diegetic music used throughout the film that in turn produces a dislocation from the familiarity of urban subculture in the use of grime and UK rap as both soundtrack and incidental music that would come to be one of the more recognizable generic conventions of the British urban film. For example, as the drunk and playful youths, joking at what seems to be Annalise's latest benign experience with drugs, are lambasted in the hospital waiting area by the emotional Agnes as she reveals that Annalise has in fact died, it is Jeff Buckley's ethereal 1994 version of Leonard Cohen's 'Hallelujah' that is played throughout a moving sequence as various characters mourn the loss of Annalise. The use of non-diegetic music emerges as a recurring juxtaposition device throughout *Storm Damage*, and it through the music's non-associativeness that the scene disturbs the audience's culturally verisimilar expectations of filmic Black death, a de-familiarity of Black urban death spectatorship produced through a visual and audial discordance that asks for a greater pathos, sensitivity and attentiveness to the evanescence of young, working-class Black life within the urban setting.

In Stefan, the film constructs an alternative to the Black urban youth as an instinctively *non-relational* other antithetical to the idea of domesticity (Figure 5.1) and this finds particular expression in *Storm Damage*'s representations of home, where Stefan's seamless return to Number 66 after evading the police while on a drug run for Bonaface presents domestic space as a constant and non-judgemental haven. The film's use of home as a leitmotif produces an interaction between two distinct variations of the home as a site of protection as Stefan, while on the run from the police, seeks refuge at the crowded, drugs-laden home of Rosa, Annalise's drug-addicted white mother. The Velvet Underground's hazy 1967 song 'Sunday Morning' accompanies the scene as the spectator is taken through Rosa's dimly lit house where Danny and Kate, in searching for the fugitive Stefan, are horrified to find a number of youths (including Paul) whom Rosa has allowed to consume drugs within the unparented sanctuary of her drugs den, further concretizing Danny's disdain for the irresponsible adult figures occupying a distanced but no less determining position in relation to the Number 66 youths. Danny earlier castigates her for her parental neglect as she turns up high when collecting Annalise's belongings from Number 66, facing her and shouting, 'Here were your choices, stay straight enough to mother your child or let her run wild and die!' For the incensed Danny, with Annalise's death and Rosa's emotional indifference

Figure 5.1 Stefan (Ashley Walters) in *Storm Damage* (dir. Simon Cellan Jones, 2000).

resurrecting the dormant feelings of abandonment felt towards his own mother, the inaccessibility of Rosa's grieving takes precedence over his own inability (or unwillingness) to consider that Rosa's deep drug addiction has rendered her incapable of responding to or recognizing the emotional gravity of Annalise's death, with the visit to Number 66 a simple interlude within an abstracted existence and the collection of her dead daughter's possessions representing a novel excursion detached from the tragic realities (and determinants) of childhood death. It can be argued that, influenced both by the film being produced at the very advent of increased mainstream presence and, resultingly, by the profitability of urban subcultural products and the film's situating within the context of PSB drama, *Storm Damage* eschews the commercial antennas that would come to unify the popular urban film genre with the urgent energy of the emergent grime and UK rap music through its distinctive soundtrack, and here non-diegetic music possesses a much more intrinsic relationship with text and serves as an additional layer of narration. The scene's characterization of the oblivious Rosa is combined with the UB40 & Pinchers reggae song 'Magic Carpet' with its tranquil, lyrical references to love, heaven, the cosmos and flying away accentuating Rosa's abstracted mental state and underscoring her disconnectedness from the realities of both life and death as she looks to the sky through Annalise's toy telescope, her incognizant mind seeing 'no ships but hardships. That's how it goes.' The film advances the family, or more specifically, parenthood, as a crucial mode of contextualizing the youths' destructive behaviour, actions that conceal the parental neglect, addictions, emotional traumas and psychological scarring underpinning the youths' disregard for both the moral standards of Danny's idealistic society and, seemingly, their own futures. In a particularly emotionally charged scene, Stefan's mother declares to both Stefan and the police that 'I don't know him' and 'I only have one son and he's inside already' when the police arrive at her flat after Stefan, with Paul in tow, is arrested for dodging taxi fares. Her rejection of Stefan through denial of his existence and Stefan's own reluctant acceptance of this reality provokes an emotional reaction in Stefan. However, Stefan's rage is motivated less by the ramifications of his latest misdemeanour with the police that Cynthia's denial of his existence has caused, but the implications of an action that has effectively rendered Stefan a motherless child through the pain of the ultimate form of abandonment – the denial of motherly love – as he is dragged away from the slammed door police screaming 'So what? Is that me and you finished then? Are we done?' Such a scene affirms *Storm Damage's* conceiving of the family as an institution whose primary responsibility is for the disciplining of ill-disciplined youth away from the socially transgressive behaviour 'of which crime is one of the most powerful indices' (Hall et al., 1978: 145). This points to a narrative ideology that positions delinquency and nihilism (which I will discuss later in this book) as the index of parental abandon. As James stated at the time of its broadcast:

> When I wrote *Storm Damage* it was with the sense that these kids had gone, 'I'm going to do what I've got to do to make sure I'm all right.' If no one takes responsibility for them, of course they are going to screw up. These aren't lovable kids, but we tend to forget they are children and we relinquish our responsibility to teach them anything. (*The Guardian*, Thursday, 20 January 2000)

Indeed, adult irresponsibility emerges as a continuing narrational theme within the film's broader endeavour to establish a relationship between the youths' familial backgrounds and their internal and external existences. However, the centrality of parenting to *Storm Damage*'s analysis of the genesis of Number 66's youths' destructive behaviour is disbalanced by the film's somewhat reductive account of gender relations. The film's representation of the family evades the construction of a racial binary identified by Young (1996) that, with particular attention to *Pressure*, conceives the dysfunctional Black family (and the Black mother at its dramatic centre) 'against the idealised image of the patriarchal white family' (141). However, the film's close attention to the discursive decrees of narrativized Black urban authenticity, here, the discourse of absent Black fathers as structuring the negative realities of Black working-class youthhood and subsequently, *Storm Damage*'s desire to reintroduce Black masculine identities within the urban environment places an emphasis on the Black maleness as the agent of reform that in turn produces a more binary characterization of the youth's biological mothers. Of course, we can find an obvious historic framework for the analysis of the drama's portrayal of gender difference through Laura Mulvey, who identified within classic Hollywood films a division of sexual labour and modes of viewing in which the text's authorship, characterizations and aesthetic arrangements were all organized for the exclusive and immediate pleasures of male spectatorship (1975). It is in contestation with the Eurocentricity of Screen Theory's Lacanian psychoanalysis of which bell hooks, in a disavowal of Mulvey's concept, would write 'The Oppositional Gaze: Black Female Spectators' (1997) in which hooks would contend that Mulvey's Gaze Theory produced particular, unconsidered ramifications for the Black womanhood, where cinema's narrative focalizations, aesthetic modes and spectatorial relations become a laboratory for the constricting of Black women into a system of representational frames and looking practices 'that reinforce pernicious gender and racial arrangements' (Winters, 2016: 143). I'm interested in how the question of gender relations as argued by both hooks and Mulvey provides a connective with *Storm Damage* in its characterizing of mothers. In this conceptual effort that asks that we approach the film as one that situates fatherhood, even in this symbolic form, as its structuring principle, I'm conceiving this aspect of the film as the site of the dispersal of a number of gazes that, in this example, appear to temporarily and partially abridge the divides of racial difference. Motherhood, as represented in Rosa, Cynthia and to an extent the teenage Massive, occupies an acute, Manichean framing beyond the maternal Agnes (a matriarchal figure which is defined by a generational departure from the film's other parents) and *Storm Damage*'s mothers are differentiated only by the degree of their disregard towards their children. In carving this homogenized view of the teenagers' mothers, the film perhaps denies the spectator a more nuanced understanding of mothering under arduous circumstances. Within the patriarchal logics of *Storm Damage*'s ruptured social universe, it is the Black masculinities in Danny and Bonaface, despite their own imperfect dualism, that are compelled to pick up the paternal tab for the irresponsibility and wickedness of the youths' dysfunctional mothers.

I want to draw attention to a central thematic that emerges from *Storm Damage*'s meditation on Black youthhood. Specifically, why is Danny fixated on Stefan? From one perspective, the film can be characterized as a slender extension of the problematic narrational ideology observed by Frederic Jameson (2002 [1981]) where, in a critique that locates its genesis in the structuralism of Claude Lévi-Strauss, texts construct a binary opposition as the means through which we can navigate the moral structures of narrative through a mediating character. Interestingly, and I will expound upon this at later points, the indexical emphasis on bleakness and fatality necessitated by the formal and thematic claim to Black realism as generic conventions means the urban text posits a variation of Jameson's stress on resolution and reconciliation of the binary positions as the structuring principles of ideological narrative form. This withstanding, Jameson's binary construction is evinced in *Storm Damage* as the liberal concern with Black youth alienation and the ideological currency of social rescue that the film assigns as Danny's *raison d'etre*, ideological insofar as it underscores the hegemonic impossibility of a productive Black youth urbanity devoid of father figures, a condition to be remedied through forms of patrimony and, in doing so, registers a simplification of the efficacy of the father/son dyad, an assertion derived from the film's privileging of one positive Black male identity (Danny) over a negative one (Bonaface). From another perspective, a less perpendicular reading of the film's understanding of the dyad posits a mutuality between the two in that while we can conceive of Danny as the redemptive guardian of Stefan's future, redemptive in the sense that as well as edification and then rescue being the telos of Danny's emotional investment in Stefan, the youth also functions as the symbolic figure that motivates Danny's confronting of his own repressed, traumatic childhood. Stefan's fate becomes the wavering and seemingly predetermined pathway to be guided by Danny's ossified moral compass as he continues to demonstrate an unbounded loyalty to Stefan, a fidelity to the youth's cause evident during another confrontation between Stefan and Shinehead where Danny places himself in front of Shinehead's knife as he attempts to stab Stefan, vowing to stand his ground as Shinehead threatens to 'pass this blade through you' to get to Stefan and convincing his former pupil to leave. It is *Storm Damage*'s interest in the complex emotional insecurities at the heart of the Black urban world and the more internal conflicts within the Black urban psyche that provide justification for the level of devotion that Stefan, deservedly or undeservedly, demands from those around him, that the film disavows a more linear protagonist's journey in favour of a characterization of the Black urban youth defined by acute, competing mentalities. Later, Stefan brutally beats up Paul over a jacket he had stolen and had refused to hand over to him. Upon the arrival of Danny and Kate (a white care worker at Number 66 who also becomes romantically involved with Danny), who rescue Paul from the beating, the camera frames Stefan in a medium shot capturing a fleeting moment of remorse on his face before recovering his instinctive sense of self, grabbing the prized jacket and running out of the house. We observe here a *spatial* difference between Stefan and Danny who, having run out of Number 66 in pursuit of Stefan, finds him with Bonaface on the Angell Town Estate. Beyond the obvious demarcation of geographic space as he walks across from the gated, detached care home to the estate streets, Danny's entry into the estate as the paragon of social and personal respectability represents a symbolic trespass into an urban setting that reinforces several spatio-cultural binaries: the thin geographical lines demarking the sharp contrast between the apparent harmonious and loving domesticity of Number 66 and the estate as an immoral, criminalized urban environment, and a territorial divide that presents the urban environment as a bifurcated landscape where Danny possesses no authoritative command or influence. Thus, the scene creates a distinction between the three Black masculinities unified by race but separated by opposing social identities, which allow for an uncomfortable cohabitation within Angell Town's urban theatre. Indeed, Danny's look of utter disgust as he faces them, spitting 'you lot are relentless' as both Stefan and Bonaface laugh at Danny's outrage over Stefan's latest act, is a further disassociation between himself and the urban Black men as a degenerate social milieu unwilling to conform to the very basic forms of propriety, an evaluation further cemented by Stefan's complete lack of remorse for the attacking of Paul and his decision to pursue a life of crime, affirmed by his retreat to Bonaface. Surveying Stefan as both an unrecognizable but familiar object of the popular imaginaries of Black youthhood, Danny's renewed contempt for Stefan now graduates from perplexity over Stefan's recalcitrance and refusal to rationally interpret his efforts towards his social deliverance to an angry resignment as he shouts, 'look at you, a couple of years from now who the fuck are you gonna be?' Stefan's smiling response of 'big super dapper!' only further entrenches his unrelatability for Danny, who counters with 'Oh what, like this man?' gesturing at Bonaface. 'The one chance you have is at Number 66 but you decide to pick stupid. And that's how he wants you, because stupid does what stupid's told.' Danny, who is then punched by Bonaface for his insult, is then turned on by Stefan, goading him to 'teach me then!' with Danny's failure to match Bonaface physically a testimony to the impotence of his version of respectability, one that is inadequate for navigating the potentially fatal realities for Angell Town's Black, working-class milieu. Stefan's rejection of Danny's pedagogical gestures is equally a rejection of the symbolisms of alterity that are bound up within questions of race, class and identity. Shouting over the stricken Danny, Stefan's denigration of Danny as 'a wannabe white man?' as Danny limps away from the scene enunciates both the tangible social barriers regulating the level of influence Danny possesses over Stefan and Danny's continued attempts at reforming the urban Other as a subversion of his Black identity. Stefan's rapid development of an emboldened Black consciousness is invoked only through the combination of his physical and mental proximity to Bonaface and the Angell Town estate that frames the three men, both energized in opposition to Danny; Stefan affirms his own authentic Black identity via the repositioning of Danny as unbelonging, as essentially 'non-Black'. In the labelling of Danny as white-aspirational, the scene reiterates the phenomenological disjuncture between the two Black identities organizing *Storm Damage*'s actualization of Black life. Stefan's description in passing of Danny as a white man on the basis of his attempts to carve a reformed, alternative pathway for him points to the limited but no less significant parameters of Stefan's urban world view in which Black masculine identity is a means of self-preservation, a suppressed and othered external existence demanding an alchemistic mode of expression, particularly when confronted with symbolic whiteness, rendering Danny's own iteration of Black maleness incompatible with the racially defined social mores of Angell Town. Here, and founded on the unabated geographically specific presence of racism, 'being Black' is an acceptance of the idea of equality, fairness and opportunity as a chimeric fantasy, the impossibility of a legitimate future within the Black urban purview and, fundamentally, an affront against an assimilatory existence that, as embodied in Danny, is one versed in the singular customs of white society. Gilroy explicates this impasse in drawing attention to what he terms as 'vernacular nihilism' (Gilroy, 1994: 70). Locating its origins in the Black vernacular cultural practices during slavery, Gilroy predicates the prospect of freedom on breaking with the racially coded rules in a challenge to white supremacy. In a later analysis, Gilroy (2001) returns to the idea of vernacular nihilism as a 'pseudo freedom' (198), defined as the structural product of, *inter alia*, the peripherality of Black social and economic life necessitating the cumulative transgressions and insubordinations performed by 'a socially-excluded underclass' (198). This iteration of Black vernacular nihilism is presented as an act of social defilement that, for Gilroy, shifts from the domain of the antisocial to one that takes on the aura of the *social* in that it allows for the coalescing of a Black identity upon a practice that 'specifies the fortified boundaries of racial particularity' (Gilroy 2001: 199). I'm interested in the utility Masood (2003) finds in Gilroy's concept of Black nihilism when applied to her analysis of the antisocial postures of the US hood films of the early 1990s. Here, Massood adopts a 'contemporary' prefix to the description of vernacular nihilism, with the gangsta culture depicted in such films indicative of a Black inner-city youth ethos of pessimistic rebellion resulting in the 'ideology of transgression with the characteristics of the urban trickster valorised in the vernacular' (170). It is from both Gilroy's and Massood's analysis of vernacular nihilism as a racially bounded defensive stance that we can understand the perspectives represented in Stefan as the internalization of dominant definitions of Black masculinity to counter what Kobena Mercer describes as the 'dependency and powerlessness which racism and racial oppression enforce' (1988: 112). My reading of the scene draws on the interplays between these three interpretations of vernacular nihilism. Danny's inability in finding the language or means to get beyond Stefan's non-relatability (Figure 5.2), and his indifference and immorality emphasizes not simply the chasm between Danny and Stefan's notions of Black identity but a continued cultural dissonance that, in this example, is engendered primarily by *antitheticality*. Stefan remains by default a creation and representative of the urban environ structuring both his interior and external life, rendering the urban as a site of subject formation, and the very arrival of Danny to within this arena and his castigation of its Black inhabitants is interpreted as an attempt at a de-territorialization of culturally specific space, and an inhibiting of his mode of being. Therefore, in this scene, a contemporary Black vernacular nihilism performs as a means of psychological and material transcendence, with Danny's presence offering no more than a resemblance of the authoritative (and white adjacent) power structures demanding only reform and constraint: school, the police and, seemingly, the care system.

Storm Damage's commitment to a multi-dimensionality of character more invested in the complex irrationalities of human behaviour and emotion within the Black urban youth existence than the popular cultural verisimilitude defining Black

Figure 5.2 Stefan, arguing with Danny while Bonaface observes in *Storm Damage* (dir. Simon Cellan Jones, 2000).

urban identities from the outside provides a logic to the apparent illogical trajectories and nihilisms of the urban sphere. Just moments after the incident, Stefan is back at Number 66, bursting into the kitchen where he finds the injured Danny and trashes the room, screaming as he throws both the stolen jacket and various kitchen objects at him, having interpreted Danny's admonishment of him in front of Bonaface as a demonstration of disloyalty and hatred. Eventually, Stefan's anger turns to tears, and as he breaks down, burying his face over the kitchen worktop, Danny tentatively moves towards him, placing a hand on his back before Stefan relents and sobs uncontrollably in Danny's arms. While Stefan's acceptance of Danny's parental love, as symbolized in the moment, reflects the kinds of power relations intrinsic to the Black family (Lawrence, 1982), the embrace is less vertical than one may denote, and the scene establishes a temporal horizontality between the two. For Danny, his uncompromising position as a moral ideologue, where an adherence to his example of moral conduct is the only guarantee of a future devoid of criminality and tragedy, has been tempered by the recognition of the difficulties within Stefan's own position as situated between two apparently incontrovertible and unambiguous future pathways. Here, Stefan's dilemma is no longer understood as a simplistic decision between a seemingly obvious right versus wrong, with Danny finally understanding Stefan's behavioural excess as a particular expression of *lack*. In this process, we observe an acceptance of Stefan as an emotional nomad whose willingness to conform to the regimented but socially rewarding behavioural modifications templated within Danny remains curtailed by the effects of a nihilistic trauma bound up in a toxic history of rejection and emotional displacement organizing his sense of trust, self-esteem and Black identity. While the sense of accomplishment Danny exhibits towards Kate in the aftermath of his and Stefan's embrace can be seen as the emotional breakthrough required to ensure the completion of the film's Black urban rehabilitation project, in the following scene we observe a continuity with the future popular urban film's generic order in which bleakness, or here, Black death, becomes the tragic mise en scène of the British urban drama's conclusion.

It is as a consequence of *Storm Damage*'s close correspondence with the extra-diegetic social circumstances underpinning the film's claim to authenticity that the film builds up to its dramatic climax from a point of apparent placidity; in its final characterizing of Stefan, with Paul and their friend MacDaddy, the scene presents an image of Stefan as a reforming self – he returns a seized stolen watch back to the delighted Paul and jokes at MacDaddy's suggestion that he is now 'under manners' by Danny, as the group enjoy the less sinister youth activities of an amusement arcade. In this scene, and affirming of the film's narrational fidelity to the reality of the urban youth experience as one conditioned by, somewhat oxymoronically, the unpredictable certainty of pending violence, where the camera frames Stefan in a close-up as he fires at the arcade screen with a light gun, the framing of Stefan serves as a visual metaphor for the perpetual cycle of violent conflict awaiting the Black boys as a familiar face emerges behind him. A shift in shot focus brings in the image of a menacing Shinehead and his accomplices into the foreground. In a highly dramatic and violent climax, the unsuspecting Stefan is stabbed repeatedly by Shinehead. Capturing what can be accepted as a variant of Massood's description of a contemporary vernacular nihilism (2003) here manifest as a nihilistic disregard for human life, Shinehead continues to aggressively taunt the prone Stefan as he is dragged away from the scene by members of his gang, as a distressed Paul attempts in vain to aid the dying Stefan up from the floor, a pool of blood emerging around him. At this point, I would like to momentarily return to the question of social realism and its relevance for the filmic representation of Black British identities, communities and cultural practices. This is not an opportunity to meditate on the discursivity of the term that, to draw on just one of the manifold and continuingly evolving definitions, categorizes social realism as a cinematic approach that articulates the relationship between socially and economically marginalized identities and the political constructs that curtail and arrest human potential, progress and ambition, with the filmmaker's specific political ideology and intention expressed through the dramatic narrative arch of a central character and the vicissitudes experienced within a social environment distressed by the effects of systemic inequalities (Lay, 2002; Forrest, 2020; Hallam and Marshmant, 2000; Wayne, 2002; Hill, 1999). Rather, my interest is in the Black urban film and its classification as a renovation, or outlier, of the formal and contextual interests of social realism, its Black themes and how it emerges with its own established set of realisms, generic conventions and expectancies that, to revisit my introduction's alluding to the conceptual position Raymond Williams argued in his historicized rejection of particular interpretations of realism (1977), is anchored by industrial and cultural dynamics as well as distinct formal methods. The point I wish to make here, in my description of the Black urban film as a social aesthetic that exists in immediate and non-interruptive dialogue with what I feel appropriate to term as the selective 'raw materials' of not simply Black life but also the crude excessiveness of a particular Black *condition* is that its capturing of the 'real' is a highly selective and deliberately dramatic form of representation. I want to consider what is being communicated in our encounters with instances of

Black mortality through a paradigm of Black Studies offered by Walcott, who arrives at the idea of the 'Black life form(s)' as a term that, in theoretical interaction with the work of Sylvia Wynter, Fanon, Derrida and Édouard Glissant, interrogates the Euro-American differentiating logics that place a non-human value system on Black life and, subsequently, Black death. It is through this reading by Walcott that the ascription of non-human black life forms to the visual dimensions of Black mortality produces what I describe as a 'prompting choreography' of violent Black death. As Walcott continues, 'when I say that Black people die differently, I mean that our deaths are simultaneously spectacularized and disregarded even as the actual conditions of our deaths might appear to mirror the deaths of others' (Walcott, 2021: 11). There are two facets to this phenomenology. It is not simply the textual form of Black death as slow death in that Black identities are subject to the cinematic temporalities and durationalities that author the affective prolonging of our audiovisual witnessing of Black mortality, but Black death as a differentiating choreography is a consequence of the spectral referentiality to the contextually flattened but textually spectacular image of Black fatality that is made voluminous by the hapitality and the multi-constitutionality of black-on-black death and its phenomenological index or, in this instance, its abstract quantum, the Black body, here performing as a useful and necessary fiction of race, a social aesthetic and as an atextual (social) ornamentation that is made distinct and spectacular only in our melanin differential. Instead of considering the Black urban death as a natural and inevitable conclusion to the realist aestheticization of the Black urban existence, this is a matter of representational and aesthetic choice. While authenticity becomes a particular aesthetic value applied to the valorizing of the representation of the Black urban, of course, death is just one reality, rather than the dominant reality of the Black youth existence. In *Storm Damage*, however, death is the *optimal* reality that ensures the most dramatic elements of the Black urban condition are maintained within its visceral depiction of an extra-diegetic reality.

In keeping with what would become the recognizable pedagogical narrative conclusion to the popular urban drama, often through either the tragic images of Black death or a moral address to bring to an end the cycle of urban conflict and violence, at Stefan's funeral the community pastor, Mister (T-Bone Wilson) offers an emotional and searing sermon to the Number 66 youths in attendance on the value of life and the need for caution when entering into a very adult world of violence that threatens the precious fragility of youthhood. Framed by an unsteady, social realist camera aesthetic that alternates between the home's grieving residents in a series of close- ups capturing the various characters' emotional subjectivities, Mister recalls an earlier life spent subjected to extreme white racism as part of the Windrush generation through which the local black identity became the foundation upon which the community was built. Mister draws a connection between the racial struggles of the past (earlier in the film Mister makes reference to the Brixton Riots of 1981 and the sense of hopeless nihilism unifying the Black youths of the 1980s to the Number 66 children) and the troubled experiences of Angell Town's youths. It is noteworthy that during this part of his speech, as part of the scene's continuous alternating of point-of-view (POV), the camera's interest is now in Paul, who throughout the film is characterized as a *bona fide* member of London's white working-class rather than as a character whose inclusion within the Black youth identities of Angell Town has been validated by the extra-diegetic appropriation of the mannerisms and vernaculars of Black urban subculture germane to South London that Les Back describes as 'black codes' (1996: 130). Paul's position as Stefan's white sidekick and the sense of loss displayed at the funeral should not be interpreted exclusively as a representation of an urban multiculture and cross-racial conviviality that, as will be examined in the following chapters, is bound together by an appreciation of Black subcultural lifestyles, products, music and a solidarity against white racism (Back, 1996). Rather, the binds here are more emotive. The Black family may well indeed be the locus of an organic Black culture, but for Paul and Celia (Tara Keatly), the other white teen at Number 66 who was also Stefan's love interest, their status as members of the care home has been accompanied by an uncontested acceptance within Angel Town's Black community. In other words, reflecting the instinctive extensivities within the care home that disavows overt racial distinctions, Number 66 is a microcosm for the social and emotional binds of a multiracial, working-class Brixton.

As Paul, Massive, Leon and MacDaddy (Daryl McCollin) cover Stefan's grave with soil, he pleads, 'don't let your life go cheap, too many people stand behind you for that', before addressing the role of the adults present, as the camera hones in on the various personalities whose displays of grief are compromised by their own complicity in Stefan's fatal trajectory: 'Hold your arrows tight. If we drop them, we have nothing!' Here, in some accordance with Claire Alexander's analysis of the Black community as both an imagined and heterogeneous set of relations, where one's membership to it is described as 'multi-layered and multi-faceted' (1996: 33), Mister's own reification of Angell Town's Black community points to the obligations of a localized and geographically bounded Black community in which even the villainous Bonaface, standing in the distance, remains a central part. Mister's speech, made to the funeral's mourners and, in the context of PSB drama's orientation towards the reflecting and addressing of the nation (Pines, 1991) equally speaks to Black Britain, represents *Storm Damage*'s final attempt to unify the unresolvable antagonisms between Angell Town's adult figures and dissolve the thin and unreliable social markers dictating where parental responsibility ends and individual responsibility begins. The spectator's attention is now on Danny, as an unstable camera frames him in a close-up, with Stefan's inconsolable mother, Cynthia, in the background and Mister at the centre of the frame, revealing three planes of emotion; the commanding oration from Mister; the neglect, abandonment and rejection experienced by Stefan at the hands of Cynthia that conditioned his youthhood; and the helplessness and sense of anger Danny feels towards those he deems responsible for Stefan's tragic but predictable fate. Indeed, just as it began, the film ends with Danny, the camera briefly cutting to Cynthia comforting Stefan's young brother, before cutting back to Danny in an extreme close-up, a momentary look of empathy in his eyes before he resumes shovelling, covering Stefan's grave with earth as the cut to the film's credits is met with the sound of Finlay Quaye's uplifting 'Your Love Gets Sweeter'. Love, or an absence of it, for others and for oneself may very well be the determining factor underpinning both *Storm Damage*'s devastating outcomes and the film's general commentary on the Black urban existence. Responsibility is a floating thematic that deliberately evades any secured or fixed position or distribution throughout the film, resulting in an almost circumscribed and mitigative social universe in which self-discipline cannot be accepted as the panacea for all the difficulties afflicting the Number 66 youths.

This also draws one into a consideration of whether *Storm Damage*'s very praxis is in the sociopolitical examination of the alienating impacts of trauma and suffering inflicted upon Black youths, an investment that accommodates within its system of representation an awareness of and responsiveness to the emergent neoliberal structuring of social life within which Black working-class men and women occupy the very lowest position. I accept that such a question may appear as *de rigueur* given the specificity of race in *Storm Damage*, and I have deliberately eschewed an analysis that orientates itself towards a mandative and inflexible realist paradigm that requires one to actively classify the film against a preordained social realist ideal, a theoretical stream that will ultimately arrive at the very analytical *cul-de-sac* Forrest cautions against in the consecrating of an established but historicized exemplar of British social realism (for example, the films of Ken Loach) against which all other versions of realism, either cinematic or poetic, are assessed (Forrest, 2020). This said, *Storm Damage*'s realist framing of Black urban death does permit one to consider if, and if so, the means by which one can position the film as a text in dialogue with its immediate sociopolitical context. Indeed, this a question that has been answered to some degree by Bourne (2002) in his suggestion that *Storm Damage* 'proved to be the best film or television drama written about the displacement and alienation of Britain's Black working-class since Horace Ove's film *Pressure*' (219). It is on the basis of the film's dramatic emphasis on problematic Black lives and tragic Black death, combined with the absence of any study of the empirical Black audience's response to the film, that one takes a slender disunity with Bourne's heuristic attempt to inscribe a definite sociopolitical agenda within *Storm Damage*'s sjuzhet. *Pressure* was indeed the first text to accurately articulate the Black youth condition in Britain, a condition marred by habitual state racism, through a documentary realist register to display both the futility of social assimilation and the necessity of a radical Black politics to expose the hokum of race relations in 1970s Britain (Mercer, 1988; Pines, 1991; Young, 1996). I accept that a concession can be made towards this assertion through the brevity of Bourne's analysis of *Storm Damage*, and the eagerness to classify the film within the canon of Black authored texts that capture Black British youth experiences within the period of adolescence is an interpretive judgement that may account for the bypassing of a film such as *Babylon* from Bourne's canonizing of films that present an account of Black youth alienation. Without wishing to reconvene historic dialogues on the meaning and implications of Black cinematic realism at this point, Bourne's analysis seems to profess a faith in the realist representations of Blackness as an instinctively political act, an evaluation perhaps constructed against the cultural significance of the definite political ethos that organized the Black British films of the late 1970s, 1980s and early 1990s (Baker et al., 1996; Pines, 1991); however, I want to suggest that Blackness's relationship to the urban film, as will be touched on in later chapters, is determined less through a continuation of what has been identified as the didactic quality of Black British film (Mercer, 1988) and towards the depicting of intra-race social conflict. I do not wish to dismiss Bourne's critical evaluation of *Storm Damage* holistically on the basis of a seemingly uncritical commitment to multiculturalist essentialism, the very analytical situation located in Hall's cautionary plea at the uncritical valorizing of films that refer to a Black experience as a trapdoor into an 'unguaranteed political argument and debate' (1988: 27) and, as a corollary to Hall's critique, my own analysis of the thin politics of race structuring the disingenuous and contradictory institutional processes through which Black PSB drama accrues an uncontested and unqualified political status (Nwonka, 2020b). However, it may be that the coarse textures and essentialist vibrations of Black film's realist apparatus has concretized a set of inherited, assumed and unimaginative interpretative practices that, in this case, render us as less alive to the possibility that the film constitutes a more nuanced understanding of the Black urban circumstance. Thus, while it is arduous to interpret *Storm Damage*'s contained fabula as advancing a definite sociopolitical agenda, I find value in the idea that the film specifically asks the spectator to engage with its characters' experience of violence and social alienation as the residual condition of a legacy of class-determined racism. From this alternative interpretation, it can be argued that *Storm Damage* offers a phasematic representation of an urban Black youthhood that arrives at the level of *affect*; the film commences its narrativizing of Angell Town at a particular phase, at the very point of which the Black community, either imagined or fixed, has been made most vulnerable to an intra-racial cycle of violence and social atrophy conditioned by an uninterrupted extra-diegetic reality of state-sanctioned racism, economic exclusion and political repression.

6

Constructing Black Urbanity

Mediatations of Black-on-Black Criminality

In language, there are only differences without positive terms
Ferdinand de Saussure, *Course in General Linguistics*, 1916

We can locate in the previous chapter's analysis of *Storm Damage* an attempt to evidence certain linkages and features that become salient as the popular Black urban text entered into a cultural and industrial moment of enunciation. First, the drama is reflective of the post-2000s diversity discourse in that it provided the narrative template for much of what would come to emerge as the primary conventions and themes of the popular Black British urban film. Second, the drama succeeded in the capturing of the vernacular experiences of a youthful Black British identity to be reconceptualized and embedded in contemporary British popular culture. I'm describing a period where capitalism began to draw on elements of urban subculture as a dynamic, economically lucrative and socially instrumentalizing strand of promotional culture. However, the uptake of Black urban subcultural forms within fashion, music, advertising and branding was perceived as a debilitating cultural presence compromising the futures of an already socially vulnerable and educationally tepid Black youth, notably for the Black academic Tony Sewell who, in considering the disproportionate number of exclusions of Black pupils from state schooling, would point to the mainstream aggrandizing of popular Black youth subcultural products and an intrenched consumerism as a particular affliction among Black teenagers, one in which he held as complicit as white racism itself in producing the negative educational outcomes for Black children. There is a particularly myopic iteration of race politics to observe in Sewell's status as an oracle of Black social commentary, a status that I argue is less an outcome of the recognition of a need for a Gramscian-esque organic intellectual to inform the official policy perspective on education and race, but the outcome of the reductive but embracing cosmopolitanism of racial capitalism and its durability through the bestowment of symbolic power that secures into the publics the position of Sewell as the ideologically compliant avatar of Black opinion. As Sewell argued, 'What we have now is not only the pressure of racism, but "black peer grouping" [which] has become another pressure almost as big as institutional racism was' (quoted in *The Observer*,

Sunday, 20 August 2000). In Sewell's diagnosis of Black underachievement, and with a willful misapplication of a Du Bois(ian) interpretation of racial progress and uplift (2014 [1903]), the affirming of Black youth identities through the commercialization of the term 'urban' as a more politically benign and socially acquiescent nomenclature for 'Black' was also responsible for the curtailing of Black scholastic achievement, a threat that requires Black youths to invest in the more palatable dimensions of English meritocracy. Evocative of a broader conservative ideology on the biological limits of Black schoolchildren's intellectual capacity, itself located within the resistant vestiges of the imperialist legacy where British educative systems established a practice of symbolic violence while equally being presented as the benevolent provision to remedy the perceived primitivity of its Black subjects, the project that is here presented is a cultural deficit that asks for the redirection of Black youth imaginations towards the pursuit of educational excellence and away from the disruptive and unproductive presence of their subcultural vernacular practices that encourages them to seek social recognition, value and emancipation in the trivial presence of Black youth subcultural trends within the British popular mainstream. While acknowledging the 'much-needed self-esteem' developed within Black youths from the public extolling of urban subculture, he goes on to argue 'that culture is not one that, for example, is interested in being a great chess player, or intellectual activity. It is actually to do with propping up a big commercial culture to do with selling trainers, selling magazines, rap music and so on' (quoted in *The Observer*, Sunday, 20 August 2000). From one perspective, one could interpret Sewell's judgement on the mainstream presence of Black youth culture as a damnation of the mechanics of racial capitalism (Bhattacharyya, 2018). In this variant, such racial corruptions manifest as the commodification of authentic Black cultural practices that succeed in extracting economic value from their non-whiteness. However, Sewell's description of the arid nature of Black popular culture is weighted heavily towards a castigation of Black youth identities located within a racialized comparative Black deficit logic in which 'intellectual activity' is instinctively attributed to whiteness, but equally a castigation of Black youths and of Black subcultural forms, rendering Sewell's evaluation of Black youth social progress as painfully fissured between negative Black culture and the exemplary white identity. What is important to note at this point is how, beyond merely the educative and extending towards discourses on crime and violence, the hegemony of a racially attributive moral crisis structured within Black identity and culture is accelerated by the popularizing of UK rap and grime music (Bramwell, 2015; White, 2017) and I want to examine the modes by which black-on-black violence, as the imperial aggregation of racially sutured discourses, became woven and embedded into the centre of the British political and social lexicon on race as urban music made a significant contribution to the development of a popular Black British urban identity within mainstream culture. The emergence of UK Garage, a strand of dance music that locates its genesis in house and the cross-pollination of ragga, soul and R&B that had developed via a number of pirate radio stations in the late 1990s, became a key vector for the increasing visibility of the urban within mainstream popular culture. Dreem Team, a Garage trio comprising of DJs Spoony, Timmie Magic and Mikee B, who had gained notoriety through underground and pirate radio stations in the 1990s, would play a prominent role in popularizing UK Garage with a Sunday morning BBC Radio One show that ran between 2000 and 2003. Indeed, by the turn of the millennium, the commercialization of the genre via the radio-friendly two-step Garage that had spawned a number of top-twenty singles through UK Garage acts such as Shanks and Bigfoot, Artful Dodger, DJ Luck and MC Neat, Wookie, Sweet Female Attitude, DJ Pied Piper and the Master of Ceremonies that were central to the broader visibility of urban cultural texts and discourses that exemplify the ways in which working-class Black British youths cultivated and circulated a culturally relevant, organic but precarious range of subcultural aesthetic practices and products that, commensurate with the exertions of capitalist accumulation, became absorbed into the logics of corporate media cultures and the instrumentalist imaginaries of cultural institutions.

However, while such acts were embraced as part of a moment in which the powerful cultural resonance of Black British youth subcultural practices and cultural production catalysed the rapid development of the *urban* as a commercial pseudonym, the development of the genre serves as a barometer for the ways in which race was adduced by dominant discourses in an attempt to advance an indexical relationship between Garage music, Black urban masculinity and violent crime. Having gained cultural notoriety through the pirate radio stations of Rinse FM, Delight FM and Supreme FM, the rapid ascent of South London Garage collective So Solid Crew accentuated the popularizing of Black urban subculture within the public sphere. Gaining further prominence through the group's 2001 No.1 single '21 Seconds', the unprecedented success of the 30-plus-member Garage act, originating from Battersea and led by the charismatic Megaman (Dwane Vincent) would establish an intra-genre conflict that found its genesis beyond the generic sensibilities and predilections that generational differences often imbue, and disquiet was directed towards the more subcultural aspects of urban music. In 2000, two members of So Solid Crew, eighteen-year-olds Alex Rivers and Mark Oseitutu, performing under the guise of Oxide and Neutrino, would sell 250,000 copies of their number one single (Casualty) 'Bound 4 Da Reload', which sampled the theme music from the BBC One television series *Casualty* (1986–) and inscribed in popular culture its use of the distinctive 'can everyone stop getting shot?' line of dialogue from the 1998 British gangster comedy film *Lock, Stock, and Two Smoking Barrels* (dir. Guy Ritchie). For Dreem Team (and others), So Solid Crew and their equally successful offshoot represented a sharp departure from the genial atmosphere of two-step Garage, and the raw urgency of So Solid Crew's more dramatic version of Garage music expedited their propelling into a media sphere where they would come to be presented as 'the controversial rap group indelibly linked with violent crime' (*The Times*, Saturday, 29 October 2005). The collective's position as the avatar of the popular urban would be further affirmed in screen culture with the broadcasting of the Channel 4 hour-long documentary *This Is So Solid* (dir. David Upshal, 2002), which itself was marred by controversy due to its production funding by the group's own record label Independiente, which some felt compromised Channel 4's editorial objectivity. Introducing the group as 'the most talk about and controversial musicians of the 21st century' and, as further credence to the popular urban as a genre of authenticity, purporting to provide 'the truth behind the hype', the documentary generally effaced a holistic engagement and interrogation of the more sinister narratives that had accompanied the collective's ascent and primarily aimed to represent them as a close-knit group of lifelong friends, devoted parents and dedicated musicians, a representation counter to their negative tabloid framing as a locus for crime, violence and gun culture. From the outset, the documentary makes reference to their media vilification in the presence of extra-diegetic features, notably through the use of voice-over narration where the collective are announced as 'the notorious group in Britain constantly associated with urban violence and gun crime' as a number of newspaper headlines are displayed across the screen. Tracing the development of the group as the brainchild of former drugs dealer Megaman, who formed So Solid Crew after spending several months on remand for attempted murder (a conviction of which he was later cleared), *This Is So Solid* sought to concretize the group's spiritual and material connection to the tower blocks and housing estates of Battersea (where many of the collective's members still lived), and the documentary takes its audience through the estate where the group describe an existence conditioned by a youthhood marred by poverty, a localized drug trade and crime, but equally conceives the estate as a locale of cross-generational community cohesion, unrecognized creative potential and innovation. Indeed, it is through its more subjective documentary practice that the audience is offered a novel insight into the collaborative creative practices, divisions of labour and authentic cultural production and entrepreneurship that would result in a platinum-selling album, two MOBO awards and a Brit Award for Best Video in 2002. Towards the end of the documentary, the crew members finally refer directly to the negative media hysteria that has compromised the group's success, and members of the collective openly discuss the incidents where interviews with the group members against the backdrop of the estate are intercut with further extra-diegetic information in the form of press vilification, with particular attention paid to the imprisonment of group member Asher D in 2001 for possessing a loaded gun. For the collective, the incident was seen as a consequence of uninterrupted socio-economic injustice and racism, and such conditions, to recall Gilroy's reference to ruthlessness, hopelessness and 'black misery' as some of the 'casual mechanisms' in which Black vernacular nihilism is diagnosed (2001: 198), derive here from a culture of envy permeating an already economically distressed social terrain, a condition further exacerbated by the hyper-locality of the urban music ecology (White, 2017) and encouraging an emphasis on the products of material culture where the relative economic prosperity indicated in the acquiring of items and possessions becomes the symbol of perceived wealth, success, status and arrival. Indeed, Asher D would insist that his ownership of the gun was the direct result of his family receiving death threats from individuals who resented the rapid success and cultural notoriety he had gained through being a member of the collective. In one of the documentary's more poignant moments, the group members meditate on the tragic injustice of the sentencing, inscribing within the documentary a momentary sociopolitical analysis of the 'haters' whose antagonisms are in part a reflection of an unequal and therefore nihilistic social environment, and the group members' own understanding of Asher D's imprisonment as an outcome of anti-Black racism within the criminal justice system (Bowling and Phillips, 2002; Phillips, 2008;

Philips and Webster, 2013). In their condemnation of the repeated failures of the police to respond to the concerns raised over the safety of Asher D and his family, the documentary offers a sympathetic evaluation of the Black men/gun-crime bind in the fate of Asher D who, according to *The Guardian*'s Peter Paphides was allegedly interviewed for the documentary while still serving his prison sentence (*The Guardian*, Friday, 4 October 2002). It is reflective of the documentary's attentiveness to the existent discourses on Black urban violence that the group offer a condemnation of gun crime, while alluding to the socio-economic inequalities of the inner city in the authenticity of their lyrics, which offers a significant mode of representation possessing a central ethos of social and cultural relationality, truth-telling and 'realness'. Somewhat indicative of the forms by which racial capitalism's venture into the cultural politics of recognition and visibility succeeds in framing Black subcultural practices within a post-multiculturalist celebratory vein while remaining steeped in the legacies of racism, the group's lyrics were to be subjected to a sustained and unfounded criticism for allegedly inciting a number of violent incidents during the previous year. In 2001, MC Neutrino was shot in the leg outside the Velvet Room nightclub in Mayfair during an attempted robbery (despite being the victim of the shooting, he was later wrongfully arrested by the police before being released without charge) (BBC News, Wednesday, 2 May 2001). In the same year, another So Solid Crew member, Skat D, would be convicted for breaking a sixteen-year-old girl's jaw (BBC News, Friday, 19 October 2001) and in November, an incident during a show at London's Astoria where two attendees were shot would culminate in the cancellation of their UK tour as the concerned venues refused to allow the group to perform on the basis of security fears born from the group's seemingly indelible association with gun terror. We can assert with some degree of authority that as an outcome of racial capitalism's circulation within the media that often seeks to hold the popular presence of Black cultural practices and subcultural expressions in some form of equivalency, opposition and hierarchy, a binary-inducing form of cultural politics bound within the dominant whiteness of the nation's cultural and creative mainstream and their accompanying notions of what constitutes cultural value, the criminalized denigration of So Solid Crew was also met with efforts to cultivate a new Black popular urban vista within the cultural mainstream. This was a modality serving as an indication of the continuing significance of music as the influential social sphere orchestrating the recognition and acceptance of Black urbanity and racial difference within the post-Macphersonist celebratory zeitgeist of the early 2000s. In many ways, this was embodied in the rapper Ms Dynamite, whose debut album *A Little Deeper* (2002) heralded a generic departure from UK Garage and would incorporate music styles such as R&B, Jazz and Ragga, offering a more politically and socially conscious form of urban music that would disavow the more elaborate (and male-orientated) lyrical concerns of Garage in favour of themes such as domestic abuse, sexism and the dangers of drug use, which would result in Ms Dynamite being awarded two Brit Awards and the 2002 Mercury Music Prize. Indeed, this period of critical acclaim would affirm the arrival of Black urban music into a domain of British culture generally perceived as the preserve of the white mainstream, when eighteen-year-old Bow-born grime artist Dizzie Rascal (Dylan

Mills) would win the same award for his album *Boy in da Corner* the following year. It is within this period that So Solid Crew's presence within the popular mainstream would be seen to diminish as rapidly as it had arisen, a descent brought into being in part by UK garage's general superseding by the popularity of Grime music towards the mid-2000s, and in part by the British media's unwavering commitment to harden the crude association between young Black men and serious crime in the continued hyper-reportage of So Solid Crew members' criminal convictions: notably G-Man (Jason Phillips), who in 2003 was sentenced to four years in prison on gun charges (*The Telegraph*, Friday, 20 June 2003), and Carl Morgan, who was sentenced to thirty years in prison for shooting dead rival Colin Scarlett in what was described by *The Guardian* as a 'wild west gun battle' (*The Guardian*, Saturday, 29 October 2005). Thus, despite So Solid Crew's involvement in a number of public campaigns against gun violence, the entrenched interest in the criminal incidents tangentially related to the group some years after their public profile as musicians had diminished contributed to the development of a certain *mediatization* of the Black urban, with Garage and Black urban music subcultures positioned at the centre of the media's construction of Black men as an existential threat to *normal* (white) society.

My analysis of the modes in which Black urban music was mobilized by State agents to assemble a tenuous pathology of Black people and violent crime and its broader relevance to the contextualization of the popular urban film draws on the central theoretical preoccupations of Hall et al.'s landmark study *Policing the Crisis* (1978), an investigation that finds its conceptual origins in Stanley Cohen's book *Folk Devils and Moral Panics* (1972). Cohen, by conducting an analysis of the immoderate social response to the Mods and Rockers conflicts of the 1960s that expands to a number of other youth subcultures, advances a theorization of moral panic as a phenomenon in which

> a condition, episode or group of persons becomes defined as a threat to societal values and interests; its nature is presented in a stylized and stereotypical fashion by the mass media; the moral barricades are manned by editors, bishops, politicians and other right-thinking people; socially accredited experts pronounce their diagnoses and solutions; ways of coping are evolved (or more often) resorted to; the condition then disappears, submerges, and/or deteriorates and becomes more visible. (Cohen, 1972: 9)

It is upon Cohen's work that a theoretical renewal is undertaken by Hall et al., and by updating the context of analysis advanced by Cohen, *Policing the Crisis* represented a major paradigmatic shift in the sociological study of crime by introducing the Gramscian concept of hegemony, deploying neo-Marxism as a methodological framework to consider the modes through which moral panics over street 'muggings' and the ostensible criminal impulses of Afro-Caribbean youths disseminated through the media ushered in the conditions of social consent that were required for the construction of and justification for an authoritarian British society. Such an authoritarianism sought to distance itself from the causes of the economic crisis of the decade and recourse to discourses of law and order as a legitimizing device for the continuation of a defunct capitalist system (1978). Defining moral panics as 'official' reactions to events that are 'out of all proportion to the actual threat offered' (1978: 16), Hall and his colleagues's position offered a departure from Cohen's original concept in that the moral panic is identified as a strategic practice rather than a social phenomenon, just one component of the topology of hegemonic practices expanding the spheres of influence within a Gramscian notion of civil society (Buttigeig, 1995; Wayne, 2018). While Hall et al.'s Gramscian-inflected iteration of moral-panic perceives a break from the theoretical corpus advanced by Cohen, we find that both epistemologies are assimilated into a unified and conflated problematic by Hayle (2013), in which, as part of a wider criticism of the prosaic application of moral-panic theory in the intervening decades which has seen Cohen's concept applied to a plethora of social situations, asks for an understanding of folk devils and moral panics as two *individual* social phenomena that, while retaining the potential for interaction, begin with a detached hierarchal order in which 'individuals can be labeled as folk devils regardless of whether or not a moral panic is taking place' (1126). It is against this assertion that Hayle finds particular dissatisfaction in Hall et al.'s analysis of folk devils, which is described as 'vague and unfocussed' (1130) paying close attention to Hall's description of folk devils as 'the alternative to all we know' (1978: 16) as an unreliable definition unable to provide the necessary ontology of folk devilling. While there is some acceptance of Hayle's general direction of analysis that, in essence, asks for (1) a more nuanced understanding of moral panics, (2) the rejecting of the dialectical theorizing of moral panics and folk devils as instinctively reciprocal and (3) a decoupling of the description of deviance as symbiotic with 'evil' and an analytical focus on the specific criminal acts that can establish evil as the defining characteristic of folk devils (1978: 16), there is a basic problem with Hayle's reading of Hall's revision of Cohen. First, one can identify a theoretical complication in the exemplars used as the basis of his argument that folk devils can indeed exist independently of any moral panic. Hayle evidences this through the analysis of the application of folk devils to the description of the murderer of twenty-seven-year-old Jahmeel Spence, stabbed and shot dead in Toronto in 1996, as 'evil' by his family, the subsequent volume of media reportage from Canada's leading newspaper, *The Toronto Star* and the societal reaction to the murder of a number of men in Toronto in 2010: sixteen-year-old Tyrone Bracken, fifteen-year-old Sealand White, nineteen-year-old Jermaine Derby and twenty-four-year-old Kevon Phillip. By conducting an evaluation of the use of the term 'evil' in the newspaper's reporting of individuals guilty of murder, and constructed by the citing of Cohen's own moral-panic criteria, Hayle's pointing to the absence of either exaggerated and/or distorted news coverage, nor any 'society-wide consensus surrounding the use of the label' (1133) becomes sufficient theoretical ground to deny the validity of Hall's legitimizing of an indexical relationship between folk devils and moral panics. However, the unreliability of this model is uncovered in the fact that all five men included in Hayle's analysis are Black, a reality that finds no real accommodation within Hayle's study. Such an omittance has serious conceptual implications for Hayle's model for a reconsidered understanding of moral panics, in that it neglects all that is exceptional within the Hall (ian) analysis, and is found in the very invoking of mugging as a phenomenon ascribed to a specific social (racial) identity, revealing an ethicizing of crime that legitimizes the demonization of an already negated social group on the basis of race and ethnicity. It is this evisceration of the social processes coordinating how the media (and subsequently the public) respond to the crime in question (and its alleged perpetrators) that reveals the critical lacuna in Hayle's disallowance of racism and racial difference to enter his general ontology of the moral panic/folk devil relationship; while one may concur with Hayle's insistence that one can exist as a folk devil without the overt presence of a moral panic, the alternative epistemology advanced by Hall demands the crucial engagement with the social processes of folk devilling, processes determined by the very tangible history of colonial othering, racial mythification and hauntological subjugation.

We find a more cogent re-theorization of Cohen's moral panic/folk devil nexus in McRobbie and Thornton (1995) who, in their paradoxical insistence that those categorized as folk devils occupy a more powerful position in contemporary society than at the point of Cohen's original analysis, also argue that folk devils have since become synonymous with marginalized social identities. Here, McRobbie and Thornton offer a sustained critique of the modes of existing media reportage and commentary to insist that folk devils 'can and do fight back' against the processes of their stigmatization within the media (566). However, the specific methods by which such contestation is performed is never fully developed within this analysis, and somewhat surprisingly given the status of their hypothesis as a natural corollary to Hall et al.'s own revising of Cohen, McRobbie and Thornton exhibit a disavowal of any kind of racial specificity to the marginal identities most susceptible to the practice of folk devilling, how racial difference may inform the description of folk devils as either deviant or evil, the material conditions of unequal social life determining one's access to mainstream media representation and the processes of racialization that act as an organizing principle for how, and to what degree, marginalized identities are enabled to fight back against their demonization. My reference to the crucial distinction between the deviant or evil characteristics of folk devils in the social imaginary chimes with Hayle's own dichotomizing of folk devils that, drawing on Edwin M. Lemert's concept of 'primary' and 'secondary' deviance (1951) with Cohen's original folk devil figure occupying the latter category, Hayle observes how the ubiquity of the term applied to social groups exhibiting 'deviant' behaviour displays a tendency to disregard criminal acts that can be characterized as 'evil'. Whereas the socially peripheral folk devil comprises of the two variants of identities understood as deviant, just a small stratum of those residing in the deviant category will go on to accrue the 'evil' description, with this status being the preserve of those groups alleged to be guilty of the most vicious and disturbing of crimes (Hayle, 2013). However, my departure from Hayle is through an advocating of an analysis of folk devilling that asks for a consideration of the racial contingencies that structure the disproportionate distribution of the 'evil' labelling; the mechanisms by which the proportion of those identified as social deviants are propelled to the status of evil is contingent on the forces of social stratification that produce an alternative set of relationalities. In other words, the machinery through which those marginalized identities are classified as 'evil' may be constructed upon existing hierarchies of race, with the socio-symbolic emphasis on racial otherness interacting with the technology by which race orchestrates the classification of the severity of the crime in question, and both considerations gesture towards the highly political processes through which the folk devil is constituted in the contemporary, processes ballast by an ideology of racism instilling the isomorphic acceptance of Blackness *as* violent crime.

I find this dichotomizing between these two modes of folk devilling useful in my broader agenda of constructing a relationship between Black identity and the media's castigation of urban subculture: What are the factors that instantize the moral panic towards Black urban identity? This is a pivotal question within the revision of moral panic offered by McRobbie and Thornton, and there are two discernible features inscribed within both the official, common-sense descriptive language forms found in the media's sustenance of moral panics that stress an organic correspondence between music subcultures and black-on-black violence that, as argued by McRobbie and Thornton, is through which we are able to derive a framework that legitimizes its application to the contemporary analysis of the media's centrality to the aestheticization of Black urban crime. First, and in a theoretical endeavour that somewhat relocates the study of moral panic to its original exegeses, that being Hall's reading of the strategic manoeuvres of mass media in which the hegemony of Black crime works to secure the binds of consensus within a Gramscian analysis of civil society, they identify the systematic quality to the cultivation and circulation of moral panics. As they suggest, 'The moral panic then becomes an envoy for dominant ideology. In the language of common sense, it operates as an advance warning system, and as such it progresses from local issues to matters of national importance, from the site of tension and petty anxieties to full-blown social and political crisis' (1995, 562–3). The idea that the moral-panic functions as an emissary supports an examination of how dominant discourses endeavoured to stabilize the perceived relationship between Black music and intra-race gun violence, and in keeping with the McRobbie and Thornton reading, one can trace the graduation of the Black/music/gun crime geometry as a moral panic from a localized concern situated within and between the police and the Black communities, to an unprecedented societal crisis demanding the cautionary attention of the nation through an analysis of the processes by which media anxieties over Black music subcultures in the early 2000s accrued a political legitimacy. In the early hours of 2 January 2003, two teenage girls, eighteen-year-old Charlene Ellis and seventeen-year-old Letisha Shakespeare were shot outside a hair salon on Birchfield Road in the Aston area of Birmingham in what was described by the police as being caught in a gang-related drive-by shooting born of a protracted territorial conflict between two local gangs, the Johnson Crew and the Burger Bar Boys. During the killing, over a dozen rounds were fired from a Mac-10 submachine gun, severely injuring three other youths who were with them as they left a New Year's party in the area. The killing of two young Black girls in such circumstances precipitated a sustained national debate on the issue of gun culture as a national crisis, the centrality of race, or Blackness, to the crisis, the role of Britain's Black communities in both instigating and remedying the crisis and the significance of Black youth music as a reliable determinant of the crisis. Notably, while the Metropolitan Police Assistant Commissioner Tarique Ghaffur would cite the 'backdrop of music' as gun crime's primary influence, chiming with the New Labour MP David Blunkett's description of the group's music as 'appalling' (BBC, Wednesday 4 June 2003), we find a demonstration of the mendacious race/music/ gun crime triangulation in more explicit tones by New Labour's Culture Minister Kim Howells who, in a series of racialized comments, would suggest that 'it is a big cultural problem. Lyrics don't kill people but they don't half enhance the fare we get from videos and films. It has created a culture where killing is almost a fashion accessory' (quoted in *Guardian*, Monday, 6 January 2003). Reserving particular vitriol for So Solid Crew's music, he went on to argue:

> Idiots like the So Solid Crew are glorifying gun culture and violence . . . . It is something new. I heard very interesting comments about [violence] in Victorian times and thugs on the street. But they didn't have these methods of popularizing this stuff. It is very worrying and we ought to stand up and say it. (quoted in *Guardian*, Monday, 6 January 2003)

If we are to follow McRobbie and Thornton's description of moral panics as 'a process which politicians, commercial promoters and media habitually attempt to incite' (1995: 559), one can immediately understand Howell's invoking of 'Victorian times' as the euphemistic process of racial differentiation, invaluating the analysis of moral panic as a practice of 'intervening in the public space of opinion and social consciousness through the use of highly emotive and rhetorical language' (1995: 562). Howell's renouncing of So Solid Crew and the description of the combinational symbolism of young Black men, popular Black music and crime as 'something new' is an attempt to present the *Blackness* of gun violence as a phenomenon which the British nation has yet to encounter, a crisis so foreign, unparalleled and potent that neither the State nor its State agents in the police have a method or process of overcoming it. Here, we observe a correspondence with McRobbie and Thornton's analysis of the evolutionary trajectory of moral panic and folk devilling as shifting from the 'unintended outcome' of media reportage to 'an actual ambition' (1995: 561). 'Mendaciousness' again becomes an apt term to interpret Howell's linguistic aptitude towards the denigrative characterization of Black men that recruits the media to substantiate illegitimate concerns over Black urban music and killings as the strategic amplification of benign interrelations; indeed, only one of So Solid Crew's six top-twenty singles between 2000 and 2003 makes any overt lyrical or visual reference to gun violence. Thus, the invective directed towards So Solid Crew becomes denotive of Gilroy's evisceration of the tariff placed on popular Black British culture's acceptance into the British mainstream circulatory as a process of racial laceration through 'the structures of the nation state and the constraints of ethnicity and national particularity' (1993: 19). For Gilroy, the apparent transgression implied in both the presence of Blackness and the associated claim to Britishness via the circulation of popular Black cultural expression is perceived by the dominant social order as 'a provocative and even oppositional act of political insubordination' (1993: 19). To this end, Howell's comments cannot be interpreted as simply 'manning the moral barricades' (Cohen, 1972: 9). Howell's calculated, specific use of 'we' is a call to arms that identifies Black urban music as a nodus point upon which an attempt is made to forge a singular national identity solely in their image as a method for 'orchestrating consent' (McRobbie and Thornton, 1995: 562). In such a rhetorical manoeuvre, Howell positions New Labour as the tribune of the nation and in doing so succeeds in revitalizing the extant racial disdain through a new Black nomenclature (So Solid Crew) and Garage music is established as a proxy for 'Black' crime (gun culture). Beyond possessing the essential tenets of disproportionality and consensus construction supporting the moral panic's fundamental telos that fulfils the Hall(ian) moral-panic criteria through which discourses of racial criminality can operate and flourish, this strategy not only provides justification for the systematic response to an alleged Black crisis. This interaction between politics and culture also sets the premise for the political dismissal of Blackness's protracted claim to Britishness, and subsequently exposes the paradoxical nature of New Labour's own political telos in that it ruptures the post-multiculturalist ideals of cultural plurality and inclusion and onto the more comfortable terrain of social division, performed here as a moral concern over violent crime but inextricably derived from a nostalgic fervour over national identity, race and racism. This, to refer again to the Hall et al model, becomes the precondition for the establishment of authoritative 'social and legislative action' (McRobbie and Thornton, 1995: 562), anointing in this strategic process the Government as the proactive and purposive defenders of the moral social order. Of course, one can recognize such methods as the continuation of a deep legacy of racial animus motivating the hyper-policing of Black cultural forms that are collapsed uncritically into the hegemonic architecture of moral panic to structure the principle of the constricting of Britain's Black population into a dissembling technology of race relations. This hyper-policing was (and remains) most notable in the Notting Hill Carnival and the cultural suppressing of the reggae Soundsystem in the 1970s (Hebdigie, 1979; Nwonka, 2022) and found contemporary manifestation in the widespread use of Form 696, a 'risk assessment' procedure that specifically decreed that public music venues provide details to the Metropolitan Police on the ethnic composition of its proposed audience and the genre of music to be performed (Ilan, 2012). My second point functions in symbiosis with the first, and is concerned with how McRobbie and Thornton advance a development of the moral panic/folk devil dialectic in which those youth identities can now contest their public castigating through making use of the very media sources complicit in their original stigmatization. It should be understood that this exercise is achieved not through a democratizing of the means of mainstream media production, one that may (despite McRobbie and Thornton's acknowledgement of the media's recruiting of pressure groups and reformed deviants-cum experts to provide sound bites for their reporting) permit folk devils to narrate their own circumstances from an authentic, oppositional vantage point, but via the dynamics of media power governing vertical social relations that entails a reliance on the benevolent offerings by media outlets sympathetic to their situation (1995). To this end, McRobbie and Thornton's theorization of modern folk devils professes an unstable faith in both the ability of the marginalized folk devils to transcend the limitations of their own negated position to successfully appeal to the better nature of previously hostile legacy media outlets, but equally, and more problematically, a faith in the idea that the media will emerge responsive to the counter-hegemonic desires of the socially devilled, the latter constructed on an indeterminate heterogeneity of mass media where organizations, journalists, newspapers, broadcasters, editors and commissioners prove resistant to hegemony. The implications revealed here are that the counter-narrative of McRobbie and Thornton's agency-laden folk devil cannot be achieved, realized or enactioned *independently* of the media organizations, necessitating a codependency in which the media remains the agency that orchestrates both the production and presence of a distinct, antithetical voice.

Despite the points of departure and disagreement within my critical reading of McRobbie and Thornton, I also find that their reconsideration of moral panic and the related position and identity of its primary actors provides a theoretical sustenance to this chapter's development of an analytical synthesis of evil/deviance through which moral panic becomes inscribed within the fictitious and non-fictitious urban text. This sustenance is found in the assertion that occupies the centre of the McRobbie and Thornton analysis: that those identified as folk devils (either deviant or evil) are bestowed with the powers of (re)representation through the media that proves conducive for an analysis of how the spectacle of racial alterity may produce a novel negotiation between the criminalization of Black male identity and the empowering dimensions of the media that allow for the amplification of voices and social dialects that have been previously disavowed and neglected. I should at this point stress that, in a reading that isolates McRobbie and Thornton's theory of a counter-narrating folk devil, what is essential to my interest in this particular rendering of folk-devilled Black identities within urban space and their hegemonic framing as a subject of social concern is how it interacts with the versatile neoliberal logics of cultural representation to be found in the UK creative industries. This kind of comparative practice, where an exploration of the Black urban crisis/ mediatization nexus finds methodological favour in the disciplinary agility of Cultural Studies which allows for a textual, formal and political economy analysis of the complex assemblages of the Black urban image system as a convention that has emerged within a historical, political and cultural context, presents a conceptual pathway for an account of how screen culture becomes positioned to mediate the imagined social crisis of Black gun crime and urban violence and the decisive role of PSB in advancing both the Black urban condition as an 'issue of national concern' and cultural diversity as the justificatory condition for 'authentic' Black cultural production and crucially, representation. To return to my reading of the development of the hauntological Black male urban *Other* as the central figure of a modern moral panic, an observable phenomenon that will later be threaded through the logics of screen industry cultural diversity and inclusion, I want to update the context of analysis offered by McRobbie and Thornton to support the entry of an institutional climate of racial inclusivity (Nwonka, 2020a; Saha, 2021) that encourages one to think about the Black urban aesthetic as an outcome of the interplay between the instrumentalist yet reductive hybridity of the screen industries and the raw, selective materials of a Black urbanity. Of course, the absence of this gesture can be attributed to cultural diversity 'theory' not yet fully entering the Cultural Studies paradigm at the point of McRobbie and Thornton's study, and in my own effort to describe the cultural commodification of the Black urban as a technology of Black world-making that finds its adapted authenticity in print media's own habitation and reorientation of the Black urban as *spectre*, is to also observe a novel interrelatedness; the popular media reportage of Black crisis exhibits a cohabitation of affects that produce at one moment desire, at others satisfaction, at another disdain, and it is from this vantage point that I want to now draw attention to the social and cultural processes that present the narrating of the inner-city identity as a process of *conversion*. In February 2002, Brendon Lawrence, aged sixteen, died after being shot several times while sitting in a car in the St Ann's area of Nottingham. On November 2003, Omar Watson, aged twenty-four, was shot dead by a gang at a unisex hairdresser's in the nearby inner-city area of Radford, and fourteen-year-old Danielle Beccan was shot dead by two gang members in St Anne's on 9 October 2004, incidents that would strengthen the denigrative, colloquial description of the city as 'Shottingham' (*The Observer*, Sunday, 5 August 2007; The Telegraph, 15 February 2006) a term that would be circulated by the media to institute within the popular imaginary Nottingham as the epicentre of Britain's Black gun crime crisis and in doing so, portray the city as an area 'ridden with crime, drugs, gangs and drugs' (McKenzie, 2016: 43). In my referencing of these shootings, I want to argue that the media coverage of these incidents, as we encounter, are marked by all the characteristics and facets suggested by Goode and Ben-Yehuda (1994) who, in aligning with the folk devil/moral-panic equation, ask that for a phenomenon to be accepted as a moral panic, the following hallmarks must all be present: (1) a heightened degree of *concern* over the behaviours of a particular social group; (2) the degree of *hostility* directed towards this social group is higher than normal; (3) a *consensus* must be achieved across society that the group's actions present a genuine and significant threat to the functioning of society; (4) there must be a clear *disproportionality* between the perception of the threat the group poses and its reality; and (5) the public reaction to the perceived social threat the group poses manifests as a multi-modal and, resultingly, unsustainable level of *volatility* towards the group, cyclical in its nature, and due to the disproportional sensationalism of media reportage, it is generally evanescent; it emerges and disappears within a short space of time (33–8). Such hallmarks become important analytical objects as they reveal what Hall defines as the subject-repositioning potentialities of media operations that seek to cloak in 'common sense' identification the representations of Black identities, formations that themselves emanate from the ideologies of racism (1981), and in an analysis of *The Guardian's* reporting on the issue of Black gun crime, we find the energizing of all the tenets cited within Goode and Ban-Yehunda's taxonomy of moral panics, with slight variations appropriate for the folk devil of a new decade. In an article titled 'Without a gun, you're dead', *The Guardian's* Tony Thompson would write:

> The new era of gun violence arrived in Britain in the early Eighties with the arrival of the first wave of Jamaican gunmen. Having been brought up in a society where violent death was commonplace, the new arrivals had a willingness to show and use guns, both against one another and the police, that was completely unprecedented . . . . Unlike most crime groups, Yardies have few qualms about shooting police officers and for this reason 24-hour armed patrols have been introduced in all major

British cities. The Jamaicans have also spawned a host of imitators, most of whom have never even visited the Caribbean. (*The Guardian*, Sunday, 21 September 2003)

Through the mythologizing racist caricature within this piece, one of twenty-five articles to be written by Thompson in *The Guardian/The Observer* between 1999 and 2005 in which the journalist displays an unconscionable commitment to the phenomenonization of Black gangs and gun violence, we see the fissures of an impending race crisis of a more immediate kind in the discursive shift from a malaise over the sadistic criminal lives of Jamaican Yardies to a concern over those who are now propelled as Jamaican gun crime's natural heirs apparent, British-born Black youths who, in correspondence with Thompson's broader project of instituting gun violence as the organic index of Black culture, 'have never even been to Jamaica' (*The Guardian*, Sunday, 21 September 2003). Hall reminds us what is at play in this example in his description of 'inferential racism' where, in a necessary distinction from an overt racism that, *inter alia*, telegraphs racist social and political perspectives, advocates 'official' racist governance or produces violent racist incitement and finds a dangerous habitat within tabloid and right-wing commentary as a 'vivid popular vernacular' (2021: 105), Hall defines racism in its inferential guise as 'apparently naturalised representations of events and situations relating to race, whether "factual" or "fictional", which have racist premises and propositions inscribed in them as a set of *unquestioned assumptions*' (2021: 105). In both manifestations, Hall observes their presence either singularly or in symbiosis within the meaning-making logics of the British media, and with specific interest in the Black gang/gun crime reportage by *The Guardian*, we find the more contemporary definition of a 'liberal racism'. Brown, Mondon and Winter (2021) argue that, in the cultural essentialist race politics that function as a particular feature of liberal societies, such liberalism draws its non-racist legitimacy only through a comparative basis separation from racism in its 'extreme and illiberal forms' (274) but, as Hall implies, subsequently works to distort and render invisible the more ubiquitous and insidious modes of racist articulation found but rarely contested in the media. Through Thompson's racialized account of gun crime we witness a rupturing of the often unsophisticated analyses that position the media pathologizing of Black criminality as a right-wing idiolect, and as we see in the narratives emanating from the broadly politically liberal *The Guardian/The Observer*, the universality of the ideology of a distinctively 'Black' gun violence and its ability to transcend the political spectrum provides further credence to Cohen's identifying of exaggerated and distorted media coverage as the principle signifiers for moral panics, distortions that typically involve 'sensational headlines, the melodramatic vocabulary and the deliberate heightening of those elements in the story considered as news' (1972: 31). To momentarily draw on Cohen's acervation, a reliance that perhaps nuances Goode and Ben-Yehuda's specifying of the temporality of media interest as a defining feature of moral panics, in headlines such as 'Yardie terror grips London' (18 July 1999), 'Gun crime spreads "like a cancer" across Britain' (5 October 2003), 'Guns, gangs and slaughter stalk the lawless West' (24 August 2003), 'The ethnic connection' (25 May 2003), 'They'll shoot anyone – even the police' (25 May 2003), 'Homegrown gangs shoot to power on our violent streets'

(26 August 2001), we observe a sustained and concerted attempt by *The Guardian/ Observer* to inscribe within the public imagination a climate of racial anxiety. However, we encounter a more immersive narrating of the Black urban imaginary in writer and journalist Graeme McLagan's 2005 book *Guns and Gangs: Inside Black Gun Crime*. McLagen, who was a BBC News and current affairs correspondent and recipient of a Royal Television Society award for his reportage, offers an account of gun violence in London framed around an examination of the clandestine activities of Operation Trident, and the potency of racial signification in the narrating of Black gun crime as a spectacle is illustrated in the promotional blurb offered in the book which states:

> In Guns and Gangs Graeme McLagan lifts the lid on a hugely unreported but important modern-day problem; an expensive problem both in terms of money and young lives. After terrorism, the single greatest worry for law enforcement agencies is gun crime, and in particular the so-called 'black on black' shootings. The statistics are shocking. Black people are the victims of three-quarters of the capital`s gun murders and non-fatal shootings. The shooters in eighty per cent of cases are also black. Most black gun crime occurs in London, but Bristol, Manchester and the West Midlands are also affected; gun crime has become a national concern. Guns and Gangs traces how the trend first started in the late 1980s and early 1990s with the emergence of the so-called Yardies and crack cocaine, and the consequent turf wars. Since then, the Police have launched numerous operations to tackle the problem, the big turning point for which came after the murder of black teenager Stephen Lawrence. Most of these operations have been kept secret over the years. Now, however, Scotland Yard is prepared to open up Operation Trident in an unprecedented way, allowing McLagan exclusive access to files and case histories, showing how black gun crime is being confronted in a joint effort by police and the black community. In 2004, there were the first welcome signs of black gun crime decreasing, but the easy availability of guns and community violence in other areas of society means that this problem is far from solved. This fascinating in-depth study, containing interviews with police officers, victims, their families, witnesses, lawyers and perpetrators, highlights this under-explored phenomena and offers valuable insights into the psychology behind this disturbing form of crime. (McLagan, 2005)

I would like to make two critical observations within this passage that, in its reliance on classic elements of fiction (character/plot/conflict/theme/P.O.V.) that prepare for the conversion of moral panics over Black men/youths and violent crime into specific modes of narrative fiction and in its promise to include the voices of victims, perpetrators and family members and understanding this inclusive process in alignment with the modalities of counter-representation *a la* McRobbie and Thornton, we are confronted with a number of signifiers within the passage that both anticipate my analysis of the ways in which the media culture and its pathological association of gun crime with Black urban identity constructs a substantive link with the annotative attentiveness of fictitious and non-fictitious film texts towards Blackness. But equally, these serve my contention that the circulatory power of the hegemony of Black crisis, conflict and death emerges as the primary tenets of a social aesthetic that immediately populate the popular Black urban film. Both are concerned with the question of *form*. Beyond the obvious racial myopia evident within the entry (Stephen Lawrence was not killed by black-on-black gun violence, thus the relationship McLagan constructs between his racist murder and an increase in police activity against black-on-black gun crime is beyond disingenuous), McLagan's prose oscillates between the detail and preoccupation with minutiae generally found within investigative journalism and the dramatic elements of crime fiction novels, with the promise of interviews with officers, families and witnesses experienced as gestural, real-life characters akin to a police procedural series. These render the accounts of Black gun crimes (and the Metropolitan Police's methods of solving them) as essential and compelling reading, and to draw again from Hall et al's reading of the hegemonic positioning of Black men and criminality within the ideologies of 'common sense' (1978), McLagan's description of gun crime as a distinctive psychological incubus within London's Black community accomplishes the spectacle of intra-race violence as a differentiating of the self from the Other through an alleged criminal culture, bound in nature. This is evidenced by his sustained focus on the Stonebridge Estate in North West London as a locus of Black gun crime and, resultingly, the Metropolitan Police's Operation Trident activity. In 2003, both twenty-one-year-old Kavian Francis-Hopwood and seven-year-old Toni-Ann Byfield and her father were shot dead in separate incidents (Hales, 2005) and in August 2005, in what would be declared by the media as an 'execution' (*The Guardian*, Tuesday, 9 August 2005), two sisters aged twenty-seven and thirty-four and their mother's sixty-two-year-old partner were murdered on the estate's Clark Court, an incident that would spark several days of widespread national news coverage (BBC News, Friday, 5 August 2005; *The Telegraph*, Friday, 5 August 2005; BBC News, Saturday, 6 August 2005; *The Times*, Monday, 8 August 2005; *The Guardian*, Monday, 8 August 2005; *The Guardian*, Tuesday, 9 August 2005; *The Telegraph*, Wednesday, 10 August 2005; BBC News, Thursday, 11 August 2005). Categorizing the incident as a 'new low in depravity', Lee Jasper, the Chairman of Operation Trident's Independent Advisory Group would describe the murder as 'one of the most horrific killings ever experienced by the Black community in London' (quoted in *The Guardian*, Tuesday, 9 August 2005). Combined with the continued reporting on a number of knife killings in North West London, these media headlines worked to substantiate media reports that the area alone had the highest murder rate in Britain (BBC News, Thursday, 15 February 2001). In the fatal shooting of Leon Labastide on the estate in 2010, the position of Black youths as the central component of the media's racist genealogies would lead the prosecuting QC to judge the crime as indicative of an indiscriminate 'law of the jungle'-culture of violence permeating the estate (quoted in *The Guardian*, Monday, 26 July 2010). Thompson and McLagan's portraiture of Black gun violence as a national crisis equally performs as a visual code, and the latter is supported by the graphic viscerality of the book, which contained a number of images of Black male suspects/convicts and their victims, including women and children, and official police forensic photographs of prone, dead Black bodies at the very scene of their murders. In unifying the two texts as possessing identical linguistic and epistemic co-ordinates, there are two observable features that paradoxically satisfy both Hayne's demand for the traits of 'evilness' to be a prime consideration for the public categorizing of folk devils and for the evolutionary fissuring of the very concept of folk devils as instinctively 'deviant'. In both Thompson and McLagan's evocative language, while making no explicit use of the term, 'evil' remains euphemized in the descriptive nature of the crimes and crucially the toxic legacies of the racist characterization of Black men. Therefore, the introduction of guns to the armoury of 'Black' crime equally heralded a transition from the folk devil of the late 1970s, which situated Black youths in the context of *deviance* (mugging) to the folk devil of the 2000s, which attempts, with evident success, to abstract Black men into an organic association with *evil* (murder). Second, we observe within their rich lexicons an additional paradox where Thompson and McLagan present moral panics and folk devils as both dialectically entwined and distinct; as we see in the earlier examples, a moral panic may not be a prerequisite for the identification of folk devils. However, within this lexical analysis we observe a novel commodification of Black identity through its dramatic language that works to present 'home-grown' Black youths as the obvious candidates for folk devilling, a conditional status driven by an accumulative impetus given the social group are already subject to a pre-existing racial hostility. Significantly, we again observe how this construction of Black youth/gun crime resides with the definition of moral panic as the 'strong, widespread (although not necessarily universal) fear or concern that evil doings are afoot, that certain enemies of society are trying to harm some or all of the rest of us' (Goode and Ben-Yehuda (1994: 11)). In their sensationalizing of Black gun violence, a classic moral panic is renewed through its reconciling with a very palatable folk devil, a unification of which neither Thompson nor McLagan make any attempt to separate. Thus, at the basis of their eager development of a contemporary moral panic in the *narrativizing* of the Black gun crime, which should not be conflated with its *reporting*, both entries perform as an effective consensus-building strategy designed to usher in an unfounded racial anxiety, where Black folk devils must occupy the moral panic's epistemological centre and social perturbation is required for the knowing, processing, subscribing and reacting to the scourge of Black youth gun crime as hegemonic. My extended engagement with the fallacies within the Black gun crime moral panic is not to counter any truth to McLagan's or Thompson's analysis; that the Metropolitan Police indeed established Operation Trident in response to the increase in gun crime among Black men in London and the demands of the Black community for action, such as the aforementioned 'Not Another Drop' campaign (Hales, 2005). More pertinently, and in slender accordance with the causality dilemma McRobbie and Thornton pose in asking us to consider if the media are the architects of moral panics or simply the conduit through which they are telegraphed (1995), the acceptance of moral panics as a process of accelerated distortion in which media outlets 'exaggerate, grossly, the seriousness of events' (Cohen, 1972: 31) is to point to the eagerness and ability of the Black urban moral panic to be converted into desirable forms of useful race fiction, with the uptake of black-on-black as a polarizing *genre*, a plausible mode of 'common sense' dramatic narration and storytelling that, presented under the guise of public knowledge, produce the twin social responses of fear and intrigue.

The phenomenon, or conditional impact of the racial moral panic, is not confined to the simple presence of 'official' disdain towards Black youths from the various spheres of white society, and in our accepting of the moral panic as a consensus-building strategy, we see how the influential scope of moral panics produces manifold expressions of anxiety in popular discourse. Indeed, in October 2003, Diane Abbott, the long-standing Labour MP for London's Stoke Newington who in winning the Hackney North and Stoke Newington Constituency in 1987 became the first Black female MP to be elected to the House of Commons, would face public criticism as a result of her revelation that she had removed her eleven-year-old son from the state school system and was sending him to the £10,000-a-year City of London School, a decision that Abbott, who had previously been a staunch defendant of the state school system and publicly criticized both Labour leader Tony Blair and the party's Solicitor General Harriet Harman for their own decisions to send their sons to selective grammar schools, would herself describe as 'indefensible' (BBC, 2003). My referencing of this debate is less invested in the charge of hypocrisy levelled at Abbott as a result of the decision, but the advancing of race and the urban as a rationale. In explaining the decision some years later, Abbott would draw on the prevailing 'crisis' of young Black males, gang culture and gun violence as a veritable fear, stating:

> I'd done a lot of work on how black boys underachieve in secondary schools so I knew what a serious problem it was. I knew what could happen to my son if he was sent to the wrong school and got in with the wrong crowd. I realised they were subjected to peer pressure and when that happens it's very hard for a mother to save her son. Once a black boy is lost to the world of gangs it's very hard to get them back and I was genuinely very fearful of what could happen. (quoted in The Mirror, 21 June 2010)

In an earlier interview on BBC Radio 4, where Abbott would contextualize the decision within a concern over the efficacy of Hackney's state schools in offering Black boys protection against the allure of violent Black youth gangs, opprobrium was directed towards her attempt to present as a *necessity* (rather than as a choice) her placing her son into independent schooling as an outcome of an undifferentiated and unified Black societal anxiety towards the fatal influence of working-class Black boys, with the obvious discordance being that in Abbott one encounters a differentiated Black identity stratified by the possession of substantial economic, social and cultural capital. Thus, criticism was levelled at Abbott on the basis of her apparent black exceptionalism; her status as a Cambridge University-educated MP with a then-parliamentary salary of £56,000, and the cultural notoriety gained beyond politics through her weekly, paid appearances on the flagship BBC politics and current affairs show *This Week* (2003–19) alongside Andrew Neil and the Conservative MP Michael Portillo. In defending her choice of schooling for her son, Abbott would tell Neil, 'I'm a West Indian mum and West Indian mums will go to the wall for their children' (*Guardian*, 27 June 2010). Here, in applying the prefix 'West Indian', as opposed to Afro-Caribbean or Black mums, Abbott invokes a term possessing an inherently political description of Black motherhood that, perhaps recalling her own working-class childhood in Paddington in the 1960s and 1970s, consecrates the West Indian mother as an identity of resistance, invoking an instinctive matriarchal protection from the varied manifestations of white racism (Lawrence, 1982; Alexander, 1996; Bryan et al., 2018). In the context of the modalities of moral panic, the anxiety-provoking structures of race-based phenomena imbue a transition in Abbott's expansion of the West Indian mother's function as a defence against institutional white racism to the West Indian mother as a defence against an intra-racial Black threat within the urban environment, impelling social extrication as the remedy and, in turn, a deliverance from a political condition in which the residual Black populace are to seek consolation in the chimeric hope of an eventual intra-parliamentary remedy to the crisis. As she went on to conclude, 'all I can do is continue to campaign on issues around education and on issues of gun crime for the benefit of a whole generation of young men in our inner cities' (*The Guardian*, Tuesday, 27 June 2010). My own hypothesis surmises Abbott's comments as a reluctant but ultimately ineluctable resignation to the hegemony of black-on-black gun- and gang-crime, and is therefore an invitation to consider the cosmopolitanism of racial moral panic that finds habitation within the very textures of Black Britain, and there are a notable set of continuities with the manoeuvres of consensus in the response offered by Abbott. First, a regime of hopeless resignation is instituted, one that implies the inevitability of gang culture and gun crime as the outcome of the state schooling of Black boys within Hackney. Second, and underpinning my interest in the relative durability of moral panics, the statement unveils the potency of the politics of race in the implications within Abbot's description of the synonymy between Black youthhood and guns/gangs within the inner-city enclave, specifically that the Black youth crime problematic can transcend the boundaries of surname, but not class, wealth, regionality and the education system, a set of considerations that implore the West Indian mother to take recourse in, as Abbot does, the ideologies of urban escape and Black uplift. It should be made clear that these factors – her status as a prominent MP and her ability to draw on tremendous economic capital to fund her son's independent schooling – should not deny Abbott her rightful inclusion into the community of proactive and protective Black mothers, West Indian or otherwise, who are situated within Britain's Black inner-city localities where peer-pressure exacerbates the problem of Black youth crime as a product of racism, systemic disadvantage and poverty that make fertile social conditions for gun violence and the very real separation of the Black mother from the Black son. This should not dissuade us, however, from pursuing a necessary interrogation of the heterogeneous forms of the contemporary moral panic, articulated through Abbott's anxiety-driven response to the phenomenon of Black death through the hegemonic vocabulary of Black youth gang-crime. In the specific case of race and criminality, this produces the very dialectical tension found in Hayle's demand for an epistemological separation of the social phenomenon from the social deviant; a folk devil may well exist without a moral panic, but my own interpretation of the phenomena of black-on-black violence asks for a reading that privileges the Hallian diagnosis of 'official' social crises and the media-accredited knowledges that sustain them as the manifestation of the hegemonic control of the postcolonial city, a triumph of social consent secured within the embracing structures of racism. Through the amplifying of racial ambivalences and intra-racial trepidations that are ballast by the hegemony of gang/gun violence, the Black working-class youth is always in the *dormant* status of folk devil, a constant and denigrated social presence in wait for dominant power to assign a moral panic to and within this process, hauntologically resurrect the Black youth into the prism of popular consciousness as an immediate threat demanding regressive modes of state action. Our mediatized encounter with the Black body and Black death creates a death-orientated understanding of gun violence that can perform hegemonically *as* Black identity, as Black culture and as the Black experience. By this, I am suggesting that we encounter a bidirectional quarry; white society is haunted by the moral panic of the Black urban folk devil hegemonically projected through the Black body, and the Black existence is haunted through the spectre of Black gun crime and death.

7

'Fuck Society'

Tower Block Dreams, Adjacent PSB and Urban Subcultural Excessivity

Nothin's equivalent to this council estate of mind
Skinnyman, 'Council Estate of Mind', 2004

By the early 2000s, at a moment where the political discourse on race had been reconfigured by the legislative notion of institutional racism, and somewhat embodied by the 'hideously white' accusation levelled at the BBC by its own Director General Greg Dyke in 2001 (Born, 2005; Nwonka, 2020a), a renewed sociopolitical context to the PSB policy frame was observed in the proliferation of the concepts of cultural diversity and creative innovation, both to be brought into being via the wider instrumentalist ideals of the UK's developing creative industries. With a reliance on the sharp Hall(ian) distinction between multiculture as a lived experience of social and cultural difference and multicultursal*ism* as a system of political governance mediating the manifold tensions and vicissitudes within the pluralistic society (Hall, 2000) and the commanding orthodoxy of post-racialism as a 'tolerant multiculturalism' that enables, accepts and accommodates the presence of the Other devoid of its otherness (Žižek, 2010), Malik (2013) identifies the highly political process through which cultural inclusion is constituted within the policies of the UK's two PSB organizations, BBC and Channel 4, and how such strategies become the technology through which race (as a question of difference) and racism (as a practice of discrimination) are now 'handled and driven underground' (228) through a periodizing of the development of 'creative diversity' as the 'official' nomenclature of post-multiculturalism. My close attentiveness to the ideological intonations at play in the creative diversity industry doxa provides a necessary complexity to the analysis of the erasure of the anti-racist premise to the representational demands of Britain's Black and Asian communities as (a) the denial of race as an aggravating factor within New Labour's Third Way doctrine of equality of opportunity and the transcendence of the structures of inequality and (b) a dissolving of the categories of identification and racial essentialism in favour of an alignment with the prevailing discourse of racial assimilation (an alignment most vividly expressed in Channel 4's then director Michael Jackson's 2001 declaration that the ethnic minorities of the 1980s and 1990s that the channel had been mandated to represent had now been fully (and equally) included within British society (Nwonka, 2015) allows for the analysis of the strategies of post-racism to be situated within the context of the UK PSB's inclusivity aims of widening access to Britain's Black and minority ethnic identities. Notably, BBC 1Xtra, launched in August 2002 as a digital radio station dedicated to Black and urban music and the national expansion of the previously regionally broadcast BBC Asian Network in October 2002 saw the industrial maximization of both the neoliberal expansion of the UK's cultural and creative industries and the implicit policy decrees in response to racial equality and inclusion inscribed within the 1999 Macpherson Report (UK Government, 1999). In addition, a key development in the rhetorical trajectory of the inclusion agenda was the establishing of the Cultural Diversity Network in 2000, where the main UK broadcasters (BBC/ITV/Channel 4/Sky) would create a collaborative forum to promote diversity within the television and broadcasting sector. In considering the modalities of PSB diversity, we observe a departure from previous modes of institutional support for Black and minority ethnic film and TV, notably at Channel 4 in the 1980s where their funding and commissioning model was specifically designed to protect extra-commercial Black and ethnic minority programming from market forces and provide fertile industrial conditions for an autonomous mode of cultural production (Mercer, 1988; Ross, 1996). There are several points through which we must consider how the politics of race become dislodged within the post-multiculturalist arena of 'cultural rights' (Hall, 1988). Saha (2018) has interrogated UK PSB's predisposition towards the culturalizing of racial politics through the symbolic actions of cultural/creative diversity. Here, PSB's evasiveness towards systemic reform, its commitment to the discursive modalities of representational diversity and its adherence to neoliberal imperatives of innovation, economic logic and cultural consumption render PSB diversity as a constellation of strategic practices that cannot prove inimical to the continued normalization of racial discrimination within the sector. In the specific example of the BBC, we find that such race politics exist on the continuum of the strategies of cultural compartmentalization, in which racism is not ameliorated by PSB diversity but redefined, rearticulated, minimized and converted into insidious but significant forms of cultural compensation, manifestations of industry pluralism which underpin my reading of creative diversity as the locus of the amalgamation of a number of competing tensions, desirables and interests. A primary example of this amalgamation in practice is found in the February 2003 launch of BBC Three, a free-to-air digital channel which had replaced BBC Choice and had a distinctive remit to offer innovation in programming to a newly identified sixteen to thirty-four target audience. Broadcast daily between 19.00 pm and 4.00 am, the analogous nature of BBC Three and other similar channels emerges in language forms that appear to suggest a homology between them, and if one can consider the launch of the channel through the prism of neoliberal commercialism, one can understand the very conceiving of BBC Three as a response to the competition presented by Channel 4's E4, launched in 2001 to similarly cater to the tastes and interests of a neglected youth demographic. However, while there were clear ideological correlations between the two channels through what Malik observes as 'their manifest derivative politics in how they attempt to "out public service the other" in their responses to ethnic minorities' (2013: 235), one can identify a point of departure in the decree that 90 per cent of BBC Three's programming would originate from the UK, with 70 per cent of this figure being of original content with a particular emphasis on new comedy, original drama, documentaries and current affairs showing as an alternative to the more traditional programming offered by both BBC One and Two. My analysis of post-Macphersonism as the primary factor in the industrial shift to questions of identity and inclusion revive what Hall refers to as a 'conjunctural moment', emerging in this example in the birth of cultural diversity within PSB and its movement towards the political logics through which PSB diversity policy operates as a decoy for the more subtle forms of post-race-making. However, in my own critical reading of Malik's examination, I want to point to an analytical neglect: that the ideological distribution of creative diversity is concentrated to within the mainstream of the two broadcasters (BBC and Channel 4). The presence of BBC Three and the specificity of its remit performed a key function in mediating the more intimate conflict between the market-based imperatives of PSB and the engineering of cultural difference and representation. The critical problem within the case studies Malik offers, which gesture towards a *homogenizing* of the main UK PSBs, and one that does not completely undermine Malik's more general evisceration of creative diversity policy as the outcome of the wider political crisis of (post) multiculturalism, is that this focus disallows a consideration of the expansion of both broadcasters through the creation of youth-orientated adjacent channels that became a key site for the pursuit of PSB diversity through a less antiquated form of programming. In the example of BBC Three's specific mandate, we can identify the energizing of the three factors that would come to concretize PSB's inclusion agendas within Malik's ontology of creative diversity – market, regulatory and social – and in sharp departure from Malik's own taxonomy of PSB rationalities, and in the use of BBC Three as an exemplar, I want to argue that such industrial predicaments are in fact interweaving, inter-reliant and cross-pollinated. First, in developing Malik's assertion that the creative diversity uptake by PSB's caters to *market* predicaments, BBC Three's mandate allows for a nuancing of the acute binary between the key principles of the BBC and Channel 4, and BBC Three represents a separation from the BBC's general emphasis on quality as the primary criterion of distinction (both economic and cultural) *vis-à-vis* Channel 4's historic association with 'innovation, imagination, flexibility, and excellence' (2013: 236). For BBC Three, creativity and innovation emerge as a definitive feature of such adjacent PSB platforms, and there is potential for us to observe a similar dynamic in its convergence on some of the characteristics that would prove conducive to the rhetorical *social* aims of creative diversity. As a holistically automated channel, its technological and stylistic features became the means through which BBC Three became a conducive platform for diverse on-screen representation and talent, and we encounter these practices of diversity and innovation in BBC Three's *60 Seconds* news bulletins, a 1-minute news report on the day's headlines screened at the end of each programme. The news segment exhibited a number of features that serve as testament to the description of

BBC Three as an alternative PSB sphere where its reconfiguring of representational difference liberated the main of the channel from the increasing obligations of inclusion, diversity and representational plurality. Notably, *60 Seconds* would become the training ground for a number of Black and ethnic minority newsreaders who would later forge careers within mainstream news programming, such as Charlene White, Sam Naz, Tasmin Lucia-Khan and Tazeen Ahmad. Further, and in accordance with BBC Three's overall aesthetic, the channel's innovative branding in the use of animation and urban music in its idents and *60 Seconds's* highly visual format proved attractive to a youth audience group less inclined to watching more traditional news broadcasts.

Despite my nuancing of the construction of PSB diversity and innovation as a technology of post-racial formation, I find value in the general proposition that the concept of creative diversity was responsive to *social* predicaments, and one can cite a further development of this social imperative in the concept of 'mobile media' (Wei, 2013), a nascent, proto-form of what would later in the decade emerge as an academic hermeneutic for 'on-demand' content that maximized the advent of new digital platforms and in turn, aided the circulation of diversity through the provision of non-linear programming and interactive televisual experiences for a young and diverse audience. The correlation between BBC Three's digital capabilities and the principles of diversity within the prevailing social and political context of the early 2000s is significant as this underpinned a staunch belief in the utility of BBC Three and E4 as a platform for diverse cultural participation and, subsequently, as an enabler of the more insidious political project of social inclusivity. Indeed, one can identify BBC Three's desire to create strategies to remedy broader social concerns in the emphasis on 'creative risk-taking' through online provision and culturally diverse content as an alternative to linear programming, heralding an amalgamation of neoliberal discourses of creative innovation cohabitating with PSB's broader economic imperatives operating within the logic of competitive global markets (Garnham, 2005). If we accept Malik's definition of *regulatory* predicaments as responsive to the new governance of cultural difference in 'enabling compliance with wider legislative and policy frameworks' (2013: 236), one of which being an adherence to the 2010 Equalities Act, we can draw credence in my situating of the ideological modalities of diversity within the decree that BBC Three should in its programming offer an iteration of cultural plurality and representation in keeping with the Corporation's broader inclusion agenda of demonstrating a commitment to creativity, innovation and a continued investment in new television talent, one in which its methods are identified within Newsinger and Eikhof's idea of implicit diversity policy as the product of macro-level, economic, infrastructural or regulatory policies that produce unintended outcomes within cultural governance (2020). Evocative of a nascent cultural politics of transference and instrumentalization, its status as an ancillary PSB platform positioned BBC Three as ideally suited to carry out the task of 'stimulating creativity and cultural excellence' (BBC, 2003) and in this endeavour, the channel becomes the axis upon which the BBC demonstrates a legislative adherence to media policies on, and significant creative and economic contributions to, Chris Smith's utopian vision of the UK's creative industries as a productive engine of social cohesion (1998). It is of significance that each of the predicaments Malik identifies – market, social and regulatory – finds habitation within the textual representations of cultural difference we find in BBC Three's output (*Being Human*, *W10 LDN*, *60 Seconds*, *Synchronicity*). This said, it is important to be cognizant of my caution at the vested processes through which the creative industries attempt to enact cultural diversity within an unchallenged neoliberal framework that both professes a commitment to meritocracy and cultural pluralism while simultaneously erecting barriers to entry, rendering the screen industries as a continuing site of inequality and exclusion (Oakley, 2004; Hesmondhalge, 2008; Nwonka, 2020a). I do not imply that such modalities of creative diversity are not, at some level, productive in the continued politics of 'the relations of representation' (Hall, 1988). Indeed, one can conceive the politics of diversity as a system of positional interplay within public institutions that permits the incremental and temporal presence of Black and ethnic minority identities, revealing creative diversity to be an ideological construct that itself avows hierarchies, exclusions and ideological coercions and through which concession, attrition, compromise *but* inclusion become *the* conditional experience through which difference remains situated within the game of cultural 'wars of position' (Hall, 1993: 107). Rather, the primary conceptual project implies a protean nature to PSB creative diversity that attempts to remedy a number of social tensions that cannot be resolved by attempts to minimize and relegate racial conflict as the basis for Black and ethnic minority exclusion. In this endeavour, I share with Hall the theoretical corpus that culture and cultural processes are forms of competing tensions, an index of broader social relations and a site of perpetual social and political contestation. However, my specific contribution to the analysis of diversity as a neoliberal gambit is an evisceration of the discursive architecture upon which notions of creative diversity and inclusiveness construct a synthetic and multitudinous response to the demands for racial and ethnic difference, a reluctant *acceptability*, and it is through this polysemicity that I identify a bipolar nature to BBC Three's position as the vanguard of representational alterity in the circumventive nature of the BBC's iteration of creative diversity that, rather than catalysing a repositioning of Black and ethnic minorities to within the centre of the channel, the regulatory, market and social impulses of creative diversity instilled within BBC Three's mandate equally imbues a sectionalization of cultural participation producing what Hall identifies as a 'segregated visibility' (1993: 107). In other words, the compartmentalizing of diverse (Black and minority ethnic) programming and representation within BBC Three's interpretation of cultural difference is condensed to within its peripheral (but innovative and youthful) platform, a telos that chimes with Saha's own admonition of such techniques of PSB diversity that reveal 'a method of including minorities but simultaneously distancing them' (2017: 90). My use of the term 'bipolar' implies that PSB diversity possesses a positive dimension in that in its galvanizing of ethnic minority optimism, utopia, participation and production (in the example of BBC Three) via their urgent coalescing upon the narrow and siloed corridors of UK PSB, the modalities of segregated distancing can be justified under the auspices of innovation, diversity and attending to the needs of new, racially diverse youth audiences, evident in the promise by BBC Three to create output reflecting the representational needs of a diverse UK society to be achieved through, for example, the setting of PSB programming outside of London and, more significantly, the advancing of 'voices and faces from a range of regional and ethnic communities'(BBC Trust, 2014). Demonstrative of how the ideology of cultural diversity, which works to efface certain race-based struggles and realities through a rhetoric-led denunciation of any correspondence between the functions of the UK's screen industries and the purging of racial and ethnic difference within them, such a critique provides a crucial uncovering of the inherently *generative* function of ideology; it produces a retreat from the currents of racism/anti-racism but equally assists in the opening up of new modes of rationality for cultural inclusivity via the cultivation of a fragile but seductive climate of optimism associated with ideas of instrumentalism and the rhetorical desire to utilize minority cultural production under a new political epoch. The conciliatory nature of BBC Three's compartmentalization of racial and ethnic difference encourages the uptake and sustenance of post-racial thought through the provision of racially diverse cultural production, and in drawing from the Hall(ian) critique of cultural practices as a continuous site of social contestation and contradiction and upon which a number of discourses engage and confront, in BBC Three we find a topology of interrelated cultural processes, industrial logics and political strategies that reside within the main contours of the 'politics of racelessness' underpinning a reading of PSB's diversity as the disingenuous, affrontive but powerfully centripetal product of the post-multiculturalist crisis of race and representation.

Irrespective of the evaluative position one may take in regard to the complex genealogies of diversity, such formations are particularly valuable for an analysis of the British urban film as a social aesthetic annotated by an array of cultural and industrial processes, and the centrality of aesthetic experience in its legitimacy as a concrete mode of authenticity, as the predicaments of cultural diversity are irreducible to merely the economic and the political, allow for the interrogation of the formal outcomes of the imperatives that configure PSB diversity; in other words, the form and content of the texts that the ideological spheres of diversity and social crises within film and television produce. I want to return to the question of how, through considering these predicaments, one can develop a critique of the urban text as a distinct extension of the consonance between the phenomena of Black criminality, diverse televisual and cinematic representation and the thematic interests of media discourses on urban identity by drawing attention to the BBC Three decree that 'drama on social issues should aim to inform as well as entertain' (BBC Trust, 2014), which exhibited particular attention to the need for the channel's programming to represent the diverse social experiences and interests germane to its younger audiences. By this, I'm referring to BBC Three's alertness to new urban subcultural practices and the lived experiences of multiculture that were to be brought into being through the channel's emphasis on documentaries, investigative journalism, current affairs programming and the broadcasting of live music. It is of particular value to this analysis that a specific ethos and public affect was mandated for BBC Three's content in that its programming, perhaps displaying a congruency with the mediatized vicissitudes of urban youthhood and peripheral social identities, should not evade the stimulating of topical debate and controversy through its subject matter while remaining within the framework of 'impartiality, accuracy and independence' (BBC, 2003). Again, and as will be expounded in the following chapters, this supports the description of television as a key visual repository provoking a number of 'sociological outcomes' (Born, 2000: 420) and in my reading of the power of PSB to construct, affirm and (re)signify social identities, I equally point to the significance of PSB as the optic through which we would come to encounter the urban text as a filmic experience that emerges from the context of a complex negotiation between a number of frames of meaning, and as a product of cultural contestation, of representational war. One such example was *Tower Block Dreams*, a documentary series broadcast on BBC Three in January 2004 (Figure 7.1). The documentary's production mode was indicative of the BBC Three ethos of encouraging the development of creative, risk-taking UK-based content through the use of new and emerging television voices. Filmed over twelve months by established documentary maker David O'Neal and new directing talent Adam Smith, the series was produced for BBC Three by Dimitri Doganis of the newly founded independent production company Raw, in one of their first major commissions for a UK broadcaster. Across three one-hour episodes screened at the show's 9.00 pm time slot, the series examined the burgeoning UK underground urban music being produced from pirate radio stations in London and the South East. *Tower Block Dreams* would several years later provide the main inspiration for the mockumentary sitcom *People Just Do Nothing* (BBC, 2014–18), which centred on an urban pirate radio station, the fictional Kurupt FM and used a faux documentary style that, as a result of the success of a series of YouTube videos, would lead to a commission for BBC Three's Comedy Feeds strand. Set around a West London council estate, *People Just Do Nothing* parodied the UK Garage, Hip Hop and Grime scene and follows a group of MCs and DJs oblivious to their lack of music talent and the absurdity of their ambitions, and would

Figure 7.1 *Tower Block Dreams* (BBC Three, 2004).

go on to win a Royal Television Society and BAFTA Television award for Best Scripted Comedy in 2017. Introduced during the BBC Three ident as a 'raw and uncompromising documentary' containing 'very strong language and explicit scenes from the outset', these statements aim to present the series as compelling viewing through the spectacle of the contemporary urban, and *Tower Block Dreams* approaches this objective through the lens of a number of young musicians attempting to secure record deals. Filmed on council estates in Islington, Archway, Tottenham, Bow and areas in Southend-on-Sea, the series is governed by a realist, observational documentary aesthetic that, evocative of the visual sensibilities found in the practice of direct cinema (Bruzzi, 2006), demands a cinematic mode of spectatorship as the audience is confronted with a group of young men using music to escape from a cycle of drugs, crime and urban deprivation, and in doing so, bringing to the screen a stratum of British society 'that did not often appear in the media' (*The Guardian*, Thursday, 11 December 2003). In the specific reference to *Tower Block Dreams* as an *alternative* mode of media representation, one that purports to break with the master frames of meaning and dominant modes of narration in its social realist ambitions, aesthetic strategies and approaches, the implicatory functions of the camera in dictating the imagined relationship between identity, spatiality and a perceptible social world permit one to meditate on the formal aspects of the documentary that frame its main subjects in a series of extreme close-ups as Killer, a young DJ/rapper profiled in an episode titled 'Ghetto on Sea' openly takes drugs on-camera, demonstrating a blasé disregard for the moral decrees of mainstream society. In *Tower Block Dreams*'s interest in urban music production, the series aligns itself with the description of BBC Three as a 'digital youth channel' (*The Guardian*, Thursday, 11 December 2003) alive to the emergent subcultures of Britain's urban youth but, in addition, extends its representational scope to the mediatized moral crisis of Britain's working-class youth identities, most notably in the third episode, *Grimetime to Primetime* (22 January 2004), in which its opening title sequence films a young white working-class boy among a group of youths on push bikes playfully dragging another white child across the floor with his arms around the child's neck (the child making choking noises) while looking to the camera and shouting 'I'm an Iraqi soldier, I'm gonna kill the English' before he mimics breaking the child's neck, throwing him to one side. It is worthy of note that this opening montage sequence is edited to the 2003 song 'We Don't Care' by the electronic/urban music duo Audio Bullys. While the song itself more generally becomes an appropriate companion to the series by its metaphorical articulation of the brutal and unsympathetic nature of contemporary society necessitating a nihilism germane to working-class life through its chorus that shouts 'in this world, its sink or swim, what the fuck?', in this opening, the sequence plays the lyrics 'There's things I have not told you, I go out late at night, and if I was to tell you, you'd see my different side', which in turn suggests the documentary will offer an encounter with a deviant social identity. The opening montage employs a rapid, kinetic editing technique that, while presenting multiple facets of estate life also produces a system of repetition through its documenting of the everyday, fleeting moments of the urban youth existence as the sequence cuts between a number of visual signifiers for the yet-to-be understood but culturally verisimilitudinous familiarity of urban,

Figure 7.2 *Tower Block Dreams* title sequence (BBC Three, 2004).

working-class life; the socially distressed symbolism of tower blocks and estates; young people on scooters riding through the confined estate spaces, a group of young Black youths MCing in unison to the camera against the backdrop of a tower block (Figure 7.2) and a distorted, out of focus close-up of a Nokia mobile phone beside a cannabis joint and a hand spinning a record player. Towards the end of the sequence, this rapid editing is accompanied by the voice of the documentary's narrator (actor Leo Gregory) who states, 'in our inner cities just across the road from the mainstream of modern life, there are people struggling though a different world'. We then cut to a clip of a hooded white youth holding a microphone and rapping among both Black and white friends before cutting to a close-up of him in his bedroom, briefly edited over a panning camera shot of a tower block, where he argues, 'like, if you move into a different area than Tottenham, and you go like, a rich area like Hampstead, and look at some 16- or 17-year-olds up there, they would be nothing like us. I'm telling you'.

Both the narration and imagery work to immediately situate the documentary within the multi-ethnic, multicultural city, while establishing the series as a sociopolitical project, with the more serious intentions for the documentary found in its narrating of the urban inner city marked by division, marginalization and otherness and these conditions become the preoccupations of the episode *Grimetime to Primetime* where the series profiles Scarface and Mini-Me, two teenage rappers from a council estate in Tottenham, North London. Demonstrative of the ways in which the documentary's images of epidermal and socio-economic difference become laden with social and cultural meanings, the camera frames the youths in a series of extreme, unstable close-ups as they discuss the meaning of their lyrics as both a defence against the manifold vicissitudes of urban youthhood and a means through which they are able to convey an understanding of their own urban identity; their painful experiences of the care system, poverty (Mini-Me describes to the filmmaker that he was unable to eat as a result of there being no food in his home) and music as a site of racial conviviality, indicative of the ways in which for Bramwell (2015) Rap music 'becomes an important part of the production of particular modes of urban living' (4). Again, and contributing to the authenticity and spontaneity of the documentary's realism in its direct address, Scarface asks to stop filming during heated arguments with both Mini-Me and the group's manager (Red) over her time-keeping and lack of belief in his own efforts to secure the duo a record deal. Despite this episode's interest in Scarface, there is little variety across the series in terms of gender identities and from the documentary's opening sequence, masculine identity is centred and problematized throughout *Tower Block Dreams*, conceiving both urban music and the council estates from which it emerges as arenas within which maleness is the dominant social and creative identity and poses a specific question to the spectator: Is there something particular about the British nation state and associatively, the urban as an existence, a concept, a condition and as a construct that produces a deeply destructive sense of masculine identity that needs to be examined and experienced? In answering this question, the series propels into the foreground the urban text as an idea and practice that emerges from the context of social volatility. An episode titled *Spittin'and Shottin'* (8 January 2004), a title that implies a parallelism between underground urban music production and drug dealing as a means of both funding it and economic survival, features two white North London rappers – Skinnyman (Alexander Graham Holland) attempting to release what would become a landmark UK Rap album *Council Estate of Mind* and Sloth (Charlie Roullion), an MC who would later forge a successful career as a Hip Hop DJ and presenter on BBC Radio One, 1Xtra and Apple Music. The episode places great emphasis on exploring their criminal backgrounds; both men have spent time in prison, curtailing their music careers and adding further incentive to their efforts to establish themselves within urban music. Indeed, for Sloth, who grew up on North West London's Somers Town Estate, his release from prison has been met with a number of death threats from rivals and former acquaintances (Sloth plays to the camera a voicemail of the latest death threat he has received) that become one of the primary motivational factors in his decision to dedicate himself to securing a record deal, an ambition that requires the abandoning of what he terms as the 'ghetto life' of violence and drugs for the liberating corrective of the urban music economy, which White (2017) has referred to as 'a transformative realm' (103). With a specific theoretical interest in the experiences of inner-city working-class Black youths and their involvement in Grime and urban music, White's conceptual project asks to demarcate urban music from other forms of creative production in that it is a culturally specific activity that can lead to the transformation of urban identities through an expanded world view, a movement across geographical and emotional borders and, eventually, economic parameters. In *Tower Block Dreams*, this sphere of social transformation presents itself as a certain form of disruption, in this instance, a disruption of a predetermined and inextricable negative life trajectory maintained by race and class disadvantage and sets the pathway for a new, reformed individual, a transformation catalysed not simply by the production of urban music, but also by the popular recognition, circulation and economic prosperity promised by a recording contract from a major label. Such is the intensity of the localized, underground economy of urban music, an endeavour to be negotiated by the vicissitudes of youth unemployment, violent conflict, marginalization and poverty that Killer, so limited by the conditions of living within what the documentary's narrator describes as 'one of the worst estates in Southend' that his existence is accepted as a simple choice between a career in music and imprisonment, is compelled to vandalize the mast of a rival pirate radio station to sabotage their broadcasts and advance his own station's success. It may be as a result of *Tower Block Dreams* finding assurance in the legibility that accompanies the hegemonic association of specific social and cultural identities with the spectacle of the council estate that the documentary's narrator never expounds on the specific social inequalities and problems qualifying the estate for such a denigrative status, beyond the combinational visage of the estate itself and young working-class people that become sufficient for an ontology of the urban environment conditioned by poverty and crime – a condition that is therefore assumed rather than fully explored. And it is from the symbolic power of the estate as the habitat of a degenerate urbanity that the documentary gestures towards an examination of the ambiguous and transitory divisions between illegality and creativity and the innovative practices and informal underground economies of urban music that, for Bramwell (2015), find their acme within the distinct cultures of the pirate radio stations.

My placing in dialectical tension the ideas of both diversity and the discursive interest in the urban social condition points to how the social, cultural and industrial contexts become critical for the examination of aesthetic modes, a methodological endeavour that reveals a multivalent textuality in *Tower Block Dreams* and the series is constituted by two distinct imperatives. First, and in recalling the BBC's comments in *The Guardian* on the series being an attempt to undo or resolve preconceived ideas, the documentary can be described as motivated by a desire to overcome the more stigmatic mainstream media constructions of urban identities through an authentic counter-representation, an agenda indexed, of course, to BBC Three's status as a platform for the televisual amplification of alternative social and cultural voices. Second, the documentary serves a general audience's horizon of expectation through the fostering of the urban identity and narrative as a televisual/filmic experience that is met with the spectator's own discourse constructed outside of the frame. Both these imperatives serve to legitimize the screening of difficult subject matter, and *Tower Block Dreams* speaks to a heterogeneous spectatorship that allows the documentary series to be evaluated against a broader critical framework and through which we can examine how, despite the documentary's aim to traffic into the popular the narratives of London's underground urban music subcultures, *Tower Block Dreams*'s telegraphing of its urban realities accompanies with it a number of problems that require, at the very least, some acknowledging. Specifically, I'm allured by the possibility that in adopting Hall's assertion that the media is a contradictory and overlapping sphere of 'representations of the social world, images, description, explanations and frames for understanding how the world is and why it works as it is said and shown to work' (2021 [1981]: 104), we can make a critical rupture in the BBC's aim to institute *Tower Block Dreams* as an uncontested mode of hegemonic agitation, in the sense that the series offers a new encounter with the unfamiliar urban other and in doing so may produce knowledges that replace or challenge certainties and foundational narratives held within the national sphere which suggest that the documentary series is primarily evidentiary; its dominant representational strategy is to evidence and then inscribe within the spectator's collective consciousness the fundamental otherness and alterity of the British urban episteme. In borrowing conceptually from Foucault (1970) the idea of the (urban) episteme, I'm suggesting that this is an alterity one cannot fully access but visually experience, an immersive but still distanced social space that is positioned and comprehended within multifaceted and intertextual knowledge derived from a number of external source texts that translate the denotive meanings of the organic creative practices and social conditions. However, although the combinational gravitas of BBC Three's production preamble and the realist narrating of hitherto ostracized urban identities aims to advance the series as a subversive mode of social representation, *Tower Block Dreams's* on-screen ideology does not necessary correspond with this ambition. Significantly, Celia Taylor, the BBC3 commissioner who was the executive producer of the documentary, would state that

> most of the time these people don't really operate within the establishment. It was a real achievement to get their trust and get them to open up. One minute you really like them and the next minute they reveal themselves as a rough lot, they reveal their attitudes. I haven't seen anything this honest and raw for a long time.
> (quoted in *The Guardian*, Thursday, 11 December 2003)

This acknowledging of the significance of the documentary's spectator as a conduit of meaning affirms *Tower Block Dreams's* situating within an array of discourses, and the ideological implications within Taylor's enthusiastic assertion that the 'revelation' of the men's true selves secures audience disdain may bring into question the very *raison d'etre* for the series, beyond the representation of urban identities and the socially and culturally defined music practices and incidents that take place within the urban geography. The invoking of descriptive terms such as 'raw' and 'honest', expressions which would later emerge as synonymous within the popular, mainstream critique of the popular Black British urban film, is applied here as a descriptive euphemism for a visual and narrational confronting of a class-determined racial and cultural alterity and emphasizes the spectacle of the unknown, here assured – in this example – through a novel proximity to the urban Other, and forms a deeply complex system of signifiers and communications between subject and spectator(s). Commensurate with *Tower Block Dreams's* adherence to the cultural verisimilitude that envelopes urban identities within the popular imaginary, the young men candidly discuss their experiences with knife and gun crime, part of a general mode of representation through which the documentary series presents the urban condition as a simple but no less turbulent pathway choice between underground, independent music production (and the social and economic liberation it may bestow upon them) and the seeming inevitability of violent conflict, criminality and prison that awaits them without it. In this moment, the audience is confronted with a modified subversive representation in which both right and wrong occupy an ambiguous position within the social/cultural causation nexus. For example, in *Spittin' and Shottin'*, Sloth is filmed in the aftermath of a violent attack by three armed men who had broken into his flat and stabbed him multiple times during an attempt to steal his drugs/money, an incident which resulted in one of the men physically assaulting his girlfriend.

Skinnyman, who had previously lost a record deal after being imprisoned for cannabis possession, would finally be offered a recording contract only to be again sent back to prison for drug dealing. These moments capture young working-class men's difficulties living within economically depressed and violent locales, and we observe *Tower Block Dreams*'s fidelity to the heterogeneity of the urban environment and the hybrid cultures and identities that inhabit it through the series's featuring of both Black and white Rap/urban music artists. While the documentary's close framing of the cultural and physical spaces within which such music is produced reveals the organic cultural relationships developed through UK rap and urban music subcultures that present the urban as a seemingly uncontested site for racial conviviality, the series does offer a very brief engagement with the impacts of race and racism in Gambit, a young Black rapper who speaks openly about the difficulties of living in the predominantly white Southend. In the episode, we see how his existence as a racialized Other is conditioned by the reality of habitual police harassment as he is filmed being apprehended by two police officers on the suspicion of selling Class-A drugs, prompting an angry reaction from both Gambit and observers to the continued injustice of racist policing (he later appears in court charged with drug offences and carrying an offensive weapon). This said, despite the variety of aesthetic registers that comprise *Tower Block Dreams* it is noteworthy that, perhaps as the combinational outcome of its narrative focalisation, homogeneity in the hegemonic fixity of the individuals to their social habitat and the significance and weightiness of composition and camerawork in conditioning the spectator's interpretation of social reality, it is the semi-distant aesthetic of surveillance that emerges as the dominant aesthetic form through which a number of deviant behaviours are filmed; the camera follows Sloth, who is currently on bail, to a North London tower block where he attempts to confront a former acquaintance in retribution for him being arrested by the police for allegedly setting fire to his car on the estate, a crime in which Sloth denies any involvement. The youth, known as Danger, evades Sloth by running into the flat of a young mother in another tower block on the estate. The woman, whose face is blurred in the documentary, later argues with Sloth on-camera as he arrives in pursuit of Danger, the mobile camera following Sloth through the estate to her front door. Confronted by the mother, who refuses to allow Sloth into the flat and lambasts him for banging on her door and scaring her young children, Sloth responds by warning her not to allow Danger to 'bring trouble to your house' while vowing to wait for him outside. Killer is filmed emerging from court saying 'fuck the judge' after receiving a driving ban and a £200 fine and later is filmed threatening to 'get a gun and kill everyone' and to cut a bouncer's throat after a coach refuses to transport a large group of young people to a club event Killer and his collective had arranged. How are we to interpret the televisual framing of these actions against my claim that the aesthetic codes that constitute *Tower Block Dreams* all combine to exhibit an indexical relationship to the stylistic and narrational conventions, thematic content and, most significantly, the industrial legitimization of the popular, fictional Black urban film? The specific modes in which the spectator encounters what can be understood as an exaggerated excessiveness of its representation of urban identities, spaces and realities are accentuated by a formal approach that assists in the

Figure 7.3 Skinnyman looking over the estate in *Tower Block Dreams* (BBC Three, 2004).

conceiving of the urban film as an instinctive claim on realism. The series employs an unsteady, observational documentary framework that on occasion is interrupted by non-realist aesthetic devices and artifice; the camera zooms in, tracks and frames our protagonists in highly stylized slow-motion shots directly against the backdrop of the council estate (Figure 7.3) reaffirming the relationship between person and place as the key, defining factor in how the documentary attempts through audiovisual means to convey meaning about the social world it depicts. In thinking through the interpretative frames which the series attempts to both dismantle and construct anew, we find some degree of conceptual allegiance in the analysis offered by Stella Bruzzi (2000) in her deconstructing of Bill Nichols's taxonomy of documentary production (1994) where six modalities of documentary practice – the *expository*, the *observational*, the *reflexive*, the *interactive*, the *poetic* and the *performative* – are advanced as the rigid subdivisions of a generic category. The fundamental challenge within Bruzzi's critique of Nichols's documentary 'family tree' genealogy is that documentaries draw on a plethora of aesthetic devices to respond to sometimes *multiple* intentions, and it is this heterogeneity – at moments explicit, then observatory and distant, in part expository in the authoritativeness of its voice-over narration, at times elaborate and hyper-obtrusive in its capturing on screen of the real and performative behaviours that satisfy the associative connections between working-class identity and urban conventions – that encompasses *Tower Block Dreams* and implies a multi-layered, multi-constituted intentionality to the series. While I purposefully evade the revising of historicized Bazanian debates over the objectivism of realism, a cohabitation between reality and representation is observed in *Tower Block Dreams*'s extensive use of non-directive interviews as a form of testimony: that the young men's accounts of crime, social alienation, violence and the struggles of urban music production traffic through the documentary a regime of truth-telling and realness as a critical posture to accentuate its sociopolitical commentary and provide the spectator a proximity to the lives of inner-city identities that may reshape perceptions and provoke a reimagining of the urban condition and the sensationalized masculine identities that populate the urban environ. The effectiveness of this testimony-as-counter-narrational-authenticity is reliant upon a specific style of representation that establishes a trialectical correspondence between who and what is being represented, the ways in which it is represented and the authorial and editorial principles and intentions that both govern and constitute its representational discourse, and one can conceive the documentary as a dynamic visual counter- public (Warner, 2002). This idea of *Tower Block Dreams* as a counterposition to the hegemonic signifiers of urban identity chime with McRobbie and Thornton's critique of the new agency afforded by the media to those described as folk devils to contest their demonization through truth-telling (1995) and, while neither documentary nor fictional drama (or a combination of both) was necessarily the object of study in their rereading of Cohen and Hall et al., this remains a valuable area of analysis in that their description of mainstream media as accommodative of the contemporary folk devil's counter-narrative strategy and my own genealogy of the urban text as an indexical product of, *inter alia*, the uncontested hegemony of Black urban crime can be unified in a reading of *Tower Block Dreams* as a filmic counterpublic, but this must also be nuanced by two additional factors: the representational *agenda* determining the degree to which the institutional arrangement permits and legitimizes the filming of urban alterity and the representational *form* within which such identities are framed and the extra-diegetic social discourses through which meaning is both derived and reproduced. This second factor points to the significance of the medium's appropriateness in its framing of peripheral social identities and the consequences of the overdetermination of realist, televisual documentary practices, particularly those invested in the presenting of race and class difference to the national audience. Perhaps to both discourage a literal reading of the actions captured in the films (although I accept that such an assertion disturbs my own critique of the documentary's claim to authenticity) and to offer the necessary nuancing and level of enquiry that secures the documentary series's criterion of value – as a separation from the more traditional, denigrative modes of representing the urban – *Tower Block Dreams* on occasions presents its protagonists in more benevolent tones as an alleviatory strategy to nuance the less experienced images and narratives of the urban existence. For example, Killer is also filmed during a more tender moment with his young daughter and partner; Gambit describes the childhood trauma of losing his father at age fourteen and his subsequent homelessness at the heart of the emotional isolation and criminal existence he must negotiate with the difficulties of his burgeoning music career; and Skinny-man reflects on his exclusion from an unsympathetic educational system and his class identity as a perpetual and demotivating hindrance to both his chances of a record deal and, with it, the possibility of a legitimate and rewarding existence. These more sentimental moments, in addition to providing further testimony, work to draw the spectator into a (temporal) emotional and sympathetic bind with these men and add a complexity to the heavily distorted otherness projected within foundational narratives, which assist in an evaluation of how *Tower Block Dreams*'s urban identities are organized by a macaronic visual language, at one moment as dedicated musicians, family men and emotionally vulnerable young people, and at another, as abhorrent and violent criminals. Of course, in such attempts at a restoration of an already stigmatized urban identity in *Tower Block Dreams*'s positive/negative representational strategy we observe the incommensurability of such media binaries Hall identified as 'adding positive images to the largely negative repertoire of the dominant regime of representation' (Hall, 1997: 274), and it is against Hall's genealogy that we arrive at an understanding of how the documentary's methods of constructing a narrational egalitarianism through an equivalency of representational structure are compromised by the omnipresence and omnipotence of the negative within both the series and the social imaginaries of its audiences, where the documentary's servility to the spectatorial desires of the negative characterizations inhabits its epistemological centre.

To interpret *Tower Block Dreams* as a work of both documentary and fiction, as both televisual and cinematic in its visual grammar as I do here, is from one perspective to appreciate the mosaic nature of the series, for it entwines diverse and disparate forms of documentary practice and elements of fiction, elements that draw on the aesthetic modalities of observational cinema verité and, in addition, in accordance with a description of an expansive documentary approach, which Bruzzi terms as 'journey films' (2006: 89), *Tower Block Dreams* produces a series of encounters between filmmaker, subject and, significantly, the spectator. From another perspective, in my reading of the series as both non-fiction and fiction, as observationalist and performative, is an analytical approach that I want to term as 'archaeological'; an exploration into the origins and complex genealogies of the popular aestheticization of urban subjects allows one to conceive *Tower Block Dreams* as a progenitor of the thematic, formal, stylistic and institutional grammars of the popular British urban film. Where the text's generic verisimilitude serves as the authenticating device for its modes of reality, representation and, therefore, truth-telling, it is its cultural verisimilitude that becomes the ideological connective between subject and audience, for an interrogation of *Tower Block Dreams* as part of an archaeology of the urban text is to define and pursue an interrogation that achieves a necessary critical distance between simply reading the documentary series as an exemplar of a visual counter-discourse through the sourcing of organic stories held within Britain's 'non-societies', and an interrogation that considers the visual and narrational modes through which *Tower Block Dreams* fulfils a particular desire within its spectator, one readied and preconditioned by the epistemological vigour of realist representational schemas. By making this argument, I do not wish to suggest that *Tower Block Dreams* is a product composed holistically of excessive performativity, exaggeration and provocative artifice. Rather, I want to propose that there is a sense of fictional constructedness in how *Tower Block Dreams* frames its urban subjects and, despite my description of the urban as a nascent genre, the series cannot be understood as a representational *tabula rasa* but one that has, at some level, successfully migrated from the media narratives of the urban problematic, the urban celebratory and the tacit decrees of cultural/creative diversity into the non-fictional language through which the series is filmed, circulated, and made distinct. There is an argument to be made that *Tower Block Dreams*'s observational realism references the very filmic and televisual codes through which official images of urbanity draw authority and credence, and that there is a sense in which the documentary's aesthetics and formations of urban identity have fed into some of the ways in which the popular British urban text would come to define itself through the definitions, imaginaries and interpretations of the dominant public sphere. This, again, is not to deny that the series captures an organic choreography of urbanity that pays attention to both the individual and collective urban identity while preserving the council estate as the foundation upon which cultural bridges are formed through music and through which the protagonists draw creative inspiration, but also that *Tower Block Dreams* can be seen to emblematize, to actually contain within itself, the desires of the primary versions of urbanity. In a reception somewhat prophesized through BBC Three's commitment to producing programming that avows controversy, *Tower Block Dreams* would be subject to criticism from the press media for its uncritical filming of criminality and deviant behaviour (*The Guardian*, Thursday, 11 December 2003), an accusation that undoubtedly stemmed from the documentary series's visceral account of the deprivation and criminality that characterize Britain's urban areas. That the BBC was subject to media scrutiny regarding the ethics of the series may in part have been a desirable outcome concomitant with the BBC Three mandate of producing uncompromising programming, and serves as an expository framework for how the aesthetics of observational documentary realism as a modality for the representing of the urban Other and the framing of an urban reality render *Tower Block Dreams* as vulnerable to an interaction with media concerns over the televisual depictions of illegal activity and youth criminality and its potential influence on a young and impressionable section of its intended audience germane to the very forms of urban music it profiles. Indeed, the BBC would later concede that throughout the production process, cognizant of such concerns, it sought to avoid the contravening of its own production guidelines in the filming of the young men's criminal activities. As Taylor would insist prior to its broadcast, 'we talked about film-makers like Scorsese, who has transformed the image of Italian-Americans. We didn't want it to be a worthy social documentary. It's a beautifully shot, heartfelt, passionate look at a bit of Britain that doesn't often get a look in' (*The Guardian*, Thursday, 11 December 2003). We should be cognizant that although *Tower Block Dreams* provides an important mode of cultural identification in its filming of distinctive social identities, situations, circumstances, practices and behaviours that may resonate with the experiences of a demographic decanted from mainstream cultural representation, this is a cultural value that is met with another audience group's segregated desire for urban excessivity through the spectacularizing of contemporary urban identities defined by crisis, and these are not twin intentions in terms of balance, emphasis and narrative focalization. I want to argue that the foregrounding of a compressed urban excessivity produces a set of meanings that in many ways curtail the ability of *Tower Block Dreams* to be evaluated as a text that can successfully follow through on the aspirations that perhaps govern, at least outwardly, some of its organizing principles. I'm insisting that the aforementioned agendas within BBC Three's editorial framework present a polysemic documentary experience produced under the official guise of both public interest and impartiality, a dynamic proximity to an inner-city lifeworld that is both instrumentalist and edificatory, in some way an acknowledgement of the imperatives of the creative industries and the politics of identification, and *Tower Block Dreams*'s detached, observational approach, its focus on Black and white working-class young men and their love of Black urban music and cultural forms and the behavioural traits that circumscribe their life chances provide a faint inoculation against the ideological binds of realist representation that are made steadfast through its claim to truth and actuality. In drawing on the analyses made by bell hooks, it is through the stereotypical circulation of the imagined cinematic representation, one further secured by dominant ideology, that a recognition, identification and interpretation of a filmic identity is achieved (2000).

If one succeeds in advancing a description of the urban text as a social aesthetic that holds within its visual textures a heterogeneity of storytelling mechanisms that are themselves the indexical offerings of a dialectical interaction between cultural identity, cultural representation and, to reframe the Marxian description of commodity fetishism, an attentiveness to the perceived needs of an audience conditioned by the media's sensationalizing of social and cultural difference as entertainment and satisfaction, this validates the reassertion that *Tower Block Dreams* is orchestrated by two distinctive imperatives: it speaks to the symbolic value extracted from the spectacularizing of urban multiculture and youthful, diverse programming, and the cultivating of a vertical and ontologically protective experience for a white middle-class gaze, both of which condition the formal and narrational elements of the documentary series and perform a decisive function in the social imaginaries within which *Tower Block Dreams* is embedded, and which it consciously cites and translates. This latter imperative, the documentary's articulation of urban pathologies, encourages one to arrive at a more pertinent question: What if, beyond being a sincere investigation into the limited life chances of young people impacted by both economic inequality and emotional trauma, beyond its semi-autonomous narration as an act of hegemonic refusal and beyond its attempted de-settling of the urban norm, the primary ideological objective of *Tower Block Dreams* is, in its social anatomy of urban life, the variated sustenance of an urban social crisis as a generic experience that, to again momentarily draw on Wayne's Marxist interpretation of the capitalist mode of film production that demands both the individualization of social problems and a particular focalization of character and social world and that can often exist on the ideological continuum of the dominant forms of identification that structure meaning (2020), is a mediatized vision of the urban realities that equally insists on an obfuscation of the real conditions responsible for its urban crisis? Let me reaffirm that in my defining of this analysis as an archaeology of the popular British urban text, which we find holds multiple contradictions and intentions in place, a productive excavation is uncovered that supports a basic premise that such questions will always be more satisfactorily answered when pursued through the examination of more than one text, more than one cultural artefact or phenomenon, medium and form. We may find an analogy in the landmark American documentary *Hoop Dreams* (dir. Steve James, 1994) in which the filmmaker follows two Black teenagers over several years as both boys attempt to win a basketball scholarship to a prestigious, overwhelmingly white College-preparatory school away from the poverty of their inner-city Chicago neighbourhoods, and favours an observational documentary form to render the film as a social 'encounter' (Bruzzi, 2006: 118). *Tower Block Dreams* equally communicates its vision of the urban environment and its inhabitants through a direct cinema in its investment in time and shot durationality, and shares with *Hoop Dreams* its interest in the aspirations of socially and economically marginalized youth identities and the spontaneity of non-fictitious dramatic action, a mode of observational documentary that Bruzzi defines as an 'open' journey (Bruzzi, 2006: 118) where the filmmaker, subject and spectator are bound in a shared social and geographic excursion without an end, an undetermined and open-ended exploration in which its conditions and outcomes emerge independently of the social relations that orchestrate the more predictable, subjective logics of dominant, determinant modes of narration. However, in considering the linguistic interplay between *Tower Block Dreams*'s production team's disavowal of any representational worthiness while also operating within the modes of realism and authenticity, we might see the ways in which a sense of futility, ending and destination nonetheless constantly reaffirms and re-establishes itself.

It is the sense that the journey is dictated by, paradoxically, an unpremeditated predictability that the documentary's journey is conducted though established ontological, epistemological, sociological and culturally verisimilar pathways, a journey with *guarantees*, and it is this encounter that remains the centre of *Tower Block Dreams*'s urban universe. By this, I'm conceptualizing the documentary's rhetoric of opacity as an ideological process that places the urban text within an 'economy of enchantment', a temporal encounter that both entices the spectator into the urban territory, one that is always framed in terms of crisis and diagnosis, and also succeeds in bringing the urban into the epistemological orbit of the dominant spectatorship. The contingent nature of this economy, contingent in that it finds fortuity upon the powerful race/class discourses and the political and cultural institutions that assemble it, support my description of the urban text as *citational*; there is a reliance on the popular source narratives of urban life that to some degree replicate the very social and cultural common senses it aims to supersede, to supplant. Like the urban geography, rendered enclosed and inactive by the twin regimes of cultural and generic verisimilitude, the camera's commitment to subject observation and performativity posits a blurring between documentary and fiction, and in the specific example of *Tower Block Dreams*'s mediated, media*tized* and instrumentalized identities, possesses a specific, tripartite industrial efficacy. First, to again reactivate the theories of McRobbie and Thornton (1995) in which the agency of the contemporary folk devils in responding to their social denigration is located in the expanded and attentive vessels of mainstream media allows for an extrapolation of their theories onto the analysis of the urban text as an architecture of 'truth-telling' and an authenticity of representation that, once funnelled through BBC Three as a product of the politics of diversity, of neoliberal innovation and creativity and the social predicaments of PSB, we find within *Tower Block Dreams* a kind of aesthetic of defence; I read BBC Three's placing of the documentary series within its regimes of authenticity and the indirect self-representation of a section of society understood only in terms of a malaise as an attempt to position the series as instinctively progressive, as vanguardist, as a site of social advocacy. Second, the inordinate attention on Black youth culture through the marketization of urban subcultural practices witnessed from the early 2000s, which permeates through *Tower Block Dreams*, finds some definition in Saha's critical intervention into the conceptual orthodoxy of the modalities of 'cultural commodification' (2021) where the popular representations of the urban otherness as a variant of racial capitalism are comprised of both cultural and economic elements (56). It is within this capitalist ecosystem that I contend that the *urban* performs as a commercial pseudonym for Blackness, a convertible and commodifiable Blackness devoid of the political history, significance and crucially, its hegemonic threat, and this produces an equally bipolar representation of the urban text, the urban identity as both sensationalized and sentimentalized, existing within the borders of white middle-class cultural consumption but remaining outside the borders of white middle-class moral acceptability. Third, in an extension of the modes in which the real and performative social logics of urban enclosure intercourse with the regimes of fear to produce an economy of enchantment that prepares us conceptually for the close textual analyses of fictional urban texts to follow, the urban possesses both a centripetal and a centrifugal force. It is centripetal in its social portraiture of epistemic peripherality that also succeeds in drawing the spectator into a temporal encounter with an excessive urban ordinary, and centrifugal in that in this process it telegraphs into the national sphere epistemologies that assist in the negotiating of – and between – confronting British cultural identities, and performs as a coda for the filmic aestheticization of an urban, inner-city grammar, one intrinsically cultivated and extrinsically defined. I accept that in taking this conceptual pathway there is a risk of collapsing a *theory* of the urban text into a reductive analysis that conceives media practices as either the passive repositories of existing ideologies of race and class or the omnipotent machinery through which everyday beliefs acquire intelligibility and become inscribed in culture, the former being at the basis of Hall's own ideological critique that marks a departure from the Althuserrian Marxist revising of ideology as the linear and determinate explanatory system for our quotidian social relations, practices and phenomena, and towards a Cultural Studies inflection that insists that the interrogation of cultural texts and the ideological spheres and instutionalities from which they are produced and embody are characterized, just as the texts themselves, by complexity and contradiction (1981). And it is from Hall's caution that I want to make clear that my archaeology of the urban text is one that conceives the fictitious or factual aestheticization of urban life as an outcome of neither manipulation nor conspiratorial media practices, nor to develop a thesis that implores us to indulge in myth. What interests me here is that the status of the urban male identity, a folk-devilled and hyper-conventionalized identity and the associated audial subcultural practices and ascribed social threat, once sublated into the constitutive creative imaginations of the screen industry as a liberal representational extensivity and as a vindication of the hegemony of the urban self-destructive pathologies, renders PSB not an independent arena but part of an ideological apparatus and resultingly, performs a specific ideological labour. In making this claim, and with an awareness of the very apposite nature of the Cultural Studies analytical focus on film and television texts and the means by which aesthetic strategies are the index of the text's own regimes of representation, which must itself be understood within a cultural, social and political context, I'm attempting to develop a methodological synthesis that places the textual analyses to follow within an analytical framework that is responsive to the possibility that we can understand the texts as conduits of an array of what Hall terms as 'ideological premises' (Hall, 2021 [1981]: 101). We cannot disregard the importance of this as an influencing practice in the formation of the popular Black urban text and its primary thematics. My arguing that such ideological antennas that constitute the accommodating, or might I say the *acquiring*, of the popular visions of the distressed urbanity within a complex system of ideological refining, a practice of aestheticization that announces itself and is made intelligible at a dynamic conjunctural moment in the epistemic and signifying discourse on race, class, crime and social peripherality, assist in an understanding of how *Tower Block Dreams* plays a decisive editorializing function in the rendering of the social conditions of the urban subject in audiovisual forms and fusing into commonality two forms of spectatorship. It establishes novel and temporal allegiances between those whose presence and non-presence within the media has been determined by race and class struggle and stigma and who, therefore, find powerful recognition and value from a mainstream representation that speaks to their vernacular experiences, and those whose social consciousness and optics through which they comprehend and make sense of urban life are developed and who remain some distance outside the social and cultural milieu from which forms of knowledge and meaning are secured and enacted upon. This, the peeling back of the contradictory, intertextual and fissured layers of cultural production rationality that reveal the urban text as a social aesthetic that, emerging from and residing in the public debate over urban violence, estate life and alienated identities, functions as a tremendously versatile social *crisis* aesthetic that doubles up, rather than masquerades, as crisis altruism, equally gives us access to the modes by which the recognizable urban within filmic and televisual representation gains public and critical currency by the coalescing upon the common sense, inner-city image streams that simultaneously work to extend the gulf between the nation and a full experience of the urban Other's alterity. Relatedly, the irreducible significance and specificity of cultural difference and representation at this critical conjuncture as located in BBC Three's sedimentation of the raw and decontextualized aspects of the austere urban existence into textual form invites a mode of analysis that both attempts to infill the lacuna we arrive at within Stuart Hall's cultural theory that was yet to fully explore the linkages between cultural texts and the subjective interests and predicaments of industrial cultural production, but speaks in concert with the Hallian identification of film and television not as the site of ideological production but as a point of ideological dispersal. Despite *Tower Block Dreams*'s interest in the social and cultural significance and affinities of urban music production and the fragility of young people's futures and the dependencies that have been constructed upon them, the documentary is unable to betray the hegemony of the urban environment, its identities and their positioning within the popular framings as a problem *for* society, as opposed to a societal problem. In other words, the very anxiety-inducing public dialogues on urban crime, the political structuring of diverse cultural production as social intervention and the formal strategies that conceive, record and project denigrative social existences onto the national imaginary prepare a new spectatorial territory through which the documentary's protean presentation of struggle and creativity within the urban environment secures within the vacant consciousness of the spectatorship the urban male, and urban*ity*, as a subject of interest and recognition, a subject of proximal identification and distanced fascination, a subject of anxiety, of allure, of desire.

8

'Kes with Guns'

Bullet Boy and the Urban Text's Ontological Suture

Like everywhere in society, coming up is a new generation ready to graduate at an ever-early age, young children who feel they have nothing to lose and a lot to gain. Whoever you are, and whatever your other weaknesses, with a gun you become someone. Instantly.

—*Bullet Boy*, BBC Films, 2002

I want to return to the question of the urban text as both constructed by a social aesthetic and circulated as a serviceable fiction of race. If the examples of the new forms of Black urban characterization found in the previous chapter's exploration of the popular urban text in both *Storm Damage* and *Tower Block Dreams* demonstrate a constellation of thematic interests and filmic and televisual conventions that by the mid-2000s had yet to translate into what one could be understood as a concerted generic model, at this stage, the progression of the urban text can be assessed by its glacial presence as a theatrical feature film. This juncture requires me to again give further attention to what is implied in the *popular* Black urban film – its official and publicly funded institutional setting that acts as a framework for how its themes are determined by the institutional arrangement within which the text is produced and its associative demands, models and intentions. Demonstrating an alignment with the general ethos of the cultural and creative industries in its emphasis on innovation and new technologies, the UKFC New Cinema Fund was established to encourage new modes of production and distribution, develop film talent working within the UK's regions and nations, attract established film talent working outside the mainstream and, significantly, 'ensure equality of opportunity and promote social inclusion and cultural diversity' (Film Council, 2000b: 15). The New Cinema Fund's public commitment to cultural inclusivity can thus be considered as on the continuum of the discourse on inclusion in the creative sector, where race was now just one component in a larger paradigmatic articulation of diversity which had by this stage evolved as a concept to refer to a number of marginal social identities while still displaying a rhetorical engagement with the vestiges of post-Macphersonism. This being so, there is a clear relationship with the issue of race to be observed in the UKFC's New Cinema Fund and its specific interest towards Black British film production, given the funding strand was primarily established to fund British filmmakers of a more cultural predilection and declared a particular commitment to support the development of Black and ethnic minority film workforces in the UK. More specifically, the fund exhibits an engagement with the emergent politics of race in its mandate to 'working with filmmakers and funding bodies in the regions and nations and those who have been traditionally marginalised or under-represented within the industry' (UKFC, 2005: 7). Such a statement is reflective of how the screen sector became interwoven with the broader politics of race in the UK, where the cultural and creative industries would revel in the instituting of the practice of integration as the major political contribution to the issue of race and ethnic difference by the insistence by UKFC executive that the fund 'would be crucial in supporting the future of black British film' (quoted in Malik, 2002: 170). However, there is a clear discrepancy between the promises of the development of Black cinema within the UKFC and the actual allocation of UKFC resources for feature film development and production, where only 4 per cent of the 106 awards granted by the New Cinema Fund and 8 per cent of the 409 development fund awards were to be given to minority ethnic-led projects and practitioners between 2001 and 2007 (Bhavnani, 2007). It was from within this space of compounded, multi-modal marginality that we encounter the circumstances that produced what I see as a primary exemplar of the popular Black urban text in the 2005 feature film, *Bullet Boy*. In this chapter, I examine the useful fictions of race that inform the film and in doing so, reveal the congregating of the previously examined industrial arrangements and Black moral panics that reconfigure hauntologically malevolent forms of Black filmic and televisual representation as a version of positive Black cultural politics. In shifting analytical attention from the production context to the text, I am interested in how a theoretical language of ontological structure can describe the film's negotiation between its depiction of inferential black-on-black gun crime and a more sentimental account of its impact upon those emotionally connected to the film's protagonist that perform as *Bullet Boy*'s claim to authenticity and counter-facticity. Further, I want to argue that the film's indexical representation of interracial Black death denies narrative closure, and in doing so, it attempts to evoke sympathy through visual trauma proffers *Bullet Boy* as a drama without ending. Finally, this chapter explores what can be discerned through the presence of the Metropolitan Police's Operation Trident as an intertextual feature within and external to the film, and this registers an intimate correspondence with the hegemony of black-on-black criminality but equally reveals a polysemicity in its use as an extra-diegetic mode of anti-Black gun crime moralism.

While I have so far developed a concept of the social aesthetic that contends that popular Black British urban representation and its immediate thematic preoccupations are the textual outcomes of the convergence of a number of social, cultural, political and industrial imperatives, at the granular level, and still pursued through the discursive language of inclusivity, the emergence of the popular Black urban film in its more dramatized inflections can be understood as the outcome of a distinctive production culture. Paul Hamann, at the time the BBC's head of documentary, and Michael Tait, then a BBC development executive for documentaries, had a film project at a nascent point of development that could emerge as compatible with the BBC's head of drama Ruth Caleb's production strategy, which involved the funding of first-time feature filmmakers from a documentary practice using a skeleton crew. Indeed, *Bullet Boy*, which at this embryonic stage had been titled simply as 'The Boys', was the debut feature film of the white British documentary filmmaker Saul Dibb, the son of noted independent television documentary maker Mike Dibb. I want to draw particular analytical attention to the modes of racial signification that are engaged in the addition of 'bullet' to the film's title, which allows for the analysis of *Bullet Boy*'s production context to extend to two key points of consideration. First, the rationale for the change in the film's title, and the means through which Dibb drew its inspiration from becomes another factor to be twined within the hauntological Black archive and is reflective of the bidirectionality of useful race fictions; in this instance, a headline of an article in the *Hackney Gazette*, a local East London newspaper, had reported on a recent gun-related incident involving Black youths within the borough. Here, we see the degree of racial signification embedded in the term 'Bullet Boy' and its alignment with the inferential narratives of Black gun crime within the media. The second point of consideration in regard to the film's production context possesses tremendous value in reaffirming my earlier contention that the specific conjuncture's forms of Black film and TV representation becomes an arena of cohabitation between racial characterization, anxiety and desire and liberal intentions, and is concerned with the film's spectacularizing title and how the film project was presented and subsequently sold to commissioning executives at BBC Films as 'Kes with guns' (quoted in *The Guardian*, Wednesday, 20 April 2005). This imaginative and contrasting comparison applied in the film's public pitching is of course in reference to Ken Loach's 1969 landmark film *Kes*, the adaptation of Barry Hines's novel *A Kestrel for a Knave* set within the coal mining town of Barnsley, South Yorkshire, and tells the story of Billy Casper, a fifteen-year-old schoolboy and the process of the unrealized personal virtue realized through Billy's training of a wild kestrel against the backdrop of an emotionally neglectful and abusive family life and domestic isolation. More broadly, *Kes* is widely interpreted as a damnation of the Tripartite System of secondary education that curtails human potential, becoming the canonical text within the consecrating taxonomies not just of British social realism but of British cinema (Hill, 1986; Forrest, 2020). There is little inherently wrong or novel in the production team's application of what can be accepted as the use of a recognizable comparative description as the film project's high concept, a somewhat standardized hermeneutical practice within the capitalist machinery of the global film industry. This being the case, the project's attempt to implant a tangible and alluring narrative image in the juxtaposing of a highly distinctive, suggestive and instantly recognizable film title with the primary and anxiety-inducing weapon essential in the construction of the race fiction of black-on-black violence as exhibiting a simple adherence to the orthodoxies of film industry lore is problematic. For it is unable to serve as a mitigating alibi for the film's drawing of its connotative image from the hauntological Black archive to accrue a sociocultural significance and spectatorial desire through the hegemony of black-on-black criminality. For what sits at the basis of *Bullet Boy*'s 'Kes with Guns' imaginary, which attempts to position the film as a site for the articulation of cross-pollinatory concerns and narrative sentimentalities that are particular to the social identities in both films, is an attempt to challenge the dominant accounts of excessive Black urbanity through the symbolic application of *Kes* to rescue *Bullet Boy* from the charge of racial depiction. Deeply embedded within the 'Kes with Guns' description is the public propagation of a range of ideas that again encourage the conditioning of our potential experience of the film that the hybridizing language of 'Kes with Guns' strives to purport – a sentimental examination of the social-political and emotional context of Black gun and gang violence – as a signifying shorthand for Blackness and masculinity given the centrality of black-on-black gun crime within the popular imagination and used here to furnish the film with the important questions of cinematic realism, naturalism and sociopolitical commentary. What are we given access to in the hybridizing of two distinctive social and geographic experiences, cultural representations and character aspirations? I am disinterested in conducting any kind of comparative analysis of the sociopolitical properties of the two films that aggrandize *Kes* as the zenith of cinematic social commentary to the detriment of *Bullet Boy*. Rather, what interests me is the narrational and contextual ellipsis to be observed in the transplanting of what is central to *Kes* – an uncompassionate educational system, an unloving familial dynamic and a newly developed self-esteem. It is through an analysis of 'Kes with Guns' as a narrational transplantation that first strips *Kes* of all the thematic assets it possesses that I am able to pursue a critique of the meaning and validity of the 'Kes with Guns' description through an analysis of what remains – a non-specific liberal concern with young lives, a corresponding sense of verisimilitude and plausibility emphasized through the use of cinematic realism. However, what may seem to imply a textual and thematic horizontality and balance is in fact a relationship of non-equivalence. In other words, all that is at *Kes*'s essence, and specifically within the character of Billy Casper, are subsumed into a much larger, spectacularizing and contemporaneous meta-representation of Black gun violence as a source of public debate, anxiety, expectation and desire. There is a particularly powerful horizon of expectation that is established through the production's mobilizing of the description that rather than desensitizing the image of the hauntological Black urban Other through superimposing it onto *Kes*'s sentimental narrative as its counter-investment in the prevailing Black crime discourse, it is instead applied as a figurative title to provide sociopolitical patina to its more extractive portrayal of black-on-black gun violence. This is both denotive of the conjuncture's prevalent politics of racism made present by the inferential discourse of Black gun crime and a hegemonically cohabiting Black cultural politics that assists in the implicating of film and television drama in a process that can be described as 'the colouring of the imagination' (Nwonka, 2020a). This alludes to the spectatorial allure drawn from the associativity of gun crime and the physicality of Black skin that is aligned with racial pathologies – and the image of the dead Black body as the linkage to the lifeworld of Black urban masculinity, and here we are confronted with forms of meaning that accompany the shift to the title *Bullet Boy* and the production's attendant juxtaposing of the conjuncture's most consensual form of Black signification and the epitome of white British working-class filmic representation. This reifies the hauntological Black urban Other as a commodity located between the continual shift between visibility and invisibility, and in this respect to some level continues the episteme's period of haunting now within the spaces of visual representation. For it is only once the hauntological Black urban Other as a social spectre begins to disturb, socially haunts, agitates and, as argued by Marriot (2007), *spooks* that the full theatricality of the Black urban criminal identity that the accounts of Black gun crime as a useful fiction of race traffics is able to reify Black male urbanity as a malevolent figure of non-being to be thrust into dramatic action, a fiction made all the more plausible by its attachment to the symbolic locations of the housing estates and Black working-class environments of the capital. Here, while 'Kes with Guns' attempts to hold racial characterization and a social purpose within an invalidating narrational horizontality, it is only the hauntological Black urban Other that appears within this liminal arena of Black urban filmic and televisual representation.

It is this understanding of the popular Black urban film as organized by an interpenetrating set of discourses and meaning that enables us to recontextualize the logic behind the endeavour to 'get something black made' and an analysis of *Bullet Boy*'s industrial documentation produced to secure its commissioning by BBC Films, and the UKFC reveals how *Bullet Boy*'s Black material was maximized by BBC Films to establish the film's credibility, despite the absence of any obvious Black reference found within the production team's ambition to 'create the human emotion of *Kes*, the iconic social power of *Made in Britain*, and the relevance and compassion of *Last Resort*' (BBC Films, 2002). Black topicality becomes sufficient to justify its economic, social and cultural investment, and I want to draw attention to the proposal that was presented to the UKFC's New Cinema Fund in the early stages of its development by BBC Films and Luke Alkin from Shine that reveal *Bullet Boy*'s commissioning logics. If it is accepted that the social aesthetics that populate the Black urban drama also carry with them the very hauntological constructions of Black life that are also captured within the conjuncture's race discourse and made culturally and economically valuable through the interaction between capitalism and Black cultural politics, then *Bullet Boy*'s preliminary material is underpinned, somewhat expectedly, by racial descriptors structured for the naturalizing of the very vertical power relations that structure Black filmic representation. While it is not possible to enter into a detailed and extensive discussion of the outline here, a critical and interrelated discourse on Black criminality is located in the passage from the film's development document:

> Bullet Boy is London slang for the children of 11–12 for whom, in certain parts of London, guns have become a way of life. They form the youngest strata of a British urban culture that has spawned headline after headline. Their world is deadly, ruthless, wild and dramatic. As the violence continues to explode onto the streets, the powerful human tragedies that lie behind each incident remain obscure. This film will tell one story. (BBC Films, 2002)

This is another mode of bringing into dialogue the framework I had earlier established, in that both the idea of the popular urban text as *social aesthetic* (the social, industrial, cultural and political imperatives that occasion its production and its narrative themes) and a *useful/necessary fiction of race* (the nature of the Black characterization and its circulatory purpose) once interacting open up fissures where the representation of Black identity are dialogically cohabited with pre-existing race discourses and representations supplemented by interweaving media forms and crucially by its alignment with historic and contemporary racism. Put differently, and to pose an exploratory question, how can the persistent presence of thematics and characterizations drawn from a heterogeneous construction of Black urban identity and married with a sentimentality to be found in the portrayal of the 'human tragedies' of Black gun crime that establishes the film as a realist encounter with Black malevolence still function as a worthy, socially purposeful cinematic experience? An answer can be found in Hesmondhalgh and Saha (2013), who remind us that 'cultural production often seeks to disseminate, incorporate, and commodify vital forms of culture from the margins of societies. Combined with racialized understandings of talent and authenticity, this can have powerful effects on cultural production' (180). Here, beyond the ability of cultural production to accommodate and commodify racial alterity within existing structures of power, the existence of a heavy capitalist market that is alive to racialized characterizations and narratives of criminalized Black life in the cinematic depiction of Black gun violence and death can be viewed as an iteration of racialized capitalism that cultural diversity not only prospers from but, in the context of the UKFC's New Cinema Fund, ushers in its conversion into a narrative formulae. Such an assertion is reflective of the more nuanced processes in which Black urban gun violence when conveyed as an aesthetic and cultural value assists in its commodification into a form of dramatic, fictitious and sensationalist narrative material. In this sense, *Bullet Boy* is by its nature intertextual, and the intensified degree of useful race fiction displayed in the BBC Films proposal displays some elements of the processes of representation that Hall defines as 'transcoding' (Hall, 1997: 270). Here, Hall describes a process of the repurposing of existing forms of meaning for the construction of new meanings, and I observe a comparable process of conversion at play in the lexicalization of black-on-black criminality as a form of dramatic storytelling. Relatedly, I'm equally gesturing towards what Hall (1993: 36) observes in PSB media in functioning as the 'theatre' where cultural diversity is constructed and circulated, made material and where different forms of representation are negotiated. What Hall's theoretical intervention demonstrates in relation to *Bullet Boy* is the significance of the texts' source language – the language out of which its Black thematic material is translated, transcoded and cited, and what is produced in its reification as a form of cinematic, televisual and narrational that will be intelligible to a target audience. While I am identifying an inherently extractive relationship, a process of Black extraction, what also accompanies this process is a Black narrational ellipsis, termed here as the deliberate shedding of the raw details of this Black subject matter that may influence the text's preferred modes of meaning construction. Thus, what becomes salient for the analysis of the popular urban film drama is a consideration of what is discarded in its process of erasure as much as a reading of the materials that survive as the migratory facets of the Black existence to be subjected to representational *distillation*, a distilling into narrational form the most dramatic, hauntological and opportune elements of black-on-black gun crime. This means considering the existing narrative accounts relied upon in the formation of the popular urban drama and how Black images are translated from one arena into the theatre of PSB drama as a kind of slanting, oblique connective. In the example of *Bullet Boy*, we observe how this practice becomes productive only when it can be energized in relation to existing moral panics and develops a tangibility through an extended inferential relationship, now between the police, the media and PSB drama. I want to consider the degree of collegiality displayed in the analysis of two corresponding texts: first, again from a sensationalist Black gun crime article by Tony Thompson in *The Guardian* and some months later in the *Bullet Boy* proposal/outline written by Dibb, Tait and Hamann that was submitted to Luke Alkin at the UKFC:

> A new generation of young guns, many of them still teenagers and almost all of them under 25, have modelled themselves on the original Yardies and now match them in brutality, cold-bloodedness and sheer bravado, particularly in the capital. Shots are now fired in London daily and incidents involving handguns are running into double figures every week. Feuds that would once have been solved by fists or knives are now settled by the bullet. (Tony Thompson, *The Guardian*, Sunday, 26 August 2001)

> Over the last few years' gunshots have become an everyday occurrence in the capital, notoriously but not exclusively amongst the black community: feuds once solved by fists or knives are now settled by bullets. The drug economy has subverted mainstream morality – even the restraining framework of the black churches – providing an alternative system of validation. In Britain's version of ghettos, British-born black kids move in rival crews and posseys, jostling to distribute the steady flow of cocaine from mules off the flights from Kingston. (BBC Films, 25 March 2002)

It was argued at the beginning of this book that the attempt to represent the 'reality' of the Black urban experience renders the popular Black British urban film as one constituted by a certain citational politics. *Bullet Boy*, as we have read here, finds its narrative source and sociocultural legitimacy in the hauntological Black archive that serves as BBC Films and the UKFC's primary exemplar of being and/or doing Blackness, sourced here from the hegemonic imagination and cast in a manner that I can describe as a haunting; it circulates through the numerous significative fields and processes that come to service PSB film and television. We can ascertain with a degree of assurance as to how the disproportionate amount of *The Observer/The Guardian* news publicity towards Black gun crime provided a significant template for *Bullet Boy* in the use of ethno-nationalistic narratives and modes of Black characterization that have been lifted *verbatim* from *The Guardian* piece. Both passages are of course useful fictions of race in all the possible ways and narrative forms that my analysis has asked us to understand and/or accept the term. An important point to stress here is that the notion of authenticity and Black truth-telling is particularly germane to the counter-narrative problematic as explored through the earlier critique of McRobbie and Thornton's moral-panic counter-narrative within sections of the media, in that BBC Films' reification of *The Guardian*'s account of Black gun violence as truth and sub-reality can represent a singular, Black perspective and secure its counter-hegemonic authenticity through Black representations firmly rooted in the realms of mythology. Taken seriously, these ideas about Black urban identity that have been narrativized are sufficient for me to problematize the foundational narratives through which Black urban identities are represented, here, as constantly abstracted as a murderous threat and one made all the more indubitable given its historic and contemporaneous presence and function as a useful fiction of race for the propagation of images of a violent black-on-blackness and its described societal effects. While some of the narrative concerns in the earlier passage, such as cocaine and its hegemonic understanding as an exclusively Jamaican import, did not come to feature in the final film, the BBC Films' identical reproduction of *The Guardian*'s sensationalism as a serviceable race fiction is to exhaust the issue of Black gun crime beyond all possible contextualization and to service a desire to abrogate the entwined narratives of Black crime and Black death with the realities of structural racism and social policy for a fixed and singular composition of Black urban crime that here is presented in a form that spectacularizes as a way of providing social and cultural insight. In this regard, the film displays a version of indexicality that ventures far beyond the cultural verisimilitudinous, here understood as the plausibility of the text's relationship to the real world it seeks to depict (Neal, 1990). *Bullet Boy*'s racial contorting of Black urban identity instead represents a constant balancing endeavour in which despite the film's ambition to supplement its reification of violent, inferential Black urbanity with sub-narrational human stories, it is primarily the spectacularizing hegemonic images of black-on-black malevolence that is thrown back into the episteme, and as I will explore, returning the story to where it is sourced from. In other words, the redirecting of violent Black urban spectrality allows for the desegregating of fiction and non-fiction and drama and factuality.

This formulation of the Black urban text as a space of verisimilitude and realness was particularly opportune to the developing of the idea of Black urban film as celebratory representation and positivity (but equally negativity, in the form of typecasting and the limited performative scope in which mostly Black actors would come to find a segregated space within in which they are compelled to conform to a hegemonic symmetry of Black urban characterization). Indeed, it is in a concerted effort to create a sense of authenticity that led the production to cast Luke Frazer through local auditions for the role of Curtis, an untrained actor who was found just four weeks before production. However, the casting of Walters, beyond his screen performance as the troubled Stefan in *Storm Damage*, was also informed by the cultural notoriety Walters had accrued in the intervening years within both Black urban youth subculture and the mediatized corpus of Black urban gun crime – notably his status as a member of So Solid Crew and more pertinently, his aforementioned imprisonment for possessing a firearm, an incident that also found reference in the aforementioned BBC Films' outline as a way to further sensationalize and crucially authenticate its filmic investment in the hauntological Black archive by evidencing that the issue of black-on-black gun crime has indeed penetrated the spheres of Black popular culture and music (BBC Films, 2002). But the moral panic of Black gun crime as a race fiction that the film builds its legitimacy on would become a veritable source of anxiety for *Bullet Boy*'s producers. Having prepared a four-week filming schedule based in Hackney, just one day prior to the commencement of principal photography, the Metropolitan Police would report to the production team that they had become aware of a death threat against Ashley Walters, forbidding the production from filming in any public place. Upon learning of this threat, some of the local location owners who had previously agreed to their premises to being used for the filming dropped out, resulting in the rescheduling of the production. Such was the concern over the safety of the lead actor and of the production itself that *Bullet Boy*'s line producer, Abbey Bach, was compelled to hire a private security team to maintain a protective presence on set. However, and indicative of the general understandings of urban violence as being orchestrated by a hyper-locality, Ashley Walters felt that the security team who were recruited by the production were not suitable for the environment nor possessed the innate cultural and geographical knowledge to both anticipate any potential attack and remain inconspicuous in their protective endeavours, a challenge that would result in Walters insisting on a security team more germane to both the urban locale and the nature of the threat posed (Interview with Ruth Caleb, 2015). Therefore, the actor's very presence can be understood as a modality of obstructing the audience's own potential suspension of plausibility, realism and association demanded by the film's Black representations through the iconography of a notable contemporary figure who occupies a varied position and source of identification within the collective imagination of the film's intended audiences.

Hall et al.'s definition of folk devils as 'the alternative to all we know' (1978: 16) provides an interesting pathway for interrogating the presence and function of the Black urban Other as a filmic experience within *Bullet Boy* as a reproduction or, to cite Godfreys's evaluation, a reinforcement of the 'normative and invariably reductive discourses of urban Black youths' (2022: 123). How can the fictions and narratives that society has been conditioned to understand as Black deviance and evil be aestheticized as the antithetical image to what is hegemonic? This is a question of medium specificity, of course, but also one of the struggles over knowledge, and the degree of excessive and sensationalism that becomes the Black urban text's criterion of value can be interrogated in this context when we remember that its other spectatorial allure, internecine Black death, is aestheticized into a coda for understanding the lives of Black youths – this is particularly salient if we accept the idea of the urban Other and the urban thematic as a recognizable non-relationality. Somewhat related to this, the popular British urban film, despite all its interest in peripheral social identities, is positioned within a tenuous and unresolved aesthetic and thematic relationship with what can be described as British social realism. It seems to me that the Black urban film, as a denigrated kind of British cinema, has occupied an equally dismissive alterative analytical and taxonomic sphere. Such a segregation within the cinematic, generic and popular imagination can be considered as an outcome of the racialized nature of the very concept of British social realism and its overwhelming association with white working-class subjects, geographies and themes, a somewhat narrow view of what constitutes the British working-class and social realism more generally in both scholarly thought and popular film criticism. As argued by Sarah Godfrey (2022), we can pursue a reading of *Bullet Boy* as a film that appears to function as a simple practice of *rehearsal*. By this, Godfrey is referring to the film's reinforcement of a violent Black urban masculinity that evidences the film as the product of an undifferentiated mimesis. I am reluctant to place Godfrey within the same corpus of critical perspectives, whose reductive comparative and categorical analyses of the popular Black urban text are birthed from the apparent limited interrogative capacity of the Black urban realist text as a noncanonical form of film culture that is theoretically simplified and made reductive by its unsophisticated, televisual ambitions and the apparent vulgarity of its primary narrative interests. However, in the context of my polemic on the faux universalism of the dominant and Eurocentric critical approaches to Black British representation and the film's own practice of knowledge creation as an essential path of analysis, any exploration of *Bullet Boy* that exenterates the cohabiting counter-hegemonic dimensions of the film within its analytical purview cannot begin to understand the most critical aspect of the film's communicative strategy – *Bullet Boy*'s practice of ontological suture, the ways that the film attempts to weave together the sensationalist accounts of Black gun crime and death with the attendant imperative of character humanization and social concern that provides the required level of self and external gratification in the recrafting of the Black urban youth as the essential Black subject. Indeed, my primary reason for the centring of the film within my current discussion is because it provides an extremely generative textual exemplar that allows us to return to one of the central features in the construction of the *popular* urban text as a form of Black film and television representation. It performs as a counterpoint, or under-narrative, to the unvaried discourse of black-on-black gun violence and its essential index, Black death. The term 'annotation' is one way for accounting for this ontological suturing, for while the idea of distillation and ellipsis suggests that the film eviscerates from the frame the more structural and racially organized factors involved in the issue of Black urban gun crime in favour of the most phenomenal and mediacentric accounts of black-on-black criminality and its inescapable outcome, Black death, ontological suture points towards the stitching together at the textual level of the crucial but absent and/or omitted experiences and perspectives that remain outside the primary media narratives of Black criminality. In this regard, *Bullet Boy* is underpinned by the practice of re-representation, but also the act of sub-narrational recreation that positions the spectator in the position of re-witnessing of the mediacentric events and incidents that are now supplemented with the ancillary and peripheral experiences and emotions outside the dominant black-on-black inferential frame.

Bullet Boy opens with two distorted images of Black youth: Ricky Gordon, filmed through the small window of a cell as the nineteen-year-old is released from a young offender's prison after serving a year for what we later learn for the stabbing of another youth during an affray, and a much coarser image of a younger Black youth curled up in what appears to be the boot of a car. The opening images accrue a significance beyond merely the subtle introduction of the film's central characters and is identified in what adjoins both images in the opening sequence. What is presented to the audience in the image of Ricky and the young boy are two subjectivities to be mediated by his best friend, Wisdom (Leon Black), a Black youth that, at least at this stage of his character journey become sufficient for him to be termed *a priori* as a 'road man', and while the specific nature of Wisdom's criminal repertoire is never divulged, one can identify him as an opportunist rather than a fully fledged gangster embedded in any identifiable organizational structure or hierarchical system, the very logics that animate the formal understandings of Black criminal gangs. Eventually, Wisdom opens the boot of his car to find Ricky's twelve-year-old brother Curtis (Luke Frazer) who has played truant from school and hid in the boot to meet Ricky upon his release. There is, for me, a much more imaginative interpretation to be made from the film's opening scenes. For while Curtis's emergence from the darkness of the car boot when adjoined with the image of Ricky in prison can of course be conceived as an attempt to unify Ricky and Curtis within a literal and metaphorical release from, and a potential return to, a period of physical and social containment, having initially left Curtis on the side of the road before reluctantly reversing back to him in the juxtaposition of two young Black people framed within a nondescript and otherwise deserted green landscape the audience naturally understands to be the countryside, the film's urban male characters achieve a situatedness through a portrayal of the Black urban Other as of place and of non-place.

Bullet Boy's opening scenes introduce the major concerns of the film: immobility, entrapment, violence and a concern with the significance of space and time in the lives of young Black men. Here, *Bullet Boy*'s interest is in the Black urban Other in its criminalized meta-representation, and the film's claim to Blackness is made sufficiently visceral through the situating of its characters in what is presented to us as a racially densified Clapton Park Estate in Hackney, East London. At this point, while *Bullet Boy* is invested in a literal construction of the symbolic location as an iconography of geographical infertility and unproductiveness, the film's initial images attempt to construct a metaphorical interpretation of the environment through *Bullet Boy*'s establishing shots and its unsteady, mobile cinematography that in crafting an austere image of the estate are firmed as the visual and narrational elements that are unable to fully free the audience from its creation of a particular 'horizon of expectation' (Jauss 1982), here, the distressed symbolic location as its primary representational vocabulary. However, the film's situatedness is also expressed through the interactions between *Bullet Boy*'s primary characters, and as Ricky and Wisdom drive into the more familiar and hegemonically symmetrical settings of East London's Clapton, Wisdom's spatial stimuli is sufficient to inaction a seemingly organic recourse to a criminal existence as indexed to the urban environment. As Wisdom exclaims, 'your people are around here and there is some dough to be made, I'm telling you we'll clean up the whole road here!' Here, the young men's friendship is structured by an indominable spirit of brotherliness that works to regulate the level of apprehension and declination that is denoted in Ricky's response of 'your way of making money, ain't the way I want to make my dough'. Ricky's paramount concern may indeed be avoiding a return to prison, but what is expressed in the relationship between their geographical settings and Wisdom's reaction is the absurdity of any other mode of economic sustenance. What is to be interpreted from Wisdom's immediate mocking of Ricky's ambition for an alternative existence within the urban is if this is an impossibility determined by circumstance or identity, and by the latter I am gesturing towards Ricky's own understanding of his identity as crafted from his internal rootedness to the urban setting, the density of its Black vernacular subcultural practices and with it, his relationship to Wisdom, as he is to find over the next days, his is equally a *conferred* identity that is unopen to change or compromise. Such dialogue attempts to immediately establish within the film that Ricky's survival in the Black urban location is inherently reliant on the possibility of Wisdom reforming as much as Ricky has, as much as the availability and provision of employment opportunities for the area's Black urban identities with the compounding burden of a criminal record. This exchange is particularly generative, and the camera now turns to a medium close-up of a scar on Wisdom's neck, serving as a vital source of narrative exposition granting access to not only the two young men's violent history but also an incident that will come to define their immediate futures and the limitlessness of their relationship. As Wisdom jokingly reminds Ricky, 'this is your scar, I'm wearing this for you', a significant moment of exposition is offered that gives us access to a history of loyalty, personal sacrifice and the brotherly ties and bonds that are called upon as demonstrations of solidarity and companionship in moments of violent conflict. Despite the jovial tone of the discussion, the scene underscores the territorial and subcultural codes and principles of a specific social milieu where a collective mentality emerges, born fundamentally from a sense of boundedness to the area.

Bullet Boy's initial moments offer an account of how localized violence escalates from seemingly innocuous incidents and encounters. Immediately on entering Clapton, the pair are thrust back into the zone of inevitable conflict, and as expected, this is ignited through the actions of Wisdom, developing a characterization that despite Ricky's release from prison remains no less incendiary than prior to his incarceration and their exchanges, while playful, construct an important binary between the two men. For Ricky, the scene presents the nature of his friendship with Wilson (and his actions) as positioned between apprehension and loyalty and for Wisdom, one marked by recklessness, irresponsibility and overconfidence as he reverses erratically after initially refusing to drive into a vacant space when they are met in a narrow road by a large approaching delivery van and clips the wing mirror of a parked car belonging to a Black youth identified immediately by Ricky as Godfrey (Clark Lawson), becoming the catalyst for an aggressive altercation with him and a group of Black men with him. This chance encounter with Godfrey opens up an important sociological dimension to the analysis of the film, for it is the result of its two central characters being subjected to the dense hyper-locality of the Black urban environment and the omnipresence of its inhabitants that Ricky, upon seeing the Black male emerge from the car instantly recognizes him and addresses him by his first name. It may well be that it is this sense of familiarity produced by the human density of the urban locale that is the incendiary factor in the escalation of trivial incidents into full-blown violent conflict as Ricky, having watched the ensuing minor scuffle from the car as Wisdom refuses to agree to the £60 Godfrey estimates as the monetary value of his broken rear-view mirror, now attempts to defuse the row. However, Godfrey, having momentarily left the scene, returns with his pet pit bull terrier, the symbolic accompaniment to the urban Black youth's sense of hyper-masculine identity, and immediately sets upon attacking Wisdom and Ricky who retreat back to the car and drive off to Godfrey's shouts of 'pusssy', an insult towards their display of cowardice. I find there is something quite diurnal about the incident, an observation that is accentuated by the film's aesthetic approach that, in the camera's tight framing of the fight within what seems to be the placidity of the everyday street, the scene reinforces that conflict and confrontation, be it minor or fatal, are the habitual experiences the Black urban male must condition himself to negotiate as part of living within the urban location. *Bullet Boy* builds on these mediated structuring logics cited in its outline, and the idea of black-on-black gun crime as the natural outcome of familial instability is secured by a number of dramatizing strategies. In this respect, *Bullet Boy* can in some ways be understood as a form of modern, moral critique. For example, Ricky elects not to return home upon being released from prison and in turn missing his own welcome home party. Here, diegetic music is employed to great effect, and the room is permeated by Janet Kay's 1979 lover's rock song 'Silly Games' to a dramatic shift in tone to the pounding 2001 track 'Danger' by the Black American rapper Mystikal as Ricky instead attends a party organized by Wisdom and his girlfriend Shea (Sharea Samuels) and situates Ricky within a more hegemonically symmetrical Black urban subcultural environment. This immediately implies a cross-generational dialectic to be contested throughout the story between the physical decrees of a street subculture and the emotional demands of a family rooted within London's West Indian community. Indeed, that Ricky and Curtis's father is never mentioned or referenced in the film, *Bullet Boy's* male characters seem to be constantly in need to find, perform and reaffirm their own version of masculinity, and having now become the subject of ridicule for his show of cowardice in front of Godfrey, an incident that has quickly circulated within the urban locale and expectedly, the immediate reassertion of masculine pride becomes a determining factor in the unstableness exhibited by Wisdom. This also speaks to how the film is organized by movement – the young men are in constant transit and within the geographical bounds of Hackney that eventually lead both men to track Godfrey to his house where Wisdom, who now has the gun in his possession, vows to reassert his sense of machismo and serves as an example of the disproportionate escalation of a conflict that the reticent Ricky is unable to intervene in. Ricky's display of shock and outrage that Wisdom, having initially promised to simply scare Godfrey with the pistol in an effort to reaffirm his sense of masculinity within the urban locale instead elects to shoot the dog, is not simply a reaction to the excessiveness of Wisdom's actions, nor that the possession of a loaded gun threatens his own freedom, but the act's more localized implications as Godfrey flees from the gunshots into the night. The film at this point seems to posit an interpretative contradiction in its conception of the dynamics of Ricky and Wisdom's friendship that attempts to use the incident to affirm the interdependence between the two men but equally displays a particularly erroneous conception of brotherhood - or at least one determined by an inflexible hierarchy of needs that are in themselves organized what appears to be a continuous flow between physical deeds and symbolic debts. For us, the imbalanced dynamic between the two men is to be discerned in how Wisdom's instinctive need to respond emphatically to Godfrey's defilement of his masculinity and pride supersedes all other possible obligations; Wisdom expresses no remorse or regret in the embroiling of Ricky, who is now compelled to kick the dead dog into the canal and in this action is now firmly re-established within the conflict-laden perpetuality of the urban existence.

From its onset, *Bullet Boy*'s mise en scène is furnished with establishing shots of housing estates that become signifiers of the physical and social boundaries and the possibility of death. For *Bullet Boy*, filmed in and around Clapton, Hackney, a distinctively Black area of East London that includes the infamous 'Murder Mile', a colloquial term lexicalized by the national media to describe a stretch of the area adjoining Lower Clapton Road with Upper Clapton Road and where in the 1990s and early 2000s was the scene of a number gang-related killings (*Independent*, 6 January 2002), the film places its central character within a bleak physical and mental commodiousness. This is exemplified by a number of shots where Ricky looks pensively over a pre-2012 Olympics Hackney Marshes (Figure 8.1). These scenes expand from Ricky's POV to offer panoramic aerial views of the symmetrically organized buildings that make up Clapton Park Estate and are presented as architecturally and socially distinct from the surrounding houses captured in the camera's overview of Hackney. Formally, and supplemented by the film's episodic narrative structure, *Bullet Boy* is documentarist in its study of peripheral Black existences and in adopting such an aesthetic approach, *Bullet Boy* represents an unvaried continuum of the realist orthodoxy of Black British film as argued by Mercer (1988, 1994). This should not necessarily be understood as a particular affliction, as the film's setting within a geographic actuality, its natural lighting and unsteady camera work generate a spontaneity essential to the film's marrying of character and location, creating the sense that its fictional action emerges naturally

Figure 8.1 Ricky looking over Hackney Marshes in *Bullet Boy* (dir. Saul Dibb, 2004).

from a real social context. It is perhaps this negotiation between its mediatized Black content and its stylistic approach that informed its critical aggrandizement as 'the nearest the British cinema has come to the power and honesty of John Singleton's 1991 picture about life in South Central LA, Boyz N the Hood, which in essential ways it resembles' (Quoted in *The Observer*, 9 April 2005). Of course, in the ghetto-centric hood films we find a less cinematic realist register, and my reading of *Bullet Boy*'s aesthetic strategies is less concerned with the transparency of its documentary realism, but in drawing on these aesthetic and thematic continuities, and bearing in mind how *Bullet Boy*'s authenticity is achieved through a realist aesthetic underpinned by a general principle of truth-telling, the film trades on its own sense of authenticity that is in many respects assumed and inherited by the topicality of its overriding thematic concerns to satisfy a set of expectations organized not only by the audience's existing knowledge of and response to the issue of Blackness and gun crime but also through the archive of previous (meta)representations.

It is this argument that the film is constructed by ideas that have been sourced from what I've described as the hauntological Black archive that in some senses chimes with Sarah Godfrey's reading that *Bullet Boy*'s interest is not in any sustained analysis of structural inequalities or racial discrimination, yet we can assert that the film attempts to appeal to a particular socio-economic interpretation of the Black urban criminal lifeworld, if only as a basis for identifying where the film has presented itself as *instinctively* citational, for *Bullet Boy*'s recourse to what remains unknown within the official grand narratives of violent Black urbanity and black-on-black gun crime – the family – is the primary means through which the film navigates through and at points attempts to expand the singularity of the official narratives of Black urban violence and death. I would describe this as a tension rather than a seamless oscillation between two systems of thought and importantly, meaning-making. Indeed, one can observe how the film offers a somewhat bipolar account of its social relations; all of *Bullet Boy*'s representations of officialdom – teachers, police, lawyers, prison officials and his probation officer – are white and implies a continuation of Blackness as being situated in vertical relationships with social power, precisely the kind of narrational convention that would require a Black narrative criminology as an intervening framework to interrogate how whiteness within the film is an invisible force of Black subjection. Ricky, having missed his first probationary meeting to roam with Wisdom, is told that missing another or his involvement in any kind of misdemeanour will result in an immediate return to prison. The film's close adherence to classic forms of narration, act structures and story craft means that *Bullet Boy* rather overemphasizes the scene's importance in setting up an impending inciting incident – the camera pauses on Ricky as he absorbs the strict caution given by officer to avoid any kind of transgression, a scenario that the audience understands as an inevitability and one that Ricky is already well on his way to fulfilling despite his recent return to his family.

One of the generally uncontested understandings of a criminalized Black urbanity that *Bullet Boy* is concerned with, as I've suggested, is the way that conflicts with the trivial origins can rapidly escalate. Related to this is Ricky's own understanding of his marginality and in turn, his inability to alter the inevitable trajectory back into violent

Figure 8.2 Ricky walking through Clapton in *Bullet Boy* (dir. Saul Dibb, 2004).

conflict. This is captured in a long shot where Ricky occupies the side of the frame as he walks through Clapton (Figure 8.2). The image of Ricky here as structured by the long shot presents an absorbing, dedramatized moment of narration that asks the audience to engage with a more capacious understanding of the spatial relationships that engulf Ricky, and he is further reduced against the buildings and streets that become signifiers of social insignificance and alienation, despite his own dissatisfaction with the inability to smother the tensions of his own social identity which is now both tethered to and abstracted from the urban environment. These images of Ricky walking through Clapton as an area of temporal and spatial uncertainty induces a disturbing air of helplessness, with the vacant physical space accentuating Ricky's limited range of possibilities and positions Ricky as extremely vulnerable to the direct and indirect, intended and unintended outcomes produced by his association with Wisdom. The audience is offered a window into the impossibility of extrication as he makes a visit to the home of the apprehensive Godfrey to resolve the conflict between them both. If Godfrey's claim that the pair are 'taking man for a pussy' interprets the shooting of his dog as a moment of disrespect to be countered by violent hyper-territorial masculinity, in Ricky's own attempts to decouple himself from Wisdom in specific regard to the killing of Godfrey's dog while maintaining his loyalty to Wisdom, we encounter the gradual coming to the fore of Ricky's anxiety towards the potential threat to his future. This is later expressed in more direct tones at a local ice rink where Ricky is able to articulate his deep desires free from peer-to-peer ridicule. His confession of 'I wanna do things' to Shea is Ricky at his most sincere as he describes the aspirations and desires that are furnished by the illusion of choice, made all the more chimeric given that individual choices are not completely destroyed but dictated by the urban locale. At this point, the abortiveness of Ricky's peace-making attempt becomes apparent, and an audial juxtaposition is established in the use of the Johnny Kidd and the Pirates 1960 song 'Shaking All Over', a sequence that displays a moment of contrasting drama by the exhibition of violent nihilism married with the enjoyment expressed by Ricky, Curtis and Shea skating as a hooded Godfrey and his accomplices destroy Wisdom's car with baseball bats while he is in a corner shop. The interacting scenes serve as a metaphor for the gradual opening up of diametrically opposing lifestyles between Ricky and Wilson. For Ricky, his escapist desires are negated by the ties of friendship and loyalty as the centripetal forces keeping Ricky within Wisdom's violent orbit. Wisdom, on the other hand, lives an existence devoid of any family structure or emotional ties beyond Ricky and some ways offers an understanding of the seamlessness in which Ricky is drawn into the conflict between Wisdom and Godfrey. The Black urban setting is conceived as a space of inescapable locality as Godfrey turns up outside Wisdom's flat with his gang vowing to kill him, and Ricky's sense of obligation is as much a commitment to filling an emotional void in Wisdom's life as it is physical support for an impending counter-attack against Godfrey, and the argument between Ricky and the disapproving Shea serves as a further source of exposition that reveals the history of violence binding the young men as Ricky shouts: 'he saved my life, and now you are telling me to turn my back on him?'. The seeming impossibility of any alternative resolution beyond the proactive and pre-emptive killing of Godfrey gives the scene a heightened sense of authenticity in placing Wisdom and Ricky in a landscape of interactions and existences that are governed by a 'kill or be killed' mentality. One may indeed wish to interrogate the plausibility of Ricky's immediate recourse to the very criminal existence he had only twenty-four hours ago vowed to forgo for a life less governed by crime and conflict, and it is this indexical eagerness within *Bullet Boy*'s narrative structure that may account for the apparent ease in which Ricky returns to criminality, having just been released from prison and faced with the reality of an immediate return to his cell. It may be as a result of the dialogism presented to us through the character of Ricky that the film, at least at this narrational juncture, seems undecided if his recourse to murderous criminal activity is a decision of culture, environment, circumstance, mentality or loyalty. What *is* clear to the audience is that the stigma of his previous crime has reshaped his outlook on life, born fundamentally from his sense of relative unfulfilment that had allowed Ricky to momentarily indulge in the chimeric idea of personal change. Despite the obvious and reverberating personal repercussions, Ricky's reaction to the threat on Wisdom's life by Godfrey summons an instinctive and unwavering loyalty to a friend that not only exhibits a code of ethics but also exposes him to the consequences of peer pressure that accompany the existence within the intensity of the urban location. Godfrey's issuing of a death threat towards Wisdom is a shared experience and therefore is to be resolved through a collective responsibility and revenge enactment, the very cyclical actions that structure the Black urban environment as an endless sphere of violent criminality. This may indeed affirm the film's referentiality to media moral panics, in that in presenting the conflict as cyclical, the scene is permeated by a distinctive homogenic energy in that it has developed a construction of Blackness, and the Black body, that casts no dividing line between those categorized as victims and those who we have identified as perpetrators.

I consider Ricky's endeavours to abstract himself from the predicament posed by Wisdom as deeply symptomatic of his own awareness of his status of being *twice* an outsider – first, a social outsider alienated from the mainstream arenas of social acceptance, a status that is accentuated by class as well as race and second, an outsider within the urban locality born from his differentiating perspective on criminality as a regressive and futile existence. For Wisdom, the genesis of his fidelity to the estate is much more than a question of territorial command and its potential as a source of Black hyper-masculinity (Alexander, 1996) but an apprehensiveness evoked by the unfamiliarity of the world outside the symbolic location and the sense of a non-being unaccommodated to a further marginal existence should one begin to venture beyond the Black urban enclave. For within the neoliberal order, the only possible mode of social existence chosen by the Black urban Other within the symbolic location is via a deeper subsumption into an unproductive criminal lifeworld and away from the mainstream economic and social spheres of white Britain, and it is this apparent construction of Black urban existence as interpreted through the film's similarly filtered optic that for Godfrey is sufficient to contend that *Bullet Boy* 'presents a neoliberal narrative in which the choices of the individual are presented as unencumbered and straightforward' (2022: 141). It is in understanding the particular tenet of neoliberalism Godfrey is referring to – the individual maximizing of opportunity and personal responsibility – that I want to argue that the film conceives Lower Clapton as an entrapped social landscape for Ricky, Wisdom and others, and to read Ricky's immediate return back to criminality (and in this case, murder) as the outcome of a simple rejection of the avenues of escape and its accompanying promise of self-actualization is to neglect how *Bullet Boy*'s subtle crafting of the physical, economic and mental relationship between space, race and identity conveys a specific social world that, for the young men embroiled in gun violence, is actually dissolved of all alternative modes of existence. In this vein, the film provides a constant reminder of how the trivial registers a powerful implication on the structural, as the scene cuts to a shot of the still floating dead dog in the canal, moving to an extreme close-up, and as the film cuts briefly to Ricky delivering his gun to Wisdom to use in the attack, the image of the pit bull terrier in the canal becomes a decomposing indicator of not just an impending conflict and reprisal but also the triviality of the ensuing conflict birthed from a culture of hyper-masculine performativity within the symbolic location. The image of the dead dog is also made significant by the film's emphasis on cause-and-effect relationships, and this is expanded through a constant duality in the intercutting between Ricky and Wisdom preparing for the attack and Curtis and Rio within Hackney Marshes as they throw stones at the carcass. The film's repetitive scenic interplaying between the two Black children and Black men performs not as a visual strategy to represent Black gun- and gang-violence as a genetic inheritance but how the tremors of the nihilistic decisions made and actions performed by individuals are felt by those in immediate emotional and physical proximity to them. Further, this should not simply be understood as a descending generational permeation but one horizontally affective through the dynamics of the friendship between Ricky and Wisdom, and is expressed in the nihilistic fatalism of Wisdom's justificatory insistence that 'if he's gonna kill me why shouldn't I kill him?' to which Ricky has no answer. Multiple interpretations of the interpellation of the discourse of Black urban gun crime and Black death to within *Bullet Boy* can be made here. On the one hand, and in some sense following the arguments of Godfrey, this demonstration of murderous nihilism by Wisdom can be understood as a simple representation of what is described as the 'long-held normative discourses around young, poor, Black men and boys' (2022: 139), but on the other, while *Bullet Boy* synonymizes the concepts of Blackness and gun crime through the superimposition of contemporary anxieties onto the images of young Black people, the image of the young boys playing on Hackney Marshes is expressed by a more poetic, neorealist aesthetic register, and like Curtis's and Wisdom's trip through the countryside to pick up Ricky, the two Black boys playing across the marshes evokes a heightened feeling of spaciousness and extensiveness when placed within a non-associative mise en scène. This is married with an aesthetically contrasting but thematically relational image as Wisdom and Ricky sit quietly on a bus, surrounded by elderly women *en route* to carry out a violent murder. Music is again a potent narrational device, and the accumulating tension of a moment of immanent gun conflict is extra-diegetically expressed through the haunting incidental soundtrack by the British Trip Hop group Massive Attack leading up to the shooting scene, where Godfrey and several of his accomplices in his urban dwelling are ambushed by Wisdom and Ricky, who plays a supporting role in the attack by keeping watch out outside the house, the camera capturing the placidity of the surrounding environment through a deep depth of field as Ricky offers a subtle gesture to a woman who walks past him. This encounter and the sense of calmness achieved by the depicting of an imminent gun murder taking place in an otherwise deserted street combine to aestheticize black-on-black gun crime as the spectacularizing unspectacular, an *ad rem* feature within Clapton that momentarily disturbs rather than fractures the diurnal flows of the everyday experiences of street and place, and in doing so offering an under-facticity to the mediatized construction of the cacophonous Black urban environment as a spectacle of relentless gun activity. This sense of quietude is unable to be unsettled by the commotion that ensues when the attempted killing of Godfrey fails, as Wisdom misses his shots. As the gun shots go off, the camera's stillness is now disturbed by a dynamic movement as Godfrey and his crew make their escape from the house. As encountered in *Storm Damage*, *Bullet Boy* exhibits no adherence to the orthodoxical use of the urban music soundtrack as an intra- and extra-diegetic marketing strategy. However, the shoot-out is able to evoke a sense of subcultural situatedness through the use of diegetic music in the sound of the Black American rapper N.O.R.E's thunderous 'Nothin', which plays from Godfrey's living room as Wisdom enters the house. Having seen Ricky's face in the aftermath of the unsuccessful attempt to kill Godfrey, and now becoming exposed to the inevitability of fatal retribution that surely awaits both young men, Ricky's scream of 'man has to get out of here' exhibits no more faith in Wisdom's hyper-masochistic confidence in fending of the impending retaliative attack in the proclamation that he 'can deal with it'. But Wisdom's status as a perpetual liability in the life of Ricky seems to momentarily erode Ricky's own perennial concern for Wisdom's immediate safety, a stance match by Wisdom's hyper-masochistic stoic as Wisdom responds with 'Blood. I'm not leaving the manor. I don't know nowhere else, I ain't got nowhere else'. Here Wisdom's disembeddedness from any emotional unit or commitment beyond the Clapton Park Estate is the barrier, rather than the enabling reality of his existence allowing him to venture beyond Clapton's confines, and in the context of the day's events, an incomprehensible alternative reality to be observed in

Ricky's response of 'This is just a place rude boy!' Again, this dialectic serves as an important point of exposition in providing further access to the friend's past which, as we can discern, has been conditioned by a continuing cross purpose, and there is an energetic subtext to the dismissive force by which Ricky ends the discussion with Wisdom, and as he turns away to leave, he shouts 'I can't keep explaining this shit to you!'. However, despite their respective reactions to the threat now posed by Godfrey, we see within Wisdom an altered sense of fidelity in the form of ownership and responsibility and with it, a reordering of the hierarchy of needs that had structured their friendship over the last days, for as he begins to walk away, Wisdom hands him his gun back for protection while offering money to fund his escape. The young men embrace, but what occurs just before this, and in many ways becomes the essence of the scene, is how the moment is framed by a prolonged look of resignation exchanged between the bredren, and the camera captures an intersubjective gaze that amplifies not just a shared sense of inevitability that the two young men will not see each other again, a consequence of the geographic distance and anonymity needed by Ricky and/ or Godfrey's impending challenge to Wisdom's mortality, but the differences between Ricky and Wisdom's sense of fidelity to the Clapton Park Estate and its surrounding geographies. In Ricky's case, difference, expansivity and redemption is a perspective achieved through his time in prison, but also revolves around their respective understandings of the exact function of the estate, their own sense of agency within the space and their individual conceptualizations of home. For Wisdom, neither superiority nor distinction is responsible for any sense of verticality now dividing the pair. However, for the spectator, Ricky's desire remains intractable for the street decrees of Clapton and subsequently for Wisdom, not simply because of a lack of courage or means of escape but equally by Ricky's inability to understand Wisdom's own desire to remain within Clapton. This scene is therefore highly important in this context of the film's endeavours to interact with but also depart from the prevailing black-on-black gang-violence narrative, as we have arrived at final stages in the film's own pedagogical imperative. This is the gradual expansion of the chasm between Ricky and Wisdom through its ontological suturing of what is severed from view in the circulation of the homogenizing narratives of black-on-black crime as a useful fiction of race; here, the behavioural, emotional and imaginative dissonance between the bredren's desires is accentuated by the reality of the seemingly inextricable conflict the young men are now trapped in and a desire that, irrespective of the murderous intentions of Godfrey and his collective, will remain bound in unrealization and stasis.

Bullet Boy's necessary moralism as a narrational strategy can be identified in its use of the family unit when Ricky is questioned by his mother Beverley's (Claire Perkins) partner and evangelical church minister Leon (Curtis Walker), who confronts Ricky at the flat during a family dinner which he had missed and refuses to join as he now attempts to leave Hackney in the immediate aftermath of the failed attempt at killing Godfrey. Standing face-to-face with Ricky in a close-up shot framing that gives greater emphasis to his words delivered in a low voice, he states, 'I know what's been going on' as he stares at Ricky, who remains stoic throughout. Just how Leon knows, a claim that is neither interrogated by the unaffected Ricky nor expounded upon by Leon, seems immaterial to the exchange. However, whether this is simply an assumption based on Ricky's current demeanour and previous criminal transgressions, an intuitive summary drawn from his own experiences of gang conflict or simply the kind of knowledge only acquired through the hyper-locality and density of the urban, his status as a church leader, a man of God and the combinational effect of his oraculist sartorial appearance that is accentuated by his black button shirt with a black beanie cap infuses the character, and his words, with a sacerdotal quality as he advises, 'it's a never ending circle that just goes round and round, it don't lead nowhere!' For Ricky, irrespective of if Leon's words exhibit a confluence between Christian evangelism and the street wisdom that Leon's seniority has accrued, his presence in the flat and attempted intervention are little more than an affront to Ricky's masculinity and his own sense of domestic proprietorship as he asks, 'you trying to preach to me?'. Indeed, Ricky is being confronted by the triple effect of Leon's interchangeable guises as a reformed gang member, a church minister, Beverley's partner or a combination of all three, but none of which are able to penetrate Ricky's aloofness, who simply walks out on the discussion, slamming the door on both his family and the chance of salvation, spiritual or patriarchal, that is offered to him. We can interpret this scene in two ways, both of which are related to the pedagogical aspects of the popular Black urban film and how its spectacularizing representations of black-on-black gun violence are to be justified by the interpellation of a passing moralism and gestural castigation of gun violence as its redemptive element. First, a moral instructive is to be located in the absence of any patriarchal guidance, and this ambition is accentuated by the camera's close framing of Leon and its capture of his resigning facial expression at the point of realization that his physical/spiritual presence in the household is not accompanied by any ecclesiastical authority or even influence. Second, in this exchange, and speaking directly to the function of the film as an intervention into the apparent impenetrability of the Black urban criminal psyche as *Bullet Boy*'s balancing counter-investment, the enlargement of Leon's anti-gun crime plea finds an extra-diegetic register; Leon is of course very much preaching, his words performing not just as an amplified instructive to Ricky but as a wider damnation of the cycle of internecine armed violence and death among Britain's Black urban youths.

Is there anything that is present *within Bullet Boy*'s hegemonically distilled fabula that further affirms the film as a social aesthetic? It is clear, for me, that it is in the need to enhance the experience of authenticity and reality that the film must also be ballast with an imaginary Black signifier. This necessitates a reading of the actual quotations that are engaged in the process of ontological suturing, and despite my claim that the film draws its themes and characterizations from the official narratives of Black fatal criminality, the Metropolitan Police occupy a less ubiquitous diegetic role in *Bullet Boy* than, say, the representations of law and order as found in *Boyz in the Hood* in a notable scene, where Tre is reduced to tears as a Black police officer holds a gun to his face after pulling him and Ricky over without any pretext beyond their race. What becomes particularly salient is the level of psychological viciousness exhibited by the police officer that disturbs even his white partner, and the Black police officer's intra-racial oppression and self-hatred as depicted by the film's director John Singleton suggest that Blackness, even when dressed in blue, functions as an undifferentiated component of a broader system of LAPD racism in which 'Tre is transformed linguistically by the Black officer from being a man to a suspected gang member' (Massood, 2003: 156). In *Bullet Boy*, the police have a more legitimate if not quite as subliminal, racially explicit and visceral engagement with Black youths in the detailed procedurality of their brief, but highly significant inclusion that allows for the film to be experienced through the spectre of the hauntological Black urban Other as an *official* figure of armed menace. Here, Operation Trident displays an intra-diegetic energy within *Bullet Boy* as a source of authenticating dramatic action as, in a scene that follows Wisdom and Ricky's attempted murder of Godfrey, the Metropolitan Police conduct an early morning raid on the family flat as Ricky, Curtis and Beverley are dragged screaming from their beds in terror as armed police units swarm the flat in what we can connote is the response to a gathering of intelligence that Ricky is in possession of gun through their Firearms Intelligence Unit. There should be a degree of perseverance exercised towards my analytical interest in what may appear to be the minutiae of Operation Trident's annotation within the text. I had previously identified Operation Trident as the signifier for a murderous Black urban masculinity, and while Trident is never directly cited during the scene, the film's depiction of the armed police raid is extremely procedural and exhibits less emphasis on the character's own narrative POV and weighs towards the formalities that are conducted during such armed procedures, and it achieves a dynamic mise en scène more akin to overt documentary practices than a work of dramatic fiction. While one could argue that the depiction of specialist police units in such a guise necessitates a heightened degree of factual accuracy, *Bullet Boy*'s inescapable alignment with the discourse of urban crime means the scene can only be accepted as an outcome of the generic, thematic and indexical relationship between black-on-black violence and its official signifier.

Despite my identification of the inferred presence of Operation Trident throughout the following scenes – Ricky is released and no gun is retrieved from the house – the police are conspicuously absent in the instance where gun possession produces a dramatic consequence, when Curtis accidentally shoots his best friend while playing hide and seek in Hackney Marches with the gun he had concealed in the mattress of his bed prior to the armed police raid, now loaded with bullets as a result of the failed killing of Godfrey. I feel this is again an example of ontological suturing, the scene is constructed from less hegemonically symmetrical logics; rather than the kids being placed within the urban settings, the scene projects a sense of asymmetricity by capturing the boys playfully shooting towards a white horse roaming on the marshes and displays a more poetic realism. Despite the presence of the gun, the scene is able to evoke a feeling of boundlessness that is enjoyed by the boys and becomes part of the film's attempt to present a counter-narrative to the idea of Black gun incidents emerging directly out of the context of nihilistic black-on-black violence. The popular Black British urban film participates in a paradox that, resourced from the Black hauntological archive as a practice of annotation and distillation, also attempts to depart from the very archive by the constructing of its own elements of authenticity and facticity to supplement the story with the sub-narratives that are kept outside of the dominant black-on-black frame. This is primarily identified in the film's interest in the functionality of the family and the emotional lives of its individual members and particularly, Beverley. Her resorting to kicking Ricky out of the family home to 'give Curtis a chance' displays some discontinuity with the familial fracturing that we encounter in *Storm Damage*, where Stefan's rejection by his mother after being arrested for taxi fare dodging is characterized by dis-recognition and indifference. Here, the sentiment is similar but less phlegmatic in its execution. Ricky is recognized but only as the defining problem in the life cycle of Curtis. For Ricky, he can only understand his mother's decision as a binary between the innocence of Curtis and the unredeemable and non-cohabitable Black urban malevolence of her firstborn, although in his shouts of 'leave the bad breed here init!' the question of causation lies firmly with a defect within Beverley's own parenting. Ricky is slapped by Beverley, a slap that I sense is motivated partly by his possessing of a loaded gun and partly out of Ricky's inability even at this point to realize the consequences of the culture of gun violence that has now entered the family home as endangering not just himself but the innocence of his young brother. Indeed, it is now, having been told that Curtis has shot Rio with his own gun and on hearing Beverley scream 'you might as well have put the bloody thing in his hand', that the tremors of Ricky's choices, all be them limited, are now fully felt, and as the camera pauses on Ricky, we are presented with two subjectivities divided by the pain of giving up a son to save another; for Ricky, the sense of familial abandonment and rejection to be further compounded by the loss of Shea who, having earlier lambasted Ricky when he revealed his and Wisdom's failed attempt to kill Godfrey, refuses to open the door when he arrives. For Beverley, she has had to endure the terrifying police raid and face the humiliating wrath of the family of Rio, particularly his father Neville (Sylvester Williams) who subjects her to a barrage of insults when she, Curtis and Leon visit the family to apologize for the incident. In Neville's damnation of the shooting as the outcome of her own rearing of her sons, *Bullet Boy* engages with the potential of the Black woman within the urban film to perform as a central character in its construction of an accompanying under-narrative to the dominant visage of black-on-black gun crime. The film's ontological suturing at this stage uses the practice of mothering as the conduit for its dispersal of hegemonically countering and under-emotions, primarily through Beverley, but also to be found symbolically in Shea's attentiveness to Ricky's emotional state. However, Beverley's maternal purpose as the suffering and scrutinizing of the Black mother, as seen in *Storm Damage*, remains generically and thematically essential to the liberal aestheticizing of violent Black urban masculinity within the frame of PSB film in this effort, to justify its dramatic interest in the traumatic image of Black corporeality; Black motherhood is only permitted to enter the inferential narrative frame of black-on-black gun violence at the very point of Black urban death.

Following my previous arguments, it is important that we spend some time considering the nature of *Bullet Boy*'s aestheticizing of the inferential construction of Blackness as the quintessential *prima causa* of the spectacle of Black death. The most traumatic forms undoubtedly come in the film's depiction of both Ricky and Wisdom's inevitable murder. The first of which, Wisdom's killing at the hands of Godfrey and his men, is the scene that awaits Ricky on arrival at Wisdom's flat. Blood covers the walls as Wisdom's dead body lies sprawled over an exercise bench in his front room, his eyes open and facing towards the wall, the room made all the more harrowing by Marcel Zyskind's cinematography that accentuates its graphicality and the power of its translation from the extra-diegetic world that gives filmic actualization to the images and narratives encountered in the dominant accounts of Black gun death. Eventually, the scene is annotated by the shouts of 'You are not alone' as the film cuts to Leon preaching in his church. This need to consciously and continuously annotate the images of Black urban gun and gang death is central to the function of the film as a useful, or in this case the *necessary* fiction of race. As Ricky stands watching the dead body, the film finds its under-narrative annotation in the intercutting of this sequence with the images of rebirth and cultural assuaging. From one vantage point, a powerful sense of haunting unease is expressed through the scene's grainy cinematography as Ricky reconciles with the graphic and perceptive reality of death and on the other, familial pain, and the camera captures the emotional tremors of matriarchal desertion and abandonment as Beverley seeks sanctuary in the spiritual space provided by the Evangelical Black church as the congregation are joined by an embracing Leon and Beverley in an emotional rendition of 'Amazing Grace' that spills back into the scene of the murder as Ricky surveys Wisdom's bullet-ridden dead body. Ricky's response at this point is reflective of *Bullet Boy*'s deliberate attempt to disrupt the simple audience identification of Black urban death as a cyclical experience without pause nor indeed pragmatism. The surviving Ricky is quiet throughout and displays little expressive change, perhaps in silent mourning, perhaps a silent rebuking of Wisdom's inability to 'deal' with the threat of Godfrey as promised by his deceased companion, perhaps silent in the realization that he is bound for a similar fate. In the context of the film's thematic trajectory, Wisdom's is an expected killing, but the degree of spectatorial anxiety and desire is secured by the unexpected viscerality of Wisdom's prone Black body, now in a state of rigor mortis, the eyes open and fixed towards the ceiling. Finding the hidden stash of money Wisdom had promised him for his escape, Ricky simply walks out of the flat and returns to his home without alerting anyone to the murder. This may be a more delicate manifestation of the Black vernacular nihilism as asserted by Gilroy that I had explored earlier. For Ricky's inexpression and (in) actions are not only a demonstration of survival as a primal instinct within the urban setting, but its accompanying ethics of silence and unspoken street codes disallow any instinctive recourse to the official forms of law and order in the police as enjoyed by the rest of society and categorize Wisdom's killing as the circular, co-complicit outcome of hyper-local gun crime that denies any possibility of true detachment or unsituatedness from the symbolic location. Indeed, as Ricky, now having returned to the family flat for a final time and explained how the chain of decisions that have left him without a family, Wisdom, a home and a girlfriend, his sense of survival is expressed here as creating the necessary distance from him and his young, impressionable brother when, as the boys look over Hackney Marshes, Ricky asks him to go to the shops for them both. Unbeknown to Curtis and exhibiting all the filmic and narrative elements that combine at a moment of humanization as the film's emotional peak, Ricky will be gone by the time he returns. The film at this point offers a tonal interchange between Ricky's leaving and the returning Curtis in a display of sibling love and obedience as he cycles home with their food towards the Clapton Park Estate. Here, and passing through an Upper Clapton Road depicted at this moment as a space of bustling human activity and Black residents, we are presented with a sense that Curtis is actually cycling through a mediatized social sphere that has aestheticized and narrativized the corpses that have littered Murder Mile's public history. For Ricky, his own trajectory is one of flotsam oblivion and emptiness, rather than of escapism and departure as Ricky leaves the estate. Unlike the promise of the college scholarships at Moorhouse College and the University of Southern California in *Boyz in the Hood* that accelerates Tre and Ricky's desire to escape the violence of Crenshaw or the prospect of love and the secure and contributive place within a family unit that awaits Caine in joining Ronnie and her son on her journey to Atlanta in *Menace II Society*, there is no visible or tangible destination or haven for Ricky to aspire towards and escape to, and no certainty in what will become of the criminal Black youth bound for a nomadic existence further debased through the severance of all that is essential to Ricky's sense of belonging.

It is this concern with the future that seems to comply with *Storm Damage*'s opaque evaluation of Black youthhood in the film's presentation of an intra-race dystopia that is firmly established as the reductive mise en scène of Ricky's conflict-laden existence. Here, while the film's contextual vocabulary is analytically benign, *Bullet Boy* makes no concerted intra-diegetic attempt to resolve the problems Ricky and Wisdom are embedded in, but rather relates them to the uncertainties of the environment as a point of social separation that determine the poles of official discourse, where gang culture within the inner city is shown to be a pervasive part of everyday life to be performed and endured only by young Black people. Here, I want to take seriously the analytical implications presented to us in the film's fabula. It is in this theoretical spirit that I acknowledge that the popular Black urban text facilitates certain ways of knowing, recognizing, interpreting and constructing social identities, responding to the moral panic of a criminalized Black urban identity, and as a result, produce different meanings and evaluations. This is constitutive of what I am terming the Black urban dialogism, and I arrive at this particular articulation of Mikhail Bakhtin's dialogism as a reliable framework for the reading of *Bullet Boy* via the analysis of filmic dialogism by Mercer, who engages with the theory of dialogism to consider the textures of radical Black British filmmaking in the late 1980s (1988). The constitutive parts of the popular Black urban film are equally available to such an analytical framework as the text is unable to function independently of the complex social, political and cultural assemblages and imperatives that unify its textual organs. Specifically, that dialogism lends itself to the description of the popular Black urban film as a social aesthetic that is itself comprised of a number of social, cultural and political imperatives with textual implications that, in our interrogation of the film, allow for a return to Derrida in recalling his disavowal of deconstructionism as a stable mode of textual analysis in that such a reading is something negotiated through the dismantling of the constitutive elements and constituent fabrics that populate the text. Given that Derrida insists that texts are absent of any self-reliant or independent fragments of meaning because any text's individual components can be comprehended only through how they become positioned within the much larger textual structure, in the case of the Black urban text, its filmic language and forms of meaning intermediate between various participant positions are not fixed and separate but are interactive. Be this termed as the social aesthetics of the urban text or its triangulation of ownership, no one constituent involved in this dialogue is able to commandeer textual meaning, demonstrative of what Hall sees as the 'negative side' of Bakhtin's dialogism (236). The complex Black urban dialogism of *Bullet Boy*'s social aesthetics that all produce their own forms of meaning makes the popular urban film as a site of continuous cultural and textual negotiation. Teleologically, *Bullet Boy* is aimed not at rupturing our received and accepted hegemonies of Black urban sociality and experience but is invested in its variability. To be precise, this variability is found in the use of the text to express a number of different meanings but where these interacting textual elements are essential to the film's interpretation. Rather than merely fragmentary, here dialogism leads to a more nuanced and tension-laden way of thinking about Black urban conflict that also enables a theoretical linkage and juxtaposition of otherwise incompatible intellectual paradigms and approaches. The popular Black urban film as a social aesthetic renders *Bullet Boy* as equally constitutive of these dialogisms, as it is comprised of different elements and interlocking discourses as it organizes its Black material as fictional narratives and indexicalities. This does not render the Black urban film as the *passive* compiler of a body of discourses, realities and hauntological imaginaries of Black urban violence and fatality but a site of the constant interaction between the tremendously dynamic and multi-constituted amplification of the mediacentric images of Black urban criminality, and highlights the complex intertextualities that embed the popular Black British urban film within a specific conjuncture as an interventive counter-narrative, as a consenting modality of Black filmic representation, as the social aesthetic, as a useful and necessary fiction of race, and with the hauntological Black Urban Other at its dramatic centre.

Bullet Boy's conclusion further demonstrates the constitutiveness of the film as a transcoded, relational and distilled aestheticization of black-on-black criminal life and gun death, albeit one which is firmly in concert with my idea of the popular Black urban film as structured of a complex dialogism. The Black body, so increasingly vulnerable to the visual approximation of externally constructed ideas and phenomena to be reified within filmic and televisual representations of Black urbanity as a templated existence, is further confirmed by the inevitability of this murder, and the film's aestheticization of Black death is particularly generative for this analysis. Here, the death of Ricky performs as a corporeal site for the symbiosis of both the regimes of verisimilitude; citational Black death functions both as a *generic* inevitability and in relation to popular urban drama as an authenticating and hegemonically symmetrical counter-investment, as a *cultural* necessity. For *Bullet Boy*, its constructing of Ricky's existence as the dictate of the hyper-local here becomes valuable for the purpose of dramatic effect that as a result of the sudden eroding of any infrastructural or practical support network around him and his geographic movements in the aftermath of the attempted murder of Godfrey and Wisdom's killing become increasingly circumscribed, Ricky's sole means of escape is via the local train station. It is on the station platform that he is passed by one of Godfrey's accomplices, having seemingly tracked Ricky as he made his way to the station, and this sense of a hyper-local sphere can be derived from how his short walk from the home to the station has been under constant surveillance. More significantly, it is this display of territoriality that reconfigures the surrounding streets of Clapton Park Estate as a novel conurbation in that its exterior and public buildings are subsumed within the sphere of a hyper-locality where even the area's train station is governed by a similar sense of muscular proprietorship, and through which Ricky is immediately confronted by Godfrey and his gang and shot multiple times on the platform. Despite the shooting's obvious and intended claim to authenticity that portrays an epidemiological version of Black urban death, the scene can also be understood as a moment of ontological suture, and its interpretation of black-on-black gun violence as catalytic of a social, cultural and emotional tremoring is conveyed again through its system of intercutting; the spectator is presented with the image of Ricky lying dead on the platform, just as Curtis arrives back at the flat to find that Ricky is gone for good. If dominant narratives and images inscribe into the anxious public imaginary the idea of Black gun crime as an inextricable feature of the vulnerability and threat of the night that is only further accentuated by its street-light illumination, *Bullet Boy*'s authenticating counter-investment attempts to agitate the hegemonic perception of Black gun violence as an all-encompassing and concealing activity of the after-dark and propels Black gun conflict into diurnality through the conspicuousness of Ricky's murder, which can only be understood as a public execution. But in the context of the broader securing of Black death within public consciousness as a convergence between interracial spectacle and anti-Black indifference, the sequence works to conceive interracial gun violence as a momentary interlude in the everyday occurrences and sights of the quotidian. This is equally an elongation of the Black gun death imaginary, which in accordance with the primary tenets of moral panic now spill beyond the symbolic locations and Black urban environments and encroach onto the public, civic spaces within East London; a train goes past on the adjacent platform just as Ricky lies lifeless on the ground, his small holdall at his feet as the camera again frames Ricky in a long shot that opens up the scene's deep depth of field as the train approaches towards the image's vanishing point (Figure 8.3). It is in *Bullet Boy*'s use of the long shot as a stylistic device that the holdall seems to serve as a symbol for Ricky's exhausted and hegemonic non-being, for despite the brevity of the scene that gives it an absorbing photographic stillness that focuses our attention towards Ricky's dead Black body, its prominent placing within the frame accrues a different but no less interrelated significance through its dialogic status, in conjunction with Ricky's corpse, as an image of paradoxicality. There seems, to me, to be an imaginative and generative under-narrative, or under-interpretation, when focusing on the scene's object that in countering the assertion that our human-object relations are determined by our reconciling of the immaterial thingness of everyday objects at the point 'when they stop working for us', as argued by Bill Brown (2001), seems to delay its relegation as a 'thing' once its basic function has been exhausted by Ricky's murder. It articulates an emptiness and anonymity conditioned by consecutive personal losses, the austerity of the image represents a life limited to the contents of a small bag, and it is this reading that allows the bag to be a metaphor for all that has

Figure 8.3 Ricky lying dead on the station platform in *Bullet Boy* (dir. Saul Dibb, 2004).

been arrested, for had Ricky arrived a few moments earlier, or caught another train, the rucksack becomes reconceptualized as the basis of a new possible existence away from the cycle of gun violence within the Clapton Park Estate. But, beyond my indulgence in such chimeric interpretations, a literal reading returns us to the analysis of *Bullet Boy* as a site of cinematic annotation, and although the film presents Black urban death as an ornamentation to the everyday, it is in the intensification of the dead Black body as a habitual feature in the distressed symbolic location and beyond that ushers black-on-black death from the sensational to the unspectacular and diurnal while retaining its crucial function as an inferential image of alluring antithetically. We again are confronted with the film's aesthetic dialogism as the film cuts back to Curtis. *Bullet Boy* is indeed unable to display a disobedience towards the hegemonic symmetry of Black urban death as a constitutive element in the hauntological Black urban Other's reification into the moral panic of urban gun violence. However, its ability to be ontologically sutured and humanized through the images of familial mourning and trauma reroutes the image towards the realm of a qualified liberal sympathy towards the Black urban Other and in this rerouting, a haptic visuality finds habitation in the liminal space that is opened up by the depicting of black-on-black gang-criminality as a structurally singular narrative that denies its ascribing to a tangible and enacted sociopolitical causality. In this liminal space, the spectrality of Black urban non-being savagery is agitated by the interpellative affect of Black trauma and mourning, and as Beverley is required to identify his body, the Black mother is compelled to perform a labour that is both tremulous and procedural in her signing of his death certificate. This may be the very point where *Bullet Boy* fully succeeds in interposing the unassorted and ossified grand narrative of black-on-black gun death so embedded in pathological sensationalism. There is of course no redemptive solution for either Ricky or Wisdom, an assertion that should be interpreted not as an *accusation* but rather as the identification of the textual and tonal specificities determined by the negotiation between *Bullet Boy*'s social aesthetics that take place at the film's molecular level and is an outcome of the industrial, cultural and social dimensions of Black aesthetic experience and visual sensibility as the dead Black body is positioned at the centre of *Bullet Boy*'s amalgam. It seems to me that the rationalizing optic of human suffering and the alluring spectacle of black-on-black death is a dialectic that is negotiated within the film's diegetic and non-diegetic spaces, and this recruits further attention to the dissimilarity of the deceased Black body as primal to our understanding of gang culture under the prevailing rhizomatic interpretive architecture. However, I want to stress that its depiction of interracial Black death that moves from the spectacular to the quotidian does not negate its power as a useful or/and necessary fiction of race, as in the endeavour to shift the audience from a position of shock and surprise to a gradual but no less anxiety-producing state of expectancy is secured through not just the replication of Black fatality but its repetition as a transmediated spectre across multiple modes of communication that finds a sense of cohesivity within the embracing and reifying theatre of PSB film and TV. In such processes, inferential Black death's dramatization is able to suspend and arrest our sense of disbelief and incomprehension and replace these spectatorial reactions with a kind of spectatorial concentration that becomes elongated and suspended. This is a temporality that is achieved through the choreography of Black death; Black trauma and death disrupt time. It is necessary to again draw on the phenomenological analysis of the criminalized Black body, and my critical understanding of the Black urban Other as a hauntological figure signified through the spectacle of Black death is complemented by Walcott (2021) in his theoretical synthesizing of Derrida's concept of hauntology with Christina Sharp's (2016) theorizing of Black people's existence within the 'Wake' as a state of conscious resistance against the persistent histories of anti-Blackness and white supremacy structuring the normativity of Black death. Walcott provides a parenthesis to Derrida's definition of hauntology in his reading of a ghostliness that is 'both an event a first time, but, importantly, it is also a repetition' (2021: 45). What is of particular importance to me in Walcott's thesis via Derrida is that he is suggesting that it is at the very point of event and repetition that we experience the denial of the spectacularizing of a fatal Black catastrophe as structured by state violence that secures its frame of knowledge and consent, and to partially draw again on Hall's reading of the processes involved in the production of news messages, Black visual injury and internecine death is rendered a story only once it is telegraphed as a *communicative event*. In *Bullet Boy*, the circulation of the reportage and imagery of Black urban violence that inspires the film and authenticates its aestheticizing of Black death performs as a tonal-suppressant in its indexicality and hapticality that seems to place the image of Black visual injury through a suspended moment of associative processing. What I am here suggesting is, and observed in the dead bodies of Ricky, Wilson and the murder of Stefan in *Storm Damage*, Black death is always a slow death, and its pacing is not a consequence of filmic exigency and stylistic artifice but the way the dead Black body is absorbed within a weighted spectatorial ecology of anxiety, desire, empathy, sensationalism and quotidianity that suspends time and in some sense, visual and narrational impermanence. Equally, and drawn from the same phenomenological conceptual stream, the discursive system of signification within the practices of film as a cultural system of narration and as the progenitor to the mythic and hauntologically present murderous Black urban Other can never fully disassociate itself from the essentiality of internecine criminality as the abstract quantum of audiovisual Black death as we experience in *Bullet Boy*. The violent aestheticizing of Black male identity as the useful fiction of race demands the gutting of the culpability of white racial systems within the official logic, and it is through the reality of Black urban criminal life and death as subject to the logics of colonial ordering that we arrive at an interesting, if highly disturbing and consequential paradox: whiteness is the *omnipresent* racial master frame through which we are implored to observe and understand the spectacularized images of Black urban death, and whiteness is equally the structuring *absence* of the realities of Black urban death.

In as much as I have identified slow Black death as being central in the gradual shifting of Black urban conflict onto the quotidian, Black death as filmic image remains no less sorbefacient, and there is a further narrational implication in the experience of visual Black urban death as slow death aestheticized through white racial frame. The desire for stories to reach an expected conclusion, resolution and ending is of course a primary tenet of narrative construction. However, and in perhaps distinguishing conclusion from resolution, the popular Black urban film exhibits a similar practice of inconclusivity as it compels us to interpret the narrative of black-on-black life and death as an open-ended one; it evades any kind of true narrative conclusion precisely because the realities it claims to represent remain present as a moral panic through the mediatized replication and hegemonic repetition of images and narratives of Black urban death with no identifiable cause or solution, and subject to ceaseless public debate and subsequently, the film becomes the source through which we attach our dominant understandings of Black criminality to and make association and inferences from. Within this, what is central to the urban drama's sense of non-ending is the presence of the dead Black body as antithetical to the dominant ideas of humanness and being, but hegemonically symmetrical to our conditioned social and textual expectations. My arguing that *Bullet Boy* participates in this practice of narrative non-closure is therefore concerned with its visual investment in Black corporeality, for while Ricky's killing can be accepted as the story's dramatic resolution that produces a sense of finality, an incompleteness can be identified in how the indexical nature of his death asks for the audience to form its meaning from beyond the diegesis and through its extra-diegetic associativity. In other words, in *Bullet Boy*, we cannot arrive at a satisfactory position on the film's account of interracial Black gun death for as the spectacular becomes the quotidian and everyday, it effaces ideological, perceptive and therefore narrational closure. The conclusive moment in the hegemonic sealing off of the Black body as an inevitable marker of violent death is equally the moment of narrational unending. For even when the hauntological Black urban Other has finally fulfilled its hegemonic purpose (a violent interracial Black death) and thus completing the *useful* and *necessary* narrative obligations as a fiction of race within PSB film and television, it is also a moment of the regenerating of the function of the dead Black body within its image system that encourages me to assert that the popular Black urban text as either a useful or necessary fiction of race is never complete or concluded, and it is this experience of black-on-black death as unending that chaperones its shift from the sensational to the quotidian while still maintaining its crucial sense of indexical desire. I favour a description of this as a schematic, as opposed to a strictly generic encounter, as the adaptive, transcoded and distilled inferentiality of the mediatized construction of black-on-black crime and death is a never-ending discourse affirmed by the replication and repetition within filmic depiction. The lingering and somewhat metaphorical final shot that concludes *Bullet Boy*'s examination of the scourge of Black urban gun violence contributes tremendously to this idea of non-closure as an index of the popular urban film as a citational and distilled representational practice, and demonstrates how its male characters are imbricated in the textual production of Black urban dialogism. The symbolism in this final scene is an attempt to again restore a constantly competing equilibrium through the provision of a moral perspective on Black gun crime as a kind of public pedagogy. Curtis, having lied to Leon and Beverley about throwing the gun away, retrieves it from its hiding place on the estate and makes his way through Clapton's Murder Mile. Our sense of dramatic non-ending is evoked by the degree of anxious desire that is created by the uncertainty of the scene that asks of the spectator to question if Curtis is on a pathway of vengeance that presents the issue of black-on-black gun crime as a perpetual condition energized not by a causeless and hauntological Black nihilism but from a place of genuine emotional hurt, spiritual laceration and familial loss as he throws the gun into the canal, for the film ceases not on the image of the gun but on Curtis, looking towards the sinking weapon. We may very well acknowledge that the hegemonic/under-narrative dialectic that *Bullet Boy* is situated within compels us to engage with the degree of symbolism in the scene as the film's counter-investing pedagogical contribution. This again reaffirms the polyphonic form of the popular Black urban text, here functioning as a necessary fiction of race that implies that Black gun crime within the symbolic location may not be as pheromonal, as secreting, and in the context of black-on-black race fictions as a mediacentric vista of Black internecine violence, as genetic as the very inferential, dominant narratives the film cites has argued. A sense of emotive and geographic immersivity is created by Massive Attack's circumspect, incidental score as the scene cuts to a close-up on Curtis. We of course are able to understand the narrational necessity of Curtis's throwing of the gun into the water. At this point, the close proximity we are now afforded to Curtis invites us to meditate on his subjectivity and in doing so necessitates a tentative approach to the interpretation of the film's intended meanings through symbolism. Perhaps this is an example of how the Black urban dialogism I earlier described is able to communicate its forms of narrative meaning through a number of characters, and the reading I arrive at through the final scene is that *Bullet Boy* neither resolves nor concludes but ceases, for only a temporal closure is reached following the restitution of the hauntological Black urban Other in Ricky to what is indexically accepted as his rightful and hegemonically symmetrical place, and Curtis's restorative rejection of the gun and with it the restoration of the film's rhetorical commitment to perform as a liberal, moralistic critique of the very moral panic of Black gun crime it has made the subject of dramatic allure. I say restorative in the sense that it is an attempt to satisfy the demands of PSB drama's Black representational ethics, here, a disavowal of gun violence. The camera, which throughout the film has oscillated between the naturalism

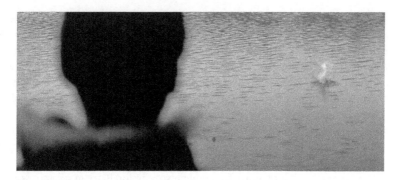

Figure 8.4 Curtis throwing Ricky's gun in the canal in *Bullet Boy* (dir. Saul Dibb, 2004).

that captures the expansivity of Clapton's urban landscapes and the realism that, in approximating the most dramatic and hegemonically distilling elements of Ricky and Wisdom's curtailed life cycle, aestheticizes criminal Black urbanity into a concerted textual experience now appears to be in a moment of stillness, acquiesce and surrender to the emotional and symbolic gravitas of the scene. Here, *Bullet Boy* disavows the use of a more concerted formal artifice, and the final scene is marked by an absorbing patience, with the camera neglecting a tracking of the aerial trajectory of the gun for a position fixated on the water, as it is thrown from the diegetic world and into the non-diegetic discourse of black-on-black gun violence through the canal, not precisely where the pit bull terrier lies, but where, in some figurative respects, the trivial source of the conflict that has resulted in both Ricky and Wisdom's murder remains (Figure 8.4). It is this reluctance of the camera to forgo its naturalist/realist aesthetic in favour of a highly symbolic, metaphorical and non-realist imagery that is also the film's reluctance to interrupt the flows of authenticity and perception that validate *Bullet Boy*'s representation of Black urban gun crime and in this effort, its intention to be encountered and understood in real time, matching the diurnal flows of Black urban and human life.

I have argued elsewhere in this book that the Black British film text as an immediate product of a post-Macphersonist impulse within PSB contexts means such films cannot be read outside of the text's circulation within existent race discourses (Nwonka, 2020a). In defining the Black British urban film as a useful and necessary fiction of race, I am also asking us to consider how its meanings, and its value, are fought over through the concerns of both racial representation and (in)authenticity, and this is precisely the kind of contestation that would welcome *Bullet Boy* after its screening at the 2004 London Film Festival, and the film would be responded to by a combination of critical praise and, inevitably, claims of misrepresentation from local Hackney residents, including an extra cast for the actual film (Evening Standard, 25 October 2004). If these pronouncements of misrepresentation are a further demonstration of the dissonance in the very structure of the UKFC's replication of Black criminalized urbanity and the ability of film and television, particularly where race is concerned, to both reflect and construct reality, critical responses such as 'the must-see British film of 2005' (Choice FM), 'a shot in the arm for British movies' (*Independent on Sunday*) and 'a terrific British film' (*Mail on Sunday*) suggest, like other forms of immediate post-Macphersonist institutional products, the urban text is identified as the basis for a hyper celebration of a new Black Britishness within a national film culture, where Black representational excessivity is again the intervention that emerges from a space of Black representational *lack*. For *Bullet Boy*, in this context, the contemporaneity and novelness of its themes as a cinematic experience are at least one way to account for the film's critical consecration. Indeed, *Bullet Boy* would be selected for the 2005 Toronto International Film Festival and would be awarded the Hitchcock d'Or at the 2005 Dinard Festival of British Film. However, despite a marketing approach predominantly aimed at Black-centric media outlets given its subject matter and opening to 75 screens, the film would return only £300,000 from the UK box office and would fail to secure distribution in any other international territory, although these industrial outcomes cannot serve as a reliable analytical basis for assessing the film's cultural resonance which, given its relatively low production budget, is embeddedness within the representational politics of the UKFC's New Cinema Fund and the triangulation of ownership that accompanies its status as a Black British text remained *Bullet Boy*'s alpha and omega. Instead, we must consider how the film's instrumentalist ideals are evidenced through its sense of social purpose that its distributors would assert as part of its promotional literature:

> *Bullet Boy* felt like a story that had been waiting to be told. There have been situations like this involving kids with guns for about the last 10 years in London. But nobody has tried to tell it from a human point of view, to get inside a family and try and show that there's more involved than what you read in the newspaper headlines. (Verve Pictures, 2005)

Herein lies the complexity of the Black urban dialogism, which, from one perspective, performs as a disavowal of the journalistic sensationalism while 'humanizing' the character immediately suggests Black identity as inherently infrahuman and requires a balancing through the depiction of non-criminal activity and family dynamics through biographical expositions that can be interpreted as a way of encouraging the audience to develop the kind of critical consciousness within its diegesis alongside the necessary degree of entertainment value. Keeping two systems of thought in operation simultaneously leaves *Bullet Boy* in an ambiguous position when considering the film's underpinning social-cultural imperative; however, both systems find their axis, in their terminological expression, in making something 'Black'. The latter aspect becomes present and meaningful not just through the film's encroaching upon the extra-diegetic contemporary discourse on Black gun crime by Operation Trident as a permeating signifier, nor by its stressing of a fact-based authenticity by the status of the film as a form of documentary realism, but more significantly in the inclusion of the Operation Trident leaflet 'RIP' inside *Bullet Boy*'s DVD inlay (Figure 8.5). The image, a white frame with the 'I' replaced with a bronze bullet at its centre and the mantra 'stop the guns' placed above the number of Crimestoppers, the UK's independent crime agency where

Figure 8.5 The *Bullet Boy* DVD inlay leaflet (dir. Saul Dibb, 2004).

members of the public can anonymously report information on crimes, function as an arresting mode of rebus, the combinational use of both images and letters to construct a word. The bold black-type font used produces a striking image as placed within the card's surrounding negative space. The card serves as a powerful form of extra-diegetic interactivity and underscores the indexicality of the film and its effort to achieve a genuinely dialogical mode of Black cultural representation that seems to compensate for the absence of specific detail within the diegesis that points to how Operation Trident as a Black signifier performs as an instrument of extratextual augmentation and as an extra-diegetic narrator. The inclusion of this leaflet offers a more manageable modality for the film's implantation of its social purpose ideals as not to overburden the film with the excessive intra-diegetic facticity that may compromise its dramatic flows and sense of spontaneous action. In such a dialogism, the film is able to be presented as an authentic Black cultural product while actively dissuading its Black audience from partaking in the culture of gun violence that attempts to secure *Bullet Boy* under its PSB guise as a tool of Black community activism and, more specifically, moral instruction and vanguardism. What I am arguing is that this use of the Operation Trident leaflet as a practice of audience segmentation is an essential part of the Black urban text's aesthetic project and as such, we cannot decouple such extra-diegetic materials from our textual and aesthetic readings and their entanglement with the social, political and cultural imperatives and meanings that inform how the institutional arrangement imagines Blackness, the Black film and Black communities to be.

As the performative and preliminary materials that populate *Bullet Boy* extract an authenticating utility in Operation Trident that is both quotational and gestural, and in some sense constitutive, the sense of a constructed 'realness' that is secured between the UKFC, BBC Films and the racially signifying omnipresence of the Metropolitan Police's anti-Black gun crime operative provides additional credence to the argument that is in some ways located in James Snead's dissatisfaction with the very idea of the Black film. As he states: 'The very term black independent film is a conglomeration of compromises, which by the time it is bundled up into a neat phrase, loses most of its intended meaning and often comes across merely as a condescending euphemism when the semantics are considered' (1988:47). Snead's dismissive position on Black independent film as a negotiated space is matched by my own disavowal of the popular British urban text's ineliminable reliance on mediacentric Black images of deviance/evil, but equally is acknowledging of its forms of racial and subcultural identification which is in itself the outcome of what has been conceived at this conjuncture as the post-multicultural iteration of Black British film. Put differently, the extra-diegetic presence of Operation Trident accomplishes the critical task of authenticating *Bullet Boy*'s depiction of Black gun crime as an accumulative and socially urgent edifice of knowledge that reinforces the impossibility of dislocating text from context, the cultural from the political, and the diegetic from the extra-diegetic.

Despite the spectacle of Black urbanity and Black death that is encountered in *Storm Damage*, my analytical aggrandizement of *Bullet Boy* as the popular Black urban *urtext* is justified through its status as a theatrical release through which we can observe and interrogate its heightened critical circulation and the subsequent modes of cultural value ascribed onto the film. This becomes apparent in its dense mediation of Black British urban identity, and we should not discount the status of the film as the UKFC's and BBC Films' very first example of the mono-racial Black filmic representation that has been sourced from hauntological, hegemonic and interconnected race fictions. Thus, what we experience in *Bullet Boy* is a depiction of Black criminal life that is in direct correspondence with other narratives that have been inscribed and cemented in culture. While there are a number of counter-narratives, under-narratives, counter-factualities to be found and appreciated in the text, it draws its meanings through a thematic hegemonic symmetry with the dominant discourses on Black masculine urbanity and the regimes of moral panic and social urgency that present filmic black-on-black criminality as a useful, and, in *Bullet Boy*'s example, a necessary and urgent fiction of race. And this is established as the axis upon which all other authenticities, realities, emotions and humanness are structured and expressed.

9

Hugging a Hoodie

Broken Britain, Conviviality and the Agnotologies of the Urban Text

Kidulthood is not really about bad kids. Even the villain is clearly suffering from neglect and the absence of love. The characters are simply children in circumstances none of us would want to grow up in. Their reaction to those circumstances is not good. But it is natural. Crime, drugs, underage sex – this behaviour is wrong, but simply blaming the kids who get involved in it doesn't really get us much further. It is what the culture around them encourages.

—David Cameron, UK prime minister, 2006

Agnotology, a term developed by Robert Proctor to describe the study of the willful and conceited propagation of ignorance (2008), is a sensibility that has been accrued by the popular urban text in its progression into the popular arena of PSB film and TV. Its etymological basis is found in the Greek word *agnosis*, or *not knowing*, which, in acknowledging what Londa Schiebinger argues is the vital distinction between epistemology (the study of how we know) and agnotology (the study of what we don't know and why) (2008), classifies the dispersal of ignorance as a political strategy of obfuscation and, finally, of securing favour and consensus. Given that Black British film and its meanings are contested within a triangulation of ownership, it is important to stress that the popular Black urban text as an agnotological practice has been carried out at the interface between the film and its critical framing, as represented by public service broadcasting contexts. However, it is the political culture as its interfacing location, as a space of liminality, that is central to understanding its agnotological intentions and underpins the appropriateness in situating an analysis of the popular Black urban film within a political economy, for the description of the urban text as a social aesthetic is bound up in a series of identical entanglements. In describing the early 2000s as a period of political crisis and cultural transition, the question posed to the nation, as in all moments of transition, is: What is revealed when one is to look at Britain, British identity and culture and politics? Here, I am concerned with how political cultures and their central ideas find their way into the representative and discursive scope of film genre. I want to suggest that One Nation Conservatism, a political philosophy that finds its genesis in the paternalistic beliefs of the late nineteenth-century Tory prime minister Benjamin Disraeli and its ideal of a collective social responsibility (1845), is a political culture that infringed upon the urban text. What I am describing here are political cultures rather than political parties, for they cross a number of different parties which are in themselves of heterogeneous formations. To think about the Conservative Party towards the end of the first decade of the 2000s, there are at least five political cultures to observe that mesh with the outgoing New Labour project: a conservatism, an economic liberalism, a strand of social liberalism, liberalism and a social democracy. Without wishing to enter into a terminological debate about the contours of Cameronism, it was marked by a fluidity and lexical coordination with other political cultures, and the One Nation Conservatism can be termed as progressive conservatism, paternalistic conservatism, liberal conservatism and crucially, a continuing form of Tony Blair-style modernism. These all seemed to interact with the discourse of 'Broken Britain', a term advanced by Cameron to describe the breakdown of law and order and social morality as an affliction particularly attributed to young working-class people. It is this chapter's interest in the Cameronist iteration of One Nation Conservatism, its manifestations within cultural discourses and how they become alive to, informing of and absorbed within film and television thematics that the urban text, as a genre, became telegraphed within a set of adjective critical prefixes: raw, urgent, hard-hitting, controversial, uncompromising, all performing as critical euphemisms for the visual and linguistic extracting of what is *really* distinctive about the urban: Blackness – as its epistemic imprint, subset within a more broader political and economic climate. First, I want to consider how the transition of both the thematic concerns of the Black urban text and the One Nation Big Society as a modality of paternalistic conservativism and as a political culture established a convergence within urban music, visual culture and subsequently, a body of necessary race fictions. Second, I evaluate these filmic and televisual examples of the popular Black urban text as a generic corpus informed by the hegemonic understanding of urban popular cultural products as representative of a placid interracial existence, the relationship between the urban genre and its aestheticization of discourses on youth moral decay, and the instrumentalist agency of these narratives in constructions and deconstructions of the One Nation vision of urban multiculture. Finally, I explore the validity and efficacy of the popular urban text's claim to agnotology as a critical context to consider the cohesiveness of the popular Black urban text as a reliable and secure form of counter-facticity and knowledge.

It is necessary, in placing the agnotological imperatives of the popular urban text within a moment of transition within urban cultural production, to return to my earlier consideration of how Black subcultural music forms were to be the focus of anti-Black moral panic. In considering this as the outcome of the political denigration of garage music and its associations with gun violence and gang activity, the major music labels exhibited an indisposition towards Black music collectives in the signing of individual artists rather than entire crews, and while the emergence of Grime music would propel a number of artists into a mainstream sphere of increased visibility, the industrial logic of individualization was to be read as a manifestation of the industrial aversiveness towards a collective Black male identity that allowed for the practice of aversive racism to be disguised behind an economic rationale of conservatism caused by the economic deficit of music piracy and illegal downloading. However, and in displaying a paradox, the spectacle of Grime music as a converging space of both individualism and collectivism was developed through the culture of low-budgeted DIY music videos as the defining characteristics of Grime, and one way to distinguish the genre from other music forms is in the significance of Channel U, a television station launched in 2003 that would become the representational epicentre of a new subversive creative economy. Like much of the post-2000s Black cultural production, Grime videos can be understood as a practice of innovation that necessitated the use of handheld DV cameras and the emergence of smartphones that were to be accentuated by the democratization of both the means of music production and associatively, digital moving image in the access to non-linear editing platforms and new modes of music distribution through the use of YouTube, Facebook and Myspace, becoming a way for Black Grime artists to assert a sense of creative autonomy over their audiovisual identities. 'Rawness', 'realness' and 'truth-telling', terms that would now be embedded within the popular Black urban text's lexicon, epitomized the Grime scene's refusal to strive for standardized representational modalities in the rejection of production artifice and finesse, while in the provision of Channel U, such videos would find an aesthetic register. However, and as observed by a number of British urban music scholars (James, 2021, Nava, 2021), one would find difficulty in positioning Grime music, at even this nascent stage, as instinctively anti-capitalist, for this a surge of video activity was propelled by a pragmatism that was attentive to the decrees of neoliberalism. I'm attempting to conceive the low-fi Grime video, just as the broader Black urban film genre outside its popular, PSB iterations, as a product of necessity in that the Grime video as a mode of Black collective enterprise may function as a deliberate counterpoint to the mainstream ecologies of urban music. The heightened Black visibility accrued in the proliferating of low-budget music video production placed control firmly in the possession of unsigned acts that provided a platform for Grime and Hip Hop artists to circumvent the established protocols of music industry engagement, and in doing so established Channel U as the pathway for those Grime artists seeking to graduate from the generative but economically confining arena of the pirate radio station. This can also be understood as a form of Black urban subcultural augmentation given that Grime music from its advent in the early 2000s had been understood primarily as an audial genre; most of its *public* interactions had been firmly situated within the pirate radio stations, and we find in the Grime genre a transient existence dictated by its illegal status and the continuous need to move broadcast locations in order to avoid detection by the authorities and by necessity, an inconspicuous and subterraneous cultural practice that affirms its colloquial synonymy with the underground. A point of fixity, identification and capture was therefore achieved by the cultural and industrial circulation of not simply Grime music but the iconographies of the Black diasporic identities that allowed audiences to locate the artists within the symbolic spaces of urban multiculture. It is these forms of narration as a visual culture that I've identified in Kano's 2005 video for his debut single

'P's and Q's'. While it is easy to observe its sharp incommensurability with the more homespun efforts that would populate the embryonic period of Channel U in that 'P's and Q's' benefits from a production value that exhibits a greater stylistic and aesthetic sophistication, I detect a cinematic odour in the video that deposits a correspondence with both the genre's more unsophisticated videos and the popular urban text. As Kano walks through the streets, the camera, which frames him in a range of different focal lengths and a deep depth of field, captures Kano under the gloom of the street lights and buildings that provide a kind of alluring social illumination to what, for those with only an inferential awareness of 'P's and Q's' more organic narrating of the particularities of 'on road' culture, is to be interpreted as an inconspicuous and predominantly night-time activity, and as congruent with how the popular Black urban film's camera constructs and telegraphs the most dramatic moments of the Black urban experience, 'P's and Q's' is essentially *noir*, with Grime music videos displaying a particular visual aesthetic that registers a durable continuity with the popular urban text.

I want to return to the presence of both cross-media and transmedia in the strategies employed by the Metropolitan Police to address gun crime among Black males aged fourteen to twenty-four within its symbolic Black London boroughs. We find a variant of community policing in the duality of Operation Trident's 'Stop the Guns' communication strategy, which used a variety of visual media to dismantle the alluring imagery of gun possession and gang activity and can be seen as an attempt to penetrate the coalescing community silence by stimulating an engagement with the police in the providing of intelligence on gun crime from within the city's Black locales.

Figure 9.1 Operation Trident 'Stop the Guns' print advertisement, 2005.

I want to consider one of the Operation Trident campaign print adverts, where its image of a light-skinned female hand placed over a darker-skinned male's hand that grips the gun reveals not only the significance of intra-community intervention into gun violence but its complex gender dynamics (Figure 9.1). Here, the image of the female hand over a gun speaks to the primacy of the role of women for the police within the Black urban environment as the silent witness to gun violence, its potential accessories, and therefore carry a particular moral responsibility for its alleviation.

The expansion of the 'Stop the Guns' campaign as a distinctive and multifaceted visual culture asserts a more substantial register upon its specific medium than the intra/extra-diegetic presence of Operation Trident in *Bullet Boy*, and while its symbolic and figurative distillation within the film can be seen as indicative of a certain opacity, I identify a more concerned cinematic texture to its creative politics in the use of moving image to dramatize the devastating effects of gun violence as observed in 'Box', a sixty-second TV advert produced by the creative agency Miles Calcraft Bringshaw Duffy, which would create a distinctive visual aesthetic that gives the impression of a video-recorded interview taking place within a prison. The advert consciously denies the audience easy identification; however, what we are able to discern is the silhouette of a Black youth who offers a lamentation on the quotidian, everyday experiences of youthhood that have now been denied to him as a result of being boxed within the confines of a prison for gun violence. To accentuate both the authenticity of its aestheticizing of Black urban otherness and the power of its moral message, the dramatic sound of a gunshot becomes the structuring point where the image is momentarily illuminated by light; however, what we now see is the image of a lifeless Black youth with a large, bleeding gunshot wound to his chest, before returning to his darkened silhouette as he continues his account of what his actions have resulted in (Figure 9.2). Exhibiting a congruence with Operation Trident's interventionalist ideals, I find that 'Box' is reflective of both a useful and necessary fiction of race as it retains a sub-irrationality and a degree of ontological suture in the tremoring impact of gun violence felt upon those most closest to the perpetrator, and his lamenting is again disturbed by the distorted sound of a young girl crying, who he describes as his sister who he cannot come to the aid of in a moment of distress and vulnerability, with a final visual fissure in the image of a distressed Black woman breathing from a hospital oxygen mask, understood as his mother, who he is unable to see after a road traffic accident as he is 'boxed' within the social and emotional confines of prison (Figure 9.3). The advert strives for a haptic affect from the imaginative aestheticizing of Black trauma and death, and it is through the claim to authenticity of the Black urban text that 'Box' can be described as a participatory practice, with the advert's dialogue being sourced through interviews conducted by the creative agency with real prisoners serving sentences for murder and gun violence. To argue that such media campaigns do not, at some level, draw its narrational form and imagery from the hauntological Black archive while performing its social corrective is to engage in one's own contradiction, in that they rely on the very forms of Black urban aesthetic that strive for a level of social impact that would equally depend on the hegemonic acceptance of a homogenous Black male criminal urbanity, and accompanying this, the acceptance of gun and knife

Figure 9.2 Operation Trident 'Box' advertisement, 2007.

Figure 9.3 Operation Trident 'Box' advertisement, 2007.

violence as the natural index of the Black urban subcultural existence. And through its permeating presence across TV, radio and print media, Operation Trident would build on the associativity of Black urban music and gun violence in the creation of a BBC Radio campaign that was further augmented by the use of music by UK Garage group NAP Syndicate in 2002.

The relationship between Grime subculture, gun violence and visual narration ventures beyond the production of audial material that serves as the associatively reliable soundtrack to the Black urban drama, and a more cogent example of the urban/ Operation Trident nexus as a site of an audiovisual convergence is to be observed in the 2006 music video/short film *Badman* (dir. Jake Nava) by East London Grime collective Roll Deep. My description of this as a film points to the function of the urban as a space of heterogeneous interactions and transmediated narrational and visual experiences, and 'Badman' is very much part of the popular Black urban text's oeuvre in that it possesses narrational elements that are informed by the social, political and cultural constituents that render the film as a social aesthetic. Further, we should also consider what is implied in the very term 'Badman', a contingent, descriptive term for young men who in this example are compelled to display a performative nihilism and hyper-masculinity within and external to the urban location. Commissioned by the Metropolitan Police's Operation Trident, and a recipient of the 2007 D&AD Graphite Pencil Award in the Viral/Use of Music category, *Badman*'s narrative project was to de-glamorize gun culture and violence among the eleven to sixteen age group within the capital's Black community through the story of a Black youth who ruins his life by his needless escalation of a seemingly innocuous traffic incident among two groups of Black youths that results in the protagonist firing a gun in the heavily pedestrian street that kills an innocent bystander. It is through the plausibility of fatal nihilism as occurring within the spatial transference from the diurnal to the dramatic that the film opens to the placidity of a family breakfast table where Badman eats with his mother and young siblings, and the film offers a vignette of the heterogeneity of criminalized subcultural Black identities that are marked by a conflicting dual existence in the contrasting but seamless transition between home and street, and between a dependent teenager and a murderous hauntological urban Black Other. The video's social message is that urban youths, once confronted with the consequences of one's actions, cannot halt the irresistible thrust of retributional violence. For Badman, now reduced to what he actually is once shedded of the hyper-local posturing and collective performativity, a mere child, he is unable to face the encroaching vengeful gang given the abandonment by scared friends, nor stop the immediate threat to his family and ultimately, evade his untimely but equally inevitable death. *Badman* displays modes of audience segmentation that are on the continuum of the Operation Trident leaflet in *Bullet Boy*, and the realities of the urban as a multi-dimensional subcultural experience produced the conditions for the staggered release of the various constitutive parts of *Badman* as a cross-mediatized product. First, such an approach was pursued in the production of 500 white-label records that were then sent to leading Black and urban music DJs, resulting in the track's airtime on both pirate and mainstream urban radio stations. Further, in an effort to maximize its uptake by its segmented audience, the track was made available to download through Myspace and other key websites onto PSPs, iPods and mobiles. Finally, and some six weeks after the track's initial circulation would be the release of the music video through a collaboration with the Metropolitan Police, who are continuously cited in the very genre as Black youth's primary source of oppression. The track required the strategic placing of the Operation Trident insignia, with the video remaining unbranded until the very final frame where *Badman* is shot dead, where the Operation Trident 'stop the guns' identikit is finally revealed. It is here that we encounter the migration of Grime video's aesthetic sensibilities, alongside the existing discourse of black-on-black violence, into the audiovisual structures of the popular urban text.

It is by the hegemony of One Nation Conservatism in its construction of ignorance that the popular urban texts are able to find self-justification as an agnotological challenge to the Tory discourse on antisocial behaviour and its focus on the fourteen to twenty-four demographic. But such texts represented not a countering but a product of hegemony, and the popular urban text would reach its industrial nadir in the release of *Kidulthood* (Menhaj Huda, 2006), a film set in Notting Hill, West London, where a group of youths have been given a day off from school after a classmate hangs herself in her bedroom after enduring what we understand as an extended period of violent bullying at the hand of other pupils. The film attempts to accurately reflect the habitual experiences of working-class youths, who spend the day undertaking underage sex, drug abuse and street fighting. The film's social address, albeit through the structuring thematic utility of Black male criminality, is an account of how the young can be damaged by the seductive pull of drugs and violent criminality, depicted in the experiences of Trife (Aml Ameen) who is compelled to punish a debt-ridden drug user by slashing his face with a Stanley knife at the behest of his gangster uncle. However, our primary encounter with youth violence is carried out through the film's chief antagonist Sam (Noel Clarke), an older pupil who pursues Trife and his two friends, Jay (Adam Deacon) and Moony (Femi Oyeniran), who had earlier bluffed their way into his home on the estate, seducing his girlfriend, violently attacking the returning Sam and then stealing his stash of drugs. The repetition and density of the instances of delinquency and crime, while important in securing a subcultural identification, disallow any moment of decompression that may produce a fissuring of its densified reading of youth experiences in the city. Indeed, given the age range of its primary target audience, the film seems to demand a televisual mode of attention, and the dramatic scenes can be seen as a source of recognition for some and for others shock, and produces a degree of triviality to *Kidulthood*'s portrayals, equally aided by the film's close adherence to narrational decrees of cause and effect. Resultingly, any moment of tonal rupture is drawn from the sentimentality of visual injury and Black youth death in the inevitable killing of Trife by Sam at the film's conclusion. *Kidulthood*'s rehearsal of the hegemonic images of the working-class and multiracial youth identities produces two, somewhat departing, agnotological issues. First, this is seen as a textual concern for Godfrey (2022), who argues that the film 'brings together two of the most familiar contemporary paradigms of social deviance: violent, drug dealing black adolescence and white, promiscuous and loud teenage girls who illustrate and perform the discourses of social and moral decay that were being rehearsed by politicians and news media alike' (127). It is undeniable that the film is holistically citational in its ambitions, and *Kidulthood*'s agnotology demands a replicating portrayal of deviancy as its consenting cultural value, which acts as a bulwark against any challenge to the plausibility or stereotypicality of the scenes. As Clarke would assert, 'The film shouldn't shock people, because it's in the newspapers every day' (Quoted in *The Times*, Saturday, 4 March 2006). We should be particularly attentive to the version of agnotology expressed by the film, which claims for the production of a counter-facticity but through the very visual amplification of already staked-out hegemonic narratives of antisocial behaviour and urban youth subcultural decay. Further, and beyond the dialogical connections made between the film and its audience in its soundtrack, the urban film as a practice of audience segmentation is also secured here by product placement in the diegetic presence of the clothing label Boxfresh, which in some parts chimes with Stella Bruzzi (1997) in her analysis of cinematic costumes and in this context, Black clothing and apparel as a form of subcultural expressivity to be observed in *Boyz in the Hood*, where the clothes worn by characters become significant for both the natural and strategic amplification of Black subcultural identity. Second, in its contextual understanding, the film would enjoy a more concerted political existence in that *Kidulthood* would become the subject of David Cameron's speech to the Centre for Social Justice, a think tank founded by former Conservative Party leader Iain Duncan Smith. Cameron, whose speech would later become synonymous with the phrase 'hug a hoodie' in developing his iteration of a paternalistic One Nation Conservativism, would suggest:

> That film is set in my own neighbourhood in London – North Kensington, Ladbroke Grove, Harrow Road. It's a very different Notting Hill from the one you see in Richard Curtis films. The film gives a disturbing insight into the pressures that teenagers round there are under. The fact is, it's frightening for a man in a suit to walk down certain streets at night. But think how much more frightening it must be for a child. Kidulthood is not really about bad kids. Even the villain is clearly suffering from neglect and the absence of love. The characters are simply children in circumstances none of us would want to grow up in. Their reaction to those circumstances is not good. But it is natural. Crime, drugs, underage sex – this behaviour is wrong, but simply blaming the kids who get involved in it doesn't really get us much further. It is what the culture around them encourages. (David Cameron, Quoted in BBC News, 10 July 2006)

There are two phases of politically engineered ignorance I've identified that become unified with *Kidulthood* as a cohabitate exercise in altruistic outrage as a way to understand the One Nation paternalistic concern with the moral crisis of urban youthhood. Cameron first draws upon the film's alternative portraiture of West London and its function for the aggrandizing of *Kidulthood* as an agnotological intervention, then argues that it is an irresistible cultural outcome. At first glance, Cameron's ideas seem to be derived from dominant colonial discourses and in its commensurability with the Disraelian version of One Nation Conservatism, but Cameron's understanding of urban crime is neither antiquated nor new. The epistemic reconstruction of the cause of Broken Britain, as examined by Slater (2012), and the various signifiers used to consolidate the image of the urban Other into its language, supports a deliberate political calculation where its individuals are responsible for their actions – a simple individual choice between right and doing wrong. But there is a second, more significant phase of ignorance that attempts to affirm the relationship between circumstances and behaviour. As Cameron would go on to assert:

> So, when you see a child walking down the road, hoodie up, head down, moody, swaggering, dominating the pavement – think what has brought that child to that moment. If the first thing we have to do is understand what's gone wrong, the second thing is to realise that putting things right is not just about law enforcement. It's about the quality of the work we do with young people. It's about relationships. It's about trust. Too many young people have no understanding of consequences – of the idea that actions have effects.

This second imperative sits at the cutting edge of Cameron's own modernist iteration of One Nation Conservatism. Here, the paternalistic and benevolent plea to a public understanding of the underlying social trauma motivating antisocial behaviour is in fact an engineered ignorance that allows for its preferred sole remedy, the Big Society, to replace rather than cohabit with the state's own complicity and therefore responsibility. The lexical unification of acceptable social behaviour and consequences with ideas of social 'relationships' is deliberately devoid of an ontological basis for our now more considerate discourse of the 'Big Society' which attempts to shift emphasis away from the responsibilities of the state and towards civil society, the charity sector and social enterprise as the foundational tenet of One Nation Conservatism's paternalism towards those described as social Others. This phase of engineered ignorance, marked by willful distortion, allows for the securing of political authority through false knowledge.

What some of the popular urban films produced by the PSB/UKFC embrace demonstrated, specifically in the co-production relationship with television broadcasters, is that the public investment in the urban film was latched with a strong sense of instrumentalism and social relevance that underpinned its claim to an agnotological address; that the images and actions encountered in the films provide some degree of sociopolitical critique and challenge, becoming the key principles that affirm the popular Black urban text's arrival as a genre, less so in terms of formal coherence or a related set of thematic and performative co-ordinates, but in the specific horizon of expectation established by its claim to knowledge. This being said, its interest in crime is accompanied by a formal atypicality and a sense of predictability in its narrative structure, characterizations and representations of verisimilitude. I risk circumventing my own taxonomic analytical and interpretative framework of the popular Black urban text as one made so by its funding by public institutions, for some texts made outside the public funding framework are able to produce a cultural resonance by the omnipresence of Grime and urban music as both a reflection of the textures of Black youth subculture and the discursive audial architecture through which the audience's encounter with realness is supplemented, and music is one of the primary concerns of the film *Rolling with the Nines* (Julian Gibley, 2006), a South London set crime drama about an up-and-coming Black Hip Hop performer who returns to an existence of violence and drug dealing after a member of their group is killed by a criminal gang. The film's authenticity is not to be identified in any claim to a cinematic realism given the degree of dramatic artifice in the highly stylized choreography of the film's fight scenes between the detectives and the gang, its frantic and undifferentiated pacing and its cross-pollinating generic hybridity that gestures towards the British gangster films that had been popularized by the release of films such as *Gangster No.1* and *Lock, Stock and Two Smoking Barrels*. Rather, and in a practice of augmentation, the film's soundtrack would allow for the convergence between Garage and Grime music artists, including Ms Dynamite, Kano, Akala, Skinnyman, Dizzie Rascal, Shy Fx, Swiss, some of whom feature in the film, to supplement its claim to 'realness'. More significantly, the convergence between urban music, the urban text and the discourse inferential gun crime was to be observed in the release of 'Rolling with the Nines', the film's lead soundtrack by the Grime collective NorthStar that would feature heavily on Channel U. The means by which the soundtrack functions as a mode of transmediality is in the video's attempts to infuse the audience with a sense of consciousnesses towards gun crime and gang violence. Here, rather than the video being simply populated by scenes from the actual film, the soundtrack produces its own additional narrative, where a young Black youth is faced with a series of dilemmas over his involvement in gun violence and allows for the video to perform as a moral counterpoint to the film's more singular representation of Black criminality.

We also find a similar, if tonally less visceral replication of the popular Black urban text's generic formula in *Life and Lyrics* (dir. Richard Laxton 2006), a story of a South London Rap group 'The Motion Crew' led by DJ Danny 'D-Biz' Lewis (Ashley Walters). The film attempts to narrate the everyday expressions of urban multiculture where music production, while being an organic space of subcultural connection and emotional bonds, is equally a neoliberal space of hyper-competitiveness, territorial rivalries and conflict, notably from a violent and antagonistic rival Rap group from the other side of London. Displaying an obvious thematic association with the kind of hyper-localized conflict and creative endeavour encountered in *8 Mile* (dir. Curtis Hanson, 2002), *Life and Lyrics* framing of the urban music scene presents this as a pathway to social and creative arrival. It may be that as a result of the eager desire for the film to be captured within the urban subcultural zeitgeist that *Life and Lyrics* elects to forgo any cinematic ambition for a highly televisual aesthetic and perhaps in direct appeal to the aesthetic sensibilities of its youthful target audience, the visual and narrational experience is extremely formulaic, a suggestion that is found in Ashley Walters's own later reflection that the director lacked a specific understanding of the film's cultural setting (GRM Daily, 21 March 2022). There is a continued focus on the themes of loyalty and geographic and emotional binds in *Shifty* (dir. Eran Creevy, 2008), a film starring the British Asian actor Riz Ahmed (Shifty) and Daniel Mays (Chris), two childhood friends who, upon reuniting within their housing estate where Shifty still lives, continue the process of the gradual fracturing of lifestyles that accompany geographic and mental departure; a middle-class existence for Chris and for Shifty, drug dealing and who at the point of Chris's return has become embroiled in an escalating drug conflict. This allows the film to be punctuated with numerous points of sentimentally, in that both young men display a desire for the simplicity of adolescence. I have earlier argued how the popular Black urban text, beyond the contingencies of the conjuncture's specific modality of Black cultural politics, was brought being by the presence of conducive production conditions, one being the BBC Films/Film London's Microwave, a co-production scheme in which filmmakers are awarded a microbudget of £100,000 to make their debut feature. The possibilities of microbudget feature filmmaking of relatively low production values with the generic framework of the urban were particularly fertile for the making of the film *Freestyle* (Kolton Lee, 2010). Here, Ondene (Lucy Kondau), a prospective law undergraduate at Oxford University seeking to unwind after a prolonged period of study, takes up freestyle basketball, and with this, the meeting of Leon (Arinze Kene), a Black youth struggling to educate himself and withstand the class-based stigma displayed towards him by Ondene's mother as a result of him coming from the symbolic location of the council estate.

The cinematic and televisual representation of young people can be understood here as the postmodern vista of diversity, and the relationship with the popular Black urban text and textual and spectatorial experimentation is one that sits within my exploding of Malik's taxonomic reading of the social, market and regulatory predicaments of creative diversity within PSB contexts. We find an example of the popular Black urban text's move towards innovation and social interaction in the Channel 4 series *Dubplate Drama* (2005–9). Set in and among the pirate radio station scene in London, the series captures the experiences of a group of young urban musicians, with the lead role played by the female rapper MC Shystie as they attempt to secure a record deal, narrated through 12 fifteen-minute episodes in the first series, 6 thirty-minute episodes in the second, and sixty-minute specials in the final series. Its responsiveness to PSB predicament of innovation is through its distinctiveness as the world's first interactive drama series that allows its youthful audience to determine the narrative trajectory of its characters, where the audience are confronted with a moral dilemma at the conclusion of each episode and invited to vote on its outcome. Further, the series would maximize the use of innovative technology by making the series available to view on both the Sony PlayStation Portable and the 3 Mobile phone network while also being screened on MTV and Channel 4's E4. The practice of innovation in *Dubplate Drama* is to be identified in Channel 4's youth series *Skins* (2007–13), and it is in the situating of youth identities within a 'branded enclosure' that David Buckingham, in an analysis of youth-orientated film and television during the period as a space of digital interactivity and participation, argues that such modes of interaction create the industrial conditions for the conflation between audience *activity* and audience *agency* (2021: 160). It is central to the definition of this iteration of the popular Black urban text as a branded enclosure that *Dubplate Drama* was developed in collaboration with the youth marketing group Livity, which devised an interactive digital strategy to secure an engagement from young people in its creation of a transmedia storytelling experience across various platforms and formats.

The combinational presence of the symbolic location, music and urban multiculture as a mode of cultural/subcultural identification is to be found in BBC Three's West 10 LDN, a 60-minute one-off television adaptation of the acclaimed collection of short stories 'Society Within' by the Black author/screenwriter Courttia Newland, developed by Kudos Film and Television and Stealth films, directed by Menhaj Huda and written by Noel Clarke, both of whom had earlier collaborated on the film *Kidulthood*. West 10 LDN centres on the experiences of eighteen-year-old Elisha (Ashley Madekwe) and her negotiating of the Greenside Estate's various gestural residents she encounters upon her arrival there. Again, agnotology is the validating framework for the popular Black urban text and despite the series' more comedic tonality, the series strives for a counter-narrating authenticity through its claim to represent a social environment encountered only at the point of the inferential reportage of Black gun violence (BBC, 2006). There are, however, moments of departure from the conventions which mark the film cycle as a whole. For example, *Shank* (dir. Mo Ali, 2010) could be read as an attempt at a dystopian account of youth ganghood, which as a result of the global economic crisis asserts control over London's now lawless streets, although the film is unable to fully free itself from a narrational atypicality, this being a result of its close reliance on *Kidulthood*'s generic and thematic framework in its depictions of gang violence and youth delinquency. This being the case, it could be argued that in *Shank*'s endorsement by the Damilola Taylor Trust, the film makes a stronger contextual claim to the popular urban text's status as a social corrective than say *Sket* (2011), a film that while exhibiting a differentiation from the generic norms of urban text in its holistic focus on girls is very much rooted in the genre's tonal and representational excessivity.

The popular urban text registers an aesthetic and narrational synonymy with the subcultural and political zeitgeist and accompanying this, an understanding of British urban film culture as firmly rooted within the capital city. However, we find a moment of variation in the fracturing of the London-centricity of the popular urban film in the Birmingham set *One Day* (dir. Penny Woolcock, 2009). Woolcock, an Argentinian-born filmmaker who would later make the documentary *One Mile Away* (2012) that used participatory filmmaking practices to explore the possibility of peace and a halt to the city's gun violence and through this performing as a filmic intermediary between two significant and warring Black gangs in Birmingham, the Burger Bar Boys and the Johnson Crew, and had earlier helped establish a temporary truce between both gangs to allow her to make *One Day*, would be inspired to make the film after herself being the victim of a violent street robbery by a Black youth in London. The film was shot within an area of the city territorialized by the Burger Bar Boys and centres on the character Flash (Dylan Dufus) as he attempts to recover £100,000 to his gang boss, the soon to be released from prison, Angel in less than twenty-four hours or face the inevitable fatal consequence. There is both a continuity with the main conventions of the popular Black urban drama in the aestheticizing of the inferential crisis of Black masculinity, drugs and gang violence and a number of departures, and *One Day* registers a more innovative narrational schema in the use of Grime music as an intra-diegetic character.

Like *Babymother*, the characters use song and performance to articulate the character's inner lives in the function of Grime music as a mode of exposition, the outcome of the practice of street-casting and the use of strictly non-professional actors, sourced by Woolcock through the distribution of flyers throughout Birmingham's Afro-Caribbean community asking for actors, music performers and rappers across a full spectrum of roles unbounded by the constrictive conventional logics of gender and age. Indeed, while it should be acknowledged that Woolcock's whiteness and age permitted the kind of access and privilege that may not have been bestowed upon Black practitioners, a point recognized by Woolcock herself, an attempt to dismantle the verticality between her and Birmingham's Black community and specifically, the city's Afro-Caribbean locale is made by the centrality of Rap and Grime music to the lives of the Black youths, and as we see in *Babymother*, this allows for Black women to take an occasional central position within the narrative. Further, the film presents a departure from the hyper-local geographic fixity and situatedness that is encountered in *Bullet Boy* and *Storm Damage*, and where the films exhibit a reluctance of the camera to venture beyond the symbolic location, an occasional spatial expansiveness in *One Day* is archived by its establishing shots and raking overhead vistas of Birmingham that frame the city's West Indian diaspora, and the film depicts the urban locale as an intergenerational social sphere that exhibits a set of cultural principles in the unchallenged display of respect towards the Black elders within the community, even during moments of violent and armed conflict. While one may immediately question the plausibility of its modes of address and vernacular expressions, notably in a moment where the film's Black male characters perform a lyrical critique of their experiences of racial stigma and white othering, given that – at least extra-diegetically – the film's spectatorship is conditioned and actively secured by the very same white gaze its characters denigrate, *One Day* does provide a novel account of the emotional connections the young men beyond the capital have both to the hyper-locality of the environment and, significantly, to each other.

It is through the status of the film as a community practice and the associated opportunity for creative expression and upskilling in which *One Day* was able to secure £380,000 of its total £750,000 production budget via the UKFC's Regional Screen Agency, Screen West Midlands, alongside additional funds from the European Regional Development Fund and the regional development agency (RDA) Advantage West Midlands, one of nine agencies set up by the New Labour government to stimulate sustainable economic development and social regeneration within the regions, with a particular emphasis on employment, skills development and innovation. However, in opening to eighty screens across the UK on November 6, *One Day* would recoup less than £44,000 in its opening weekend, a box-office performance that for the director, and providing an example of the historic denigration of Black cinematic representation as a vessel for the inferential dispersal of a moral panic, was attributed to the film being withdrawn from the Odeon Cinemas chain due to concerns that the film's screenings within Birmingham would incite violent conflict between the city's rival Black gangs, a decision that, for the director, was carried out on the behest of the West Midlands Police.

The narrational practice of agnotology within the description of One Nation Conservatism as a political culture finds a presence not just through the medium of film but within the spaces of non-theatricality, and it is the social function of PSB and the articulating of the state-of-the-nation that the discourse of Black youth moral crisis is able to entice otherwise representationally and thematically white dramas by the mainstream broadcasters to precipitate the habitual presence of not just the Black urban text but Black urbanity as a dramatic, gestural theme within the social practice of televisual drama. This is much more than a question of verisimilitude but how Black representation gains its social legitimacy in the depiction of a Black thematic contemporaneousness, here most evident in the dramatizing of Black youth violence and postcode conflict. This is precisely the citational and annotative sensibility found in a two-part episode of the long-running BBC One forensic pathology drama series *Silent Witness*. In 'Safe', broadcast on 1 and 2 October 2008, it is the widespread public concern with Black youth violence that takes the series to the more novel settings of Black South London, where the forensic team investigate the killing of a young Black mixed-race girl who has been gang-raped and stabbed to death in what the police and the forensic investigators believe was the result of a gang initiation. Further, one of their forensic investigators, Leo (William Gaminara), having been sentenced to a period of community service after a drink driving conviction that leads him to the Battersea council estate, is paired with AJ (Amal Ameen), a young Black youth worker whose resentment towards the perpetual white One Nation paternalism embodied in Leo is matched only by his disdain for the estate's unrelenting culture of gun- and gang-violence. However, the episode follows the tragic trajectory of another Black youth on the estate, Errol (Daniel Kaluya) who, having made unsuccessful attempts to extricate himself from the sphere of violent ganghood, turns his ameliorative attention to his younger brother Levi (Kendar William Sterling) who is gradually seduced into the world of gang culture by Keenan (Charles Mnene), the leader of a Battersea-based gang and former friend of Errol. The episode's thematic investment in the spectacle of habitual Black violence is observed in the stabbing of Errol and the shooting dead of a Black teenager in a packed youth club hall, where the killing is filmed by the perpetrator on a smartphone. Later Errol, who has acquired a gun to kill Keenan as the only means of protecting Levi, tracks his brother to a location in Brixton to stop him from delivering drugs at the behest of Keenan and finds himself trapped within the geographic territory of the Brixton Crew Brotherhood, a rival Somali Muslim gang whose more frightening forms of violence is attributed to what AJ describes as their 'Sharia law and that'. Confronting Errol, and mistaking him for one of Keenan's gang members, he is attacked by the group. My specific criticism is how the next scene is drawn from the archive of the hauntological Black urban Other and the conjuncture's reassociation of the folk devil from deviance to evil – not only has the Somali gang killed Errol but also satisfied the generic requirement for a hegemonic display of Black nihilism in placing the corpse in full public view against a tree in the area of green in-between the tower blocks of the estate and the playground, the very location where Levi would later be mauled to death by a pit bull terrier at the command of Keenan. However, the episode's adherence to the hegemony of black-on-black as the (visual) nomenclature for anti-

Figure 9.4 Errol's dead body in *Silent Witness* (BBC Studios, 2008).

Figure 9.5 Errol's dead body captured photographically by the forensic team in *Silent Witness* (BBC Studios, 2008).

Black non-humanness is observed in how Errol's killing is presented as a particular example of ethno-centric sadism; the gang had both beaten Errol unconscious and doused him in wood-tar creosote and goose down. The episode's categorization as a necessary and useful fiction of race is determined by what is produced in the image of Black corporeality, here in its depicting of Errol's dead body (Figure 9.4). The spectacle of Black death is interrupted only by a camera shutter sound as the audience is met with a monochrome, forensic image of the youth's mutilated face, an image that is both diegetically silent and extra-diegetically spectacular (Figure 9.5). While the image's claim to cultural value and knowledge is primed for the production of Black trauma, its racism is compelled to find refuge in the safe haven of PSB film and TV narratives.

Unable to fully emancipate itself from the sense-making and voyeuristic gazes of Black urban life and violent death, the episode's version of One Nation politics becomes a permissive sphere for a Black hauntological recourse to extract, transcode, migrate and distil the narratives of Black savagery, but equally gain legitimacy in their own myopic attempt at an aesthetic agnotology of the Black urban youth crisis. Here, Errol's defiled Black body is no bestowment to the Black gaze but is an ever-extractable image that is severed from its context and reconstructed as a moral and forensic examination for whiteness; through PSB as a validating framework, Errol's Black death is denied any kind of escharotomy.

What we find in my assertion that the function of PSB as the validating architecture upon which the imagery of Black youth violence is accepted as possessing a cultural value is that the urban itself becomes a space of conflicting agnotology where One Nation Conservatism's paternalistic dictate of the Big Society seemed to provide such dramas with a thicker sense of duty and public engagement. I identify a further textual example of how the interaction between the popular Black urban text and the social address instincts of PSB as a bidirectional agnotology renders One Nation's Broken Britain diagnosis as a dialogical political culture where different imperatives compete for the authoritative analytical position over the crisis of Black youth urbanity in *Fallout* (dir. Ian Rickson, 2008) a feature-length television drama broadcast as part of Channel 4's Disarming Britain series, a season of programming dedicated to exploring the culture of gun violence that would register a particularly powerful resonance in the session's print and TV campaign. While the Channel 4 promotional advert, at nearly four minutes in duration, would attempt to present itself as a agnotological counter-narrative in the dismantling of the hegemony of gun crime as a Black lexicon, the film is unable to decentre Blackness as its discorded menace, even when such reconstructions are positioned through a series of interwoven scenes that attempt to portray gun violence as a multiracial and cross-generational social affliction: a group of hooded Black youths are shot at from a passing car, a white working-class family's dinner erupts into violence as a boy shoots his father as a result of long-standing domestic abuse towards his mother; a group of hooded youths' attempt to rob an off-licence ends in one of them shooting the shopkeeper; a Black youth is shot in a restaurant in front of his girlfriend by a love rival; the tower blocks of a council estate again become the signifying backdrop for the moment of hauntological anti-Black black-on-black death as a hooded Black youth points a gun towards the head of another Black youth in what can only be understood as a pending execution; a scene where a young Asian child simply surveys a playground populated by his oblivious classmates, a moment that, rather than satisfy the audience's anxiety in showing an instance of gun fatality within the spaces of innocence, is simply followed by the on-screen text 'getting a gun has become child's play'. It is particularly significant within the context of One Nation Conservatism's interest in the condition of adolescence and childhood that the advert begins and ends with the image of the young child pointing gun-like towards the screen, the very part of society in need of urgent remedial and preventative intervention. Indeed, at the centre of the print advertisement is a striking image of a Black child mimicking a gun (Figure 9.6), an action that replicates the hand gesture

Figure 9.6 Channel 4's Disarming Britain print campaign (Channel 4, 2008).

made by a seventeen-year-old towards the back of David Cameron while visiting the Benchhill Estate in Wythenshawe, Manchester, and this intertextual image of a working-class youth in his hooded apparel against the geo-sociological backdrop of the symbolic location engages with the signifier firmly established within conservative media as the totalizing embodiment of Broken Britain.

Its status as a Black 'event' becomes the faux cultural value for *Fallout*, written by the Black playwright Roy Williams, who based the film, adapted from his own 2003 play of the same title, on the death of Damilola Taylor, a ten-year-old Nigerian boy who was stabbed in Peckham by a group of youths in 2000. This incident is given loose filmic dramatization in the story of Kwarme, an academically gifted sixteen-year-old who, after being bullied by a group of Black youths, two of which are girls, is chased, stabbed in the stomach, has his trainers stolen and is left to die, his pleas to one of the girls in the group ignored, who stands over him after the boys have run off but refuses to help. This incident occurs at the very opening of the drama, and in the following ninety minutes the film takes the characters through various points of exposition as the group members struggle to come to terms with the consequences of their murder. Again, we find that the discourse of Black violence performs as all-encompassing, since the film is concerned not with gun violence but with the culture of knife crime. The description of *Fallout* as a social aesthetic is born of its interplays between the hegemony of Operation Trident as a hauntological Black signifier inscribed in discourse and the popular Black urban text as a useful and necessary fiction of race, in that the film displays a dependency with the hegemonic acceptance of gun/knife crime and gang violence as both *of* the Black community and sustained *by* the Black community through the absence of investigative co-operation within the symbolic location, and as we encounter in *Safe*, the police struggle to find witnesses as an impenetrable wall of silence stymies the police investigation. Indeed, it is the racial and geographic specificity of the murder that necessitates the introduction of Joe (Lenny James), a Black policeman and former resident of the Cleveland Estate, whose own emotional history towards the estate is bound up in his identification of Kwarme as the victim of internecine violence and the exploration of the murder as an outcome of ethnic racism. Given that the Big Society edict is the dramatic centrepiece for Channel 4's Disarming Britain season, *Fallout*'s social value claim is supported by a feature in the *Telegraph*, where a group of pupils at Henry Compton School in Hammersmith, West London, are interviewed after watching the film, a location made significant given that just a year earlier sixteen-year-old Kodjo Yenga, a Congolese A-Level student at the same school, was stabbed to death in the area after being pursued by a group of youths (*Guardian*, 16 November 2008). Indeed, the film's status as a One Nation intervention is further accentuated by Williams's instance that 'We have to teach kids to be less materialistic . . . it's all about greed – wanting a mobile phone or a pair of trainers and just taking them. Everything is done so quickly, without thought for the consequences' (*Telegraph*, 3 July 2008).

My analytical interest in *Fallout* as a One Nation inflection of the popular Black urban text not limited to its depiction of gang violence and internecine Black death, or how its status as a Black 'event', is sourced by its hegemonic Black subject matter further validated through Channel 4's Disarming Britain season, but in the specific gender relations that are prevalent within the popular Black urban text's generic conventions. I want to draw from Lola Young's reading of the politics of race, representation and shadism to be found in Black women-focused print magazines. I find the ideas explored by Young as a valuable framework in identifying the popular Black urban text as a permissive aesthetic for the naturalizing of 'intra-black colour-based antagonisms' (2000:422). There is great value here in drawing upon some of the thinking within the distinctive field of critical mixed-race studies, specifically, Black mixed-race identity's negotiation with normative ideas of Blackness and social/cultural privilege (Campion, 2021). Despite my own parenthesis to Campion's ethnographic study in my asserting of the importance of visual culture and narrative representation in the construction of mixed-race identities, I remain cognizant of the inconclusiveness of on-screen racial identities as a point of categorization in my analysis of how the popular urban text appears to esteem mixed-race Black female actors. Specifically, I purposely circumvent the application of mixed-race as a description for the characters cited in the urban text, not solely as mixed-race Black identity has yet to emerge as a *material* thematic concern within the popular Black urban film but also because the Black mixed-race representations that have a presence within screen characterizations may also imply skin fairness, as since the popular Black urban text generally exhibits an exclusive focus on the inferential experiences of Black urban masculinity, the audience is often denied of the narrative representation of bi-racial parentage, family life or domesticity that would help situate its female characters in an empirical understanding of their racial composition. This being the case, and while such hierarchal colour coding remains as the combinational historical outcome of the legacies of colonial orders and the racist genealogies of pigmentocracies, the critical reading of the fair urban female character as not instinctively mixed race but light-skinned does little to negate her external construction as the 'mulatta' within urban popular visual culture. The overtly reductive and highly serviceable representational status of Black women within the urban text has always appeared to me to be structured by a binary of either mothering and matriarchy or narrational disposability in their function as the subject of collateral gang death or/and the subject of male sexual desire and misogyny. A less critical perspective may interpret the omnipresence of light-skinned women within the urban genre as an un-intervening practice of mimesis, where the films are simply reflecting the everyday in-keeping with their general principle of authenticity – here, in capturing within its (re)representative and quotational purview the urban environ as the real without any overt intertextual intervention or dramatic reconfiguring. However, such a degree of self-awareness or introspection does not seem to chime with the general narrative predilections of the popular Black urban text where, and by no means exhaustive or finite, the construction of fair-skinned female characters to be observed in Massive (*Storm Damage*), Shanice (*Bullet Boy*), Elisha (West 10 LDN) and Shana (*Safe*) implies a specific interest in such identities, and despite the genre's investment in youthhood as the sphere of modernity and multiculturalism, the popular urban drama's privileging of light-skinned young female characters can be understood as a participation in an antiquated system of representational pigmentocracy. In building on Young's reading of the phenotypical positioning of light skin-ness as the esteemed and photogenic iteration of Blackness, such desirability is incorporated into the peer-to-peer competitive desires in the securing of a 'lighty', a colloquial epithet that (not exclusively) remains present within the vernacular social life of Black urban males. The term possesses a polysemicity in that within the domain of urban male vernacular expressions it is accepted as a positive differentiation; it is derogatory in that it equally functions as a form of female objectification by the specific privileging of fair-skinned complexion as the corporeal marker of masculine sexual triumph and sociocultural and subcultural status. But my interpretation of the popular urban text as engaged, like any other variant of popular visual culture within the structuring logics of capitalism in the organizing of human life within a structuring racial codification, renders the popular Black urban text particularly fertile for the practice of pigmentocracy, or to refer to a more hegemonic description, the consecrating and taxonomic logic of colourism. My interest in *Fallout* in this context is focused on the way its characters, both male and female, appear to exist upon the axis of its only light-skinned character, Shanice (Gugu Mbatha Raw), who is immediately introduced as 'the pretty one' when observed from a towerblock balcony. Such a statement is an entirely comparative observation, in that the only other girl in the frame is the much more dark-skinned and physically larger Ronnie (Bunmi Mojekwu), her best friend and the continued subject of aversive racism in that it is Shanice that is immediately identified as the object of male attraction by both the Black youths, the white racist police officers and later Joe, an assessment contrasted by her proximity to the dark-skinned Ronnie; she is continuously denigrated by the boys as a 'troll', a term that functions as a disparaging form of identification where Ronnie is positioned to simply accentuate the beauty, femininity and attractiveness of Shanice, and one that is primarily determined by skin-tone differentiation. My specific criticism is in no way towards the presence of a light-skinned actress in the role, which of course may be the indeliberate outcome of casting practices, but in what emerges as the representational by-product of the *positioning* of Shanice as the central point of narrative attention; Shanice is the only one in employment, that is seen to be performing in school and, at least at this stage of the film and offering justification for Joe's immediate identification of Shanice as potentially the most reliable source of intelligence, appears to be the moral and authorial compass of the group as their pact of silence is challenged by the mental fragility of the murder's primary perpetrator, Emile (Charles Mnene). For Dwayne and Emile, Shanice functions as an additional point of violent conflict between the two dominant Black youths in their continuous reference to Shanice's beauty and their escalating struggle over her affections, and the One Nation diagnosis of a social/moral decay and the subsequent prognosis of paternalistic understanding and affection becomes discernible after an altercation between Dwayne (Aml Ameen) and his father Manny (Clint Dyer), a drunken beggar and incomprehensible peripheral figure throughout the film whose occasional presence becomes the source of sympathy towards Dwayne from the other youths, but for Dwayne himself, a figure of disowning personal shame. Dwayne is enraged by Manny's inability to remember his own son's name nor recognize him when he begs the youth for £1. For the emotional Dwayne, he is simply one of multiple children dispersed across different parts of London that Manny has fathered. If the necessity of the scene is to accentuate the cultural, familial and environmental factors behind their violent act, the sentimental social embrace congruent with the One Nation Big Society motif of hugging-a-hoodie is reflected through the figure of Shanice to provide the otherwise nihilistic Black youth access to a suppressed emotional life and with it, the possibility of social understanding and the chance of redemption and transformation. For Shanice's orchestration of both the masculine sexual desires surrounding her and the relegating of Ronnie into the fixed position of emotional servitude is a narrative feature that cannot be divorced from the epidermal difference bestowed upon her and her own awareness of her status as an object of cross-generational and transracial male sexual desire and intra-gendered admiration. This is further accentuated in Joe's description of Shanice as 'not like them', a distinction that within the context of the police investigation could be viewed as a glacial process of witness manipulation, but equally attempts to delineate Shanice in all her epidermal fairness from the denigrative non-humanness of Black urbanity. This, in some respects, can be seen through a more Fanonian inflection of what Winston James (1993) termed in his reading of Caribbean societies and Black men's marrying of light-skinned women as a means of social and cultural emancipation as a 'self-immolating' practice (234) in understanding the Black youth's pursuit of Shanice as the source of social orientation and emotional rescue that undermines the social critique implied in Joe's cry to his investigation partner that 'there is always a reason' (for interracial murder). This is of course an extra-diegetic reality, but in correspondence with the discursive aspirational narrative conventions of the popular urban text, this reason is kept outside the narrative frame. What does enter the frame is how the issue of class trajectory and the hyper-local constructions of Blackness inform the gangs' disdain for the other Black males: for Kwarme, the juvenile rejection of his Black identity is determined by his scholastic achievement and Africanness; Joe's white adjacency is identified by his status within the estate as the Black police officer tasked with investigating his murder and his apparent indifference to the injustices faced by Black youths. However, and perhaps as part of the film's authenticating project, there is no internal evaluation into how the roots of their Black heterosexual desire is captive to the psychological stronghold of pigmentocratic femininity, one internally developed and externally expressed. Indeed, we later learn at the concluding moments of *Fallout* that Kwarme's killing was a direct consequence of his rejecting of Shanice's sexual advances at school, and as the girl faces his mother seeking absolution through the provision of African forgiveness, *Fallout*'s revelation of this backstory at such a point completes Shanice's characterization as a contemporary jezebel within the landscapes of Black urban masculinity.

There is a particular instrumentality in the popular urban text's attempts to define itself as an agnotological aesthetic, for I identify a thematic shift from the anxiety-evoking spectacle of Black Yardie violence and towards, in concert with One Nation Conservatism's formulation of the Big Society, a concerted interest in youthhood as the utilizing vista of postmodernism that renders such texts as extremely fertile for the practice of creative diversity and the amplification of the socially redemptive potential of the screen industries. Such urban film's visual agnotology is contextually claimed but textually devoid of any substantial political analysis or accusation, beyond the fact that such themes occupy a sustained and heightened presence within political and media discourses. Buckingham's critique of the paradoxicality of youth screen identities offers an important distinction between youth films and the representation of youth identities *on* film, and this is a separation that has particular implications for my reading of the popular Black urban genre in that certain texts 'implicitly view youth from the perspective of adulthood' (2021:4). These films display an authenticating horizontality in that such texts are born from or informed by the organic experiences of its youthful characters and racially diverse authorial talent, the casting of non-professional actors and the sense of cultural recognition that is drawn from the condensed and sustained period of visibility and the nature of the films as both a product of and a reaction to the very adult-created inferential moral panic around youth delinquency, violent crime and antisocial behaviour. However, in the context of the function of the popular urban text in this moment as a form of agnotology, this insists on an engagement from the very institutions and figures complicit in their public denigration. I see the creative practice of the use of street-casting as a deliberate and conspicuous convention, in that the interconnected and overlapping cultural, social and industrial imperatives embedded in the idea of cultural verisimilitude mean the films are expected to display a correspondence between the actor, their on-screen character and the social world, its images of authenticity firmed as the popular urban text's primary point of value. Such a practice is also supplementary to the popular urban text's choreography through the density of its dialogue that, in a concerted endeavour to augment its sense of accuracy, places great emphasis on the distinctive vernacular expressions and oral specificities within the urban lexicon. Here, hegemonic symmetry is also an understanding of how actors are made visible through the standardization of its production practices within a neoliberal framework through the instrumentalism of creative participation. By participation, I am of course gesturing towards the promoting of youth creative endeavours as a sphere of diversity and inclusion that requests its young actors and creative talent to invest in the One Nation dictate of personal responsibility that had been eroded by the paternalism of New Labour's big government and the myth of meritocracy, specifically at a moment of social and economic crisis in contemporary Britain. I would argue that this is one of the most significant ideological frames of the popular Black urban text, and the popular Black urban drama organized by a hegemonic symmetry serves well as a fictitious vessel of agnotology, given that particular sections of its audiences do not reside within, and therefore do not understand, the social world the characters inhabit. Thus, hegemonic symmetry as an agnotological endeavour services a need for not just stylistic commensurability but also knowledge production, a logic that can then activate the 'deficit model' of training and upskilling as a social corrective (Newsinger, 2012). However, the practice of hegemonic symmetry as a primary generic tenet of the popular urban text as a permissive social aesthetic asks for the conceptual explosion of the very term 'typecasting', which from a more traditional position may be understood pejoratively in the practice of performative fixity and stereotypical identification. This example reveals a positive dimension in the opening up of a concerted and generally mono-racial performative arena for actors who may have otherwise found themselves denied of acting opportunities through both the paucity of Black and ethnic minority characters and themes within the film and TV industry and the racial exigency denounced by Adrian Lester and the rejection of the very practice of a hegemonic correspondence. There is an embodiment of the urban as a creative visual experience to be encountered in Ashley Walters (*Storm Damage, Bullet Boy, Life and Lyrics, West 10 LDN, Sket, Anuvahood, Top Boy*), and we encounter in the popular urban text an interchangeable platform for emerging actors such as Riz Ahmed (*Shifty, Ill Manors*), Aml Ameen (*Kidulthood, Shank, Fallout, Safe*), Charles Mnene (*Life and Lyrics, Shoot the Messenger, Fallout, Safe, Dubplate Drama, NW*), Janine Winstone (*Bullet Boy, Kidulthood*), Ashley Madekwe (*Storm Damage, West 10 LDN*), Adam Deacon (*Kidulthood, Adulthood, West 10 LDN, Dubplate Drama, Shank, Anuvahood*), Jacob Anderson (*Adulthood, West 10 LDN*), Chanel Cali (*Dubplate Drama, Adulthood*), Duane Henry (*West 10 LDN, Dubplate Drama*), Ashley Chin (*Storm Damage, Anuvahood*), Alexis Rodney (*Storm Damage, Life and Lyrics*) and Jerome Holder (*Shank, Fallout*). This kind of performative density allows for the popular Black urban text to trade on the cultural associations to be constructed upon the presence of such acting talent. However, the urban film as a genre of creative access is also accompanied by a certain boundness, in that many of these performers would experience generally intermittent acting careers that, given their synonymy with the urban text, were to remain fixed within the racial, classed and evidently generic lores of the UK film industry. Such an assertion finds some exceptions, as was the case for Noel Clarke, who would win the BAFTA Rising Star award in 2009 for his 2008 film *Adulthood*, the sequel to *Kidhulthood* which Clarke would both write and direct and would reunite much of the cast from the first film. Here, Clark revises the character of Sam, now returning to the area after a period in prison for the killing of Trife, rendering the sequel as a story of revenge and personal redemption. *Kidulthood* would go on to become one of the highest-grossing British films of 2008, a feat supplemented by the increasing popularity of urban youth subculture and its economic success through ancillary markets such as DVD sales (BFI, 2009; Nwonka, 2015). This would also be the case for the final film in the hood trilogy, *Brotherhood* (2015), which would continue the urban crossover as a system of reception in the casting of the Grime artist Stormzy as a central character in the film. However, this success was to be diminished by the controversy that would surround Clarke immediately after receiving the BAFTA Lifetime Achievement award in 2021, where over twenty women would accuse Clarke of multiple incidents of sexual assault, misconduct, bullying and harassment, some of which were said to have taken place during the production of the 'hood' films (*The Guardian*, Thursday, 29 April 2021). Within the Black urban text's presence in the industry, an enthusiasm for subcultural difference seemed to inaugurate a specific protocol of engagement, criticality and cultural politics. This is what Herman Gray terms the 'emotionally charged trajectories' (2013: 787), pointing to how high-profile award ceremonies allow for the visage of cultural celebration to be fixed upon a faux democratization of the film industry. For us, the urban actor becomes the contradictory demark of a *modus vivendi* between the film industry and the popular urban text as a platform of visibility and a compartmentalizing instrumentalization. The nature of the popular Black urban text as both an emancipatory landscape of youth inclusion and a hyper-celebratory but equally segregated achievement allows one to consider the omnipresence of Adam Deacon in such films and the success of Deacon's own self-directed feature debut *Anuvahood* (2011), which would offer a parody of the urban film/TV genre in its depiction of deliberately hyper-contrived caricatures within the symbolic location and would lead to Deacon being nominated for the same BAFTA Rising Star award in 2012.

I am particularly cognizant that such texts succeed in registering a powerful cultural resonance among its targeted demographic in both inspiring young minds and the realizing of creative aspiration, and the nomination would place Deacon, of Moroccan descent and from a working-class background in Hackney, against a crop of established and less hegemonically symmetrical and generically bound performers, most notably, the Eton and Cambridge educated Eddie Redmayne and the Tom Hiddleston, who at this point had already been firmly identified as being in possession of the performative lineage and continuity with the normative image of the UK film industry, for both actors would be positioned as the emergent ambassadors of the British acting class. We should be particularly attentive to the issue of acting and social class, specifically the very nature of the film industry as a site of tremendous social inequality (O'Brien, Friedman and Laursion, 2016), an experience that becomes more exacerbated when considered within the intersecting context of race. That Deacon, who had referred to the significance of social class in his own nomination and the potential for a social and cultural change in the sector should he succeed in an interview with ITV London News in the days leading up to the BAFTA ceremony, and my own observation of the specificity of the Rising Star award as the only BAFTA Film Award to be publicly voted for produces different forms of social meaning to be placed within the episteme. Deacon would indeed triumph on the evening, and the highly public 'spectacles of visibility' Gray (2013: 787) identifies within such a practice performs here as the industrial, Big Society ambassadors for the One Nation dictate of social uplift, personal transformation and moral and individual responsibility as the prerequisites of national belonging, and allows for the awarding to be conceived as a welcomed defilement of not just the BAFTA Awards as the preserve of white middle-class normativity but more significantly permits the film industry to herald its arrival at the zenith of diversity and inclusion, with the moment performing as the exemplar of the potential of the cultural and creative industries, and the screen sector specifically, as a highly generative sphere. However, the reductive but liberally tolerated presence of racial and classed otherness in such films alongside the much more prestigious examples of British cinema means that the popular Black urban text can function as a socially transformative sphere for some, but an ultimately immaterial consecrating interlude for others, who are able to accrue tremendous career cache through other forms of social, cultural and economic capital. Hegemonic symmetry here possesses a bidirectional dynamic in that it is accompanied by the devaluation of the urban actor through the reductive margins of race and class, but also by its attendant generic hierarchy organized by forms of cultural taste and normative notions of aesthetic value. In the hailing of hegemonic symmetry as a necessary and virtuous industrial phenomenon, those who wish to question the artistic merit of the popular Black urban text were also compelled to exhibit a degree of liberal tolerance towards its apparent vulgarity as a film genre. Naturally, both Redmayne and Hiddleston would continue their Hollywood ascent propelled by racial and class privilege, and the validity of my reference to both career trajectories as comparable cannot be undermined by Deacon's highly public demise that would culminate in him being sectioned under the Mental Health Act after being convicted of harassing Noel Clarke and possessing an offensive weapon. Rather, the comparative legitimacy of the reference to Deacon, Redmayne and Hiddleston is developed from the nodal point of the BAFTA Rising Star award, the temporal and segregated celebration of diverse acting talent but fixed within a hierarchy of value and esteem that is framed as the reinvigoration of the film industry by the representations of racial and cultural alterity.

I arrive at a particular point of paradigmatic departure in my reading of the popular urban text as a sub-category of Black British cinema, one that questions the cohesiveness of the films within the urban generic corpus to be organized under a singular and inherently implicatory racial prefix, for the popular Black urban texts that have been considered in this chapter generally exhibit a departure from the Black representational density that accompanied the more adultified aesthetic of Yardie gangs and inferential gun violence and towards the narratives of working-class youthhood that allow the popular Black urban texts to be captured within the accommodative extensivity of Black urban visual culture as a theatre of multi-raciality, a cohabitation that performs as an elongation of urban multiculture. The writings of Paul Gilroy on the question of conviviality are particularly salient to the analysis of the urban text's claim to an organic multi-raciality. For Gilroy, the convivial is to be understood as 'a social pattern in which different metropolitan groups dwell in close proximity but where their racial, linguistic and religious particularities do not – as the logic of ethnic absolutism suggests they must – add up to discontinuities of experience or insuperable problems of communication' (Gilroy, 2006: 40). It is against this understanding of conviviality that Valluvan, in a conceptual challenge towards the interpretive swelling of the very term, arrives at an interpretation of the convivial as 'how everyday multicultural practices rest on a radical and complex ability to be at ease in the presence of diversity but without restaging communitarian conceptions of the self-same ethnic and racial difference' (2016:205). Such a reading of conviviality as a space of homogeneity is one that provokes an interrogation of the popular Black urban text as an amalgamating aesthetic where in its implied function as an integrated multi-raciality in both composition and reception becomes a site for the aggregation of a number of cultural experiences to be aestheticized in film and television culture's representations of young people and its ability to present a communitarian horizontality between different racial and ethnic identities. There is, I believe, an already present theoretical response to Valluvan's later concern with the issue of 'how ethnic and racial difference is navigated within convivial formations' (208) and is to be observed in a number of scholarly endeavours. It is certainly an example of the convivial in the generative (if also conflictual) interactions between Black and ethnic minority and white inmates that Coretta Phillips observes inside 'the multicultural prison' (2012) and can also be located in De Noronha's more recent interrogation of conviviality as a phenomenon within the spaces of state-administered racism and violence within deportation centres (2022). My specific extension of Valluvan's concern is how convivial engagements are presented as purged of racial antagonisms in the placid spectacle of white existence within a space of Black majoritarianism, and an additional response to Valluvan's critique can be sourced from Hall's purview of the *popular* in Black popular culture (1993) and his temporal-resistant reading of the capitalist orchestration of Black representation that in the context of my own historicization inaugurated a shift from the experience of multiculture to the urban (diversity) as an instinctual and institutionally affirmed practice of post-multiculturalism. Like Valluvan, I share a dissatisfaction with the unsophisticated analyses of racial integration as an ontologically simplified reading that finds accomplishment in the presentation of the assumed rather than explored existence of conviviality as an everyday, quotidian accordance within the multiracial city. But my reading of multi-raciality and interraciality both within the Black urban text and in its circulation as equally alive to the possibility of conviviality as an 'indifference to difference' (Amin, 2013: 3), or as advanced by Gilroy, as diurnal and unspectacular is a critical point of departure. This, I want to argue, is an impossible task. For this becomes compromised when our experience of the attenuate veneer of the convivial is negotiated through the powerful and hegemonic resonator that is popular culture, a sphere that is of course not the subject of either Valluvan or De Noronha's analysis but one that provides a quite crucial and generative parenthesis to Valluvan and allows for a critical rather than a duplicative reading of the convivial culture. While his examination of conviviality is purposefully devoid of textual analysis, it does pay paradigmatic attention to the potential for the exemplars of the experience of difference to move from an epistemic concern and into the spectrum of the aesthetic. In this endeavour, I find some reassurance in Valluvan's ethnographic referencing of Gilroy's interest in cultural artefacts as produced and consumed through the spaces of difference, and the possibility for the practice of racial verticality to be found in the epistemic demand for the uncritical acceptance of urban visual culture and performance as the arena of an organic convivial sensibility was to be asserted by the author/rapper Akala, who would make a number of public animadversions towards the 2011 song 'Jungle' by the white Grime/Rap artist Professor Green (aka Stephen Mandleson). Green, who in the previous year had won both a MOBO award for Best Hip Hop/ Grime Act and was nominated for several Urban Music Awards, appeared to flourish within the legitimacy of the urban genre as a source of uncontested convivial authenticity through his raising on the Northwold Estate in Clapton, Hackney, his self-confessed involvement in a localized drug trade and his own interracial childhood friendships, symbolic ties and associations that allow for a Black urban adjacency that, at least within the commodificatory function of the urban as a promotional (sub) culture, is secured through recognizable and hegemonically incontestable forms of racial signification. Here, we encounter a portrayal of a convivial experience that is expressed both in the video's imagery and in the track's chorus sung by the white Irish singer Maverick Sabre in a distinctive Jamaican patois and the video, which would be filmed in Hackney, would exhibit the very authenticating modalities found in the popular Black urban text's aesthetic practices in the use of non-professional Black actors cast from the local area. It is of course beyond the ambit and interest of this chapter to conduct a complete enumeration of the sequences that unequivocally aestheticize Black urban masculinity as a hauntologically durable and consenting figure of social anxiety. But there is a commensurate presence of the hegemonic representations of Black Otherness as a point of racial meaning to be found in the opening of the video to an image of a Black youth laying in a coffin placed in a living room. Directly referencing Hackney in his opening bars, Green is framed at the front of a group of posturing hooded Black men as he declares 'its wild round here, you don't wanna spend the night round here' (Figure 9.7), an establishing image that is intercut throughout the video with instances of the violent and lawless nihilism encountered in

Figure 9.7 Professor Green's 'Jungle' music video (Virgin Records, 2010).

the inferential narratives of internecine black-on-black urban criminality as a useful fiction of race and aestheticized in *Bullet Boy*; a group of balaclava-laden Black men burst into a flat and attack a younger Black youth for, from what we can discern, a stash of money; a Black man is seen tied up and bloodied with a gun held to his head. Here, the video takes us through the repertoire of violent acts within the hyper-local confines of the symbolic location. Throughout these sequences, Green's lyrics of Hackney's criminalized Black urbanity provide an augmenting narration to the images of Black discorded menace, but the primary moment of racial description is heard in the lyric 'and your chains looking like fresh fruit to a hungry ape', the particular point of Akala's disapprobation by the video's immediate cut back to a close-up of the young Black youth in a coffin. The continuity between the video and the idea of the Black urban text as a necessary fiction of race is open to some challenge here, in that 'Jungle' is absent of any ontological suture, sub or counter-narration or facticity, as its audiovisual schema makes no attempt to unsettle the contiguity of the video's Black hauntological image system. I identify a specific utility in the reading of 'Jungle', which by 2022 had amassed 27 million views online, in the context of the broader analysis of the urban as a site of uncontested and seemingly primordial conviviality and a free linguistic exchange that is demonstrative of the 'lexical traffic' Roger Hewitt described as the vernacular flows between Black and white adolescents within the multicultural landscape who use Black diasporic language forms and gesticulations (1986). It is this assumed understanding of the convivial that licences the hegemonic acceptance of the urban as absent of racial verticality through the conjecture's development of diverse cultural and creative production as the visual intermediary between young Black and white people, and allows for a return to the Black urban dialogism as a theoretical framework. Specifically, it is within the visual representations of popular Black urbanity as a social aesthetic that I am able to identify and interrogate the constituent parts of the text, and its resignifying of the hauntological Black urban Other through visual ideas is resourced from the hauntological Black archive, and the construction of the urban as the multi-modal, multi-dimensional and cross-mediatized site for the rejection of representational and communicative artifice is paradoxically reproduced by the capitalist frames of promotional culture as a site of multiracial authenticity.

In arguing that this version of conviviality that is produced within the urban space cannot be guaranteed through any proximity to or embeddedness within the Black geography, Akala arrives at an inevitable impasse in that the highlighting of the video as a denigrative mode of Black characterization, to take one aspect of the Akala critique, may also annul the necessary interrogation of the reality that Black men/youths may draw a sense of recognition, however myopic this may appear, in seeing their identities and experiences affirmed, albeit indirectly, within popular visual culture. I am carefully approaching this idea that the hauntological images of violent Black masculinity and death may attend to a utopian desire is an example of subcultural insularity or of a variating double consciousness, for this myopia may be the very contradiction identified by Hall in the conjunctural specificities of Black cultural politics and symbiotically, capitalism's tariff for the incorporating of Black creative artefacts and forms of representation into the popular. Thus, while one concurs with Gilroy's insistence that indifference to difference is the necessary condition for the organic experience of conviviality, the 'unremarkable' (Gilroy, 2004: 105), the indifferent, the commonplace and the everyday diurnal is not the *immaterial*. The Black urban text as the convivial is unable to achieve a disentanglement from the politics of diversity as a commodifying intermediary negotiating the terms and textures of Black visual identity and cultural representation. This question of ownership is the central argument made by Akala, who comparatively points to a degree of proprietorship and contested autonomy established by African American performers through the struggle to not simply come into visibility but assert a social-cultural and industrial ownership of Hip Hop as an unquestionably Black social and cultural practice. From Akala's formulation, this means that for non-Black artists who are afforded entry into this sphere, it is one to be undertaken with a certain representational ethics and is found in his example of the white US rapper Eminem, whose status as one of the most successful figures in contemporary Hip Hop as a distinctive Black cultural form is conditioned by a sense of performative reticence in that his music is concertedly sanitized of any stereotyping lyrical trespass or racial figuration in the constructing of pathologizing images of Black America. Therefore, the cultural inclusivity of Hip Hop is marked by a degree of guardship and propriety, and it returns us to the issue of the social life of conviviality, in that Valluvan's ethnographic analysis argues that the production and experience of conviviality can be considered within the context of urban sociology in that the convivial experience as a politics of multiculture is negotiated by the geographic and hyper-local decrees within the multi-ethnic social space commandeering over the expressions of Black vernacular cultures. In the case of Jungle's video, it is the text's existence outside this space and into capitalism as a sphere of negotiation and inextricable commodification that expedites the disintegration of the already degradable thin borders of cultural appreciation/appropriation that presents the urban as a representational utopia that denies and repels racism, heightened by the popular presence of Black masculine identity as a durable and naturalizing entry point for an engineered racial inclusivity. It is when it enters the commodifying spheres of mainstream cultural production and exploded within the carnivalistic spheres of racial difference that conviviality triumphs in an evading of the hyper-local structures of proprietorship that commandeer the use of Black language forms by white peers, and it is by capitalism's amplificatory logics that conviviality is able to succeed in a contravening of what Hewitt terms the 'private arrangement' (1986: 163) of the Black majoritarianism's allowance of racial difference. But in identifying the *popular* as an instinctive field of racism, conviviality, in this guise, is unable and unprepared to disturb the ossified system of racial verticality that racial capitalism's abstract quantum interests find in Black urban cultural production. The conjunctural specificity of Black cultural representations of convivial culture as the exemplar of communities as the unspectacular and quotidian is orientated through a process of shedding through its development from the geographic situatedness of the pirate radio stations to the spectacularizing gaze of mainstream audiovisual performance and importantly PSB film and television. My thinking here, one that chimes with Valluvan's suspicion towards the paradigmatic pronouncements of the 'convivial turn' within the academe that inflicts no damage to the continued politics of race structuring these relations, the accentuating of its function as a popular and multiracial product is assured by capitalism's reconfiguration of the urban as the all-encompassing descriptor for all that may purport and appear to be racially integrated, aesthetically subversive and youthful in its representational orientations. Indeed, a semblance of this conjuncture's dissonance around the question of race and the subjectivities of the urban can be observed in the 2014 publishing of the BBC's 1Xtra's 1XtraPowerList that would vote the white singer-songwriter Ed Sheeran as the 'most important UK artist in the black and urban music scene' in the placing of the then 23-year-old Sheeran at number one in its consecrating list of influential performers within the urban sphere. Not dissimilar to the industrial aggrandizement that was enjoyed by Professor Green, the very practice of popular consecration serves as a tremendously unreliable foundation from which one can assess the urban as a seamless convivial experience. In an understanding of the urban as a term that oscillates from the classification of the urban as the physical representation of Black people to the undifferentiated nomenclature for youthhood, diverse cultural production and multiracial cultural consumption that remains attuned to Joy White's reading of the urban, just as James Snead's historic theoretical challenge to the concessions and compromise that constitute the very idea of Black independent cinema, Black urban visual representation as a sphere of convivial identity remains beholden to the strategic, instinctive and the continuously shifting and irregular predilections of capitalism's extractive and amplificatory interests in the verisimilitudinous construction and presence of racial difference. This means that we cannot accept wholesale the urban text as the undifferentiated convivial continuum in its aestheticizing of the hauntological Black urban Other, however proximal this imagery is to the realities of the Black urban experience or how embedded one is to this demographic through any spatial attachment or cohabitation, but as an inevitably extractive aesthetic that may display moments of commensalism. To assert that the *popular* convivial as a natural index of the urban text is laden with the racial verticality it claims to disavow is not to advocate that we surrender what has been accrued culturally, socially and creatively from the very real interactions and everyday forms of multiculture and our both dynamic and placid urban subcultural practices and vernacular expressions to the atavistic dictum of ethnic absolutism. Rather, and in returning to the thinking offered by Back in his rebuttal of what he views as Hewitt's totalizing and somewhat limited framework in his insistence that 'dialogue between Afro-Caribbean and White working-class youth may have little or no impact on the use of racist discourses that are applied by whites to other minorities' (1996: 13), my reading re-emphasizes the need to develop a more radical assessment of conviviality and the normalizing naturality of racial and ethnic difference under the hyper-celebratory and commodifiable spheres of the urban *as* industry. Put more simply, urban conviviality as the visual and narrational is unable to truly achieve the unspectacular and indifferent while being both mobilized and immobilized by the insatiable cosmopolitanism of whiteness that reappropriates organic urban cultural production as a vital variant of diversity and inclusion that become readied for the seductive, indexical, mimetic and the culturally and generically verisimilitudinous visual frames of the popular Black urban text, of which 'Jungle' lays claim to in its existence within the sphere of the urban text as a *liminal* space.

I want to consider the implication of the textual representations of urban multiculture as a sphere of conviviality. On 4 August 2011, Mark Duggan, a 29-year-old Black man from Tottenham, North London, would be shot dead by the Metropolitan Police, an incident that would catalyse the largest moment of civil disobedience within a generation in the UK. Duggan, who was under surveillance by Operation Trident, had been followed by a specialist firearms unit who would apprehend the mini-cab he was travelling in by performing a 'hard stop' manoeuvre that would force the vehicle to pull over. Here, Duggan would be shot twice by the police upon exiting the taxi, and the highly ambiguous nature of the incident would become the basis for the Duggan family's public campaign for justice given that Duggan was neither armed nor posed any threat to the officers at the moment of his killing and the gun he was in possession of during his taxi journey was found some 7 metres away from his body, despite both the forensic pathologist and the biomechanical reports commissioned by the IPCC concluding that it would be highly unlikely that Duggan would have been able to throw the gun such a distance either at the point of or immediately after his shooting (Forensic Architecture, 2021). The spectacle of Black male death justified under the protective veneer of police protocol is of course no novel occurrence, and a similar public instance of Black male death at the hands of the police is to be found in the death of 24-year-old Azelle Rodney, a Black man from West London who was killed by a Metropolitan Police marksman in Edgware, North London. Azelle was shot six times in 2.1 seconds by an assault rifle through the passenger window of the Volkswagen Golf he was seated in and was the subject of the 2010 Public Enquiry that would conclude Rodney was unlawfully killed. In the example of Duggan, what was a defining factor in motivating the violent nationwide response to the killing, beyond the outrage at the two days that would pass before the police would contact Duggan's family and the police indifference that would meet the 200 peaceful protesters that had gathered outside Tottenham Police Station, is the resonance of the incident as a historical colonial legacy and contemporary practice of anti-Blackness and class-based policing among a multiracial youth living within a specific political condition that seemed to speak to their social and cultural existences. It is the personal impact of the very public tremor of the killing and the riots that were to be captured in George Amponsah's 2015 documentary *The Hard Stop*, which exhibited a particular attentiveness to the condition of loss created by the killing. *The Hard Stop* would commence its story in the aftermath of both the killing of Duggan and the nationwide riots and the conclusion of the judicial inquest that would return a verdict of lawful killing, all telegraphed through the perspective of Duggan's two closest friends, Marcus Knox-Hooke and Kurtis Henville, and their return to a mournful existence within the Broadwater Farm Estate and the struggles of coping with the mental implications of the fatal practices of the Metropolitan Police. The relevance of the Duggan killing and the subsequent England Riots to an analysis of the urban as synonymous with the concept of conviviality and its popular textual representations as an aesthetic of agnotology is that the uprisings occurred at the point of an unprecedented period of economic austerity and the symbolic and material social violence that accompanied the electing of the Conservative-Liberal Democrat Coalition government in 2010 who, in administering the most comprehensive system of welfare cuts seen in Britain, would greatly extend the fractures of a nation already deeply organized by the sharp divisions of race and crucially, class. My concern with the riots is not necessarily rooted in how the uprising was to be understood in the context of policing, poverty and government policy alongside the Duggan killing (Lewis, 2011) or the general attribution of the riots and its spectacle of nihilistic looting and lawbreaking to an improvident culture of hyper-consumerism alongside the crisis of both economic and social liberalism (Lammy, 2012), but how the equally powerful spectacle of the cross-racial experience of austerity and the violent rebellion against it served as the epitome of Broken Britain as racially indiscriminate phenomena for the historian and broadcaster David Starkey, who would provoke a storm of criticism after a televised discussion for his evaluation of the seemingly novel multi-raciality of the riots. Appearing on BBC2's Newsnight, and speaking of 'a profound cultural change' and one that for Starkey would demand the urgent re-reading of Enoch Powell's 'rivers of blood' speech, Starkey would insist that 'His prophesy was absolutely right in one sense. The Tiber did not foam with blood but flames lambent, they wrapped around Tottenham and wrapped around Clapham. . . . But it wasn't inter-community violence. This is where he was absolutely wrong'. At this point, Starkey then gestures towards the other panel guest, *The Guardian* journalist Owen Jones, the author of *Chavs: The Demonisation of the Working Classes*, and would go on to assert:

> What has happened is that the substantial section of the chavs that you wrote about have become black. The whites have become black. A particular sort of violent, destructive, nihilistic gangster culture has become the fashion. . . . 'Black and white, boy and girl operate in this language together. This language, which is wholly false, which is this Jamaican patois that has intruded in England. This is why so many of us have this sense of literally a foreign country.

Starkey's accusation towards the prevalence of Black urban multiculture and its culpability for the riots as a racially transcendent defilement of white working-class identity should of course be understood as a demonstration of mournful melancholia that streams from the deep resentment towards the nation's Black presence as a racial defilement of British national identity that is masked as an intellectual contribution to a contemporary moral issue. The riots, as a multiracial phenomenon where both Black and white youths find themselves being subject to the social and economic lacerations meted out by the Coalition, find a presence in the period's popular urban texts as both useful and necessary fiction, in that their depiction of a criminalized multiracial youthhood is equally claiming to perform as an agnotological aesthetic. Social inequality is certainly a discursive concern, if not easily located *within* the thematic features of *Ill Manors*, the feature film of the rapper/singer Plan B (Ben Drew). Drew, whose 2006 song 'Kidz' had featured in *Kidulthood* and had played the role of Dabs in its sequel, would employ music as a mode of narrating the story of Aaron (Riz Ahmed) and Ed (Ed Skrien), two childhood friends who grew up in a care home and would become embroiled in a series of criminal situations before redeeming themselves in demonstrations of unrecognized responsibility and virtue, but only before the audience is taken through a number of citational, set-piece instances of Black gun violence, drug dealing and the coercing of a woman into prostitution as a quid pro quo payment for drug debts. Developed from Drew's short film *Michelle* (2008) and produced through a £100,000 budget between Film London's Microwave Scheme and BBC Films, the film would later gross £453,570 from the UK box office. I earlier described the elaborate conventions of popular Black urban texts in the practice of street-casting and the use of non-professional actors; music also serves to authenticate the film's own claim to a convivial urbanity through urban cultural production, and there is a form of segmenting subcultural appeal to be encountered in the film's poster which would be populated by endorsements by a number of urban artists/performers, including Tynchy Stryder, Alesha Dixon, Professor Green, Tinie Tempah and Ed Sheeran, but also by the release of the soundtrack album of the same title. Indeed, the liberal media's fervour upon its release in March 2012 was an attempt to contextualize the 2011 England Riots through a damnation of austerity Britain and the Coalition Government's destruction of the welfare state and public services and the positioning of working-class youths as the central antagonists within the fiction of Broken Britain through the media. The issue of social class is addressed in the song's video, which uses to great effect both broadcast and CCTV footage from the riots that are interspersed with images of both David Cameron and Coalition's Liberal Democrat Deputy Prime Minister, Nick Clegg. *Ill Manors* is constituted by series of intertextualities in the inclusion of the film's soundtrack, which features cast members from the film who seemingly reperform their screen characters and in this establishes a continuity with the film in the endeavour to resituate its cast within a political framework as an attempt to recontextualize the film itself through an interaction with the music video as a distinctive transmedia activity. As Plan B goes on to rap:

> There's no such thing as broken Britain/ We're just bloody broke in Britain/ What needs fixing is the system/ Not shop windows down in Brixton/ Riots on the television/ You can't put us all in prison! (Plan B, *Ill Manors*)

How can we understand *Ill Manors* and its presence within the crisis of urban youthhood as a liminal space of agnotology? For all its hyper-aggrandizement as a form of political commentary, 'ill Manors' exhibits a number of inescapable continuities with Professor Green's 'Jungle', none of which are specifically concerned with the question of the riots, although this has provided an important entry point to consider how *Ill Manors* conducts a critique of the fallacies of the economic programme of austerity finds significance as an extra-diegetic presence, and the urban as a multiracial experience conditioned by austerity allows us to assess the bidirectional permeation of the One Nation Conservative discourse of Broken Britain through the film's cognitive and discursive architecture. 'We are all products of our environment . . . some environments are just harder to survive in.' The agnotological intention implied in the film's tagline comprises of two, somewhat interconnected, phases. In its second phase, *Ill Manors* suggests that the audience is to embark on a polemical account of how the distressed fabrics of its social environment are preconditioned for the production of the very worst demonstrations of national unbelonging. However, it is the first claim that the characters are simply displaying the natural behaviours germane to the symbolic location that is of particular importance, as neither phase is abridged by the crucial analysis of an antagonistic oppressive political system, further emphasized by Drew's insistence that the characters 'act the way they do because of the shit that happened to them that wasn't their fault' (*The Observer*, Sunday, 27 May 2012). Like the manufactured ignorance of Cameron's Broken Britain, where instead of social policy, social pathology sits at the basis of the crisis of a multiracial working-class social breakdown, it is here where the film displays a structural dissonance in its own agnotology, for its analysis of manufactured political ignorance is not conducted by its interrogation of structural inequality within its diegesis but by the critical context through which the film would be circulated. What can account for this clamour? The agnotological positioning of the film through the media is identified in *The Observer*, who in a sprawling feature on the film, would convene a range of notable figures from film, politics, music and popular culture and the burgeoning arena of social commentary on the film's value as a form of confrontational politics. It is somewhat indicative of my reading of One Nation Conservatism as an inchoate and liminal political culture that *The Observer* feature is able to combine and unify the thoughts of former Conservative MP Edwina Curry and the Labour MP Walthamstow Stella Creasy alongside the perspectives of the Grime artist Lethal Bizzle and musicians Goldie and Tinchy Stryder. Here, in the unequivocal and unified championing of the film under the aegis of *The Observer* as sufficient to secure its embeddedness within a political project, it is the significance of its critical context that seemed to anoint *Ill Manors* with a political agenda that finds its value in the hegemonic image of delinquent youth identities and economic improvidence as its textual language of agnotology. I want to re-emphasize that the very idea of the popular Black urban text as a social aesthetic is concretized through its inescapable adherence to the shifting and regenerating political cultures. What develops here is a particularly myopic mode of agnotology that does not base its knowledge excavation of the myth of Broken Britain at its structural, but that there is some doubt as to the existence of urban violence and decadence located somewhere between government, the media and the public, despite both the media and government's complicity in the very inferential discourse of urban crime. As Drew argued, 'A lot of people outside this environment don't believe it exists. . . . So in the film, rather than glamorise it, I'm trying to say to people this is the true, dark reality. This is what happens. It's not cool. No drug dealer really has the last laugh' (*The Observer*, 27 May 2012). At this moment, we are asked to accept the film's examination of ignorance, or as asserted by Slater, the advancing of a Broken Britain as 'cunning terminalistic screen' (2012: 964), as agnotological in the densified behavioural aspects of its demographic, argued by the Conservatives as the genesis of Broken Britain establishing a wilful practice of distortion as a concerted political strategy. Relatedly, *Ill Manors* becomes a site of ideological conflict by its ability to recruit the eager liberal applause of Big Society agents and their desire to consecrate the film as Broken Britain's article of faith. Notably, Camila Batmanghelidjh, the founder of the now-defunct Kid's Company that would be aggrandized by David Cameron as a primary exemplar of the One Nation mantra of the Big Society, would describe *Ill Manors* as 'an incredibly accurate portrait' of the crisis of youth in British society. But given that its facticity is telegraphed through themes and characterizations serviceable to the Conservative practice of willful dis-knowledge, its agnotology can only be secured in *The Guardian* exclamation that 'social commentators are already talking about its political significance, and reviewing last year's riots through the prism of its lens' (2012). My own reading points to an interest in the cultural terms by which the film can be filtered through such a prism, and the interrogation of the credibility of the film as an agnotological study in some ways supports my claim that the urban text is constituted by social and political dynamics and the One Nation Conservatism precipitates an interpretative reading drawn from the liminality of its social context, and the validity of *The Guardian*'s own claim can be read as a practice of discursive augmentation, sourced here from the spectacle of public discussion and debate. To read the film from an alternative perspective, a critique of the uncritical acceptance of the film as a tool of agnotology is to be found in the comments of Fraser Nelson, the editor of the Conservative publication *The Spectator* who, in drawing attention to the film's recourse to the Broken Britain discourse, identifies the film's attribution of its characters' deviance to the absence of the nuclear family as sufficient to evaluate *Ill Manors* as 'a very conservative film' (*The Observer*, 27 May 2012). Such an analysis of the text seeks to establish continuities between the One Nation Conservative taxonomy of Broken Britain in the abdication of personal responsibility and the film's aestheticizing of crisis urbanity, albeit with critical intentions. I'm compelled to ask what is revealed to us if we momentarily overlook the historical political binaries latent within the question of the Big Society's strategic practice of ignorance in our evaluation of the film? In doing away with the crucial antagonism between government and society, the film's defining agnotology operates at the level of the individual and their moral and cultural code. This asks for the nuancing of the understanding of the urban as the reliable tribune of austerity Britain and the question of race, for as neither of its two lead characters in the British Pakistani Riz Ahmed and the white British Ed Skrien are Black, the hegemonic acceptance of the urban film as a commercial product, a subcultural practice and more significantly, conviviality remains constructed upon the ossified axis of Black gang and drugs criminality. Therefore, an agnotological chasm emerges at this particular political culture due to *Ill Manors* inability to identify and articulate a position outside of the One Nation political discourse's incorporation of the popular urban text. In other words, the film's own political intervention is sutured to the broader politics *of* intervention into the myth of Broken Britain. These popular urban narratives reveal an interesting ideological, contextual and contingent negotiation with One Nation Conservative politics on the one hand but an implied digression from it on the other. Within the contested field of cultural production where both film and television texts are powerful processes of social formation, which produce different regimes of perception, identity and the grounding of dominant knowledges in what are unequal zones of power, the popular urban text at this political conjuncture as agnotology is an aesthetic form and narrational practice that, rather than dismantling its structures of ignorance, attempts to make whatever is known or believed about the condition of Broken Britain's multiracial youth available to us in new ways.

10

Defensible Black Spaces

Race, British Identity and Architecture in
Attack the Block

> The politics of race in this country is fired by conceptions of national belonging
> and homogeneity, which not only blur the distinction between race and nation,
> but they rely on that very ambiguity for their effect.
>
> —Paul Gilroy, *Ain't No Black in the Union Jack*, 1987

My contention that popular urban films have tended to efface critical questions of racial
inequality within their diegetic representation of the urban reality is not to imply that
the evacuation of a structural analysis of the urban world represents a failure on the part
of the films. Of course, the inclusion of such apparatus within the diegesis is much more
than a decision of political predilection or the degree to which a director may evaluate
broader social structures as *influential* factors in the urban character's repertoire,
circumstances, behaviour, decision-making processes and narrative trajectory.
There are additional generic factors embedded in the urban film that, in privileging
the spectacle of cinematic urban violence, can prevent the spectator from engaging
textually with the broader causes and contexts of urban conflict. For Neal (1990), film
genres represent 'systems of orientations, expectations and conventions that circulate
between industry, text and subject' (19). This triangulation of factors underpinning
the primary function of film genre poses a particular problem for films attempting to
represent urban conflict vis-à-vis the deep public conditioning of both popular image
streams of Black youths and the established generic expectations of the urban film. It
may be that as such violence is so inscribed within the popular urban oeuvre that to
depart from them and enter into a more didactic mode of representation would be to
relegate the very criterion of value within popular urban films – the spectacle of urban
'street' realism – to the narrative background. Indeed, it may be that a reorientation of
the very generic model for the urban film may provide the narrational flexibility to also
interrogate the relationship between Black working-class youth existences and racism.
In other words, for the spectator to be alive to the alternative textual modalities within
the urban film, a generic *rupture* is required to dismantle the ritualistic processes of

representation and spectatorship that challenge the usual filmic conceptions of Black urban identity and difference. It is with this ambition in mind that this chapter examines the 2011 film *Attack the Block* (dir. Joe Cornish) and explores the possibility of locating an alternative mode of the filmic articulation of Black youthhood, stigma, racism, class difference and state oppression within the urban film oeuvre. Undoubtedly, *Attack the Block*, *Bullet Boy*, *Adulthood* and many other films referenced within this study are linked by a continuity in the themes of Black youth criminality that map onto broader horizons of expectation for the urban text. However, despite the generic corpus within which the urban films are unified, and the centrality of the urban norm to these expectations, I must stress that representational comparison is not in itself the centre of my focus, although it forms a useful framework for the discussion. The focus is, instead, on the narrational modes and cinematic aesthetics through which an alternative visage of the urban landscape emerges within the urban film itself, the ideological interpretations of these and its validity in shaping the contemporary debates on the Black working-class existence. In terms of the representation of the urban norm, the familiar performance of crime, violence and delinquency emerges as the recognizable introductory repertoires of *Attack the Block*'s primary characters. However, within this immediate familiarity, a new allegorical representation of Black youth oppression is observed, and I want to draw attention to this political expression as a conscious process of incorporating whiteness, both literal in its description of the social tensions between Black youths and the white middle classes and metaphored in an extra-terrestrial attack on a housing estate as a system of state oppression, into the main fabric of the film. To achieve this explorative aim, this chapter adopts an analytical approach that equally pays diligence to the more formal and textual properties of the urban film that provide a broader description of its social commentary while simultaneously suggesting conceptual and dramatic narrative techniques and generic hybridities for incorporating this expansive view of social inequality within the urban text. An analysis of *Attack the Block* also permits an interrogation of the filmic registration of the housing estate constructed through, as I'll argue, an allegorical representation of the tumultuous relationship between Blackness, Britishness and the dominant political cultures, and how the film's activation of the housing estate as a physical site of political conflict reappropriates these locations not simply as the urban film's aesthetic backdrop but as an active, multi-layered physical space that performs as a crucial vector for its filmic treatment of the structural relationships between environment, racial identity and social injustice in contemporary Black Britain. Within *Attack the Block*, the urban landscape, made active through the iconography of the council estate, is never simply a (re)representation of an extra-filmic social reality, and this chapter investigates *Attack the Block* as a radical exploration of racial and social tension, anxiety, nationhood and resistance. Here, a metaphorical critique of race and class antagonism is developed through an examination of the crisis that emerges from the intrusion on the tower block by extra-terrestrial power. To further understand the film's novel use of space and location to narrate the conflict between the estate's Black indigene and a greater systematic force, I consider how the tower block constructs an imaginary defence against an oppressive force to uncover the film's socio-spatial representations, their associated political and sociocultural properties and the allegorical meanings that emerge from its modes of critical realism.

As my analysis of the production context of *Bullet Boy* and the textual properties of *Ill Manors* demonstrates, a tension can be identified in the British urban film's desire to provide a more expansive view of Black urban life to counter the reductive analyses offered by mainstream media while equally relying on an 'excess of Black convention' (Nwonka, 2020a). This refers to the modes in which the films' close adherence to the more traditional generic conventions of social realism, combined with the culturally verisimilar visage of Black urban youth conflict bound up in notions of representational authenticity, produces a horizon of expectation that, paradoxically, requires at some level an alignment with the very representations they seek to counter. Consequently, the films are unable to redress or contextualize the delimiting image constructions of Black youths, representations that Woods (2015) describes as 'young black men's struggles with masculinity, gang warfare, drugs, teen parenthood and conflicts with authority' (235). I've previously described how the social realist ambitions of the urban drama (particularly endemic to films in receipt of public funding) are often defined through their advancing of a version of realism heavily reliant on themes of violence and criminality that are assumed to be pathologic to the urban environment, and an additional convention unifying *Bullet Boy*, *Shifty*, *Ill Manors* and *Adulthood* with an analysis of *Attack the Block* is the centrality of the inner-city housing estate as the defining but equally unexamined component of the British urban text. Such spaces are denigrated in the popular imagination as sites of violent urban conflict, crime, moral deficit, unemployment, social exclusion, antisocial behaviour and problem families (Ravetz, 2001; Hanley, 2007). Resultingly, tower blocks and council estates have formed an opportune and primary visual backdrop for these representations in British film and television but have equally recruited divergent meanings from the estate. The narrational use of the estate as a social landscape has at times occupied the epistemological centre ground of films attempting to offer an analysis of peripheral identities within a divided society, at other times function as a recognizable negative visage of decontextualized image streams supporting the further entrenchment of class prejudice and disdain.

Perhaps unsurprisingly, scholars have previously had very little to say about *Attack the Block* within the various analyses of both contemporary social realism and the Black urban film (Nwonka, 2017). An exception is Woods (2015), who, in describing the tenets of what she terms as 'telefantasty', constructs a taxonomy of film and TV dramas that rely on the generic hybridity of British social realism, youth TV and elements of fantasy, science fiction and horror. With a specific focus on the E4 series *Misfits* (2009–13) in which five young offenders carrying out community service are caught in an electrical storm and acquire occult, supernatural powers, a definition of telefantasy is advanced that for Woods 'explicitly draws on the late 2000s media panics around urban and underclass youth focalised through the threatening figure of the "hoodie"' (237). Wood acknowledges the significance of the council estate as a recurring motif to her classification of the telefantasy genre, drawing on the iconography of the tower block beyond the Thamesmead Estate-set *Misfits*, recognizing that 'the telefantasy tower block plays a central role in a cinematic comic-tinged take on the urban youth cycle, *Attack the Block*' (2011). As she goes on to assert:

> Echoing *Misfits*, it puts a science-fiction spin on the urban youth film's familiar tales of turf-wars and white plight. . . . Amid the genre-hybrid capers, the film manages to construct a compelling, nuanced depiction of conflicted young black masculinity as the boys' leader, Moses, is forced into a struggle bigger than hoodie-clad muggings and the temptations of gang life. (2016: 236)

Wood attempts, with some degree of success, to establish a vision of urban youth representation within *Attack the Block* that departs from both normative expectations and stylistic practices of the urban film while equally existing within the bounds of British social realism. However, there are at least two basic problems with this endeavour. First, beyond a taxonomy that limits *Attack the Block*'s telefantasy credentials to its marrying of sci-fi with cinematic tropes deriving from particular repertoires of Black youth delinquency in popular media (and in this obfuscating any alignment with the didactic dimensions of British social realism), there is a general instability in Wood's entry about the relationship with telefantasy to questions of race, Black identity and masculinity, given its primacy in both the very forms of representation Wood terms as 'urban youth exploitation cinema' (*Top Boy, Fallout*) and its overt associations with Black youths and criminality. This makes any attempt to unify *Misfits* and *Attack the Block* within an analysis of race and class injustice extremely arduous. For example, in terms of their representational focus, just three of *Misfits* central characters across its five series were Black/Black mixed-race, rendering unstable the reading of its significance to questions of race and its subsequent alignment with *Attack the Block* (beyond its obvious generic elements). Finally, and related to this observation, where the characters in *Misfits* have been bestowed with supernatural powers, further cementing its alignment with the sci-fi sensibilities of the telefantasy genre, for Moses and his collective, despite the significance of the film's digital manipulations, these do not dismantle the character's indexical relationship with reality, and the methods with which the group resist the alien attack rely on the very human means so associated with urban youthhood. In other words, *Attack the Block*'s ambitions lie firmly within the real.

I want to suggest that it is possible to free *Attack the Block* from a generic and epistemological fixity and advance an alternative interpretive framework through an analysis of the film's non-conventional uses of its physical landscape. In doing so, I want to draw on how its representation of place, space and environment assist in an allegorical reading of its account of Black youths and the processes of racial othering. In his 1973 book *Defensible Space*, the American architect Oscar Newman offered a sprawling (and equally controversial) analysis of the impact of physical design on the relationship between flat and street. The explicit focus of his study was the New York high-rise housing projects that, as a result of its specific architecture, produced a fertile landscape for criminal activity. However, this analysis also considered the impact of the buildings' design on the environment's social dynamics, becoming an influential factor in the creation of an enclosed urban milieu. In examining the 'non-street', high-rise housing blocks, separated from the main transit of the surrounding city streets, he advances a description of how the construction of symbolic and physical barriers both demarcates the restrictive limits of public access and affirms an informal but uncontested proprietorship of the building and its parameters, conducive to the residents' surveillance, identification and interrogation of the non-resident and their purpose in crossing the defined territories of public to private spaces of the locale (Severs, 2010). I will return to this crucial dimension and its usefulness as a framework for understanding *Attack the Block*'s cinematic registration of location as the process within which the film articulates racial, spatial and class relationships at a later point in this chapter; at this stage, I would like to draw attention to the description Newman offers of the high-rise block's physical design, particularly at ground level: the undefined entrances and exits elevated beyond the street, the interconnecting walkway systems and the secluded corners and underpasses the walkways create. These physical features would prove opportune for external threats and leave residents vulnerable to attack, predominantly in the form of criminals. While his analysis was concerned with the housing projects in the United States, particular elements of the defensible space model are easily recognizable in British state-built housing of the same period, and we find examples of this in both the Heygate Estate in Elephant & Castle and the Bemerton Estate in Islington, where much of *Attack the Block* is shot. My interest in the idea of the housing estate as a defensible space is motivated by its utility in articulating a more allegorical interpretation of *Attack the Block*'s representation of the relations between race, class and the city space. In what ways can the Wyndham Tower, as is mediated through *Attack the Block*'s cinematic optic, provide an allegorical account of spatial injustice and social stigma, and in a moment of attack from an external threat, in turn, become a defensible space? What relationships are established between the urban landscape, the camera and the film's Black political bodies?

Released just prior to the 2011 London riots, *Attack the Block*'s relevance to the increased cultural representation of Black urban youths is validated in part by virtue of its dialogue-led narrational style, an authenticity that can equally be attributed to a script that was developed alongside children from South London, where the film's naturalistic, street vernacular was captured collaboratively with young actors sourced from local schools and drama clubs. It is perhaps indicative of both the film's use of a generic approach not traditionally associated with representations of Black identities within British cinema and the general tendency for mainstream urban texts (or some variation of it) to be made by directors who are not drawn (at least along racial lines) from the very social milieu the films depict (*Storm Damage, Bullet Boy, Life and Lyrics, Fallout, NW*) that *Attack the Block* is the work of a white British director, Joe Cornish, who had established himself as a comedy writer and performer prior to writing and directing what would be his debut feature film. Although identifying as middle class and attending the independent Westminster School in Central London, Cornish was raised in Stockwell and through this had developed a particular attentiveness to the race and class struggles that had defined the areas where the film is set in the late 1970s and 1980, becoming an observer of the critical points of racial injustice and Black political expression through, among other moments, the Brixton Riots of 1981 and 1985 and the general race and class-based inequalities germane to the Black existence in South London. Indeed, such is the film's commitment to an accurate sociopolitical critique of social relations that marries a concern with the disadvantages and stigmas affecting Black British youth with a reference to the white anxiety felt towards this demographic that Cornish based his script on his own experiences of being mugged in South London. The film was made with the intention that *Attack the Block* would, at some level, address the demonization, apathy and lack of understanding displayed towards Black youths at the height of the 'Broken Britain' and, in exploring the backstories behind the youth identities he encountered during his own mugging, this would provide a contextuality to the decontextualized and depoliticized tenor of the contemporary descriptions of Black working-class youths within both political and media discourses.

Attack the Block's departure from the accepted generic forms of the British urban films with a tonality and genre hybridity in closer alignment with spoof comedy can be attributed to the presence of the British director Edgar Wright as the film's executive producer, who had by the end of the decade gained critical acclaim for directing a number of British comedy shows and films, including the cult Channel 4 series *Spaced* (1999–2001) and the film *Shaun of the Dead* (2004), a comedy-horror film upon which *Attack the Block* draws its generic references. Indeed, some of the influential texts that Cornish has cited as informing *Attack the Block*'s generic and narrational approach speak to a desire to reconfigure the cinematic representation of Black British youth identity within the textual binds of horror: *Assault on Precinct 13* (dir. John Carpenter, 1976), *Night of the Living Dead* (dir. George A. Romero, 1968) with its delicate social subtext critiquing issues such as war and American foreign policy, mass media and racism, and more prominently, the Korean film *Attack the Gas Station* (dir. Kim Sang-jin, 1999), where a group of delinquent youths take a gas station hostage before later running the station and serving customers. Such influences point to Cornish's faith in the allegorical traditions of sci-fi and horror to produce a social/political examination of the present (Blake, 2008) or in *Attack the Block*'s specific example, race, racism and the class-based social stigmas experienced by Britain's urban youth.

An additional factor driving the distinction between the established canon of British urban films and *Attack the Block*, determined in part by its more expansive generic repertoire in which its visual affects become a key component of its storytelling approach, is *Attack the Block*'s £8 million budget. This sum, which represented a considerably high production value for a first-time feature film, was one of the final films to be financed under the newly reformed UK Film Council Production Fund, which had unified the previously separate Premier Fund and New Cinema Fund as part of a reorganization as a result of cuts to the UKFC's grant-in-aid funding. The film would go on to recoup just £4 million from its budget, financed through a co-production between the UKFC and Film 4 and Big Talk Productions, with distribution from StudioCanal UK. Basement Jaxx, the South London music duo, would produce the film's distinctive score combining electronic music with the city's emergent Grime genre, a cross-pollination used to great effect at key points in the film to further support its claims to authenticity through reference to urban subcultural products. However, despite its high production budget, *Attack the Block* remains on the continuum of urban and low-budget film casting approaches in the use of first-time, emerging and non-professional acting talent. Beyond being the breakout film roles for British actress Jodie Whittaker and actor Luke Treadaway, *Attack the Block* is also notable for being the acting debut of South London-born actor John Boyega, who, aged seventeen, would play the film's main protagonist, Moses.

In considering the visual representation of London within British cinema, Charlotte Brunsdon suggests that South London 'tends to be produced through that matrix of stylistic practices associated with realism, naturalism and documentary' (2007: 76) and a combination of these aesthetic codes can be discerned in the film's opening sequence. We see an image of a meteor-like object soaring through space before gradually panning down and emerging into a tangible realist image: an aerial shot of scores of human traffic emerging from Oval station and, against a backdrop of fireworks, out to a modern-day South London. At first observation, this human traffic possess a range of narrative trajectories and possibilities from which *Attack the Block* will subsequently decide upon as a protagonist. Here, a young white woman (Sam) emerges from the station talking to her mother on the phone as she walks through an array of public bodies. As she continues her journey through the street full of markets, conversations and activity, this sequence is intercut with production credits. Sam's non-London, regional accent is made apparent as she continues her phone conversation, coming off a main road as she heads down a dark residential street, where we see young white children running down the street with their parents towards a fireworks display. Here, Sam appears very much within an accepted filmic understanding of person and place as she walks through a street of South London townhouses. However, the film's score suggests an impending danger as she passes graffiti-laden walls. A firework goes off and she quickly turns, startled. The spectator is presented with Sam at the point of both a geographical and territorial crossing – the dramatic shift from the public activity of the high street to a deserted non-street locale and subsequently a shift in her sense of personal safety. As she continues into the openings of the estate, she sees a group of five hooded youths on BMX bikes in the distance, who stand in a triangular formation with Moses positioned at its tip. The spectator, just as Sam, understands immediately what to expect of them by their physical attributes and apparel. As the youths turn their attention to Sam she stops walking forward in the realization of an impending confrontation. Sam reacts with 'Oh Fuck' as both pathways, the entry to and exit from the estate, are now blocked by the youths. Sam's petrification is sustained by the sharp visual binary established between the white, female Sam and the much taller Black male now confronting her as the camera pans dramatically from a point-of-view shot of the three youths standing behind her to introduce Moses, the gang's ringleader, half of his face covered with a scarf and a baseball cap underneath a hoodie, only his eyes visible as he shouts 'give me the phone!' Moses takes Sam's phone, before demanding money from her purse. She fumbles, panicked, before Moses snatches the purse from her and throws it to one of his crew members behind him. In the context of filmic and televisual representations of Black working-class youths, the film retains the excessive violence associated with Black youth gangs on housing estates, as Moses reveals a knife and threatens to merk (stab) her unless she gives him a ring on her finger. Hesitating, Sam is then pushed to the ground by Moses as they scuffle for her ring. The camera now frames the four youths standing over Sam as she lies on the ground, emphasizing the power relations inherent in the exchange and Sam's sense of vulnerability as she finally hands over the coveted ring, with the gang seemingly unconcerned with the very public attack that may attract the attention of the police.

It is important to note that despite the highly stylized, almost parodic characterization of the gang members we see later in the film, at this stage, the fear and anxiety displayed by Sam in *Attack the Block* is real and signals the dramatic intrusion of the real into the film's generic hybridity. Her mugging at the hands of Moses and his gang is no less visceral and culturally verisimilitudinous than the media discourses of Black youth violence and the texts that have been informed by such narratives (although beyond the examples found in *Storm Damage*, this viscerality is generally reserved for intra-race violence rather than towards white women). However, this anxiety is interrupted by the generic elements of sci-fi. At this point, they all notice a beam of light as the alien emerges from the sky, crashing on to a nearby car, an interruption that allows Sam to escape as the gang are momentarily distracted by the explosion. Presuming it was a stray firework, Moses's attention now turns to the possible valuables inside the now-wrecked car. As he reaches through the window and searches the glove box, a mammal-like creature attacks him, throwing Moses to the ground. Instinctively, Moses stabs him with his knife before it runs away. Now sporting battle wounds across his face, knife in hand, he vows to kill it, stating, 'I'm chasing it down, I'm killing it. Watch.' Such threatening language, usually reserved for rival gang members within the lexicon of urban warfare, is now directed at an unidentified creature. The gang, armed with firework bangers and iron bars, pursue the creature to a nearby shed where, in an act of bravery that will be repeated throughout the film, Moses (a name that possesses obvious character associations derived from the Biblical story of Moses in the Book of Exodus) runs into the shed and kills it. Concluding that the creature is an alien, they take pictures of their kill on smartphones while shouting that the alien has arrived 'in the wrong place!'. Phrases such as 'welcome to London!', 'this is London, the ends!' and 'this is the block! Nobody fucks with the block!' often the identifiable vernacular for the urban film's claims to authenticity are used here to reinforce the youth's sense of territoriality. For the group, the alien represents a simple variant of an outside threat encroaching upon their turf. In keeping with the film's intertextual ambitions that attempt to hold some of the generic conventions of sci-fi and the familiar 'common sense' representations of Black youths within a symbiosis, such a transgression must be met with an attack akin to a statement being sent to violent rivals on the consequences of infiltrating enemy territory. This statement of hyper-locality is reinforced when, as the gang hold the carcass up to the sky in triumph and a collection of meteor-like objects are now shown descending on the estate, the camera pans down and we see a map of the Clayton Estate with the Wyndham Tower at its centre.

My analysis of *Attack the Block* relies on these notions of hyper-locality and territoriality, and in the context of the film's investment in the relations between marginalized social identities and physical space, the film offers a framing of a Black youth existence that is overwhelmingly spatially determined. As Moses leads the group as they drag the dead alien through the Clayton Estate, we observe how the film navigates the physical facts of the estate: its division from the mainstream of the area's cultural and economic activity, the symbolic barriers of entry and custodianship created by the youth's omnipresence, its dark, unlit, convoluted walkways and enclosures and the close proximity between the private spaces of the estate and the public spaces of the city – all of these are woven into the opening scenes. The film's use of juxtaposition as a narrational device is particularly striking in a sequence where, having just mugged a defenceless young woman and violently killed what appears to be some sort of mammal, one of the youths, Biggz (Simon Howard), calls his mother to assure her that he'll be home by 10 pm and that he's eaten. The scene achieves two key points of exposition; first, such conversations reaffirm the age of the boys despite the violence of the mugging, and second, they display the youth's ability to oscillate seamlessly between two distinct identities – at one moment, violent street muggers, and at another, vulnerable young teenagers whose parents worry about when and what they have eaten and what time they will be returning home. In the same scene, we also observe the film's attentiveness to the youth's own understanding of the markers of class and wealth. Having searched through Sam's purse and discovered her occupation, Dennis (Franz Drameh) declares 'she's a nurse, they get paid nothing. Why you always picking the poor people, Moses?' Here, *Attack the Block* reveals the discriminatory nature of hyper-local crime and one that is inherently territorial. For Sam, and as implied by Dennis and many others previously, wealth is the status ascribed onto the gang's victims, and the presumption of affluence is a decision informed by their victim's alleged outsider identity, one that is frequently (and in Sam's specific case) found to be an incorrect one (the gang would later claim that they would not have mugged her if they knew she lived on the estate).

In these opening scenes, *Attack the Block* reproduces a series of recognizable stereotypes highly compatible with the urban norm, to be both confronted and distorted throughout the film. In her home, shaken and distressed by the attack, Sam is tended to by a fellow Wyndham resident, a white elderly woman who shares Sam's displeasure at having to negotiate the gang's presence on the estate, 'walking around with knives and great big dogs like they own the block. . . . They're fucking monsters, aren't they?' At this point Sam looks up to her with a severity in her eyes. 'Yeah, fucking monsters'. Sam's disdain for the estate's youths as a contaminating threat to British society through the characterization of Moses and his collective as street muggers permits a re-engagement with the key themes of the landmark study *Policing the Crisis*, and the idea of moral panics remains a constant reference throughout the film. As explored in my analysis of both *Bullet Boy* and *Adulthood*, the central premise of this study was that the framing of Britain's Black youths as a 'social problem' became the ideological basis for the synonymity of Black youths and street mugging gaining both public prominence and social credence from the 1970s, a model which Hall et al. categorizes as a *political* phenomenon (1978). For Hall and his colleagues, the accompanying narratives of Black youthhood, unemployment, poverty, alienation, lawlessness and unstable family cultures within a distressed inner-city enclave were drawn from hegemonic image streams of Blackness and housing estates and produced public anxiety over the condition of 'second generation' Black British identities and their place within society. The initial construction of *Attack the Block*'s Black youths as a social problem, a status to be dismantled through the course of the film, is achieved through the film's close adherence to a thesis/antithesis/synthesis narrational premise, which through its plot presents a negotiation and resolution of a previously binary position, circumstance or identity. We see the film's temporary positioning of the youths as a morally bankrupt and contemptible social problem (a problematization the film later asks the spectator to interrogate) in an early scene where, as Sam describes the assailants to the police, they are seen walking through a long walkway inside the tower. A neighbour comes out of her flat, peering behind a barred gate and threatens to call the police simply at their mere presence. In the juxtaposition of these two scenes with the sound of terror in the neighbour's voice, the gang are indeed characterized as modern folk devils (Cohen, 1972), a constant, recognizable and culturally verisimilar menace to the very safety of the estate's residents.

In a similar vein to the parodic performance of Black urban youthhood we see in *Anuvahood*, *Attack the Block*'s own comedic imitation of the Black urban repertoire in part further supports a subversion of the cinematic Black realism that, as suggested by both Mercer (1988) and Pines (1981), has produced, somewhat paradoxically, a negative association with the depiction of Blackness and Black life. It is this racial specificity of cinematic realism, where the spectators' perception of Black life is guaranteed through the primacy of realism as the dominant visual mode in which Blackness is encountered, narrativized and crucially absorbed in the white imaginary, that Forrest, while recognizing that his New Realism is a representational strategy in which 'the nation is imagined as overwhelmingly white, and almost always English' (2020: 4), appears to neglect in his analysis of the potential of New Realism to move 'beyond a deterministic account of social, economic and cultural forces' (2020: 2). For *Attack the Block*, the utility in the coordination of parody and realism to its socio-spatial analysis of Black youth marginalization is located in the introduction of the block's drug baron Hi-Hatz (Jurmayn Hunter), where we see the hierarchical modes in which youths are seduced and cohered by elders as Hi-Hatz, suggesting that there are easier ways for Moses to make money on the block than by selling weed, instructs Moses to sell cocaine on his behalf instead, handing him a cigarette box with cocaine bags inside. Although clearly located within the generic bounds of the urban film, there is tremendous sociological value in the scene's construction of the ease in which adolescents are enticed by older, more violent peers, a seduction that is made all the more potent by the social, economic and geographical parameters within which the Wyndham residents must exist. Such parameters are equally psychological and point to the methods in which localized, criminal, influential power becomes an alluring force for fertile young minds disallowed from venturing beyond the spatial and social territories of the estate as a region, a city with its own ecosystem. Making it clear to Moses that upon accepting the upgraded responsibility of selling cocaine that 'you are my boy now', the conditional demand embedded in the exchange is the ownership of another's life, an ownership that transcends the influential but sometimes fragmented bounds of family belonging within the estate. As Moses comes out of the weed room, he is congratulated by his friends on his triumph. Here, the graduation from weed seller and mugger to cocaine dealer under the wicked tutelage of Hi-Hatz is presented as a successful rite of passage for Moses; for the gang, such a graduation is also the realization of the ultimate and shared personal ambition for the youths, seemingly unaware of or incapable of resisting the gravitational, centripetal force of capitalism and hyper-local status, where prosperity can only be defined and achieved within Hi-Hatz's criminalized orbit.

Allegorically, *Attack the Block* can be understood to be preoccupied with two central concerns: first, the racial character of the public perception and social controlling of Black youths and their defence against their continued demonization and marginalization and second, the impact of hyper-local territoriality on Black youths existing within a spatial structure of containment. Indeed, social compression is a constant motif throughout *Attack the Block*, and to this end, there is something to decipher in the images of the Wyndham tower block (Figure 10.1). A sense of entrapment and immobility presents itself as the tower is framed from a low-angle shot as the camera descends, eventually opening up the image to reveal the gang walking along a low-lit walkway leading to the tower's entrance. Indeed, in contrast to other popular urban films where the combination of a visual contrast between the specific (the estate) with the general (the city) and the depiction of 'on-road' culture is a central tenet of the urban genre's aestheticization of London's spatial boundaries, where the protagonist's mobility is characteristic of the urban social world, all of the film's dramatic activity takes place within the confines of the estate's internal and external borders. *Attack the Block* is spatially bounded, and I want to explore how the film can be read as demonstrative of how the Black urban youth's negative characterization within the spatial parameters of the council estate is an identity conferred onto them externally; it is the multi-modal discriminations produced from outside the estate's social, economic, racial and physical boundaries that *maintain* the ghetto, concretized in the popular imagination as 'no go' estates that architectural theorists describe as

Figure 10.1 The Wyndham tower block in *Attack the Block* (dir. Joe Cornish, 2011).

'characteristically high-rise, modernist and "non-street" (Severs, 2010: 450). This supports an architectural observation of Wyndham's external layout: the estate as a whole is a *cul-de-sac*, both literally and figuratively, and the effects of this social enclosure are seen when Moses, on venturing out of the block to deal with a swarm of newly arrived aliens on the estate, is apprehended by police and searched, where they recover both the knife and the Class-A drugs he's now selling. An intensification of the relationship between the Black youth and authority within the urban locale is produced in the image of Moses being pinned to the floor, handcuffed and bundled in a police van where Sam, who identified Moses to the police, also sits. These opposing identities momentarily (and uncomfortably for Sam) become reluctant allies as both become trapped in the police van after the aliens attack the police officers, the rest of the gang, having observed the aliens devour the police from a balcony, rescue them by both using fireworks and driving off with the van, evading the latest alien attack. In this reliance on the familiar images of race and space, the film momentarily occupies, in a similar vein to *Storm Damage* and *Bullet Boy*, a very conventional place in terms of its representation of Black youths, but the dialects of location, territory and environment give the scene an additional political dimension. The arresting of Moses at the site of the estate's public and private, street and non-street crossover is equally where we see the city's segregated geography, where the estate's exterior spaces mark a point of the imagined and experienced separation of two national identities determined by race and class and rendering the estate's outlining streets leading to its exit and mainstream social activity an unclaimed field of perpetual nation versus the Other antagonisms.

The estate is therefore pivotal to the political world the film seeks to reconfigure, and it is within its architectural layout of *Attack the Block* that the film's allegorical devices are most dramatically visible and where its relationship to the estate as an enclosed territory is most evident. The ability of the Clayton Estate to offer a 'defensible architecture' to the exclusive benefit of the gang is made apparent in a violent confrontation with both the aliens and Hi-Hatz in the underground parking bay underneath the tower block. Having survived the latest alien attack that sees Hi-Hatz's accomplice devoured by an alien (an incident that was the result of Hi-Hatz ignoring Pest's pleas that the estate has been taken over by aliens) the gang, who escape the scene to the sound of violent threats by Hi-Hatz on the cowardice the gang display by deserting him (and again enforcing the ownership and control Hi-Hatz asserts over the young), conclude that the safest place for them is 'off the streets' and 'back in the block'. There are several key observations to make from these scenes, both of which offer a correspondence with the social, political and spatial analysis that forms *Attack the Block*'s broader critical realist ambitions. First, the identification of the estate's external spaces as 'streets' offers a reinterpretation of Newman's general thesis that suggests on the one hand a differentiation between public and private spaces within the estate's boundaries that the gang now attempt to cross to reach 'safety' from outside predators. Second, the juxtaposition between the cultural verisimilitude found within the idiolects associated with urban conflict in the exchange between Hi-Hatz and the gang, with the very genre-specific conventions seen as Hi-Hatz's sidekick is mauled by an alien, creates a novel moment in which *Attack the Block*'s genre hybridity is inscribed within the scene itself, where elements of sci-fi, horror and comedy combine to perform as parallel, complementary sensibilities that accentuate the film's approach to an urban sociopolitical reality.

My description of the Wyndham Tower as a bounded cityscape, one in which the capacity of the allegorical to offer a reconfiguration of the relationship between character and the cinematic environment, is captured in a sequence of overhead shots as the gang ride their mopeds and bikes to the safety of the tower block while being perused by the aliens. The gang navigate the complex labyrinth of the Clayton Estate through a forensic, indigenous knowledge of the estate's architecture, public spaces and escape routes in moments of pursuit as we see Biggz jump across the dangerous and potentially fatal gap between two overlapping walkways to escape one of the aliens (Figure 10. 2). This use of the estate's physical space as a defensive strategy for the gang is a pattern revisited throughout the chase scene, a sequence exhibiting the very physical arrangements that Newman identified as facilitating urban crime: multiple escape routes for criminals (the connecting walkways), the unregulated access to block entrances allowing strangers (or here, aliens) to pass undetected and the lack of 'natural surveillance'. If this, for Newman, evidenced the potential for these kinds of spatial arrangements to create a 'defensible space' (1972) in *Attack the Block*, it is the foregrounding of the relationship between the public and private realms, the physical and spatial expression of the territorial claims of the residents together with a judgement of the moral worth of those residents which produces both allegorically and physically a defensible architecture, one that is maximized at this particular moment due to the invading force's inability to equally navigate the intricate architectural layout of the estate, and the alien is evaded only by Biggz's natural and instinctive understanding of the estate's escape routes. Here, Wyndham Tower is an intimidating and impenetrable labyrinth not just to the extra-terrestrial force or beyond but also, allegorically, in the minds of outsiders, the press, the middle classes and particularly, the police. Both of these ideas promote the architectural expression of Wyndham as a private territory that encroaches on (or overlaps with) public spaces and bodies. Indeed, such a reading chimes with the spatial analysis of the urban ethnographer

Figure 10.2 Biggz escaping the aliens in *Attack the Block* (dir. Joe Cornish, 2011).

Suzi Hall (2012) who, in another field of study that identifies the local spaces of the city street within urban multiculture as an affinity space bearing a 'politics of nearness', considers how the term 'territoriality' can function as 'a defensive strategy used to combat the effects of change or the perceived threats of difference' (108). But in what ways does a radical characterization of the council estate as a defensible space that offers a re-representation of Black urban geographies emerge here? The answer here lies in the point of view of the text and the definition of whose 'defensible space' it is. While the physical design of the estate should, according to Newman, prove opportune for criminals from outside to prey on the residents, in *Attack the Block*, the estate turns its defensive mechanisms towards outsiders and intruders, and the Clayton Estate as a confusing labyrinth is accentuated as an overhead shot captures the gang as they run and ride their scooters, bikes and mopeds to the eventual safety of the block. What I'm suggesting within *Attack the Block* is a model for understanding the relations between marginalized bodies and urban territories which sees the youths, in defending themselves from attack, simultaneously maintain a fidelity to the Wyndham Tower. Whereas for outsiders, the block is a confusing architecture unable to be navigated, and for Sam, an intimidating environment to escape from in moments of danger, for the gang, in times of an external threat, they *retreat* to the very same location.

Why is the estate in *Attack the Block* able to activate these architectural and social connections? The narrational theories of Georg Lukacs, often obscure within the various analyses of cinematic realism despite its clear relevance to film, remind us what is at stake here, as on the surface of *Attack the Block* we see what he terms the 'extensive totality' (1962). For Lukacs, the work of art must attempt to represent what he described as *der mensch ganz*, or 'mans totality'. This refers to the relationship which exists 'between the subject and the social environment during a particular historical conjuncture' (Aitken, 2006: 74). Certainly, the application of Lukacs may appear incompatible within an analyses of what can be described as Black or urban cinema's iteration of cinematic realism, but the attraction between the realist theories of Lukacs and the utility of an allegorical interpretation of *Attack the Block*'s aestheticization of the Wyndham Tower as a defensible space gives rise to a new analytical structure that forms an alliance between the depiction of urban youth alienation within the built environment and a *geographic* reality. Here, the film's activation of the estate as a process of meaning-making recalls what Paul Willemen, drawing on Bretch, termed 'complex seeing', a mode of dynamic active spectatorship which requires 'the reading of landscape within the diegesis as itself a layered set of discourses, as a text in its own right' (Willemen, 1993: 141). In acknowledging Raymond Williams's own renovation of Bretch that situates the very process of complex seeing within the context of the text itself (Williams, 1961) for Willemen, in considering the significance of the environment within the mode of complex spectatorship, the film's physical space must not be subservient to the demands of character or plot development but should emerge as 'a discursive terrain with the same weight and requiring the same attention, as the other discourses that structure and move the text' (Willemen, 1993: 31). In making connections between the inhabitants' maximizing of urban space and the space itself as metaphor, it captures the explanatory power of *Attack the Block*'s mediating of the council estate in the advocating of what I will describe as a *geographicality of representation*, a ballasting of the characters in their physical boundaries, revealing itself in a sense of fidelity and connection to the environment. Crucially, such geographicality requires the participation of the social context (here, the architectural and the locational as the sociopolitical) within the film as an independent character, one so definite that it grows to influence, if not determine, the protagonist's physical, physiological and emotional trajectory.

In the case of *Attack the Block*, its geographicality of representation is observed in the contextualization of the relationship between Black youths and whiteness during an exchange between Sam and the gang that points to the mixed demographic of its South London council estate that reflects the change in tenure and appearance brought about by the rising costs of living, and the film accurately displays its impact on former socially homogenous council estates, where differing social groups now live side-by-side, if not fully integrated. This equally points to the gradual hyper-deskilling of public service labour, where even a nurse such as Sam has been forced to find accommodation within the crime-ridden Clayton Estate. Having forced their way into Sam's flat with the injured Pest (Alex Esmail) and demanding she uses her nursing skills to attend to his severe leg wounds sustained during a fight with the aliens, Sam reveals to the gang that she has only been living on the estate for a couple of months and is considering leaving as she 'don't like the area'. One must situate such an answer, directed at the gang members as a result of their mugging of her just moments before, in the context of *Attack the Block*'s use of the estate as the instrument through which a range of social violences are inflicted upon Black youths. In the gang's sharp rebuking of Sam as the camera cuts to Dennis (Franz Drameh) as he aggressively responds with 'what's wrong with the area?' the exchange reveals the Black youth's own awareness of the stigmas associated with both their race and class status and the social space they inhabit. The term 'residualization' is particularly conducive here, referring to the processes by which the perceived undesirability of a neighbourhood or location catalyses the gradual but no less damaging evacuation of one demographic, leaving a social residue of the less mobile demographic to endure the multi-modal effects of prejudice, stigma and socio-economic inequality (Burrows, 1999). For Sam, her ability to even consider leaving is both an affront to the boy's sense of hyper-locality and a demonstration of a race and class privilege of escape and mobility beyond the reach of the estate's less-advantaged residents. This reinforces the significance of the film's other white characters who, while appearing to provide only comic relief, contribute to *Attack the Block*'s notions of territoriality and the film's polarization between the middle class and the working-class youths on the estate, for whom a greater sense of fidelity, connection, belonging and boundness to the physical environment is apparent. In a notable scene, a white, middle-class student, Brewis (Luke Treadaway), having ventured into the estate in search of his white weed dealer, Ron (Nick Frost), displays his anxiety towards the Black youths (prior to collaborating with them in the alien fight) through his reluctance to share a lift with them, all while listening to hip hop from earphones. Brewis's dislocation from both the estate and its inhabitants is further emphasized as he talks in his middle-class accent to his dad on the phone before adopting a more performative urban vernacular when met by the gang. In addition, the kinetic cinematography used as the collective prepare to fight the aliens provides a sense of the transient existence of the youths' home life and how their sense of locality and identity is accrued more by the external 'block' realities than from the internal family spaces. Jerome (Leeon Jones) pushes past his sister who, in the disruption his entrance has caused, shouts 'some of us have exams tomorrow!' as he runs to his room and pulls a machete from his bedroom drawer before running back out to join the gang. This demonstrates the striking coexistence of contrasting identities within the bounds of family, where educational prosperity and murderous intention can cohabit within the shared spaces of the sibling's social and domestic life. However, it is not simply within the private realm of home within which the film draws its analysis of urban dwelling but also its relationship to the more public spaces within the Wyndham Tower. Here, the film juxtaposes two social spaces to accentuate the urban youth's ability to exist between the estate's hyper-masculine 'streets' and the seemingly safe and predominantly feminized domestic spaces of home. This also provides an exploration of the associations that different classes have to council estates in contemporary times: for Sam the tower block provides an intolerable temporary accommodation for the mobile middle class, for Brewis, an equally mobile and temporal pathway to safely accumulate the cultural capital associated with aspects of Black subculture without its stigmas or consequences. But for Moses and his collective, the tower offers a home, a community and an identity. In this way, *Attack the Block*'s polemic is located in the film's organizing ideology; it presents a Luckacian sense of characters participating in a socially dynamic situation within politically demonized territories on the periphery of society.

For *Attack the Block*, these dialectics of place and identity merge to present contemporary racial prejudice as essentially a function of the British political structure, and in this endeavour, allegory becomes a particularly adept narrational device for the analysis of social stigmas and isolations, with the Clayton Estate being central to such allegorical strategies. However, *Attack the Block* equally makes references to the more direct sociological concerns over racism, and while realism, science fiction and comedy remain in tandem, it is here that *Attack the Block*'s more traditional realist modalities come to the foreground to critique the racist social relations dictating the conditions of Black youth existence. Again, the film carves this alternative iconography through the figure of Moses. The gang, with Sam now in tow, escape to the flat of Biggz's teenage cousin Tia (Danielle Vitalis) among her and her female friends. As Aitken reminds us, a central tenet of the Lukacsian realist narrative is its ability to 'situate working-class characters within social and cultural environments marked by poverty, social hardship and injustice, and also depict the relationship between character and environment in considerable empirical detail' (2006: 113). However, Lukacs's realist paradigm, while conducive to a broader analysis of *Attack the Block*'s modes of critical realism, is not limited to its utility for understanding the significance of the tower block as a socially specific physical environment ushering the compartmentalization of Moses and his peers, and there is a further Lukacsian interpretation to be derived from this scene's action. Here, it is the relations between character and its context that become the focus of attention: the character's own recognition and criticism of the racism that continue to determine the very conditions producing inequalities within the contemporary Black urban existence. The very external definition of Black youths as pathologically delinquent, as argued by Stuart Hall et al. (1978), possessed the potential for a 'second marginalization', where the denigration of Black youths as a social problem is compounded by an equally racialized characterization as violent and dangerous criminals. It is clear that for the youths, the attitude of the police towards them, where the hegemonic categorization of Black youths as natural members of a criminal subculture has been internalized to the extent that they continue to carry out the very misdemeanours society has been conditioned to associate them with. Pest's reply that 'they arrest us for nothing already' to Sam's naïve suggestion of calling the police to deal with the alien attack may seem inconsistent within the diegesis given that the group had earlier mugged Sam, but this both points to the reality of race-based harassment for the youths and reveals the different relationships that exist between the police and sections of society in times of emergency as a result of race and class. It is this acceptance that calling the police to deal with the aliens will expose the young heroes to further prejudices of the criminal justice system that prompts Moses, sitting alone and deep in thought, to suggest 'I recon the feds sent them anyway. Government probably bred those creatures to kill Black boys. First, they send drugs to the ends. Then they sent guns. Now they send monsters to get us. They don't care man, we ain't killing each other fast enough, so they decide to speed up the process.' On hearing this, the youths burst into laughter, at the absurdity of the assertion that a conspiratorial association exists between state authority and extra-terrestrial power, but equally at the political analysis displayed by Moses, one at odds with the evaluation of the intellectual capabilities of working-class Black youths that exist both beyond and within the diegesis. Pest's weed-induced response of 'yes man', in support of Moses's insights, affirms *Attack the Block*'s novel use of comedy, generally delivered in such one-line responses, within its generic hybridity to both remain palatable to its youth-themed audience and to accentuate the more serious implications for the boys. This is a crucial scene as it uses humour to both detract and emphasize the acts of social violence towards the estate's Black indigene. While his peers all laugh, Moses is making a sombre point on the systemic forces, both literal and metaphorical, responsible for the continued othering and marginalization of Black boys, and for Moses, the alien attack is interpreted as a simple variant of state-driven, violent oppression. Yet, the emotion displayed here by Moses is more of despair than anger; it is a lamentation as well as an accusation, and the scene is constructed to show the social violence (real and symbolic) that is done to both Moses and Black youths like him. The destruction of the Black working-class youth, for Moses, is conditioned by a state-led ideology of racism but performed through state agents: the police, the government, media and the whiteness of a localized drugs supply chain. On the other hand, as Moses's phenomenological statement (and the reaction to it by his peers) reminds us, this is a question of perspective as much as affect. The urban Black youth now sees himself beyond the perspective of the dominant force that has othered, objectified and excluded him, and the realization of his negated position within this system is equally a call to arms. Here, devoid of social power, and economic power, the Black underclass must resort to a *physical* power as a defence mechanism against a sustained and violent state attack.

Despite *Attack the Block*'s expanding of the parameters of urban film's generic conventions by relocating elements of the urban norm, its realism is interrupted by the occasional parodic treatment of its characters and situations. These moments serve a polemical function in the context of ridiculing the critical attitudes towards Black youths, perspectives that are born from the prejudices and stigmas associated with the film's environmental setting. Indeed, as the alien's track down Moses and the gang to Sam's flat, Sam's screams at the youths not to embroil her in 'whatever gang war bullshit you are involved in' as the boys arm themselves to fight reveal the cultural assumptions that align with the hegemony of media narratives of the intra-racial violent conflict between Black youths and in Pest's insistence that the attack has 'nothing to do with drugs or gangs, or rap music or violent video games!' the film offers a satirical reference to the repertoire of moral panics created within political discourses to explain Black youth delinquency. We find a more allegorical understanding of how *Attack the Block* engages with the destructive politics of social and spatial confinement and territoriality in a later scene where Hi-Hatz makes it back to the block via slaying a number of aliens in an effort to exert revenge upon Moses for his actions that have attracted both the aliens and the police to the block. Moses and the gang reach Ron's flat on the nineteenth floor only to be met by the waiting Hi-Hatz. He confronts the unsuspecting Moses, pointing a gun towards him and telling him that his refusal to join him in his wicked ways will now cost him his own life. For a moment, this scene is constructed within the literal boundaries of Wyndham's hyper-localized power structures as Hi-Hatz reminds him that 'this is my block, you get me?'. However, unbeknown to Hi-Hatz is the swarm of aliens approaching the window behind him. In gesturing towards the impending attack, Moses is now cognizant of an imminent deterritorialization of the block as the pack of aliens surround Hi-Hatz before subjecting him to a gruesome death. The arrival of the aliens on the block also announces the dismantling of the power structure that had previously defined the Wyndam Tower. Hi-Hatz no longer has an ownership or command within the block and subsequently over Moses and the block's youthful denizens; the previously uncontested spaces of the estate, as a contained city, have been taken over by another, much more powerful force with no regard for the established hierarchies or power relations that had been the organizing principle of social life on the Wyndham Tower. Moses's response of 'not really' to Hi-Hatz's renewed claim to the block before escaping with the gang under a hail of bullets just prior to Hi-Hatz's death should be understood beyond a simple rejection of a criminalized lifestyle and its promise of a hyper-localized upward mobility, infamy and micro-celebrity. The scene offers a reaffirmation that *Attack the Block*'s state-of-the-nation allegory is located firmly in the private, contained spaces of the Wyndham Tower, an analysis that chimes with the conspiratorial assessment Moses had made earlier of the motivations for the alien invasion. The uncontested omnipotence over the tower block that Hi-Hatz had enjoyed may simply have been a temporal or even phantom power simply afforded to him by a greater, more insidious force. Such systemic forces, having previously displayed apathy towards the destructive reality of

Figure 10.3 Hi-Hatz surrounded by aliens in *Attack the Block* (dir. Joe Cornish, 2011).

urban life, have simply permitted the localized authority represented in Hi-Hatz to exist solely within its own volition and when most conducive to its aims for an intra-racial Black death, either literal through violent conflict or spiritual by its localized drug trade, damaged futures and the self-exclusion from a broader social life produced by racial inequality. For a moment, the camera frames Hi-Hatz prone on the floor, eyes filled with terror as he is confronted by the aliens. In keeping with the film's reluctance to provide excessive exposition and describe the aliens in *explicit* terms of state power, we don't see the aliens – the camera circulates around Hi-Hatz's blooded face in a point-of-view shot privileging the aliens as they look over the now powerless Hi-Hatz (Figure 10.3). This is very much an allegory to the covert, clandestine *modus operandi* of state power and its relationship to Black life; we can only identify it by its damaging effects. The screen turns black before we again see Hi-Hatz, this time with his face disfigured as *Attack the Block* reverts to horror film aesthetics; sound becomes crucial to this endeavour as we hear only screams and the sound of Hi-Hatz's ripping flesh and organs. Within a broader narrational schema where the oscillation between its generic repertoires permits a scenic equivalency of generic convention, at one moment sci-fi, horror, comedy and the urban, in combining these diffuse generic modes the film displays its engagement with multiple, *colliding* urban realities. Specifically, it is within the unification of these two shots where *Attack the Block*'s allegorical devices perform as a devastating political critique of racial injustice. The state, conceived here as the locus where the force of law and law of force correlate in tremendously powerful ways, retains an enduring but invisible dominion over the lives of the estate's Black youths, and the unwillingness of Moses to accept his fate within this racialized domination has simply catalysed the deployment of a vastly superior authority to expedite the very intra-racial state-sponsored genocide of Black youths that Hi-Hatz and the localized drug trade he operationalizes was mandated to carry out. Such a reading engages with Cedrick Robinson's classic analysis of racial capitalism's ability to simultaneously include, empower, exploit and destroy the non-white identity within the ruling class' own system of domination (1983), an ability with particular ramifications for Hi-Hatz. Where he was at one moment an unconscious ambassador for the structure of inequality they sought to maintain, the disequilibrium catalysed by Moses's Black rebellious challenge to the system, and Hi-Hatz's failure to restore it, has summoned the systemic force to now reassert formal control over its racially oppressive regime. And in doing so, Hi-Hatz, and the authority he once represented, has now been made redundant within it.

This appears to be exactly the *affective* tension Wayne (2002) mandates in his description of the 'anti-national, national film', in which he declares that these films 'are national insofar as they display an acute attunement to the specific social, political and cultural dynamics within the territory of the nation, but they are anti-national insofar as that territory is seen as a conflicted zone of unequal relations of power' (45). For Wayne, anti-national films constitute a narrative strategy that disrupts the myth of social horizontality projected by mainstream cinema, and such cinema should be considered as a major repository for the production of counter-narratives about contemporary British society and hence a visual source of sociopolitical articulation. This emphasis on narrational intention as the defining feature of the anti-national, national film resists a reliance on film form and the traditional markers of realist aesthetics as the determining modality for the production of a critical realism, and *Attack the Block*'s central protagonist's psychology is revealed by offering the spectator a glimpse of Moses's interior existence to accentuate the subsidiary role that poverty occupies within both parliamentary and media debates on the social causation of Black urban youth criminality. That we see the internal spaces of Moses's home, of his child's status, poverty and social vulnerability is crucial to the film's analysis of spatial disadvantage within the urban locale as again *Attack the Block* attempts to link his ability to excel in the public world with his mere survive within the domestic. Sam is sent to Moses's nineteenth-floor Wyndham flat to assist in luring the aliens into a trap that has been devised by Brewis, where she will create a gas leak that, upon Moses luring the aliens to the flat, will set off an explosion that will permanently rid the tower block of the remaining invaders. As she continues through his home, she's shocked at the flat's poor condition, which is littered with an array of takeaway food boxes, unwashed clothing and dirty plates. Moses's voice is heard throughout as he guides her over the phone, and this provides narration to Sam's tour of his private space as he reveals he is raising himself alone in the flat, making reference to an occasionally present 'uncle' who, according to Moses 'comes and goes, goes mostly'. The film at this point attempts to situate Moses's criminalized existence within the explanatory context of a youth deprivation and poverty also born from family neglect and absent parenthood, a set of culturally bound afflictions that are somewhat in concert with the very 'problem family' discourse New Labour would advance throughout the decade. Indeed, when Sam, upon entering Moses's bedroom, is amazed at his Spiderman beddings and kids posters on the wall, the film offers a visual sermon on how the racial stigmatization maintained within the British political structure could be dismantled through enquiry and understanding – here, the very encroachment by a social outsider into the seldom experienced private domestic space of the Black urban youth. However, Sam's expression of surprise at Moses's age (he reveals when asked that he is only fifteen years old) and response of 'you look a lot older' also produces a particular representation of whiteness and its associated notions of Black physicality.

While Moses responds with 'thanks', there is something much more consequential at stake here beyond the complimentary ego-boost it provides for teenage boys who are deemed to be closer to manhood than they actually are. The development from childhood to adulthood, as explored by Lawrence (1982), also required the passage of youthhood, which exists within 'that area of transition between these two apparently fixed states' (54–55). It is within this very province of youthhood that for the Black youth, the development is expedited, bypassed and made ambiguous by hegemonic notions of Black physicality and its associations with racialized violence, criminality and danger, a set of characterizations that for the Black male youth exposes them to the very sphere within which the Black child can now be subjected to the full force of the police and other manifestations of state authority. For *Attack the Block*, Moses's arrested childhood as identified by Sam is a testament to the courage, responsibility and leadership he's demonstrated to this point, but also an outcome of his racially determined status that ushers in a forced separation from the innocence of childhood and into the very damaging (and potentially fatal) status of youth/adulthood, with all its negative connotations and consequences.

My contention that *Attack the Block* articulates the social anxieties towards Black youths through a subversive realist aesthetic strategy may appear to be in alignment with Forrest's claim about New Realism: the ability of the films of Clio Barnard and Andrea Arnold to offer a richly textured aesthetic that cultivates an intimate and partial reality that succeeds in 'making emphatic selected elements of lived experience for their particular poetic and political ends' (2020: 6). However, *Attack the Block* functions through a more expansive, spatially situated realism referring to a classic hero's journey that, in its stressing of the interconnected and multi-modal stigmas and social oppressions germane to the environment, aids in the creation of a less atomized social realism, and Moses's eventual return to elixir carries with it both his atonement for his previous behaviours and in this redemption, a recovered social, cultural and political identity to be fully realized in the film's final act. Having found safety in Ron's weed room, Brewis identifies Moses as carrying a pheromone trail that, as a result of his slaying of the female alien upon landing on the estate, has attracted the male aliens to both him and the Wyndham and subsequently led to both the attack on the tower block and the death of his friends, the police and others. In another act of leadership, having realized the consequences of his own actions, Moses uses his pheromone trail to lead the aliens to his flat where, having asked Sam to create a gas leak, he fires a firework towards the alien pack causing a huge explosion, killing the aliens and sending Moses through the flat window to his presumed death. In the film's dramatic climax, Moses emerges from the smoke clouds, clinging onto a Union Jack flag hanging from a flat window on the tower as the estate's residents, the community he has rescued from the alien invasion, watch on from the ground (Figure 10.4). It is in this symbolic moment that *Attack the Block* offers an analysis on the textures of race and British nationhood. I want to explore the ways in which we can consider the significance of this scene beyond its literal representation of Moses hanging from a flag on the nineteenth floor of the block. Moses's Black body is now rendered as a political object, as he struggles to maintain its survival under a sustained attack. A police spotlight now

Figure 10.4 Moses clinging onto the Union Jack in *Attack the Block* (dir. Joe Cornish, 2011).

frames Moses, delivered from one of the numerous helicopters dispatched to the estate to respond to what they naturally believe to be is a major criminal incident involving armed Black youths on an inner-city housing estate. However, in doing so the camera also frames Moses within a range of social, cultural and political identities. I want to suggest that the central preoccupation in this scene is the reconstructing of what Alexander (1996) observed as the perceived 'anomaly' of Black and Britishness (4) and the reimagining of national identity and belonging, a challenge found through the combination of three distinct planes of epistemic intention: Moses's status as a Black, working-class urban youth now under attack by the police, the social architecture that binds him within the cultural and political imagination as a locus of race and class exclusion and demonization, and finally, the heavily contested claim on the British flag and with this, the Clayton Estate resident's forced separation from a nationhood where, within the dominant political discourse, the perceived pathological cultural practices of the council estate's inhabitants are representative of explicitly non-British values. For Moses specifically, his griping of the Union Jack is a protracted claim by Black people on a national identity that is compromised by the phantom history of race relations and the Black position within a white national sphere where for Gilroy, the categories of Black and British are 'mutually exclusive' (1987: 63). As Gilroy goes on to argue, 'it is still felt today as Black settlers and their British born children are denied their authentic national membership on the basis of their race and, at the same time, prevented from aligning themselves within the British race on the grounds that their national allegiances inevitably lies elsewhere' (1987; 46).

Attack the Block's symbolism of Black Britishness possesses several layers of meaning to it: from serving as a sign of disempowerment, to a sign of defiance, to the estate as a renewed discursive space of possibility where a renewed British identity can emerge. I want to situate the iconography of Moses's Black screen image within the social and political context of contemporary Black British popular culture, and an identical imagery is noted in the Union Jack imprinted bullet-proof vest the UK Grime artist Stormzy wore throughout his 2019 headline performance on the Pyramid Stage at

Figure 10.5 Stormzy performing at Glastonbury Festival in June 2019 (BBC, 2019).

Glastonbury (Figure 10.5), a set usually the historical preserve of white guitar-based acts and represented for many a historic cultural intervention (indeed, mainstream media would aggrandize the Glastonbury performance as the 'first headline show by a black British artist' (*The Guardian*, Saturday, 29 June 2019)). The performance, described as a 'glorious victory lap for black British culture' (*The Observer*, Saturday, 29 June 2019), drew national attention and praise, particularly in response to Stormzy's use of the platform to speak out against the racism, injustice and disproportionate policing experienced by Black youths, sampling a House of Common speech made by David Lammy in response to racial discrimination within the criminal justice system. In locating the triumph of Stormzy's performance within a hyper celebration of a Black popular culture embraced as inherently British, its meanings oscillate between, on the one hand, the rejection of the traditional cultural manifestations of Black British identities, and on the other, the assent of a politically demonized Grime music subculture and the Black British male bodies that constitute it to the apex of the British cultural mainstream. Structured through the iconographic power of Stormzy as a young, tall and powerfully built Black British man, the performance of Black Britishness represents the possibilities for new, positive Black masculine identity to emerge that, rather than occupying a tenuous position within the nation, offers an alternative, counter-hegemonic image of young Black British men. However, the Black Britishness that Stormzy and Moses make claim to is marked by both continuity and departure. While both Black men, in their adorning of the Union Jack are now rendered as political bodies, Stormzy's Banksy-designed bullet-proof vest is only partially transgressive.

The Union Jack is distressed, drained of its red and blue and in favour of a Black and grey, a defilement of the very triumphant visions of imperialism and empire still held dear within the British imaginary and a dismantling of the historical amnesia in the national psyche permitting the unconflicted nostalgia among nativist British nationalism that sees the Union Jack as bearing only the colours of global power, rather than of colonial conquest. However, in displaying the repertoires of a contemporary racial capitalism, where whiteness extracts economic and cultural value from Black cultural products, Stormzy's hyper-consecration by Britain's white cultural mainstream also exposes the thin politics of racial diversity at the very centre of cultural elitism where Black excellence, creativity, performance, exceptionality, success and entrepreneurship are the conditional exemplars in white elite imaginations of a modern, integrated and valuable Black Britishness where the identities of 'Black' and 'British' are no longer in tension. However, in contrast to Stormzy at Glastonbury, Moses cannot exist as a fully accepted and autonomous Black British body; he exists as such only by virtue of whiteness's own valorizing of his identity and its place in British social life. His is a *contested* body politic, a Black Britishness only in relation to the immediate social and societal architectures that frame him. Such a moment has a particularly striking political resonance. As Moses's clinging body, framed within a police spotlight, comes into view with the Union Jack, an alternative range of sociopolitical epistemologies emerge. This Black body politic, as Moses shows us, emerges in a dialectic between the subject, the location and the nation, producing a synthesis of race, nationality, class and the capturing of the spectacle of Black youth criminality within which the police, state agents and the dominant political culture are all imbricated. In this moment, as he lifts himself to safety onto a balcony by climbing up the Union Jack, Moses's Black body becomes simultaneously disarticulated from its cultural verisimilitude and reconstructed as the axis of a new articulation of national identity. Moses's political body is one not just of survival, fortitude and self-preservation, but represents the very politicization of the Black British youth identity that rejects the contradictions inherent in the very idea of a Black British identity which, for Mercer (1994) ideologically, 'society regards as mutually exclusive' (85). Here, both Black British men pose a challenge to the myth of an integrated post-multicultural Britain, whether on the large-scale, mediatized, mediacentric and liberal cultural platforms of Stormzy's Glastonbury Pyramid Stage or the more stigmatized urban spaces of Moses's Wyndham Tower. But for Moses, his is an alternative Black Britishness. In becoming a body politic, he has temporarily affected a redefinition of a social milieu declared as unrepresentative of the British way of life. For a moment, in his clinging of the Union Jack, we see a renewed reclaiming, even a demand, for the acceptance, inclusion and appreciation of a rejected race and class identity germane to the very socio-geographic location that, within the political imagination of New Labour, produces cultural practices, values and existences that 'shame us as a nation' (Tony Blair, quoted in Social Exclusion Unit, 1998). To this end, the symbolic power of Moses, his Blackness and his possession of the national flag within the tower block as a distressed social architecture unify to confront a destructive political discourse that seeks to present the urban estate (and the working-class indigene that inhabit it) as a separate nation of its own; a peripheral infrahuman nation of racial and classed others unwilling to be included into the preferred, prosperous and positive image of Britain, a morally defunct physical landscape whose inhabitants continue to reap the economic benefits produced by mainstream British society while making no active or recognizable contribution to its construction.

Such moments in *Attack the Block* align with the imperative that the Lukacsian film must efface a focus on individual situations and circumstances to critically address the collective experience, motivated by what Aitken describes as 'the fundamental Lukacsian principle of the need to connect the particular to the general, in order to express totality' (2006: 100). Moses, clinging to the Union Jack and framed within the Wyndam Tower, holds the reclaimed national identity of underclass Britain in his hands. Let me suggest that this flag-hanging scene is not the end of the film but its actual beginning, as the individual becomes multiple through the construction of a collective political body, where Moses's heroic acts produce both a personal and collective redemption that is derived from the respect and acclaim of his community, even as he is being arrested by the police and placed in the back of a police van, an image in keeping with the more hegemonic relationships between state authority and working-class Black youths, but one where the redemptive elements of the story are secured through the community's chants of 'Moses!' just before the end credits.

These final scenes in *Attack the Block* represent more than the triumphant finale to an extra-terrestrial attack on an inner-city council estate. Beyond its significance for understanding the ways in which Black youthhood is defined within the popular imagination, for its two central protagonists, we see how their respective character arcs do not necessarily unify to provide the eventual resolution of previously binary positions. Rather, such character transitions are siloed and individual, although both arcs have required an engagement with the politics of location and law enforcement that also possess distinctive racial dimensions. For Sam, the collective rejection of racism, classism, stigma and police harassment is integral to the rite of passage she must perform to credibly defend what she now sees as a systemic attack on what is now *her* community. Identifying Black oppression and injustice, Sam's advocacy of Moses and his innocence is equally her recognition of her white privilege. For Moses, the realization of unrealized virtue has culminated in him saving the block from an alien attack and acquiring hero status among the community that had previously seen him only as an object of fear, although this still does not liberate him from the force of law. Despite Moses's moral progress, one must resist the temptation to situate Moses's arc within a predictable 'structure of sympathy' (Smith, 1995), in which the text ushers the spectator into a position of advocacy for the protagonist's moral journey. In *Attack the Block*, for all his initial urban malevolence we find in Moses a character worthy of empathy, of our understanding that his frustration may be the index of the symbolic violence he and many others like him are subjected to. Moses's final smile, however, should not be interpreted as an attempt at humanization, the often-cited narrative methodology where the urban protagonist is depicted in moments that seem to offer a more three-dimensional characterizing and a broader set of emotional sensibilities. Rather, and representing the completion of the Lukacsian principle that the critical realist text should produce an altered political perspective within its audience, it is the transitionary affect on the *spectator* that is now primary. Moses's character trajectory produces a defamilarization of the cultural verisimilitude within the spectator's imagination, where our protagonist is reterritorialized within and beyond the cinematic apparatus, as the spectator's Black gaze is also reoriented. Just as *Attack the Block* had pre-constructed in Moses an example of the contemporary folk devil, the film has asked us to incrementally dismantle him, and within this dismantling process, to deconstruct our own culturally verisimilar modes of spectatorship and accept a new configuration of Black youth identity, the very identity Moses has reconstructed. In this way, *Attack the Block*'s relocating of the Union Jack to the racial, social and geographic environments of the council estate equally demands the recasting of those who have been deemed undesirable British citizens. Here, architecture, social environment and racial identity become powerfully interwoven, with Moses rejecting the identity conferred onto him by a political discourse, resisting the neoliberal ethos of individuality and, collectively and simultaneously, reaffirming the intrinsic but contested Britishness of the socially excluded that both the emergent and existing political culture had so denigrated.

Attack the Block retains all that would be considered culturally verisimilar in the context of Black urban representations of the housing estate: youth gangs and criminality, a localized drug trade and the informal social hierarchies within its community. However, its critical realism emerges through its interrogation of social stigma and power, both via the imagined and literalistic spatial logics maintaining the racist ecologies within British social life and the social prejudices and discriminations of the system. In effect, *Attack the Block* reveals an interesting cinematic negotiation with Britain's racial politics, a politics that comes from how character and environment are operationalized to demonstrate a concern with the conflicts and inequalities experienced when different social groups and authoritative power interact, rendering the film a key text enabling a dialogical and immutable encounter with anti-Black racism. Indeed, having remained in the popular imagination as a film of only cult status, a renewed interest in *Attack the Block*, some nine years after its making, was inspired, somewhat fittingly but equally tragically, by an impassioned speech on racism given by John Boyega during a demonstration with Black Lives Matter movement in London's Hyde Park on 3 June 2020 in response to the killing of an African American man, George Floyd who, after being arrested by the Minnesota Police, died after the arresting officer knelt on Floyd's neck, despite his pleas that he could not breathe. The video of this killing, captured on a phone and circulated across social media, sparked worldwide protests, and in the aftermath of Boyega's appearance at the Hyde Park demonstration, a revisitation of *Attack the Block* as an optic for understanding the continued marginalization and violence inflicted upon young Black men, police brutality and the broader social, political and economic dislocation processes excluding them from equal participation in mainstream society. Standing among other Black Lives Matter protesters, Boyega, who declared that 'I don't know if I'm going to have a career after this, but fuck that', after his speech offered a searing attack on racism within British and American society, earning international attention and acclaim. As he went on to state:

> Black lives have always mattered, we have always been important, we have always met suffering, we have always succeeded, regardless. And now is the time. I ain't waiting. I ain't waiting. I have been born in this country. I'm 28-years-old. Born and raised in London. And for a time, every black person understands and realizes

the first time you are reminded that you were black. You remember. Every black person in here remembered when another person reminded you that you were black. (quoted in *The Guardian*, Thursday, 4 June 2020)

Like Moses's speech, Boyega directs his invective at the social infrastructures preserving a system of anti-Black discrimination; his words speak of the effects of a collective experience of racism that attempts to unify the tragic moment in Minnesota with a quotidian racial violence that transcends generation, gender and nationality. As he continued, 'we are a physical representation of our support for George Floyd. We are a physical representation in our support for Sandra Bland. We are a physical representation of our support for Trayvon Martin. We are a physical representation of our support for Stephen Lawrence, for Mark Duggan' (Quoted in *The Guardian*, Thursday, 4 June 2020). The references made by Boyega to Stephen Lawrence and Mark Duggan are of particular relevance. Both Lawrence and Duggan are two young Black men from London, whose deaths were the catalyst for two seismic moments inscribed within the history of British racial justice: a public campaign over several years by the Lawrence family for an enquiry into Stephen's murder and the police incompetency and malpractice that allowed his killers to evade justice and, as explored in the previous chapter, the killing of Mark Duggan (which sparked the 2011 riots) and the Duggan family's own fight against the legality of Mark's shooting at the hands of the police. Both campaigns, while separated by nearly two decades, are unified by their challenge against the permanence of institutional racism within the Metropolitan Police specifically and race and class inequality more broadly. This is the precise critique found in the speech by Moses in *Attack the Block* and its articulating of a critical perspective on racism, a perspective that seems less permissible within the popular urban film's generic conventions, where the economic structures of the UK film industry condition the popular urban films' realism to narrationally satisfy a primordial desire for the pleasurable cultural familiarity of the urban excess. It is perhaps this stylistic approach that permits *Attack the Block* to be understood within a definite political context, one conditioned by specific sociopolitical imperatives and by a distinctive visual strategy that operates within an allegorical film grammar that is able to position Black youths and state power within a Manichean cinematic representation of good and evil. It is the very atemporality of allegory combined with the digital effects associated with sci-fi that, rather than compromising its realism, further concretizes its indexical relationship to reality. *Attack the Block* therefore acquires its political dimension via a novel representation of the urban environment that presents the tower block as a geography of intricate social relations producing a diagnostic account of Black youth oppression and injustice, one that stresses the connections between race, class, physical landscapes and the sociopolitical apparatuses determining the racial contours of British identity.

11

Of Simulacra, Performativity and Language

Top Boy, Black Cultural Visibility and the Popular

what is essential to the definition of popular culture is the relations which define 'popular culture' in a continuing tension (relationship, influence and antagonism) to the dominant culture. It is a conception of culture which is polarized around this cultural dialectic.
>—Stuart Hall, *Notes on Deconstructing the Popular*, 1981

One does one's body.
>—Judith Butler, *Performative Acts and Gender Constitution: An Essay in Phenomenology and Feminist Theory*, 1988

I'm particularly cognizant that my inclusion of *Top Boy* (2011–23) into the corpus of the popular Black urban text is a paradigmatic disturbance that requires a further textual and contextual exploration of what can be seen as a bipolar meaning of the *popular*. We remain within the liminal space of Black cultural politics in that the popular Black urban text and the various mediacentric expressions, representations and production cultures within the Black urban corpus that accrue different meanings become accommodated within new cultural and industrial logics and, consequently, are accommodative of the cultural shifts that will inevitably redefine what we understand and accept to be the value in media's representations of Black identities. As noted earlier, while my general conceptualizing of the Black urban text as the popular cannot be described as necessarily Hallian in its construction that emerges from a PSB production context where the very concept of public funding for film and PSB as the paradigm in which television and its construction of social identities 'act as our forum for interpretations of the world' (Ellis, 1999: 69) and pulls into its sphere a number of cohabiting and competing cultural, social and political imperatives and predicaments, a much more Hall-influenced formation of the popular Black urban text can very much exist within what he sees in the popular as 'the space of homogenization where stereotyping and the formulaic mercilessly process the material and experiences it draws into its web, where control over narratives and representations passes into the hands of the established cultural bureaucracies, sometimes without a murmur' (108).

A similar conceptual elasticity is applied here in a critical analysis of *Top Boy* as a nodal point from which a divorce from the PSB orthodoxy finds its manifestation in the production of not just new forms of Black representation but also new protocols of audience engagement. Crucially, these reform the urban as the axis upon which a new phase of Black cultural politics and visibility emerges, determined by a claim to authenticity and verisimilitude so heavily layered with the residual elements of previous and concurrent modes of Black urban representation that have been constructed for our pleasures, social anxieties, our serviceable race fictions (either necessary, useful or both) and our forms of knowledge and racial identification that sourcing its 'realness' is a spectatorial practice that cannot access its original quality and is subsequently compensated by lateral forms of communication established between the text, its audience and certain learned, expected and strategic valorizations. Within the term 'popular', we are confronted with an iteration of culture that carries with it a definitiveness of purpose and cultural intention. As Hall argues, 'in one sense, popular culture always has its base in the experiences, the pleasures, the memories, the traditions of the people. It has connections with local hopes and local aspirations, local tragedies, and local scenarios that are the everyday practices and the everyday experiences of ordinary folks' (1993: 107). Here, there is a relationship with the formal, representational and thematic orthodoxies as native and essential to the popular Black urban text that, as I have previously examined, draws on the kinds of hyper-visible social pyrotechnics that can be sourced in Bakhtin's idea of the 'carnivalesque' (1984) that carries with it the very modes of evaluation and segregated acceptance that position the popular urban text within the period as primed for the instinctive association of filmic and televisual Black popular with a vulgarity, grotesqueness, primitivity, the unformed and unsophisticated. For Hall, this compartmentalizing of the Black popular within a relegating disposability that he observes as 'counterpoised to elite or high culture' (108) is a framework fluent with the critical reflexes that have been present in the negotiation of the popular Black urban text as a credible part of screen culture and in chiming with Hall's assessment 'that is why the dominant tradition has always been deeply suspicious of it' (108). The moral perturbation and hollow liberal applause that has accompanied the glacial encroachment of the urban text and the Blackness that it embodies into the more powerful vines of cultural recognition have always been marked by a certain cultural vanguardism, and the popular poses a threat to its commandeering proprietorship over the pathways of mainstream visibility. Therefore, *Top Boy*'s arrival in 2011 as 'an honest and gripping rendition of inner-city drug and gang culture' (Channel 4, 19 October 2011) invites me to consider how its initial presence on Channel 4 and its relaunching on Netflix in 2019 become two very different iterations of the popular Black urban text that produce particular textual and interpretative outcomes as it moves into a space of popular visibility.

Channel 4's *Top Boy* serves as an exemplification of the collision between the two regimes of the Black popular that structure our engagement with the series, developed after its creator/writer Ronan Bennett witnessed a young child conducting a drug transaction in a supermarket car park in Hackney. *Top Boy* affirms its claim to Blackness by the degree of Black spectacularism based primarily around the violent criminal activities of 26-year-old drug dealers Dushane (Ashley Walters) and Sully (Kane Robinson) and their ambitions to seize control of the then hyper-localized East London drugs economy. Despite the serendipitous nature of Bennett's influencing encounter, it is undeniable that *Top Boy* finds its primary influence in the HBO drama series *The Wire* (2002–8) which in its dramatization of how gangs, users and the police are imbricated in the drugs economy in Baltimore also offers a sociological study of Black urban life and the city that 'focuses on the economic impact of the decline of the public sector, the effects of the globalisation of finance, the far flung production of all commodities and the massive social inequality resulting from these policies and practices' (Corkin, 2017: 8). In this London-centric offshoot, its cause-and-effect narrative interweaves a number of storylines that attempt to demonstrate how the hyper-local drug trade impacts various lives on the fictional Summerhouse Estate. Visually, we find an aesthetic continuity in the formal approaches of both directors, Yann Demange (series 1) and Jonathan van Tulleken (series 2), where both attempt a social realist framing of Black British working-class identity within an economically depressed Hackney by the use of natural lighting and *cinéma vérité* deep-focus cinematography that evoke a sense of spontaneous dramatic action built upon the linkages between its cast and its geographic setting. As suggested by Ellis (1981), there is a development of a 'narrative image' to be observed in *Top Boy*'s promotional practice that attempts to augment its formal claim to a Black urban authenticity. This is captured in the promotional poster for *Top Boy*'s first series (Figure 11.1). Here, and above the copy 'an incredible 4 nights of drama', the two principal characters, Dushane and Sully, and the acritical source of public paternalistic sympathy towards the vulnerability of Black youthhood in the young Ra'Neil (Malcolm Kamulete) are pictured standing

Figure 11.1 *Top Boy* Series 1 print advertisement (Channel 4, 2011).

across a low brick wall, a dustbin and a damaged BMW car that all mimic an Olympic podium and are positioned against the backdrop of two high-rise tower blocks. The juxtaposing of these epistemologies, in clear reference to the forthcoming 2012 Olympic Games in the London borough it is set and within the distressed urban landscape, reveals the hierarchies of the varying, antagonistic statuses of its characters to be explored, but also performs as powerful signifiers to establish *Top Boy*'s 'generic corpus' (Neale 1990). Indeed, a contribution to this corpus is undoubtedly observed in *Top Boy*'s first episode's opening images, which display raking, establishing shots of East London housing estates and the unstable camera framing of Black youths engaged in a drugs deal that is then interrupted by an armed, all-Black rival gang who rob Dushane and Sully's young runners of their drugs/money against the soundtrack of urban music. This authenticating triangulation of the symbolic location, Black identity and criminal activity is a modality of Black representations that for Andrews (2017) exhibits a highly problematic continuation of the media's system of depicting the Black urban physical and social landscape as a signifier for Black violence and criminality. Andrews's attempt reveals a much more deep and critical epistemological fracture than the one encountered in Akala's more considered reading of the negative racial characterization found within Professor Green's 'Jungle' video.

Andrews pursues an analysis that privileges an interpretation of Channel 4 in its post-multiculturalist guise as a commercial broadcaster and by this, its aestheticizing of the most hegemonic forms of Black representation is one that does not identify the complicity of the broadcaster's PSB ideals in the spectacularizing orthodoxy of Black deviance, and leads him to contend that, consequently, 'It is no coincidence that both *Dubplate Drama* and *Top Boy* draw on recognisable stereotypical tropes of black representation' (112). Andrews's reading situates its denigration of *Top Boy* in the concept of the 'iconic ghetto', drawn from Elijah Anderson's analysis of Black American 'Gangster Rap' music and how Black artist's performance of Black nihilism within the symbolic location exhibit a complicity in the creation, circulation and uptake of criminalized Black characterizations more broadly (2012). Resultingly, Andrews's analysis is informed by the kind of representational indexicality that insists that *Top Boy* should, and subsequently does not, work as a critical tool through which it can present the true social context of Black criminality to a broader public. However, my contention that the conjunctural field of Black representation is neither fixed nor stationary but mobile is to assert that *Top Boy* is produced within a highly cosmopolitan cultural and industrial apparatus that is subject to and constituted by extratextual cultural and market dynamics that determine *Top Boy*'s form and meaning(s). It is within this idea of Black textual representation as contingent that a generative reading of Black popular culture can be predicated upon, and as a result requires a specific set of analytical tools that here, at least conceptually, are declared out of bounds. The neglect of this particular explanatory framework for an antiquated stereotype analysis is not inherently problematic on its own. Rather, Andrews's criticism of *Top Boy*'s denigration of Black identity as the outcome of Channel 4's authorial verticality and leaning solely towards its commercial imperatives in its creation of the iconic ghetto means that we are unable to place *Top Boy* within a critical conjuncture in which

Black representation as a social good is shaped by different regimes of agency. Consequently, Andrews's extrapolation of Anderson's iconic ghetto and application to the textual features of *Top Boy* is developed upon a highly unstable and singular conceptual terrain by insisting for an accurate and facsimiled form of Black representation that affirms a relationship between the Black urban existence and social inequality, an investment that would organically disturb the persistence of racial stereotype and sever ossified associations between Blackness, criminality and social malaise. As stated here, 'Black communities consistently complain about police harassment and though all of the negative signifiers of the ghetto are littered across *Top Boy* there is not a single stop and search' (125). It should be made clear that my own analyses of *Top Boy* share a number of points of congruency, although these are developed, evidently, from quite differing epistemologies. Chiefly, there is no basis for any contention to his reading that there is no interactive relationship between *Top Boy*'s characters and any broader social apparatus, notably schools, and Andrews is very correct in his insistence that *Top Boy* compromises its own claim to realism in the absence of the police as an antagonistic institutional force within the Black urban existence. However, and recalling my earlier extrapolation of Richard Dyer's idea of filmic utopias that it is in the ideological positioning of the screen industries within a political project of cultural diversity, marginalized racial identities are able to draw identification and satisfaction from when the textual representation of Black masculine urban identities, in all their discorded menace, is finally affirmed within the popular spheres of the screen industry, or to use a more Hallian phrasing, 'the theatre of popular culture', where the image streams of criminalized Black urbanity as a counter-identity have come into a space of not just visibility but *recognition*. The denial of this by Andrews in exchange for an uncomplicated analytical correspondence between *what* is being represented and *who* has authored and consumed this representation reveals a conceptual excavation that, if unattended to, is unable to note that the popular has created arenas of Black participation in both the production and the marshalling of the images of Black urban identity. This asks for an epistemic reconfiguration of what does remain a neocolonial space of representation and attendantly requires an analysis that therefore cannot function independent of the cultural and material constructions and reconstructions of the Black popular, irrespective of if (and how) such text's attempt to place Black people within a homogenizing mono-aesthetic spectacle. However, and remaining crucial to the critique of Andrews's formulation of the iconic ghetto as divorced from the question of subjectivity that, as a result, cannot appreciate the interrogation of its approximation of a Black urban reality, this being achieved through either intra-diegetic textual features or extra-diegetic critical clamour, any reading of *Top Boy* must be placed within a pluralistic body of meanings. I want to describe *Top Boy*'s depiction of Black urban realness as a Baudrillardian 'simulacra'. In drawing on the postmodern theories of Jean Baudrillard (1981), this describes the representation, or copy of someone or something that in its later theorization became associated with the idea of imitation, inferior reproduction and, as argued by Baudrillard, a claim to truth but is devoid of its original source or true text/reality. Relatedly, *Top Boy*'s circulation, reception and cultural consumption can be seen as a 'language game'. Here, the German philosopher Ludwig Wittgenstein (1953) argued that words gain meaning through their function, which are woven into the social practices and relations within which they are embedded. Simplified, we interpret and respond to language through the 'rules' of the game encoded in the language, and its purpose is both provincial and contingent and is enacted by choice and influenced by discourse. In my contention that *Top Boy*'s depiction of realness and authenticity points to a Baudrillardian simulacra, and our discursive engagement with representations of Black identities as presented in *Top Boy* through the popular is indicative of a Wittgensteinian language game, we should remember that what I am describing in *Top Boy* is a modality of Black popular culture that produces its representational excess from a position of lack, and consequently, develops its realism upon the migratory thrust of the performative Black masculinity of Grime and urban music and the characterizations and thematics of the popular Black urban text within an authenticating symbiosis. Indeed, such is the powerful convergence within *Top Boy* between the sounds and iconographies of Black urban music, Black cultural production, Black subcultural representation and the Black popular urban text that the audience is left with the particularly arduous but ultimately generative task in making the textual distinction between what is real and germane, and what is synthetic and gesture. It is at this point where we see the symbiosis between language game and simulacra, for the popular Black urban text's pathways to cultural recognition has to include the dead Black body as collaterally positioned to be textually encountered but then either bypassed or walked over for the hyper celebration and cultural visibility of Black identity, and renders the urban Black popular cultural production and representation as a self-referential discourse with a particular protocol of reception that is contextually dependent. This means the language game at play within *Top Boy* is dialectically entwined with its simulacra. Whereas in another context we reject the hegemonic framings of Black corporeality and (anti-Black) black-on-black death, the popular Black urban text presents and impels us to place a different value system on the very same images that are to be recruited from integrated, competing and linear fields of representation, the aggregation of different elements of Black urban culture in the relatability secured from the lyrical and thematic content of Grime, UK Rap and Drill music. *Top Boy* is an aggregational realness of both simulacra and language game. The popular's project of reconciling our imaginations with Black urban images in the meshing of authenticity within the textures of Black cultural visibility is how its recreational simulacra, the re-enacting of historical or contemporaneous events and issues, is identified. What we encounter in the urban text are the fictions of Black urbanity that have undergone a long process of discursive veneering, for its (re)representation of (re)representations means the Black urban body when performed under the auspices of authenticity is no longer a claim to the aesthetic, or textual, real; the heavy layering of discourses, rationalities, performative, technological and promotional artifice and the multiplicity of cross-textual encounters with Black urbanity means that we are unable to source its original point of 'realness'. The Black urban is now at the apex of its representation as a criminal identity, and this is the version of Black urban performative visibility that spills into the *truly* popular; we are all now all fully committed to whatever constructions of Black urbanity are offered and are therefore imbricated in a racially and (sub)culturally distinct language game.

Judith Butler's project of performativity must take a central position within this formulation (1988, 1990, 1993, 2004). For Butler, bodies, and what they come to represent, cannot be assessed through an organic claim to reality, truth and facticity but as produced by the interaction of the object with a range of cultural symbols, languages and gestures. In terming such bodies as social agents, Butler considers the body 'as object' as formed *by* rather than producers *of* any social reality, and like the concept of the hauntological Black Other that is subject to a continuous discursive process of (re)signification, social bodies are constructed by different matter (1988). This aligns with the application of the idea of a social aesthetic to the popular Black urban text as inherently constitutive, for as present within Butler's emphasis on the body as the site of repeated performative gestures, movements, vernaculars and expressions, the body is inherently dramatic, reactive and accumulative, and once unified, it represents a preferred and interactable construction of the body that we are asked, and in some cases impelled to accept and engage with its bodily acts, in all its performativity, that create and present the body as an 'object of belief'. *Popular* Blackness is very much of the hyper-visual and performative, and in remembering that we are within a new moment of popular Black urban visibility and its coming into being from lack to excess, the idea of performativity as a strategic posture positions this as an affective dimension of Black urban life that works through the gaze of whiteness but makes powerful registers upon young Black urban identities as a culturally negated group now within a shift from invisibility, exclusion to proliferation, hypervisibility and a necessary and inevitable exaggeration where, as Butler stresses, 'one does one's body' (156).

In returning to the context of fictitious televisual Black urbanity, the hyper-performativity of Black urban masculinity as an audiovisual identity is one such bodily expression that accentuates the realism of its textual representations. This is not lost on Hall, and in some ways, his description of popular culture as 'profoundly mythic' (113) provides a framework for considering the unreliability of the popular urban Black text as a stable point of truth, identification and authenticity, and applied to *Top Boy*, that necessitates a critical nuancing of Bignell et al.'s claim that 'at its best, television drama has provided not only a window to the world but also a critical interrogation of it' (2000: 1). Rather, Hall views the popular as a source of benign and playful integrations with representations that permit Black men to 'live' out and 'replay' fantasies of Black hyper-masculinity. Where Hall's formulation reaches a natural temporal juncture is that popular Black urban representations as fictions of race cannot be reduced to the servicing of the fantasies of Black masculinities, even if such representations are ballast through its displays of misogyny and homophobia. However, we are taken back to Hall when considering that in his singular critique of *Top Boy*, Andrews is making a theoretical attempt to escape the very *politics* of representation through which, as Hall reminds us, is the very paradigm where 'the political rightness or wrongness of a particular cultural strategy or text can be measured' (Hall, 1993: 111). Such a reading poses questions over how we are able to intellectually grapple with the cultural permeation of a series that would achieve one million Channel 4 On Demand online views, over 23,000 plays of its soundtrack and during its opening week would be referenced in 123,000 tweets, becoming the most digitally engaged Channel 4 programme since they began analysing online interaction vis-à-vis the decision of Hackney Council to refuse the production's filming in Hackney and would argue that 'it was not fair on residents to run the risk of having their neighbourhood stigmatised on national television as riddled with drugs and gangs' (*Hackney Citizen*, Friday, 23 September 2011). How are we able to account for the tremendous incommensurability identified in Bennett's defence of *Top Boy* as essential *to* the Black community? Or how does Ashley Walters own feelings that 'we didn't have a genre back then that represented Black people in the way that they're represented now . . . so most of the parts you [would] play didn't really ring true, or relate to a Black audience. There weren't things like Top Boy back then. There weren't things that were authentic. Stories that are written by ourselves and for ourselves, that didn't exist' (Quoted in Okundaye, 2022) work against Andrews's insistence that 'the show was written, directed and produced by white people, for a mainstream, largely white audience' (128). This too is an analytical lacuna worthy of Hallian interrogation, for his valuation of Black popular culture as a contradictory arena of 'strategic contestation' (1993: 108), as encoded in its forms of operation, proves resistance to the critique of Black urban criminality through otherwise reliable binary positions of good/bad, authentic/inauthentic or negative racial characterization/positive cultural identification. *Top Boy*'s claim to Blackness, just as Andrews's accusation that *Top Boy* is the autonomous product of the white imaginary, cannot be seen simply as the product of a singular imaginary and therefore one axis of opposition but as having been brought into visibility and value by a constellation of cultural dynamics. Its representational approaches are organized by not an institutional space that asserts a singular domination over the terms of representation but a popular space where text and audience participate in an endless system of positional interplay and representational reconfiguration. This also means that such discourses naturally and inevitably capture within its sphere the emergent climate of Black cultural politics which, in this case, is the emancipatory state of Black urban representational fervour. Ultimately, the popular Black urban text is an instinctive and restless text of postmodernism, in which its definitions, meanings and sense of the real are predicated on what the particular juncture has decided to accept as the political, the social and the authentic. The issue of authenticity is primarily, but by no means exclusively, a question of textual *address*.

Our ability to both identify and disavow the simulacra present within Black urban performativity is specifically what the postmodern Black popular text displaces and is a conjunctural shift that moves us away from Hall's 'positive/negative strategy' critique that argues that the insertion of positive interludes within the dominant, negative frames of representation cannot instinctively displace the negative reception for as such binaries remain fixed, negative connotations continue to be drawn from such images (2001). Instead, and as asserted by Gray, it means we cannot find assurance in the presumption that

> a corrective to the image would repair lost dignity, redress resources imbalances, and help generate recognition, empathy, and trust that might lead to more

care and protection for all of us. However, getting the story straight in terms of authenticity, generating more and better facts, and telling better and more accurate and representative stories seem no longer sufficient to redress injury or generate new practices of equality in the moment of racism after race. (Gray, 2013: 792)

For so ossified is our accepted depictions of Black urban criminality, *Top Boy*'s 'real' as simulacra is authenticated by the popular and brings us into a language game that occupies a space within the celebratory arena of Black urban visibility. In other words, it is through the popular performativity that *Top Boy*'s aestheticizing of the Black urban locale and its hauntological Black subjects are neither positive nor negative but simply *are*.

The media, particularly screen media and its cultural representations, are a powerful terrain from which such modes of the cultural reconfiguration of Black popular culture are able to produce the capacity to accentuate the desires among marginalized racial identities for mainstream cultural visibility. The reaction to the 2013 cancellation of *Top Boy* by Channel 4, pursued without prior discussion with the creative team or rationale, serves as a demonstration of the incommensurability of Black cultural politics and is to be derived from its creator/writer Ronan Bennett's contention that its cancellation 'felt like a slap in the face to the community it was representing' (Quoted in Harrison, 2019). The argument that *Top Boy* is an indispensable part of Black British identity and culture seemed to place demands upon the residual public service ideals of a post-multiculturalist Channel 4 on the pretext that the esteeming of Black visibility, by whatever tonalities or thematics, as possessing distinctive Black cultural value. The arrival of Netflix to within the popular Black urban text's constitutive ecology, both of which serve as a subsidiary of the popular, poses an interpretative challenge to both the ideological basis of PSB and, significantly, the relationship between Black Britain and Channel 4 in particular (Ross, 1996). Netflix, the US subscription streaming platform and production company that would now acquire *Top Boy* as a Netflix Original Series and would stream its final three seasons from 2019 (as well as its first two), can be seen as an exemplar of what Hall saw as the axis of global cultural production in US-centricity. But while Hall saw this as a shift from high culture to the vulgar, I see that this introduces a new system of value and esteem in *Top Boy* as a transformed site of 'American mainstream popular culture and its mass-cultural, image-mediated, technological forms' (1993: 104). In its Netflix guise, *Top Boy* is a mode of televisual Black British representation that is now presented to its expanded audience via streaming but requires a cinematic mode of attention. I want to argue that Netflix is also central to the accentuating of *Top Boy* as the *popular* through the significantly increased production values that allowed for a narrative expansivity to 10 one-hour episodes from the 4 during its two Channel 4 series, which were condensed within 4 consecutive weekday evenings and supported my initial description of *Top Boy* under its PSB auspices as 'Black event' PSB drama. My contention here is that *Top Boy*'s adherence to the hyper-commercial imperatives of Netflix as a streaming platform liberates *Top Boy* from the PSB responsibilities to a much more genre lore/market logic of popular value that, in the context of Black representation, can be reclaimed as authentic cultural and aesthetic value, and this is to be observed in two distinctive manifestations. First, this can be identified in the intervention of the Canadian rapper Drake, who can be understood as serving a critical function in the placing of *Top Boy* within the popular not merely as an economic gatekeeper in his role as executive producer but as a cultural intermediary, for his position as an avatar of the global popular Blackness and his visibility across *Top Boy* quickens Black British popular culture's incorporation of what Hall had termed 'Black American popular vernacular traditions' (1993: 105). Hall of course resists a specific taxonomy, but allows me to offer a parenthesis to his reading. The flows of our mass consumption of the cultural products and representations of Black America that have carried with it the various language forms, expressions and terms that have a natural presence within the Black British urban lexicon establish an intertextual Black visibility constructed upon the global resonance of Black music subcultures and allow *Top Boy* to achieve a certain commensurability with what Gilroy had identified in the fusing of Black Atlantic cultural forms (1993). Second, Black British urban representation becomes captivated by the popular and, in turn, is rendered a space where individualism becomes a collective entrepreneurial identity, a collective performative endeavour where Black urban identity can be constructed in a different key and imagination. That the departure from the PSB logics of Channel 4 permits the series to enjoy a certain sociocultural and economic unrestrictiveness does not render *Top Boy* any less 'event' Black visuality; indeed, Netflix can be seen as an arena where such Black event representations are placed within an expanded narrative scope. For example, as explored by Bowling (2009), we encounter a textual example of the said transnationality to drugs and criminal activity within the Black locale, in that the vast majority of its dramatic action takes place within estates of East London but retain rhizomatic entanglements with Jamaica, Morocco and Spain. What *Top Boy*'s Netflix existence produces is a conditioning of the economic, cultural and technological media terrain for the exploding of Black cultural entanglements and assemblages that Herman Gray sees as 'difference as the basis of (brand) distinction' (780). With this in mind, *Top Boy* as a space for a popular Black cultural convergence in the recruitment of Black producers, directors and creative talent reconfigures the Black urban text as the sphere of Black subcultural iconography and performance that in its dependent interactions with the popular Black cultural mainstream embolden its claim to a Black authenticity and is observed in the strategic casting of Dave the Rapper, Little Simz and the model Adwoa Aboah. The presence of such popular Black figures orientates our experience of the Black cultural popular as inaugurating a process of authentic cultural augmentation that, as has been observed by Gray (2013), is part of a palatable system of Black accumulative individualism that is accrued not just through the logics of mainstream film and TV commissioning but by the visibility accrued through Twitter, Instagram and the essentializing of Blackness and urban subcultural vernacular expressions through the economies of brand culture. This economy naturally includes fashion and urban apparel, and is observed in Drake's own production of a *Top Boy* imprinted clothing line as part of the series launch and *Top Boy* production's sponsorship of Hackney Wick FC, a grassroots football team based within *Top Boy*'s geographic setting to deter youths from the gang violence the film aestheticizes, attempting to ballast the series brand with a tangible community-based praxis. Alongside what I can only describe as an unprecedented cultural interest in *Top Boy* through media publications/outlets as diverse as *The Observer, Evening Standard, GRM Daily, Rolling Stone, Face* and many others, the series becomes an exemplar of the popular Black urban text as an all-encompassing sphere of Black popular culture. *Top Boy*'s transition through Netflix's 'global streaming platform' is equally an inevitable shift in its status from a Black televisual event to a Black cultural experience, and finally, *as* Black culture.

I am attempting here to formulate a means of analysing *Top Boy* that can rest within Butler's theory of bodily performativity. Hall's dissection of the flows of Black culture as a product of the popular and the general thrust of the show's textualities display elements of simulacra and language game and asks for the consideration of the posture of performative Blackness as a strategic tactic of visibility. What, in accepting that the urban text, like all texts, are constitutive of what Paul Willemen's cultural studies reading terms as an 'economy of discourses' (1993: 13) and his identification of both textual theme and characterization as the site where such intersecting pluralities are to be exploded is revealed to us as Netflix's spectacularizing of the Black British urban text through *Top Boy* moves Black popular culture into a new position of esteem and celebration, and with this, establishes a new protocol of cultural visibility and engagement? Relatedly, how does the celebrated but protracted visibility of Black urban identity as a branded experience accentuated by global media technologies and new exhibition and distribution platforms inaugurate a distinctive culture of representational ostentatiousness that come to underpin and inform screen representations of Black identities, gender and sexual difference? What I am suggesting is that in considering the new Black urban visibility through *Top Boy* and its high-end marketing campaigns and a critical reception that espouses the show's attempts to interact with social concerns, particular narrational strategies emerge where Black visibility, simulacra, language and performativity combine to produce a distinctive textual implication. *Top Boy* Season 3 on Netflix continues its dissection of the Summerhouse Estate from the point of Dushane and Sully's rehabilitation into a post-2012 Hackney annotated by gentrification, urban renewal and social injury within an urban locale that signifies both change and stasis, in that its demographic changes are obfuscated by its own antiquated version of nihilistic social Darwinism and the attendant inevitability of fatal interracial violence. Where Homerton was once Dushane and Sully's indigenous habitat of urban Blackness, it is now an unapologetically gentrified, colour-coded and class-organized existence where buying coffee is now a curatorial discipline and a spatio-economic privileged experience where crucially, the capitalism underpinning the discourse of urban regeneration and the drugs economy is both imbricated in an ecology of new economic forces that come to be energized by physical coercion. The area is now governed by a violent paedocracy that for Dushane and Sully carry with it the threat of a generational eclipse through the ambitious energy of a London Field's gang, ZT (Zero Tolerance) and their attempts to regulate Hackney's drugs economy by driving out their competitors through violence, including an acid attack on one of Dushane and Sully's young teenage drugs shotters.

I find particularly generative here how *Top Boy* places its hegemonic representations of Black internecine violence within a pictorial dialectic between the diurnal and the sensational, for what can be seen as the spectacular in Dushane's incomprehension at the when and the whys of the introduction of scarring chemical products as the criminalized urban Gen-Z's weapon of choice, the stabbing of one of Dushane and Sully's young gang members and its expressive mis en scéne ushers the image of Black urban violence back into the quotidian. As he is stabbed at the foot of the estate and the perpetrators flee, the camera slowly opens up to the illuminated image of the block on the estate where its residents stand across various levels, oblivious to the very latest instance of Black injury (Figure 11.2). As we see, life simply continues as knife attacks are domesticated as the habitual mise en scène weaved into the everyday tapestry of an atypical evening within the Black symbolic location. Like the *Wire*'s final three seasons, *Top Boy*'s most dramatic actions offer a spectatorial navigation of the vicissitudes of an older criminal generation unaccustomed to the new orthodoxies of the internationally sourced but hyper-locally contested drug economy. However, my primary interest at this point is how the series in its most spectacularizing 'Blackness' produces themes and images that are reflective of what I see as its *acceptable antilogies*, or contradictions, for the popular's reinvigoration of Black fictional representation appears to licence a cohabitation with a number of communicative tensions that in a previous conjuncture would otherwise be read as being caught in an irreconcilable textual/contextual dialectic between cultural and structural forces. However, whereas Hall's paramount conceptual investment in the meaning of Black popular culture is at the point of cultural circulation and reception, there are a set of *narrative* implications to what Hall sees as a natural indenture of Black popular culture. We encounter a range of thematic issues to be addressed in *Top Boy* that are not necessarily interwoven by their linear narrative chords but are primarily held together by their presence as contemporaneous Black subject matter: the sub-themes of the Windrush Scandal and the human indignities experienced by those living at the very cutting edge of

Figure 11.2 The habitual nature of urban violence in *Top Boy* (Netflix, 2019).

Britain's hostile environment, or the familial tremors of gun violence approached via the continued use value of Black female bodies as consequential collateral; a girl who is on a date with ZT's leader Jamie (Michael Ward) is left brain damaged after being shot in the neck during an attack on the ZT's by another gang. Later, where Jamie is confronted by her father at the hospital, the scene functions as the show's moral instructive against gun violence that has reduced his daughter to simply another victim of an arrested innocence, and while powerfully emotive in its delivery is neither capable nor truly willing to disturb the necessary subsuming of its social address into the popular's required performing of the most verisimilitudinous and identifiable aspects of the Black urban experience. This said, the series strives for a more expressive visual style that, in the opening episodes, is heightened by the direction by Reinaldo Marcus Green, where a cinematic visual language is introduced to *Top Boy* that is also found in Barry Jenkin's *Moonlight* (2016) and *If Beale Street Could Talk* (2018) where the absorbing framing of its characters as they face towards camera teases towards the breaking of the fourth wall. It is appropriate for *Top Boy* to be described as cinematic television, and the series is infused with cinematic aesthetic properties and the textual features of high-end drama in how it responds to the spectatorial demands of the popular and produces a formal flourishing. We see this in a notable opening sequence to episode 4 where, having found the £10,000 demanded to secure their first Jamaican drugs supply and placing Dushane and Sully momentarily 'back on top' of the hyper-local drugs economy, the highly stylized sequence trails the drugs economy in Hackney, and its capitalist machinery from production, purchase, consumption to finally profit is conducted to Wreckless Eric's 1978 song 'Take the Cash' as the screen is populated with pound notes and later frames a rejuvenated Dushane in a double dolly shot that carries him through the estate (Figure 11.3). Here, and as metaphored in its title, *Top Boy* frames criminality as a simple means of accumulative social mobility and the unlicensed acquiring of wealth that violently and extractively implicates the estate and its indigene.

Figure 11.3 Dushane 'back on top' in *Top Boy* (Netflix, 2019).

Top Boy as the performative Black popular inaugurates a shift in terms of Black cultural visibility. This renders Black urban subcultural identity as both a distinct and commodifiable iteration of performativity to consolidate our place within the screen sector and the subcultural recognition that its images of Black urbanity reflect back onto us. But there are moments of emotional alterity that are placed within the fissures of *Top Boy*'s depictions of drug activity and fatal gun violence to reanimate the popular Black urban text with a social purpose. Humanizing, which in this context can be understood as the development of a more benevolent characterization to dimensionalize and nuance, rather than counter the racial othering that has been encountered through other inferential media frames, is a narrational strategy that exits both within and beyond Hall's positive and negative binary problematic, in that it is this balancing that can licence an exposure to the full range of human emotion and character dimensions while remaining within the popular's infrahumanizing frames of reference. Here, the pursuit of its hauntological Black humanizing efforts via fictional means is unable to extract itself from the general understandings of Black urban life. By this, I am suggesting that we are to observe a bidirectionality in humanizing as a textual practice as its foundational logic is positioned in and constructed from an acceptance of Black corporeality as firmly positioned outside of human categorization. The term therefore can be understood as both a generative, authenticating 'truth'-telling modality and a central structural problematic in the popular urban text's attempts to re-represent young Black people that for *Top Boy* flows from a cultural liberalism that is exemplified in Season 4's tagline 'family before everything', a thematic thread that unifies the motivations behind its characters most deviant expressions of crime and violence. But we also see an engagement with the characters' Caribbean identity that consolidates its textual presence through representations of emotional duress and cultural memory that, for example, is seen in the death of Dushane's mother in Season 4. My specific point of critique is that the problems in the popular urban texts' humanizing practices are identified in the geometricity of its characterizations that are determined not by the dimensions of depth – that the excavating of a character's inner being and internal life produces a significant register on the narrative trajectory of both character and those around them – but by breadth – that the counter-hegemonizing humanization of the hauntological Black Other represents an elongating of its actions within a narrative fissured by tonal difference, moments of tenderness with their blood families and a sense of kinship towards their road families. It is this latter narrative action and its refusing or inability in constructing its humanization from the rejection of Black criminality as an instinctive and pathologized act of non-human being that the Black urban text as the popular Black cultural experience is extracted of any ontology of Black humanness and instead develops its genealogies in an acceptance of the hegemony of fatal Black internecine violence and deviance as normative, achieved here by the exploding of one inferential identity (evil/deviance), the extracting of human emotion as the hauntological Black urban Other's redemptive element and the placing of this humanizing in a temporal shift within another category of identification (altruism). This is a primary facet of the urban text that presents a much more compelling set of contradictions that Hall's Gramscian reading of the arrival of Black culture into the popular cannot account for nor can it, without the culturally verisimilitudinous elements of Black urban representation and its voyeuristic function that services what Jauss (1982: 79) terms as the 'horizon of expectation' accrued from the proliferating impact of Black subcultural performativity, theorize itself through the competing tensions and contradictions that such facets produce. The Black popular allows, and in some instances insists, in the first instance that its representational frame must first be hegemonic in its attempt to be *counter*-hegemonic.

My reading of the problems embedded in the textual practice of accepting and then working through hegemonic understandings of the hauntological Black urban Other as a validating process of humanization is not to argue that the series cannot produce highly important moments of character introspection however, and the bulk of *Top Boy*'s humanizing project is pursued through Sully, where the disruption of the urban archetype is here concerned with expanding the dimensionality of expectation and meaning to be extracted from our inferential Black urban masculine constructions. This somewhat delicate strategy of humanizing begins from Sully's release from prison to Ramsgate, where he has reconnected with Jase (Ricky Smarts), a young boy who he had rescued from his drug-addicted mother and a desperate state of malnutrition, neglect and physical abuse as part of Season 2's depiction of fatherhood and paternal extensivity from its Black males as a sub/counter-narrational thread to create a three-dimensionality to its otherwise singular characterizations. The reintroducing of Sully away from the cultural symmetry of Homerton's Summerhouse but instead to a decrepitating seaside townhouse is where Sully would reconvene his drugs activity, an endeavour that involves the exploiting of a young refugee family. *Top Boy*'s engagement with the hegemonies of Black crime is interspersed with moments of provincial racism and anti-Muslim resentment in the resurgent nationalism of Brexit; the refugee family are subjected to perennial attacks by a group of local white racists who later set the house on fire where the escaped Sully, unable to rescue the trapped Jase from the night-time blaze, watches in horror as he's overcome by the flames. The complexity of Sully's characterization encourages us to resist an understanding of humanizing in emotive terms of loss and tragedy, and could equally be ascribed to the consequence of the attempted venture, be it spiritually or materially, beyond the drug trade. We of course find this in *Wire*'s Stringer Bell (Idris Elba) and his attempts to carve out an external, non-linear existence outside the Barksdale Crew and towards self and re-education and his subsequent investment of his drugs dividends into Baltimore real estate projects and local politics, a set of desires that would lead to the loss of his money, a separation between him and Barksdale and eventually, his death. Similar to Stringer Bell, and following *Top Boy*'s general schema of how men are broken and rebuilt anew, made more nihilistic, expand and recoil by the expression of emotion and the provision *of* and exposure *to* love, a humanized Sully only leaves him more vulnerable to not just the feeling of futility towards his existence that catalyses a deeper recourse to a violent nihilistic world view but an attack on his life by rival gang members Leyton (Kola Bokinni) and Jermaine (Bashy) at the behest of Mouldy at a graveyard immediately after being the sole attendant at Jase's funeral. Again, the popular has a register on the crafting of our aesthetic engagement through its form, and the scene is bestowed with a cinematic

Figure 11.4 *A Prophet* (dir. Jacques Audiard 2009).

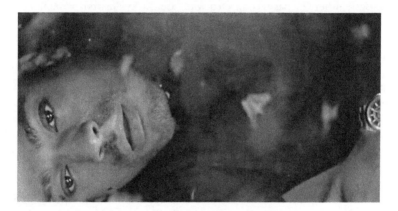

Figure 11.5 Sully, under attack in *Top Boy* (Netflix, 2019).

textuality that rejects the hegemonic documentary instincts of formal realism for the expressionistic aesthetic devices to be identified in Jacques Audiard's *A Prophet* (Figure 11.4). Sully, crouched at the floor of his car as a hail of bullets shatter the windows above him, the frame's tight concentration on him is perhaps a moment of reflection at the futility of death as Sully listens, eyes fixed to the camera as he waits for the final shots from the gun clip, before running out of the car to the camouflaging safety of the graveyard park (Figure 11.5).

For Sully, his character is driven by an emotional trauma that would spill into Season 4, for while Dushane, whose every action, be it business or personal, is to be indexed to capitalist accumulation to service his expanding status as a multimillionaire top boy, Sully's own motivation is to outrun and exorcize the combinational pain of the premature death of Jase and the management of his own sense of remorse and shame for the killing of *Top Boy*'s tritagonist, Driss (Shone Romulus). Prior to this graveyard

Figure 11.6 Sully and Jase in *Top Boy* (Netflix, 2019).

scene, having returned to Ramsgate to avenge Jase's death by finding and then beating to an inch of death one of the racist locals who had terrorized the migrant family, Sully retreats to the beach where he and Jase had enjoyed not just a moment of mental expansivity that accompanied his first experience of the sea but also the location where he was to realize his own function as a source of human dependency born from Jase, whose needs provide Sully with a feeling of a reciprocal fatherhood, albeit one brought into being by a kind of surrogacy (Figure 11.6). Sully, tearfully submerging himself into the water before dawn, presents us with a powerful visual, cultural and spiritual juxtaposition. Thus, my reading of this scene asks us to resist the desire to think of this solely as a moment of human catharsis, nor for his entering into the sea as a form of baptism or rebirth; his inability to protect Jase does not necessarily catalyse a renewed desire to rebuild a relationship with his own young daughter. Instead, *Top Boy*'s horizonal break from the Black urban representational normativity is in providing the audience with a glimpse of Sully's nomadic existence beyond the symbolic location and its violent orthodoxies, a spatial asymmetry where his sense of loneliness and emotional solitude become more heightened through a hegemonic juxtaposition that, paradoxically, reveals a correspondence with Sully's subjective experience.

I have been unable to fully measure the range of discourses present within what has been circulated socially in the 'post-George Floyd context', a phrase that despite the receding critical juncture of racism and structural inequality confessionalism to be found in the temporal fragilities of white institutional consciousness has maintained an epistemic presence as an industrial, institutional and textual hermeneutic for the bountiful, open ended and extractive thematic of (anti) Blackness as a pluralistic practice where economic and cultural value are to be extracted from and enacted through Black popular culture and its various representations, fictitious characterizations and narrative thematics. *Top Boy*'s own claim to this exploding context can be observed in the form of police brutality. This depiction is informed by none of the agnotological residue that marked the show's first two Channel 4 series, where a liberal critical discourse attempted to situate its Blackness within a One Nation interventionalist cultural paternalism that would be forcefully instrumentalized as the narrational antidote to Broken Britain and the 2011 Riots. Instead, *Top Boy* is presented as social pedagogy, and this was emphasized by Saffron Hocking (Lauryn) in a BBC News interview publicizing the fourth series, who would state, 'The Black Lives Matter protests opened everyone's eyes. . . . But I think that what Top Boy already did before BLM was show black people on TV, and it was exposing to show black people on TV, and we continue to do that' (Quoted in Lawton, 17 March 2022). Here, we again find the celebration of mono-racial Black density that may very well be constitutive of 'the essentializing moment' of a fragile and inversive valorization of Black identity that finds its politics in utilizing Black urban visibility in itself as political representation. Visibility, as a particularly novel valorization of racial difference, positions *Top Boy* as a cultural experience drawing its sense of necessity from the essentializing of Black identity that, as argued by Hall, bestows the popular Black with a guaranteed political texture and meaning in the attentiveness to a particular racial climate or, as described by Raymond Williams, in the mobilizing of existing 'structures of feeling' through the dramatization of the various antecedents of the Black social experience: child poverty, domestic abuse, housing and spatial injustice. Black Lives Matter is here facsimiled onto *Top Boy*'s political project through the experiences of three of the young Black gang members with the police. Refusing to get out of the car after being pulled over by a swarm of police units, the three are then dragged out by the officers, with the most violent expressions of excessive policing reserved for Kieron (Joshua Blissett), who is thrown to the floor by several officers to a chorus of resistant screams. This scene's composition, specifically the capturing of the assault of Kieron through a low-angle framing, gives emphasis to the sense of optical unease in the unorthodox physical positioning of the Black body that remains increasingly vulnerable in such spaces, an unease that is further heightened by the inevitability of this incident. Here, a sense of bleakness is being expressed through the tonal rather than the formal elements of noir as not through any high-angle shots or lighting techniques but how the scene evokes a quality of despair as the dramatic moment is punctuated by their expletives towards the disreputable actions of key public institution. These dimensions of its mise en scène bring its audience into an engagement with a familiar situation through which *Top Boy* exhibits a number of intertextualities, and the prominence of the Black police officer in the carrying out of the violence can be seen as a node to the non-white officers complicit in the killing of George Floyd. What we are asked to interpret from its reconstruction of our most contemporaneous manifestations of systemic racism is that the incident is a demonstration of a muscular system of anti-Blackness, of which our Black police officer is a mere adhering component. Our own sense of Black trauma is not necessarily derived from the episode's dramatic reconstruction of the police and the racialized technology of stop and search, which is accordingly littered with the spectacular acceptable antilogies that the urban text as the popular seems more than capable of holding in an uncritical and unrepellent symbiosis. That the violent accosting is depicted as the result of a clandestine police surveillance operation (the three could very easily have been in possession of weapons or drugs) is, of course, immaterial to the forms of meaning that the scene endeavours to disperse among its audience, meanings made all the more haptic by a receptive stability conditioned by the Black Lives Matter sentiment circulating within its episteme. Rather, the narrative strategy of first isolating the scene as a contemporaneous interlude rather than as a *thematic* and then placing it within a widening context of racial inequality suggests that the moment functions as a source of topicality for *Top Boy*'s expanding social aperture that licences the counter-hegemonizing humanization of its characters; drug dealers who exploit, damage, criminalize and kill the very young yet are publicly outraged at the official practice of gentrification and community displacement. Black gang members who operate at the very centre of an indiscriminate murderous drugs economy that defiles the Black community as the habitat of internecine death inflicted upon and most felt among Black people yet are incandescent at the injustice and indignity of police stop and search. What are we to make of these tensions? It may be that these antilogies supplement *Top Boy* with a multi-dimensionality of characterization and is therefore simply emblematic of a criminalized social world organized by a moral complexity. In this sense, the annotative cultural relatability of the Black urban text as the Black popular means that the scene cannot be easily dismissed as gestural in its depiction of racial policing, of which the scene's language appears to stress but never returns to pollinate the thematic or incidental moments of any of the following episodes. *Top Boy*'s claim to 'tackling current issues' is therefore a statement comprised of a body of contingencies and subjective positions that are structured by the presence of 'Black' as a political placeholder, a positioning further augmented by the character's racial identities, their acts of defiance in the face of the habitual technology of police violence and harassment that subsidize of *Top Boy*'s claim to a Black social address – the incontrovertible exemplars of racial discrimination that completes the series as a race-making project and one that is not compromised intra-textually by the incident later being evaluated by Dushane as a 'routine stop'. The scene asks its audience to develop the kind of critical consciousness that dialectally validates its inclusion, however fleeting, of Black death and corporeal laceration as entertainment value; keeping two systems of thought in simultaneous operation leaves *Top Boy*'s audience and their subjective positions locked within a Wittgensteinian language game, where our interpretations and responses are regulated by the feeling of expectation, desire and relatability recruited by its depiction of very specific racial and geo-social experiences. The audience is asked to take a detour through the identification of Black visual injury and violent fatality if we are to be permitted access to the recalcitrant energy and emotion of the Black Lives Matter protests that structure the scene, and this includes evading the element of nuance suggested in the highly regimented demeanour and actions of the Black police officer that may imply that the scene strives for an equivalency of scenic organization and resultingly, perspective. For as they return to the car, it is the impact upon the young Kieron that is our focus, and the camera that frames him in a close-up that ultimately requires us to concentrate on just his own subjectivity. The three characters do not and are not required to verbally address the incident as an example of racist policing, and this inexpressiveness is not an act of silence, for this scene is to be interpreted as a moment of inexpression as a specific political modality laden with expressive meanings, rendering his silent and still image as particularly absorbent within a Black social contemporaneity. This may be a site of the modes of visual relationality implied in the Black gaze that for Tina Campt (2021) describes an audiovisual-looking practice that rather than extracting from its distressed Black moving image disperse forms of meaning that are severed from the Black perspective instead 'renders our relationship to Blackness in an anti-Black world palpable, in ways that require us to reckon with our distance from or intimacy with the disposability of Black bodies' (2021: 1). Indeed, this is a Black gaze that is neither ruptured nor negated by our next encounter with Kieron, where he instructs a very young child, one of many in the room, how to plant cocaine into rubbish cans as part of his role as a primary instructor in a co-ordinated and fatal system of exploitation where children are enticed into Dushne and Sully's broader transnational drugs operation. His inability to find not only the words but the means of talking about the incident in its immediate aftermath when questioned by Jaq (Jasmine Jobson) is an internal state of anti-Black trauma made haptic through our own physical, emotional and visual life with police racism.

As I explored in Chapter 9, this dominant representation of Black males renders the popular urban text in all its iterations as an inherently masculine project. As a result, the prominence of female characters within the Netflix-produced series allows us to consider its mono-gendered dynamics and how *Top Boy*'s representations of gendered and sexual difference can be considered within what Kara Keeling terms the ghettocentric film's 'Common Sense'. As Keeling argues, 'official common sense uses the glaring sexism and homophobia of these references (bitches, hoes and faggots) and their politically incorrectness as locations into which it siphons off the pernicious homophobia and sexism that maintains its intelligibility' (2007: 123). Although the first two *Top Boy* series included characters that were conducive for the disrupting of the urban male norm, with young female gang members such as Chantelle (Letitia Wright) in Season 1 and Nevaeh (Monique Day) and Nafisa (Weruche Opia) in Season 2, it is undeniable that the Netflix-produced seasons represent a more concerted attempt to subvert the heteronormative framework of its criminal Black urban landscape through the supplementing of its gendered alibi with a sexual one as a hegemonically transgressive politics of representation. It could be argued that as a result of *Top Boy*'s reliance on *The Wire* as its chief narrational influence, the Black popular's incorporation of gender and sexual politics necessitates the production of its own representational facsimile of the *Wire*'s 'Snoop' (Felicia Pearson), the sole female member of the Stanfield Organization who exhibits much of the ghetto-centric's violent hyper-masculine performativity. It's through *Top Boy*'s attempts to implant within the masculinity of its Black gangs a dramatic embodiment of femininity that we find an analogous, citational figure of sexual difference in the character of Jaq, a young Black mixed-race girl who, while presented initially as part of the band of urban dwellers under the dismissive instruction of Dris as one of gang's teenage drug shotters, eventually surpasses him in being appointed by Dushane and Sully as the gang's third in command and the show's narrational tritagonist. This performance of gender and sexual identity displays a further defiling of the generic understanding of gun crime and gang violence as the exclusive domain of Black masculinity and demands that we are at least open to the possibility to contend that Jaq's presence can be considered not as a mimetic capturing of all that is present and natural within a criminalized Black urban sphere but as a specific valorized intervention, and *Top Boy*'s challenge to its own heteronormativity in the strategic essentializing of sexual difference is by how Jaq seemingly enjoys a harmonious existence at least within the hyper-masculine structures of the gang.

This aesthetic practice of branded distinction is a concerted effort in *Top Boy*, for it is set in place from the first episode's opening dialogue. Jaq's gender is questioned by two Turkish drug barons who mock her for her alleged gender ambiguity and later her interest in competing with males when playing basketball with two young boys she later coalesces into running drugs for the gang. Jaq's gender commands much greater narrative attention than not just both the other female characters who have featured in the show across its previous two series, but equally, the rival gang's female member Farah (Seraphina Beh) who, while she can be accurately described as a background character, her heterosexuality is firmly established in her calling of another rival female gang member a 'fucking lesbian!' during a public knife fight, and whose presence within the spaces of Black urban masculinity is not depicted as a source of ambiguity or contestation, or in Jaq's example, narationally worthy of identificatory celebration and an essentialist subject position. In carving out this reading, I am drawn again to the writings of Kara Keeling and her analysis of the queer representational politics to be observed in the film *Set It Off* (1996), where a group of four Black women undertake a series of armed bank robberies. Such a film was embraced as a Black feminist tribune, representationally subversive of a ghetto-centric masculinity in the all-female R&B group En Vogue's 'Don't Let Go' soundtrack, displaying the popular Black culture's converging within the frames of Black American cinema. Keeling's analytical interest here is on the character Cleo (Queen Latifa), who for Keeling is an embodiment of what she terms as the 'Black Lesbian Butch-Femme' who occupies an ambiguous motivational position within the film vis-à-vis the other female robbers who are driven to carry out the robberies by racial injustice, economic hardship and the threat of social services taking away a member's young child. For Keeling, the film provides little expositional material to account for the criminal enlistment of Cleo, and her function as the film's gestural embodiment of Black masculine nihilism deposits a specific kind of gender performativity. As Keeling observes, 'While the other three primary characters in the film have some rationale for getting revenge and making money by robbing a bank, Cleo's masculinity seems to be enough justification for her resort to crime' (Keeling, 2007: 124). This argues that Cleo's sexuality becomes the basis for the film's characterization of her as the group's aggressive, gun-carrying and masculined 'butch', and the film's representation of Cleo's queer identity as ontologically deflated is cause for Keeling to contend that 'Within the context of the film's valorisation of ghettocentric black masculinity via the character Cleo, Cleo's homosexuality is simply a by-product of her female masculinity' (Keeling, 2007: 127). For Jaq, an equally valorizing practice is to be discerned in *Top Boy*'s labelling of her gender and sexuality as the vessel through which the series asserts its feminist/queer politics in the championing of sexual difference as the postmodern emancipatory existence within the urban; a boxer/boxing coach who spars (and beats) men, and a drug dealer and a murderer within an otherwise hyper-masculine cartel who commands the respect and acceptance of those around her despite her youth and the immediate sense of peer subservience in relation to Sully, Dushane and Driss implied in her sexuality and gender. If this is an example of how the Black popular insists on a representational pluralism as it latches onto new forms of visibility through the intersections of race, gender and sexuality, in congruence with the analysis made by Keeling in how *Set It Off*'s Cleo's queerness functions within Black masculine modes of meaning, Jaq's presence within *Top Boy* as a performed point of postmodernism and its eager and necessary representation of sexual difference enjoys only a conditional accommodation under the sanctioning Black hyper-masculinity of Sully, Dushane and the rest of the gang. Jaq's queerness is a product of the representational politics of sexual difference that poses no intertextual threat or concern to the masculinity of Dushane, Sully and the gang and with this secures the viability of her full acceptance into the gang but produces no contextual or extratextual laceration or challenge to homophobia as the authenticating posture of its social and cultural universe. This presents an avenue for the introduction of homosexuality to the augmentative arena of Black popular culture as the real, the other forms of Black urban expressivity that *Top Boy* makes a lateral connection to (grime/urban subculture) and the centrality of homophobia to its very modus operandi. As Keeling suggests, 'The sexism and homophobia endemic to the ghettocentrism that has pervaded mass culture in various ways since the early 1990's undermines ghettocentricism's own ability to articulate a conception of the world that enables a social movement that is radically different from that currently perceptible' (2007: 122). My interrogation of *Top Boy*'s simulacra and language game therefore speaks to how from one perspective, Jaq's lesbianism enjoys a seamless cohabitation within the heteronormative space of the gang, but from another, the presence of a male sexual difference would require and represent a fundamental deconstructing of *Top Boy*'s mode of Black male representation and relationality, an unreconcilable challenge to the legibility of the urban as a sphere of hyper-masculine Black heterosexuality and in turn would be a defilement of the very Black urban subcultural performativity that *Top Boy*'s authenticity is constructed upon. One may reach for an immediate counterpoint to this assertion in *The Wire*'s Omar Little (Michael K. Williams), a character whose open and depicted homosexuality, a decision of dramatic licence given that the character is facsimiled from the real-life story of the heterosexual Baltimore hitman/robber Donny Andrews, is one that possess no fracture to *The Wire*'s intradiegetic complexing of Baltimore as a geography of violent heteronormative Black nihilism or the extra-diegetic claim, among other things, to a Black urban sociological realism, and Omar's Black homosexuality is asymmetrically accommodated within the contours of the show's fictional Black identities and themes of Black male ghettocentrism. However, there is a clear contextual and therefore *conceptual* remiss in resourcing a critical position on my argument through the citing of Omar's sexual difference. For while *The Wire* indeed retains some obvious textual points of connection with *Top Boy*'s British version of a Black orchestrated and rhizomatic drugs economy within the inner-city and its physical spaces as the arena of a criminalized Black hypermasculinity, in significant *industrial* departure from *Top Boy*'s strategic use of Black urban music and the casting of Black urban performers to racially aggregate the series as the spectacular Black urban event, *The Wire* maintains an acute non-relationality to the powerful capitalistic corpus of Black audiovisual and cultural celebrity, notoriety and recognition, where the show's realism *as* Black cultural value (and its accompanying Black heteronormative ghettocentrism) does not demand an interdependence with the artefacts of hypervisible Black America (music, fashion, media, television, etc.) as an elaborate source of *popular* Black cultural augmentation. In other words, *The Wire*'s semi-fictional Black male universe and its accompanying claim to a Black narrational authenticity, of which the homosexual Omar takes a central dramatic position, is not threatened textually by Black male sexual difference as the show is neither a creation of, supplemented by or reliant upon on the artifices of male, ghettocentric, popular Black American cultural production. Such arguments ask for a partial questioning of *Top Boy*'s claim that Jaq's character offers a *universal* critique of anti-LGTBQ+ violence. While *The Wire*'s referential detachment from Black American Hip Hop as an intertextual presence liberates the show from any possible incorporation, even culturally, into the material spheres of Black male ghettocentrism which in turn disburdens Omar's homosexuality to negotiate only the homophobia of *The Wire*'s intradiegetic world (as opposed to any extra-diegetic appeal to Black male ghettocentricity as a marketing strategy), Jaq's sexual identity, its attack, her defence of it and its acceptance within the otherwise all-male gang, is a powerful presence across the series as the popular's politics of recognition, but benign in the context of dismantling a broader hyper-masculine homophobia within *Top Boy*'s aggregational sphere and its positioning within a popular Black cultural domain where homophobia remains an essential generic thematic to the hyper-masculinity of the urban.

In returning to the different social meanings that are formed within the urban text through apparel and costume, *Top Boy*'s use of the hood as worn by its various male characters within a specific socio-geographic context, performs as a marker of both subcultural identity and Otherness, and despite the hood being worn by female gang members, this does not liberate the hood from its cultural association with a particular social and gendered phenotype. Therefore, the series produces a set of *gendered* associations that are deeply embedded in the hood and becomes *Top Boy*'s performative aesthetic motif in two significant moments in the series that I now want to briefly consider. First, this association takes place where Jaq and her date Becks (Adwoa Aboah), upon kissing each other while walking home, are subjected to a violent lesbophobic attack by a group of five youths that carries with it an attendant misogyny. The aftermath of the attack is initially framed by a long shot where Jaq is momentarily prone on the pavement, the camera now frames the couple in a medium close-up as, in an action of tremendous symbolism, Jaq gets up. But Jaq's action is not merely a getting up from the floor but an *arising* and one that strives for a social relatability drawn from its depiction of everyday anti-LGBTQ+ violence. Her arising can be seen as a politics of resistance that performs as an anti-lesbophobic defiance unaffected by the emotional or physical impact of hate-motivated attacks. However, we can only fully understand this as a sexual politics through the meaning that is

Figure 11.7 Jaq placing the hood over her head in *Top Boy* (Netflix, 2022).

derived from its second phenomenological move, made significant not simply in its presence but in its execution. The scene's own sense of importance is accentuated by a slow-motion effect as Jaq places her hood over her head (Figure 11.7), before turning her attention to the wellbeing of Becks. Given that the hood had been worn down by Jaq prior to the attack, I interpret the turning of the hood, in all its deviant associations, as a performative identity of *unidentification*. This is similar to the actions of Tyler (Charles Mnene) prior to his killing of Felix (OT Fagbenle) in *NW* (Saul Dibb, 2016) where the placing of the hood over his head becomes the decisive moment of hegemonic adherence by performing the 'conventional prelude' to the securing of a Black urban cultural verisimilitude to service the desirable anxieties of an audience readied for the internecine performance of Black violent death (Nwonka, 2020a). Indeed, this scene's moment of masking as a practice of social *un*masking holds a number of direct interactions with the second moment of performativity when the gang come to the aid of Sully, having been kidnapped by another gang, beaten and held at a drugs lockup in South London. However, while the primary interest in the scene's armed rescue mission is how Dushane's business separation from Sully does not completely sever the binds of brotherhood in the ensuing shoot-out that secures Sully's rescue, the specific point of meaning to be extracted through the sequence is in the actions of Jaq, who shoots dead at point-blank range the rival gang's lieutenant, Khadeem (Khali Best). The scene produces a deeper resonance beyond its significance as her first 'kill', the momentary emotional distress in the aftermath of the shooting, or as a rite of passage where Jaq completes her graduating from a street shotter to a fully fledged gun slugger in earning her stripes, to term this graduation more colloquially. This moment is less about direct physical identification (the audience can see that this is indeed Jaq) but a social-cultural identification that is attempted in the slow uncovering of her face that remains unidentifiable until the assailant's snood is lowered to reveal her full identity (Figure 11.8). In Jaq's ritualistic uncovering of her face after shooting dead one of the male rival gang members, it is only through bringing her to within a hegemonic identification of fatal Black

Figure 11.8 Jaq reveals her face after killing Khadeem in *Top Boy* (Netflix, 2022).

malevolence that *Top Boy* strives to dye queerness into the everyday fabrics of hyper-masculine Black urban criminality.

The commodification of urban subculture through the popularizing of the creative products of Black British culture Grime and Drill is embodied in *Top Boy*'s entry into the very popular arenas of global culture. But these have also produced different kinds of valorizations, realisms, representations and forms of meaning. What would remain in the attempts to sequester the entirety of Black urban representation away from the popular? Like Hall, I am convinced that there are positions to be won in mainstream culture that demand performative gestures as an intervention in the white-dominated field of mainstream popular culture, pointing to Hall's own reference to both bell hooks and Gayatri Spivak in arguing that essentialism, strategic or otherwise, is both a necessary and inevitable cultural manoeuvre. But, if we accept that this strategic performativity remains an essential strategy for navigating Black identity through these new forms of cultural visibility that postmodernism's politics of difference present, we must also accept the contradictions that accompany the positioning of the popular Black urban text within the primary entanglements of neoliberalism: digital life and cultural participation, promotional cultures and the commodification of racial and subcultural difference as the popular's recognition of marginality. This means that the context of our analysis, and its attendant analytical tools, must therefore be continuously relayered to be attuned with what I have explored as the most salient considerations for the popular Black urban text as it enters into a new phase of visibility. This also requires an attuning to the racial, cultural *and* the technological in the (re)formations of Black cultural politics and how Black cultural practices and subcultural performativities, eagerly migrated over from one cultural domain to another, alter both how we identify and respond to its claim to value and authenticity within a process of Black cultural augmentation. *Top Boy* is indeed of simulacra, language game and performativity but is made a real and essential part of Black urban culture by its shift from invisibility to visibility, a cultural experience that becomes authentic only by its mobilizing through other related forms of Black urban identity.

12

Conclusion

The (Un)Exceptional Textures of Black Urbanity

In concluding this book, I want to consider the possibility that the popular Black urban text may be able to establish an independence from the hegemonies governing its production and reception and the positioning of its representations as the unquestionable means through which we are able to construct, understand and act upon Black British urban identity. Given this book's investment in the significance of the cultural, social and institutional dynamics in the visual representations of Black urbanity, my reflecting on the possibility that the Black urban text can exist outside of its constitutive framework and push back against the authenticating indexicality of Black film may appear to be a disavowal of the very conceptual project this book has pursued. It may therefore be more helpful to frame this consideration as a lamentation or a utopian desire that emanates not strictly from the text itself but from the social context that continues to place tremendous importance on the Black urban text. This was certainly the lamentation/desire I applied to the film *Blue Story* (dir. Rapman, 2019), which can be placed within the expanded understanding of the popular Black urban text in its status as a film produced by BBC Films, it being co-produced by Paramount Pictures, the ways that the film finds an urban cultural augmentation and authenticity through the YouTube series *Shiro's Story*, made by Rapman (Andrew Onwubolu) which would secure a contract with Jay-Z's ROC Nation, and the mono-raciality of *Blue Story*'s cast and the majority of its key production crew. The film opens to a series of CCTV images of a number of violent incidents and attacks predominantly involving and being inflicted upon the young: hooded gangs fight in the street, bullets are fired from cars, images of crime scenes and floral tributes to the deceased. These non-diegetic images are supplemented with the audial power of real news reports on urban violence and a voice-over narration in the writer/director Rapman's rap lyrics that attempt to contextualize the images of urban discorded menace. These opening images are a series of augmentations that, for the audience, are meant to mimic the real experience of encountering urban violence through the lens of factuality. There is a particular significance in this attempt to reappropriate what actually are the very images that are fixed at the centre of our perceptive commitment to the discourse of Black urban violence as a social epidemic. The film, a story of two Black childhood best friends whose brotherhood is severed by the nihilistic fatalities of rivaling gang warfare that is narrated through the lyrics, is an attempt to reveal the futility of hyper-local violence and provide a filmic sermon on the devastation such actions leave behind. Expectantly, while the film's positive, pedagogical moralism was positioned as the film's justificatory optic, it is in the privileging of the negative elements of *Blue Story*'s representations that would become the basis for the decision by Vue and Showcase Cinemas to pull all screenings of *Blue Story* from their theatres. The film, having opened to 60 screens across the UK and Ireland on Friday 22 November 2019 would be withdrawn after a mass public brawl between up to 100 youths from rival groups took place at a Vue Cinema in Birmingham during the film's screening, one of over 25 'significant incidents' that were reported in 16 separate cinemas within 24 hours of *Blue Story*'s release. Notably, the cinema chain would argue that the number of associated incidents was the biggest they had ever encountered for any film within such a timeframe, and despite putting a number of safety measures in place, including the increased presence of security guards, reducing its screening and limiting the existing ones to day-time only showings, the decision to completely withdraw *Blue Story* was made within twenty-four hours of its release on the grounds of public safety.

In many respects, this response is perfectly consistent with the modalities of a contemporary moral panic. But my engagement with the anxious racial fervour that surrounded *Blue Story* is not to provide an already well demonstrated and unnecessary example of how the popular urban film genre represents both a response to and is informed by racial hegemonies, nor a means of evidencing that Vue and Showcase were now implicated in the toxic legacy of moral panics over the cultural representation of young Black men. For it is accurate to define Black film censorship, either official or de facto, as an antiquated social practice; *Pressure* was denied its theatrical release for almost three years by the BFI due to its documentary realist images of police brutality towards Black people, *Babylon* was given an X-rating by the British Board of Film Classification which believed that Black youths may see that retributional violence against whites was their only option available in their resistance against habitual British racism, and both *Bullet Boy* and *Top Boy* would be denied permission to film in Hackney at various stages of their production by a local council reluctant to have the borough stigmatized on national television as a location marked by violent Black gangs and drugs. Further, my referencing of the Vue incident for thinking through the possibility of an unexceptional Black urban textual encounter is not necessarily drawn from the racialized colouring of our public imaginations in the mediatized hysteria over the banning that, as I had forecasted, would allow the film to accrue a certain public notoriety as a form of outcast cinema when the ban was eventually lifted. Indeed, *Blue Story* would become one of the highest-grossing British films during its opening weekend in 2019 and would go on to return nearly five million in box-office takings. Rather, my specific concern was what specifically made *Blue Story* homogenously dangerous? Instinctively and universally dangerous? What kinds of materialities, indexicalities and facsimiles does the film possess to position it as a catalyst for violence? It is made an immediate social threat not from its content but from its generic and formal approaches, the geographicality of its representation and its textual investment in the spectacle of Black death within an anti-Black discourse that for the cinemas indicated a racialized mode of perceivability. This assertion may appear to chime within the very rationale given by Vue that it was not the film's content that was cause for moral concern. However, this is an assertion that must be understood in a comparative context: it is undeniable that the ultra-violence of the James Bond franchise has made an unmeasurable imprint within the British imaginary that was yet to be framed in such language. Thus, the issue of race, and more specifically Blackness, is firmly placed at the axis of a moral contestation and anxiety where those represented, the audience and institution, are all bound by an aesthetic and sociocultural claim to authenticity that from one perspective presents the popular urban text as an essential cultural value and at the same time the very same modalities of representation become subjected to a disguised system of racism and colonial organization. This suggested to me that the film's withdrawal isn't about the content of the film as the inciting source of violence per se but about a certain audience who are drawn to the cinemas as a space of representation and the idea encoded in the official responses that the film is attractive to a racialized demographic predisposed to displays of nihilistic violence, a rationale that remains predicated on the idea of an inability of a predominantly Black spectatorship to distinguish fiction from reality – that the alternative, antithetical and correct responses to the film's reconstruction of urban violence are somehow beyond the psychological capabilities of a particular audience.

Black Boys: The Social Aesthetics of Black Urban Film is a conceptual and theoretical invitation for us to dabble at the very marrow of the various questions that have remained unasked and unapplied to the Black urban text, and curates a heterogenous and multidisciplinary space for us to congregate, consider and potentially reimagine Black urbanity in the arena of cinematic representation and its social and cultural presence. As I've explored through a range of conceptual frameworks, our engagement with the popular urban text is bound by the hegemonies that fill the hauntological archive of Black urban otherness. Now, this idea of the unexceptional urban textual experience has stemmed from the racialized hysteria towards *Blue Story* in a variety of ways; what motivates its production? What governs its cultural, critical and institutional responses? How accurate are these narratives? To whom are they real? Do *we* recognize *ourselves* here? In pondering over how (un)exceptional textual materials of Black urbanity may reveal itself within the popular Black urban text, what I am continuously confronted with is the absence of a stationary normative centre from which we can potentially construct an approach that can account for the power of the various imperatives involved in the filmic and televisual representations of Black urban life and vernacular subcultural practices and the racial, social, cultural and aesthetic meanings we have and are able to draw from in the sight and the sounds of Black urban life. The purpose of this book, therefore, is also to open up an opportunity for us to consider the tremendous subjectivity of the urban text as a source of racial, cultural and social identification. It is because of the constitutive nature of the urban text that I ask if the presentation of Black urban death as the index of Black urban life is able to find a balance between demonstrating an ethical attention to Black visual care and what may be felt as the essential dramatizing of the explicit experiences of Black working-class identities within the urban environment. In that sense, the popular urban text is a contingent and unstable aesthetic modality, at once a source of anti-Blackness and a mechanism of counter-hegemonic agitation and social repair. By integrating surveillance footage at the very opening of *Blue Story* as its establishing contextual schema, the film invites an engagement with familiar images. But we cannot afford to, as I have stressed throughout, be dismissive or disinterested in the ways that the cultural politics so implicated in the production and circulation of the urban text reconfigure how we are able to accept the hegemonic images offered to us in one field of representation as part of a politics of visibility and our structures of Black filmic engagement, and disavow the same imagery within another. Authorship, context and intention are of course important factors, but the presence of different looking practices and racially distinct gazes may not be a sufficient response in this example, for it is in the production of representational excess from a state of lack that we are compelled to develop a reliable visual modality of Black representative density and visibility that the mainstream screen sector had and continues to fail to truly recognize or remedy adequately. As Hall reminds us, the contradictory nature of Black cultural politics and its attendant representations are orchestrated by the specificity of the conjunctural moment, and in the early 2000s conditioned the context where Black urban subcultural visibility became socially, culturally, politically and economically significant for the increasing of the cultural visibility of previously marginalized racial and classed identities. Some years later, it was the postmodern fascination with the young Black popular combined with the emergence of new democratized technologies that allowed for Black urban identities to craft their own communicative representations within the platforms of Facebook, YouTube and Instagram that not only created new augmentative material for authenticating the urban text but also, as examined by ˙Abenna Owusu-Bempah in her analysis of Grime, Rap and Drill videos (2022), serviced as admissible evidence within instinctively racialized criminal procedure. This represents a new frontier in the discourse of Black urban criminality. In one frame of representation, subject and institution become unified in a shared carnivalizing of the elevated visibility of Black urban youths in the cultural popular while within another but interacting sphere of representation become the basis for a sustained state assault on young Black people, specifically those who have been historically subjected to secondary marginalization within the shifting economic and material positions of Black Britain. But this does not mean that we cannot observe moments of textual and thematic variation and the unspectacular within the filmic representations of Black youth identities. For example, *The Last Tree* (dir. Shola Amoo, 2019) is in some ways demonstrative of Forrest's conceptual project of a New Realism in that the film possesses a more poetic and lyrical representation of the urban Black youth identity, and as presented to us through the trajectory of its central character, the urban can be understood as identity, environment and as *activity*, and it can be suggested that it is through the film's desire to exist outside the purview of the augmenting Black urban subcultural *popular* that the film is able to take up a space between Black urban representational continuity and departure. Similarly, *Rocks* (dir. Sarah Gavron, 2020) is also a film which offers a much more expansive and understanding of the popular urban text that finds its authenticating power within themes of poverty and friendship within the urban location. More recently, the urban romantic comedy *Rye Lane* (dir. Raine Allen Miller, 2023), a BFI/BBC Films production which affirmed its Black cultural value via a marketing approach that placed tremendous emphasis in the valorizing of the historic but vestigial racial specificity of the film's setting/location in Peckham, South London, is consciously disembedded from the epistemic markers of Black urbanity (hypermasculinity, crime) and further advances the very term 'urban' as a liminal and unbounded generic category for Black racial, cultural, representational and creative alterity/diversity. This is not to place these films within a competing positive/negative binary with those texts, where urban violence and internecine Black death are essential narrational features – remember, the popular urban text in this guise is neither positive or negative but simply *is*. Rather, it is to highlight how central spectacular Black fatality is to the urban text's associations with stylistic vulgarity and unsophisticatedness, and how the dominant culture's aversion to Black urban representational density in all its realisms is feinted within the accusatory hermeneutics of glorification and glamorization, without ever providing an affirmative understanding of what these terms mean, their measurable manifestations, or actual sociocultural impacts.

To close, and in summarizing the ideas pursued throughout this book, it is clear, I think, that the possibility of an unexceptionality to the popular Black urban text is one that is predicated on the conjunctural alignment between the very preliminaries, be them industrial, political and cultural, that constitute the social aesthetics that, as I have argued, constitute the Black urban genre. This naturally is also rooted in the sustainability of the film, television and streaming platforms, in this undoubted moment of institutional clamour over racial difference and structural change, to attend to the full textual and contextual experience of Black life. Given that Black Britain's own claim to Britishness is consistently overwritten by our apparent epidermal incommensurability to the nation, this means that these moments of Black urban visibility become sufficient, just, to make us believe in the cultural value of the most hegemonic and hauntological forms of Black urban filmic and televisual representations that have been carried along in that shift from post-multiculturalism to diversity. But this does not mean that all we have done, and can do, is to watch the filmic constructions of Black urban identity within the frame through which British society watches us back. Where there is a continuation of Black death and bodily injury as a mode of authenticating testimony that is placed within the transcribing images of popular urban text as a citational experience, the forms of authorship and Black cultural popularity seen in *Top Boy*, *Blue Story* and the countless other texts that reside outside the popular of PSB and mainstream contexts but exist within the popular of cultural recognition through new and alternative viewing and exhibition platforms have offered alternative representations to be constructed to see the urban, in all its meaning, from various perspectives, in a shifting audiovisual field where there is a developing sense of proprietorship over what and who is being represented and in what social, cultural or formal context. This is undoubtedly a post-2020 conjunctural outcome, the outcome of a critical juncture of race and difference, but we know that this happens and has a deep historical pedigree in the cultural politics of Black cultural visibility. So, with this, we cannot forget that the social, political and industrial preliminaries, when combined, contribute to this kind of urban aestheticizing. Thus, there is still too much inter-reliance in the production and circulation of the popular Black urban text to arrive at a point where its images can be de-spectacularized, or they can exhaust its audiences, be it through the images of Black bodily casualty and once circulated through either white imaginaries or Black self-representations, of the aesthetic anxieties and pleasures attached to the image of hegemonic racial difference. This is why, as this book has attempted, the multi/interdisciplinary analysis of the popular Black urban text in all its contradictions, preliminaries, useful and necessary race fictions and constitutive social aesthetics provides one way to navigate the field of UK film and screen culture and the racial dynamics that sit at the basis of our filmic and televisual encounters with Black British urban identities.

Bibliography

Adorno (1991) *The Culture Industry*. London: Routledge.

Aitken, I. (2006) *Realist Film Theory and Cinema: The Nineteenth-Century Lukácsian and Intuitionist Realist Traditions*. Manchester: Manchester University Press.

Alexander, C. (2008) *(Re)thinking Gangs. Runnymede Perspectives*. London: Runnymede Trust.

Alexander, K. (1996) *The Art of Being Black*. Oxford: Oxford University Press.

Alexander, K. (2000) Black British Cinema in the 90s: Going Going Gone, in R. Murphy (ed.) *British Cinema of the 90s*. London: British Film Institute.

Althusser, L. (1984) *Essays on Ideology*. London: Verso.

Amin, A. (2013) Land of Strangers. *Identities* 20 (1): 1–8.

Anderson, E. (2012) The Iconic Ghetto. *The Annals of the American Academy of Political and Social Science* 642 (1): 8–24.

Andrews, H. (2014) *Television and British Cinema: Convergence and Divergence since 1990*. Basingstoke: Palgrave Macmillan.

Andrews, K. (2017) The Iconic Ghetto, in S. Malik (eds) *Adjusting the Contrast: British Television and Constructs of Race*. Manchester: Manchester University Press, pp. 111–31.

Anthony, A. (2008) The Killing of Kodjo. *Observer*, Saturday 15 November.

Arnheim, R. (2006) *Film as Art*. Berkeley: University of California Press.

Arnold, K. and Wambu, O. (1999) *A Fuller Picture: The Commercial Impact of Six British Films with Black Themes in the 1990s*. London: British Film Institute.

Austin, M. (2011) *Useful Fictions*. Nebraska: University of Nebraska Press.

Back, L. (1996) *New Ethnicities and Urban Culture*. London: UCL Press.

Bainbridge, L. (2012) Plan B's iLL Manors: 'This is the True, Dark Reality'. *Observer*, Sunday 27 May.

Baker, Jr, A., Diawara, M., and Lindeborg, R. (eds) (1996) *Black British Cultural Studies: A Reader*. Chicago: Chicago University Press.

Bakhtin, M. M. (1981) *The Dialogic Imagination*, ed. Michale holquits, trans. Caryl Emerson and Michael holquist, 425/253. Austin: University of Texas Press.

Bakhtin, M. M. (1984) *Problems of Dostoevsky's Poetics*. Minneapolis: University of Minnesota Press.

Barthes, R. (1972) *Mythologies*. London: Paladin.

Baudrillard, J. (1981) *Simulacra and Simulation*. Los Angles: Semiotext(e).

Baudy, L. (2002) *The World in a Frame: What We See in Films*. Chicago: Chicago University Press.

BBC (2004) Who Killed PC Blakelock? *BBC One*.

BBC Films (2002) The Boys Memo. 24 March.

BBC Films (2004) Co-Production Meeting Minutes. 16 December.

BBC News (2001) Garage Star Escapes Jail for Assault. Friday 19 October.

BBC News (2003) Abbot Speaks Out on School Row. Friday 31 October.

BBC News (2006) Cameron 'hoodie' Speech in Full. Monday 10 July.

BBC Trust (2014) *Service Licence Review: Review of BBC One, BBC Two, BBC Three and BBC Four*. London: BBC.

BFI (2009) *Statistical Yearbook 2008*. London: British Film Institute.

Bhattacharyya, G. (2018) *Racial Capitalism: Rethinking Racial Capitalism: Questions of Reproduction and Survival*. London: Rowman & Littlefield.

Bhavnani, R. (2007) *Barriers to Diversity in Film*. London: Film Council Publication.

Bignell, J., Lacey, S. and Macmurraugh-Kavanagh, M. (eds) (2000) *British Television Drama: Past Present and Future*. Basingstoke: Palgrave Macmillan.

Bird, S. (2005) So Solid Crew Gun Killer Gets 30 years. *The Times*, Saturday 29 October.

Bizzle, L. and Currie, E. (2011) iLL Manors Reviews. *The Observer*, Sunday 27 May.

Blake, L. (2008) *The Wounds of Nations: Horror Cinema, Historical Trauma and National Identity*. Manchester: Manchester University Press.

Born, G. (2000) Inside Television: Television Studies and the Sociology of Culture. *Screen* 41 (4): 404–24.

Born, G. (2005) *An Uncertain Vision; Birt, Dyke and the Reinvention of the BBC*. New York: Vintage.

Bourne, S. (2002) *Black in the British Frame: The Black Experience in British Film and Television*. London: Continuum International Publishing Group Ltd.

Bowling, B., Parpar, A. and Phillips, C. (2003) Policing Ethnic Minority Communities, in T. Newburn (ed.), *Handbook of Policing*. Devon: Willan Publishing, pp. 611–41.

Bowling, B. and Phillips, C. (2002) *Racism, Crime and Justice*. Harlow: Longman.

Bradburt, D. (2000) A Boy's Own Story. *The Guardian*, Thursday 20 January.

Bramwell, R. (2015) *UK Hip-Hop, Grime and the City: The Aesthetics and Ethics of London's Rap Scenes*. New York and London: Routledge.

Brook, O., O'Brien, D. and Taylor, M. (2020) *Culture Is Bad for You: Inequality in the Cultural and Creative Industries*. Manchester: Manchester University Press.

Brown, B. (2001) Thing Theory. *Critical Inquiry* 28 (1): 1–22.

Brown, K., Mondon, A. and Winter, A. (2021) 'I'm not "racist" but': Liberalism, Populism and Euphemisation in the Guardian, in D. Freedman (eds) *Capitals Conscience. 200 Years of the Guardian*. Bristol: Pluto, pp. 274–91.

Brown, M. (2007) *A License To Be Different; The Story of Channel Four*. London: British Film Institute.

Brunsdon, C. (1981) 'Crossroads'. Notes on a Soap Opera. *Screen* 22 (4): 32–7.

Brunsdon, C. (2007) *London in Cinema: The Cinematic City Since 1945*. London: BFI.

Bruzzi, S. (1997) *Undressing Cinema: Clothing and Identity in the Movies*. London: Routledge.

Bruzzi, S. (2000) *New Documentary: A Critical Introduction*. Abington: Routledge.

Bruzzi, S. (2006) *New Documentary*. 2nd edn. Abington: Routledge.

Bruzzi, S. (2020) *Approximation: Documentary, History, and the Staging of Reality*. Abbington: Routledge.

Bryan, B., Dadzie, S. and Scafe, S. (2018) *Heart of The Race: Black Women's Lives in Britain*. London: Verso.

Buckingham, D. (2021) *Youth on Screen: Representing Young People in Film and Television*. Cambridge: Polity.

Burrows, R. (1999) Residential Mobility and Residualisation in Social Housing in England. *Journal of Social Policy* 28 (1): 27–52.

Butler, J. (1988) Performative Acts and Gender Constitution: An Essay in Phenomenology and Feminist Theory. *Theatre Journal* 40 (4): 519–31.

Butler, J. (1990) *Gender Trouble, Feminism and the Subversion of Identity*. London: Routledge.

Butler, J. (1993) *Bodies that Matter: On the Discursive Limits of Sex*. London: Routledge.

Butler, J. (2004) *Undoing Gender*. New York: Routledge.

Buttigieg, J. (1995) Gramsci on Civil Society. *Boundary* 22 (3): 1–32.

Caleb, R. (2015) Interview with author, London, 12 May.

Campion, S. (2022) *Making Mixed Race: A Study of Time, Place and Identity*. Routledge.

Campt, T. (2017) *Listening to Images*. Durham: Duke University Press.

Campt, T. (2021) *A Black Gaze: Artists Changing How We See*. Cambridge, MA: MIT Press.

Cathcart, B. (2000) *The Case of Stephen Lawrence*. London: Penguin.

Chrisafis, A. and Mace, M. (2002) British Actors Say Outlook is Bleak in 'Institutionally Racist' Film Industry. *The Guardian*, Tuesday 26 March.

Cohen, S. (1972) *Folk Devils and Moral Panics: The Creation of Mods and Rockers*. London: MacGibbon & Kee.

Cole, T. (2023) *Deadpan: The Aesthetics of Black Inexpression*. New York: New York University Press.

Coleman, A. M. (1985) *Utopia on Trial: Vision and Reality in Planned Housing*. London: Hilary Shipman.

Corkin, S. (2017) *Connecting The Wire: Race, Space, and Postindustrial Baltimore*. Texas: University of Texas Press.

Costa Vargas, J. and Jung, M. (2020) Antiblackness of the Social and the Human, in J. Costa Vargas and M. Jung (eds) *Antiblackness*, 1–14. Durham: Duke University Press.

Critcher, C. (2003) *Moral Panics and the Media*. Buckingham: Open University Press.

Deans, J. (2003) BBC3 Unleashes 'Killer' Documentary. *The Guardian*, Thursday 11 December.

Deleuze, G. and Guattari, F. (1993) *A Thousand Plateaus*. Minneapolis: University of Minnesota Press.

Department of Culture, Media and Sport (1998) *A Bigger Picture; the Report of the Film Policy Review Group*. London: DCMS Publication.

Derrida, J. (1993) *Specters of Marx: The State of the Debt, the Work of Mourning and the New International*. London: Routledge.

Derrida, J. (1994) *Specters of Marx: The State of the Debt, the Work of Mourning, and the New International*. Abingdon: Routledge.

Diawara, M. (1993) *Power and Territory: The Emergence of Black British Film Collectives. British Cinema and Thatcherism*. London: UCL Press.

Dickenson, M. and Harvey, S. (2005) *Film Policy in the United Kingdom: New Labour at the Movies: Political Quarterly*. Hoboken: Wiley-Blackwell.

Disrali, B. (2018) *Sybil, or The Two Nations: Is an 1845 Novel*. Scotts Valley: CreateSpace Independent Publishing Platform.

Doyle, G. (2014) Film Support and the Challenge of 'Sustainability': On Wing Design, Wax and Feathers, and Bolts from the Blue. *Journal of British Cinema and Television*, 11 (2–3): 129–51.

Doyle, G., Schlesinger, P., Boyle, R. and Kelly, L. (2015) *The Rise and Fall of the UK Film Council*. Edinburgh: Edinburgh University Press.

Du Bois, W. E. B. (1898) The Study of the Negro Problems. *The Annals of the American Academy of Political and Social Science* 11: 1–23.

Du Bois, W. E. B. (1903) *The Souls of Black Folk*. Chicago: A. C. McClurg.

Dyer, R. (1977) Entertainment and Utopia. *Movie* 24 (Spring): 2–13.

Dyer, R. (1997) *White*. London, Abingdon: Routledge.

Ellis, J. (1981) *Visible Fictions: Cinema, Television, Video*. London: Routledge.

Ellis, J. (1999) Television as Working-Though, in J. Gripsrud (ed.) *Television and Common Knowledge*. London: Routledge, pp. 55–70.

Fanon, F. (1952) *Black Skin, White Masks*. London: Penguin Classics. First published 1952. Copyright © Éditions du Seuil, 1952. English Translation Copyright © Richard Philcox 2008. Reprinted by permission of Penguin Books Limited.

Film Council (2000a) *Film in England, A Development Strategy for Film and the Moving Image in the English Regions*. London: Film Council.

Film Council (2000b) *Towards a Sustainable UK Film Industry*. London: Film Council.

Film Policy Review Group (1998) *A Bigger Picture: The Report of the Film Policy Review Group*. London: DCMS.

Fiske, J. (1994) *Television Culture*. London: Routledge.

Fogg, E. (1994) Crack Dealers Bring Gun Law. *Independent*, Thursday 30 June.

Forensic Architecture (2021) *Forensic Architecture Reports #1 The Police Shooting of Mark Duggan*. London: ICA.

Forrest, D. (2020) *New Realisms. Contemporary British Cinema*. Edinburgh: Edinburgh University Press.

Foucault, M. (1970) *The Order of Things*. London: Tavistock.

French, P. (2005) When Young Guns Go for It. *The Observer*, Saturday 9 April.

Freud, S. (1991) *New Introductory Lectures on Psychoanalysis*. London: Penguin.

Friedman, L. (1993) *Fires Were Started: British Cinema and Thatcherism*. London: UCL Press.

Gaertner, S. L. and Dovidio, J. F. (1986) The Aversive Form of Racism, in J. F. Dovidio and S. L. Gaertner (eds) *Prejudice, Discrimination, and Racism*, 61–89. Orlando: Academic Press.

Garnham, N. (2005) From Cultural to Creative Industries: An Analysis of the Implications of the 'Creative Industries' Approach to Arts and Media Policy Making in the United Kingdom. *International Journal of Cultural Policy* 11 (1): 15–29.

Gilroy, P. (1982) The Myth of Black Criminality, in Martin Eve and David Musson (eds) *The Socialist Register*. London: Merlin Press, pp. 49–76.

Gilroy, P. (1987) *There Ain't No Black in the Union Jack*. London: Unwin Hyman.

Gilroy, P. (1988) Nothing But Sweat inside my Hand: Diaspora Aesthetics and Black Arts in Britain, in Kobena Mercer (ed.) *Black Film British Cinema*. London: ICA.

Gilroy, P. (1993) *Black Atlantic: Modernity and Double Consciousness*. London: Verso.

Gilroy, P. (1994) After the Love Has Gone: Bio-Politics and Echo Politics in the Black Public Sphere. *Public Culture* 7 (1): 53.

Gilroy, P. (2000) *Between Camps: Nations, Cultures and the Allure of Race*. Abingdon: Routledge.

Gilroy, P. (2001) *Against Race: Imagining Political Culture Beyond the Colour Line*. Cambridge, MA: Harvard University Press.

Gilroy, P. (2003) A New Crime, But the Same Old Culprits. *The Guardian*, Wednesday 8 January.

Gilroy, P. (2004) *After Empire: Melancholia or Convivial Culture?* Abingdon: Routledge.

Gilroy, P. (2006) Multiculture in Times of War. *Critical Quarterly* 48 (4): 27–45.

Glifford, L. (1986) *The Broadwater Farm Enquiry*. London: Karia Press.

Glifford, L. (1989) *Broadwater Farm Revisited*. London: Karia Press.

Glynn, M. (2021) *Reimagining Black Art and Criminology*. Bristol: Bristol University Press.

Godfrey, S. (2022) *Masculinity in British Cinema, 1990-2010: Troubled Times*. Edinburgh: Edinburgh University Press.

Goffman, E. (1963) *Stigma: Notes on the Management of Spoiled Identity*. London: Penguin.

Goode, E. and Ben-Yehuda, N. (1994) *Moral Panics: The Social Construction of Deviance*. Cambridge, MA: Blackwell.

Gordon, A. (2008) *Ghostly Matters: Haunting and the Sociological Imagination*. Minneapolis: University of Minnesota Press.

Gray, H. (2013) Subject(ed) to Recognition. *American Quarterly* 65 (4): 771–98.

Grimshaw, A. (1997) Anthropology on Television: The Work of Melissa Llewelyn-Davies. *Journal of Museum Ethnography* 9 (1): 49–64.

Guardian (2005) So Solid Crew Killer Gets Life Sentence. *The Guardian*, Saturday 29 October.

Guerrero, E. (1993) *Framing Blackness: The African American Image in Film*. Philadelphia: Temple University Press.

Hales, G. (2005) *Gun Crime in Brent*. London: London Borough of Brent.

Hall, S. (1981) Notes on Deconstructing the Popular, in R. Samuel (eds) *People's History and Social Theory*. London: Routledge & Kegan Paul, pp. 227–40.

Hall, S. (1988) New Ethnicities, in K. Mercer (ed.) *Black Film/British Cinema*, London: ICA, pp. 27–31.

Hall, S. (1993) What Is This 'Black' in Black Popular Culture? *Social Justice* 20 (1–2): 104–14.

Hall, S. (1997) *Representation: Cultural Representation and Signifying Practices*. Milton Keynes: Open University Press.

Hall, S. (1999) From Scarman to Stephen Lawrence. *History Workshop Journal* 48 (1): 187–97.

Hall, S. (2000) Conclusion: The Multi-Cultural Question, in B. Hesse (ed.) *Un/Settled Multiculturalisms: Diasporas, Entanglements, Transruptions*. New York: St. Martin's Press, pp. 209–41.

Hall, S. (2001) The Spectacle of the 'Other', in S. Hall (ed.) *Representation: Cultural Representations and Signifying Practices*. Milton Keynes: Open University Press, pp. 223–79.

Hall, S. (2012) *City, Street and Citizen: The Measure of the Ordinary*. London: Routledge.

Hall, S. (2018a) *Essential Essays*, vol. 1. Durham: Duke University Press.

Hall, S. (2018b) *Essential Essays*, vol. 2. Durham: Duke University Press.

Hall, S. (2021a) *Selected Writings on Race and Difference*. Durham: Duke University Press.

Hall, S. (2021b) *Writings on Media: History of the Present*. Durham: Duke University Press.

Hall, S., Critcher, C., Jefferson, T., Clark, J. and Roberts, B. (1978) *Policing the Crisis: Mugging, the State, and Law and Order*. London: The Macmillan Press.

Hallam, J. and Marshmant, M. (2000) *Realism and Popular Cinema*. Manchester: Manchester University Press.

Hanley, L. (2007) *Estates: An Intimate History*. London: Granta Books.

Harker, J. (2010) Dianne Abbott Must Confront this Crisis Head On. *The Guardian*, Sunday 27 June.

Harrison, E. (2019) Top Boy: Creator Ronan Bennett Says Channel 4 Cancellation 'Felt like a Slap in the Face to the Community it was Representing'. *Independent*, Wednesday 11 September.

Hattenstone, S. (2017) The Strange, Sad Story of Adam Deacon: 'I Started Thinking, will I ever Act Again?' *The Observer*, Sunday 19 November.

Hayle, S. (2013) Folk Devils without Moral Panics: Discovering Concepts in the Sociology of Evil. *International Journal of Criminology and Sociological Theory* 6 (2): 1125–37.

Hebdige, D. (1979) *Subculture: The Meaning of Style*. London: Routledge.

Hesmondhalgh, D. (2008) Cultural and Creative Industries, in *The Sage Handbook of Cultural Analysis*. Thousand Oaks: Sage, pp. 553–69.

Hesmondhalgh, D., Oakley, K., Nisbett, M. and Lee, D. (2015) *Culture, Economy and Politics: The Case of New Labour*. Basingstoke: Palgrave Macmillan.

Hesmondhalgh, D. and Saha, A. (2013) Race, Ethnicity and Cultural Production. *Popular Communication* 11 (3): 179–95.

Hewison, R. (2014) *Cultural Capital: The Rise and Fall of Creative Britain*. London: Verso.

Hewitt, R. (1986) *White Talk Black Talk: Inter-Racial Friendship and Communication amongst Adolescents*. Cambridge: Cambridge University Press.

Hewitt, R. (1996) *White Talk, Black Talk: Inter-racial Friendship and Communication amongst Adolescents*. Cambridge: Cambridge University Press.

Hewitt, R. (2005) *White Backlash and the Politics of Multiculturalism*. Cambridge: Cambridge University Press.

Hill, J. (1986) *Sex, Class and Realism: British Cinema 1956–63*. London: British Film Institute.

Hill, J. (1999) *British Cinema in the 1980s*. Oxford: Oxford University Press.

Hill, J. (2012) 'This is for the Batmans as well as the Vera Drakes': Economics, Culture and UK Government Film Production Policy in the 2000s. *Journal of British Film and Television* 9: 333–56.

Hills, J. (1998) *Thatcherism, New Labour and the Welfare State*. London: LSE.

Hinsliff, G. and Bright, M. (2000) Black Youth Culture Blamed as Pupils Fail. *Observer*, Sunday 20 August.

Hobbs, D. (2013) *Lush Life: Constructing Organised Crime in the UK*. Oxford: Oxford University Press.

Hobson, D. (2007) *Channel 4: The Early Years and the Jeremy Isaacs Legacy*. London: I. B. Tauris.

Holmans, A. (1987) *Housing Policy in Britain: A History*. London: Croom Helm.

hooks, b. (1996) *Reel to Real: Race, Class and Sex at the Movies*. Abingdon: Routledge.

hooks, b. (2014) *Black Looks: Race and Representation*. Abingdon: Routledge.

Ilan, J. (2012) 'The Industry's the New Road': Crime, Commodification and Street Cultural Tropes in UK Urban Music. *Crime, Media, Culture* 8 (1): 39–55.

Inwood, S. (2000) *A History of London*. London: Papermac.

Inwood, S. (2005) *City of Cities. The Birth of Modern London*. London: Pan Books.

James, M. (2021) *Sonic Intimacy*. London: Bloomsbury.

James, W. (1993) Migration, Racism and Identity Formation: The Caribbean Experience in Britain, in w. James and C. Harris (eds) *Inside Babylon: The Caribbean Diaspora in Britain*. London and New York: Verso, pp. 231–87.

Jameson, F. (1981) *The Political Unconscious: Narrative as a Socially Symbolic Act*. Ithaca: Cornell University Press.

Jauss, H. R. (1982) *Towards an Aesthetic of Literary Reception*. Brighton: Harvester Press.

Johnson, A. and Mendick, R. (2002) Eight Men Shot Dead in Two Years. Welcome to Britain's Murder Mile. *The Independent*, 6 January.

Johnson, S. (1992) The Harder they Come: We the Ragamuffin is Peckham-Born, Peckham-bred. Sheila Johnston Attended its Premiere. In Peckham. *The Independent*, Thursday 16 July.

Kale, S. and Osborne, L. (2021) 'Sexual Predator': Actor Noel Clarke Accused of Groping, Harassment and Bullying by 20 Women. *Guardian*, Thursday 29 April.

Keeling, K. (2007) *The Witches Flight. The Cinematic, the Black Femme, and the Image of Common Sense*. Durham: Duke University Press.

Kelly, L. (2016) Professionalising the British Film Industry: The UK Film Council and Public Support for Film Production. *International Journal of Cultural Policy* 22 (4): 648–63.

Korte, B. and Sternberg, C. (2003) *Bidding for the Mainstream? Black and Asian British Film since the 1990s*. Amsterdam: Rodopi B.V.

Lammy, D. (2012) *Out of the Ashes: Britain After The Riots*. London: Guardian Books.

Lawrence, E. (1982) Just Plain Common Sense: The 'Roots' of Racism, in P. Gilroy (ed.), *The Empire Strikes Back: Race and Racism in 70s Britain*. London: Hutchinson.

Lawton, M. (2022) Top Boy after George Floyd 'will be Eye-Opening' for Some. *BBC News*, 17 March.

Lay, S. (2002) *British Social Realism: From Documentary to Brit Grit*. New York: Wallflower Press.

Leich, L. and Low, V. (2004) Star's Film Role Angers Estate. *Evening Standard*, 25 October.

Lemert, E. M. (1951) *Social Pathology: A Systematic Approach to the Theory of Sociopathic Behaviour*. New York: McGraw Hill.

Lentin, A. and Titley, G. (2011) *The Crises of Multiculturalism: Racism in a Neoliberal Age*. London: Zed Books.

Lévi-Strauss, C. (1963) *Structural Anthropology*. New York: Doubleday Anchor Books.

Levi-Strauss, C. (1978) *Myth and Meaning*. London: Routledge.

Lewis, P. (2011) *Reading the Riots Investigating England's Summer of Disorder*. London: The Guardian/LSE.

Lukács, G. (1962) *The Historical Novel*. London: Merlin Press.

Lukacs, G. (2005 [1970]) *Writer and Critic and Other Essays*. Lincoln: iUniverse.

MacCabe, C. (1974) Realism and the Cinema: Notes on Some Brechtian Theses. *Screen* 15, Issue 2 (Summer): 7–27.

Macpherson, W. (1999) *The Stephen Lawrence Enquiry*. United Kingdom Government.

Maikle, J. (2010) Footballer Gavin Grant Jailed for Life for Gun Murder. *The Guardian*, Monday 26 July.

Malik, S. (1996) Beyond 'The Cinema of Duty'? The Pleasures of Hybridity: Black British Film of the 1980s and 1990s, in A. Higson (ed.) *Dissolving Views: Key Writings on British Cinema*. London: Cassell, pp. 202–15.

Malik, S. (2002) *Representing Black Britain: Black and Asian Images on Television*. London: Sage.

Malik, S. (2008) 'Keeping it Real': The Politics of Channel 4's Multiculturalism, Mainstreaming and Mandates. *Screen* 49 (3): 343–53.

Malik, S. (2013) Creative Diversity: UK Public Service Broadcasting after Multiculturalism. *Popular Communication: The International Journal of Media and Culture* 11: 227–41.

Malpass, P. (2005) *Housing & the Welfare State*. Basingstoke: Palgrave Macmillan.

Marks, L. (2002) *The Skin of Film. Intercultural Cinema, Embodiment, and the Senses*. Durham: Duke University Press.

Marx, K. (1990) *Capital: A Critique of Political Economy*, vol. 1, trans. Ben Fowkes. New York: Penguin.

Mason, R. (2008) Channel 4 Fallout Film Exposes 'Real' Face of London Knife Crime. *Telegraph*, 4 July.

Massood, P. (2003) *Black City Cinema*. Philadelphia: Temple University Press.

McKenzie, L. (2016) *Getting By: Estates, Class and Culture in Austerity Britain*. Bristol: Polity Press.

McLagan, G. (2005) *Guns and Gangs: Inside Black Gun Crime*. London: Allison & Busby.

McRobbie, A. and Thornton, S. (1995) Rethinking 'Moral Panic' for Multi-mediated Social Worlds. *The British Journal of Sociology* 46 (4): 559–74.

Mercer, K. (1988) Recoding Narratives of Race and Nation, in K. Mercer (ed.) *Black Film/ British Cinema*. London: ICA.

Mercer, K. (1994) *Welcome to the Jungle. New Positions in Black Cultural Studies*. London: Routledge.

Mills, H. and Ward, S. (1995) Condon Resolute over 'Black Muggers'. *Independent*, Tuesday 11 July.

Moody, P. (2017) The UK Film Council and the 'Cultural Diversity' Agenda. *Journal of British Cinema and Television* 14 (4): 403–22.

Mulvey, L. (1975) Visual Pleasure and Narrative Cinema. *Screen* 16 (3): 6–18.

Nava, O. (2021) Grime' Music Video Production as Radical Counter-Mapping. *Living Maps* (11): 1–11.

Neale, S. (1990) Questions of Genre. *Screen* 31 (1): 45–66.

Newburn, T. (2016) The 2011 England Riots in European Context: A Framework for Understanding the 'Life-Cycle' of Riots. *European Journal of Criminology* 13 (5): 540–55.

Newman, O. (1972) *Defensible Space; Crime Prevention through Urban Design*. New York: Macmillan.

Newman, O. (1973) *Defensible Space: People and Design in the Violent City*. London: Architectural Press.

Newsinger, J. (2012) British Film Policy in an Age of Austerity. *Journal of British Cinema and Television* 9 (1): 133–44.

Newsinger, J. and Eikhof, D. (2020) Explicit and Implicit Diversity Policy in the UK Film and Televi-sion Industries. *Journal of British Cinema and Television* 17 (1): 47–69.

Ngai, S. (2007) *Ugly Feelings*. Cambridge, MA: Harvard University Press.

Nichols, B. (1994) *Blurred Boundaries: Question of Meaning in Contemporary Culture*. Indiana: Indiana University Press.

Noronha, L. (2022) The Conviviality of the Overpoliced, Detained and Expelled: Refusing Race and Salvaging the Human at the Borders of Britain. *Sociological Review* 70 (1): 159–77.

Nwonka, C. J. (2015) Diversity Pie: Rethinking Social Exclusion and Diversity Policy in the British Film Industry. *Journal of Media Practice* 16 (1): 73–90.

Nwonka, C. J. (2017) Estate of the Nation: Social Housing as Cultural Verisimilitude in British Social Realism. *Filmurbia Screening the Suburbs*. Springer.

Nwonka, C. J. (2020a) The New Babel: The Language and Practice of Institutionalised Diversity in the UK Film Industry. *Journal of British Cinema and Television* 17 (1): 24–46.

Nwonka, C. J. (2020b) The Black Neoliberal Aesthetic. *European Journal of Cultural Studies* 25 (3): 843–62.

Nwonka, C. J. (2022) The Black Neoliberal Aesthetic. *European Journal of Cultural Studies* 25 (3): 843–62.

Nwonka, C. J. and Malik, S. (2018) Cultural Discourses and Practices of Institutionalised Diversity in the UK Film Sector: 'Just Get Something Black Made'. *The Sociological Review* 66 (6): 1111–1127.

O'Brien, D., Friedman, S. and Laursion, D. (2016) 'Like Skydiving without a Parachute': How Class Origin Shapes Occupational Trajectories in British Acting. *Sociology* 51 (5): 992–1010.

Oakley, K. (2004) Not so Cool Britannia: The Role of the Creative Industries in Economic Development. *International Journal of Cultural Studies* 7 (1): 67–77.

Observer (2012) Ill Manors Reviews. *Observer*, Sunday 27 May.

Okundaye, J. (2022) Ashley Walters on 'Top Boy' Season Four, Turning Forty and Lasting TV Success. *Rolling Stone* UK. Issue 004, April/May.

Owusu-Bempah, O. (2022) The Irrelevance of Rap. *Criminal Law Review* 2: 130–51.

Paphides, P. (2002) Crew's Control. *Guardian*, Friday 4 October.

Petersen, R. D. (2000) Definitions of a Gang and Impacts on Public Policy. *Journal of Criminal Justice* 28: 139–49.

Petridis, A. (2019) Stormzy at Glastonbury 2019 Review – A Glorious Victory Lap for Black British Culture. *The Guardian*, 29 June.

Phillips, C. (2008) Negotiating Identities: Ethnicity and Social Relations in a Young Offenders' Institution. *Theoretical Criminology* 12 (3): 313–31.

Phillips, C. (2012) *The Multicultural Prison: Ethnicity, Masculinity, and Social Relations among Prisoners*. Oxford: Oxford University Press.

Phillips, C. (2020) The Pains of Racism and Economic Adversity in Young Londoners' Lives: Sketching the Contours. *Journal of Ethnic and Migration Studies*. DOI: 10.1080/1369183X.2020.1850246

Phillips, C. and Webster, C. (2013) *New Directions in Race, Ethnicity and Crime*. Abingdon: Routledge.

Pines, J. (1991) *Representation and Blacks in British Cinema: BFI Educational Documents*. London: BFI.

Pines, J. (1992) *Black and White in Colour: Black People in British Television Since 1936*. London: BFI.

Pitcher, B. (2012) Race and Capitalism Redux. *Patterns of Prejudice* 46 (1): 1–15.

Power, A. (1993) *Hovels to High Rise: State Housing in Europe since 1850*. London: Routledge.

Proctor, R. (1995) *Cancer Wars: How Politics Shapes What We Know and Don't Know about Cancer*. New York: Basic Books.

Proctor, R. (2008) Agnotology: A Missing Term to Describe the Cultural Production of Ignorance (and its study), in R. Proctor and L. Schiebinger (eds) *Agnotology: The Making and Unmaking of Ignorance*. Stanford: Stanford University Press, pp. 1–33.

Proctor, R. and Schiebinger, L. (eds) (2008) *Agnotology: The Making and Unmaking of Ignorance*. Stanford: Stanford University Press.

Pulwar, N. (2001) The Racialised Somatic Norm and the Senior Civil Service. *Sociology* 35 (3): 651–70.

Rankine, C. (2015) The Condition of Black Life is One of Mourning. *New York Times*, 22 June.

Ravetz, A. (2001) *Council Housing and Culture*. London: Routledge.

Robinson, C. (1983) *Black Marxism: The Making of the Black Radical Tradition*. Chapel Hill and London: The University of North Carolina Press.

Robinson, C. (2000) *Black Marxism: The Making of the Black Radical Tradition*. Chapel Hill and London: The University of North Carolina Press.

Rose, D. (1992) *A Climate of Fear: The Murder of PC Blakelock and the Case of the Tottenham Three*. London: Bloomsbury.

Rose, D. (2004) They Created Winston Silcott, the Beast of Broadwater Farm. And They Won't Let this Creation Lie Down and Die. *The Guardian*, Saturday 17 January.

Rosenthal, J. (2005) *By Jack Rosenthal: An Autobiography in Six Acts*. London: Robson Books.

Ross, K. (1996) *Black and White Media: Black Images in Popular Film and Television*. Cambridge: Cambridge University Press.

Rowe, M. (2004) *Police, Race and Racism*. Devon: Willan Publishing.

Runnymede Trust (2000) *The Future of Multi-Ethnic Britain: The Parekh Report*. London: Profile Books.

Saha, A. (2013) The Marketing of Race in Cultural Production, in K. Oakley and J. O'Connor (eds) *The Routledge Companion to the Cultural Industries*. London: Routledge, pp. 512–21.

Saha, A. (2017) The Politics of Race in Cultural Distribution: Addressing Inequalities in British Asian Theatre. *Cultural Sociology* 11 (3): 302–31.

Saha, A. (2018) *Race and the Cultural Industries*. Cambridge: Polity Press.

Saha, A. (2020) Funky Days are (Not) Back Again: Cool Britannia and the Rise and Fall of British South Asian Cultural Production. *Journal of British Cinema and Television* 17 (1): 6–23.

Saha, A. (2021) *Race, Culture and Media*. London: SAGE Publications.

Saha, A. and van Lente, S. (2022) The Limits of Diversity: How Publishing Industries Make Race. *International Journal of Communication* 16: 1804–22.

Saussure (1993) *Course in General Linguistics*, trans. Roy Harris. London: Duckworth.

Scarman, L. (1982) *The Scarman Report: The Brixton Disorders 10–12 April 1981*. London: Penguin.

Schlesinger, P. (2013) The Creation and Destruction of the UK Film Council, in K. Oakley and J. O'Connor (eds) *The Routledge Companion to the Cultural Industries*. London: Routledge, pp. 464–76.

Severs, D. (2010) Rookeries and No-go Estates: St. Giles and Broadwater Farm, or Middle-Class Fear of 'Non- street' Housing. *The Journal of Architecture* 15 (4): 449–97.

Shoard, C. (2020) John Boyega's Rousing Black Lives Matter Speech Wins Praise and Support. *The Guardian*, 4 June.

Sivanandan, A. (2008) *Race, Culture and Globalisation*. London: Pluto Press.

Slater, T. (2012) The Myth of 'Broken Britain': Welfare Reform and the Production of Ignorance. *Antipode* 46 (4): 948–69.

Smith, C. (1998a) *Creative Industries Mapping Document*. London: Department of Culture, Media and Sport.

Smith, C. (1998b) *Creative Britain*. London: Faber & Faber.

Smith, M. (1995) *Engaging Characters: Fiction, Emotion, and the Cinema*. Oxford: Clarendon Press.

Snead, J. (1988) 'Black Independent Film': Britain and America, in K. Mercer (eds) *Black Film British Cinema*. London: ICA, pp. 47–50.

Snead, J. (1994) *White Screens/Black Images: Hollywood from the Dark Side*. London: Routledge.

Social Exclusion Unit (1998) *Bringing Britain together: A National Strategy for Neighbourhood Renewal (Cm 4045)*. London: Stationery Office.

Solomons, J. (1988) *Black Youth, Racism and the State: The Politics of Ideology and Policy*. Cambridge: Cambridge University Press.

Solomos, B. and L. Back (1996) *Racism and Society*. London: Palgrave.

Squires, P. (2000) *Gun Culture or Gun Control?* London: Routledge.

Sutcliffe, A. (1974) *Multi-Storey Living, The British Working-Class Experience*. London: Croom Helm.

The Mirror (2010) Dianne Abbott: I Sent My Son to a Private School so He Wouldn't End Up in a Gang. 21 June.

Thomas, P. (2011) Multiculturalism and the Emergence of Community Cohesion, in V. Bryson and P. Fisher (eds) *Redefining Social Justice: New Labour Rhetoric and Reality*. Manchester: Manchester University Press, pp. 57–77.

Thompson, T. (2001) Homegrown Gangs Shoot to Power on Our Violent Streets. *Observer*, 26 August.

Thompson, T. (2003a) The Ethnic Connection. *Observer*, 12 May.

Thompson, T. (2003b) They'll Shoot Anyone – Even the Police. *Guardian*, 25 May.

Thompson, T. (2003c) Guns, Gangs and Slaughter Stalk the Lawless West. *Observer*, 24 August.

Thompson, T. (2003d) Without a Gun, You're Dead. *Observer*, 21 September.

Thompson, T. (2003e) Gun Crime Spreads 'Like a Cancer' across Britain. *Observer*, 5 October.

Times, The (2006) Kidulthood, Saturday 4 March.

United Kingdom Film Council (2003) *Film in the UK 2002, Statistical Yearbook*. London: UK Film Council.

United Kingdom Film Council (2005) *New Cinema Fund October 2000–February 2005: An Overview and Report to the Board*. London: UKFC.

United Kingdom Film Council (2009a) *Scenario Planning for 2010–2013: Discussion Paper. How Effective have Our Policies and Interventions been to Date?* London: UKFC.

United Kingdom Film Council (2009b) *Stories We Tell Ourselves: The Cultural Impact of UK Film 1946–2006*. London: UKFC.

Valluvan, S. (2016) Conviviality and Multiculture: A Post-integration Sociology of Multi-ethnic Interaction. *Young* 24 (3): 204–21.

Valluvan, S. (2020) *The Clamour of Nationalism: Race and Nation in Twenty-First-Century Britain*. Manchester: Manchester University Press.

Vice, S. (2009) *Jack Rosenthal*. Manchester: Manchester University Press.

Vinen, R. (2010) *Thatcher's Britain: The Politics and Social Upheaval of the 1980s: The Politics and Social Upheaval of the Thatcher Era*. London: Simon & Schuster.

Walcott, R. (2014) The Problem of the Human: Black Ontologies and 'the Coloniality of Our Being', in S. Broeck and C. Junker (eds) *Postcoloniality - Decoloniality - Black Critique: Joints and Fissures*. Frankfurt: Campus Verlag, pp. 93–108.

Walcott, R. (2021) *The Long Emancipation: Moving toward Black Freedom*. Durham: Duke University Press.

Walker, A. (2019) All Hail Stormzy for Historic Glastonbury Performance. *The Guardian*, 29 June.

Walker, J. (2012) A Wilderness of Horrors? British Horror Cinema in the New Millennium. *Journal of British Cinema and Television* 9 (3): 436–56.

Walsh (1986) Hosing Down Comedy. *the Independent*, 8 December.

Wambu, O. (2003) *Babymother. Screenonline*. London: BFI.

Warner, M. (2002) *Publics and Counter Publics*. Cambridge, MA: MIT Press.

Wayne, M. (2002) *The Politics of Contemporary European Cinema*. Bristol: Intellect Books.

Wayne, M. (2006) Working Title Mark II: A Critique of the Atlanticist. *International Journal of Media and Cultural Politics* 2 (1): 59–73.

Wayne, M. (2018) *England's Discontents: Political Cultures and National Identities*. London: Pluto Press.

Wayne, M. (2020) *Marxism Goes to the Movies*. Abingdon: Routledge.

Wei, R. (2013) Mobile Media: Coming of Age with a Big Splash. *Mobile Media & Communication* 1 (1): 50–6.

West, C. (1993) *Race Matters*. Boston: Beacon Press.

White, J. (2017) *Urban Music and Entrepreneurship: Beats, Rhymes and Young People's Enterprise*. Abingdon: Routledge.

Willemen, P. (1993) *Looks and Frictions: Essays in Cultural Studies and Film Theory*. London: BFI Publishing.

Williams, R. (1961) The Achievement of Brecht. *Critical Quarterly* 3 (2): 153–62.

Williams, R. (1977) A Lecture on Realism. *Screen* 18 (1): 61–74.

Wilson, A. (1991) *Black-on-Black Violence: The Psychodynamics of Black Self-Annihilation in Service of White Domination*. New York: Afrikan World Infosystems.

Wilson, W. (2009) *More than Just Race: Being Black and Poor in the Inner City*. New York: W. W. Norton & Company.

Winters, J. (2016) *Hope Draped in Black. Race, Melancholy, and the Agony of Progress*. Durham: Duke University Press.

Wittgenstein, L. (1953) *Philosophical Investigations*. Oxford: Blackwell.

Woods, F. (2015) Telefantasy Tower Blocks: Space, Place and Social Realism Shake-ups in Misfits. *Journal of British Cinema and Television* 12 (2): 229–44.

Young, L. (1996) *Fear of the Dark: 'Race', Gender and Sexuality in the Cinema*. London: Routledge.

Young, L. (2000). How do we Look? Unfixing the Singular Black (Female) Subject, in P. Gilroy, L. Grossberg and A. McRobbie (eds) *Without guarantees: In Honour of Stuart Hall*. London: Verso, pp. 416–29.

Žižek, S. (2010) Liberal Multiculturalism Masks an Old Barbarism with a Human Face. *The Guardian*, October 3.

Index